Minerva Britanna

By Henry Peacham

With an introduction by Josephine McCarthy

Digitally restored for reprinting by Michael Sheppard

For more information, please visit www.quareia.com

Published by Quareia Publishing UK

ISBN 978-1-911134-23-7

Dedicated to
HRH Charles, Prince of Wales, Duke of Cornwall, Duke of Rothesay,
King in Waiting, and beloved of the Faery Queene.

Thanks to Duke University Library Emblem Collection,
for making this reprint possible.

Introduction

Minerva Britanna, published in 1612, is an enigmatic magical puzzle. It is an *emblem book*, a form of literature that first became popular in the Elizabethan era, and which was still the height of fashion in the reign of Elizabeth's successor, King James I, when *Minerva Britanna* was composed.

The first ever emblem book was *The Emblemata* by Andrea Alciato, which was first printed in 1531 (though it had been 'born' some nine years previously, on the ninth of December, 1522). Each page of *The Emblemata* had a motto, usually in Latin, a puzzle image, and a poem; together, these three elements made up the 'emblem.'

Alciato, an academic lawyer, wrote *The Emblemata* just to entertain his friends, but the book quickly became popular with the chattering classes of Europe, and soon everyone began copying its format. Emblem books were churned out by lovesick poets, political writers of intrigue, esoteric adepts, and writers looking for royal patronage. Even school masters made use of the format, as it could be used to get points across to students in a memorable way. So by the time Henry Peacham created *Minerva Britanna*, nearly ninety years after *The Emblemata*, the emblem book was a very well-known and successful genre of literature.

Minerva Britanna mixes together Renaissance faery magic, Elizabethan codes, Hermetic wisdom, and kingly advice.[1] It is intended to teach a future king how to connect with the sacred female power within the land, how to keep balance, and how to rule justly. It also advises nobles on how to be magical upholders of truth and justice, and gives warnings on what dangers lie ahead and how to avoid them. It is a puzzle book of those magical Mysteries that have to do with the land, the monarch, the sacred duties of the nobleman, and the faery secrets of Britain. It also deals with ascent and inner rebirth, which were absolutely central parts of the early Rosicrucian pattern.

---

[1]Some of that kingly advice was sourced from King James' *Basilikon Doron*, a book on kingship he wrote for his son Henry.

Some modern writers who have analysed the text have concluded that it was written to flatter, by imitation, King James. I disagree: though it is similar in tone and subject matter to the King's *Basilikon Doron*, it is a very different book. The magical aspects of the images in *Minerva Britanna* point to Peacham himself being an initiate of the Mysteries, or at least a follower of British faery magic, which was deeply integrated with sacred kingship and the Faerie Queen, the goddess of the land of Britain.

I think our friend Henry dedicated *Minerva Britanna* to the Prince of Wales in 1610 not to flatter King James, but to protect his book. Reflecting James's ideas about kingship and dedicating the book to his son ensured the book's survival—and reduced the chances of Peacham being executed as a witch. For extra insurance, *Minerva Britanna* also includes the names of other royals and aristocrats, along with appropriate emblems. Flattery got you everywhere in Jacobean England.

Minerva Britanna was released to the public two years before the Rosicrucians declared their existence in 1614 with the *Fama Fraternitatis*, by which time they had already existed secretly for one hundred years.[2] And we know, from various historical sources, that the *Minerva Britanna*'s illustrated manuscript was already being passed around privately in 1609. It was birthed just before the Rosicrucians were ready to out themselves, and nine years after the death of Queen Elizabeth I.

This was a very magical time. Europe in the early 1500s to the early 1600s was a melting pot of exciting magical thought. Hermetic philosophy and alchemy were on the rise, and magical artists, writers, and thinkers swarmed through Venice, London, and throughout Germany, enjoying noble patronage. This was the age of magicians such as John Dee, and of powerful magical texts such as *The Arbatel of Magic.*

---

[2]Article six of their agreement states "The Fraternity should remain secret one hundred years." There is a modern misconception that the writers were making that declaration from that point on: that they should remain secret for one hundred years from 1614. However, by publishing the Fama, they would have been breaking that oath of secrecy. In fact, their hundred years were already up. Their declaration was revealing, finally, their existence.

After the death of Queen Elizabeth I, things shifted a little. Her successor, James I, had a keen but unhealthy interest in demonology, witchcraft, and folk magic, and it was on his watch that executions for witchcraft[3] really got underway. He wrote a book on demonology in 1597 before coming to the throne, and in 1604, one year after ascending the throne, he passed the Witchcraft Act, which made "raising spirits," or anything that could be considered witchcraft, punishable by execution. People had to be careful, and that included nobles.

For magic to survive, it had to be hidden in plain sight. Wrapped in the trappings of mathematics, classical philosophy, religion, poetry, drama, history, and art, it hid safely, nestled in places where it could not be recognized by the uninitiated, but where it could be spotted by initiates who paid attention. In this way, magicians could wave to other magicians and pass on ideas, concepts, advice, and magical patterns at a time when letters and conversations could get you executed.

Intense pressure and restriction always encourage innovation, and *Minerva Britanna* is a wonderful example of this. Henry Peacham used a popular literary genre—the emblem book—to hide secrets within layers of meaning. Any adept magician who reads his book will spot its messages, advice, reflections, humour, and its finger pointing the way to the future. Its very first image, of a person hidden behind a veil with an exposed hand writing a motto, should suffice to reveal the book's overarching message.

The book's motto, "Mente Videbor," means "in the mind I will be seen/understood." This is an instruction to work with the book in vision: it is a book of visionary constructs, gateways, and keys, hidden among flattery, humour, mathematical puzzles, and historical reflection.

It is sort of an Elizabethan version of the Egyptian *Book of Gates*, only even more obscure, more mathematically complex, more jumbled, and containing less magical knowledge. Putting the book under the protection of Minerva, and leaning her persona towards that of Britannia, the goddess who is the land of Britain and the Faery Queene, hints at the Mysteries of sacred kingship and the king's marriage to the sacred land/goddess.

---

[3] By burning in Scotland, by hanging in England.

Here is an interesting quote about *Minerva Britanna* by Roger Stritmatter, PhD:

> Peacham's antidote to the ambitious impulses that lead to political disaster at court is spiritual purification through ascent, a widely influential consideration of Medieval aesthetics, rooted in Neo-Platonic, Kabbalistic, and Christian sources. Mystics of all three traditions shared the common goal of facilitating the ascent and union of the soul with God or The One. ... For Plotinus, the rungs on the soul's ladder of ascent are comparable to the stages of initiation into a mystery religion. The metaphor became widely accessible to a Christian readership through Boethius, who exposes the connection between the doctrine of ascent and the Platonic ideal of memory or "return": His exhortation to "Let us now raise our minds as high as we can towards the high roof of the highest intelligence" is explained by personified Wisdom: "so that you may most speedily and easily come to your own home from where you previously came."

While Stritmatter feels that *Minerva Britanna* is an ascent text (a subject that does indeed form part of the book), as a working magician, I don't fully agree. I feel it is more of a faery magical text, with some ascent work included within it, as opposed to specifically an ascent text like *The Arbatel of Magic.*

Though the text does highlight the magical steps that a king or noble should take towards climbing the spiritual and mystical ladder of ascent, it does not explain how to climb the ladder itself. Rather it shows the reader who can penetrate its puzzles how to work towards being a good candidate for acceptance on the ladder. It shows how to avoid the many traps, mistakes, and dead ends that people can get stuck in; and most of all, it roots everything within the sacred land of Britain and sacred kingship. For those wishing to delve into the deeper Mysteries of traditional English Renaissance faery magic, *Minerva Britanna* is the perfect book to work with.

About Henry Peacham

It would be rather remiss of me not to bring “goode Henry” into the limelight for a moment and to give you a bit of background on his life. Having the same name as his father, Henry Peacham was known as the “younger,” and was born in 1578 in North Mimms, Hertfordshire. He graduated from Trinity College, Cambridge at twenty-five years old.

He became Master of Wymondam School in Norfolk, and later, a personal tutor to the two sons of Thomas Howard, Earl of Arundel. This would have brought him firmly into the orbit of many nobles. According to Trinity College’s records, he remained unmarried and gained a gentle fame as a painter, musician, and mathematician. He wrote and presented *Minerva Britanna* to the Prince of Wales in 1610, and soon after gained a modest stipend from King James that would let him continue writing.

In 1622 he published *The Compleat Gentleman* as a guide for young men, which contained advice on poetry, arts, philosophy, music composition, and the most important influences of the time. Here is an example from the text, in which Peacham is discussing recent poets:

> In the time of our late Queene Elizabeth, which was truly a golden age (for such a world of refined wits, and excellent spirits it produced, whose like are hardly to be hoped for, in any succeeding age) above others, who honoured Poesie with their pennes and practice (to omit her Majestie, who had a singular gift herein) were Edward Earle of Oxford, the Lord Buckhurst, Henry Lord Paget; our Phoenix, the noble Sir Philip Sidney, M. Edward Dyer, M. Edmund Spencer, M. Samuel Daniel, with sundry others: whom (together with those admirable wits, yet living, and so well knowne) not out of Envie, but to avoid tediousnesse I overpasse. Thus much of Poetrie.

The Compleat Gentleman is stuffed with names, as Henry was a terrible name-dropper, and the book is a veritable who’s who of the Renaissance art world. As such, it has remained a necessary reference book for those who study the art and poetry of that era.

Henry died in London, still unmarried, in 1643.

How to work with *Minerva Britanna*

The most basic thing to be aware of when you read *Minerva Britanna* is a couple of alphabetical peculiarities of Jacobean text. V and u are often interchangeable, and there is a second form of the letter s, ſ, which can look very much like an f.

If you are mathematically minded and a good sleuth, and are good at putting puzzles together, then you will have great fun finding the number patterns in the book's poems and mottoes, and following the classical references that unlock pieces of the puzzles. The whole book is a group of puzzles within puzzles that, solved, take you to the threshold of English faery magic.

If your mind does not work so analytically, then another way to unlock *Minerva Britanna* is to reproduce its images on card and work with them as a divination deck. Some of the images are obviously related to certain Tarot trumps. You will have to figure out which of the others are decoys, which are jokes or flattery, and which are magical.

You will find that there are three main magical themes. First divide the images into these three themes, then add back the humorous and flattering images, which are also markers on the path and act as parts of the jigsaw. You will see three distinct stories emerging, and three different visionary constructs that you can work with to connect to the sacred land, the faery realm, and Underworld prophecy, and to activate the bond between the goddess of the land and yourself.

To have the images trigger for you magically, you have to do the investigative work yourself. Finding the keys is part of the process, and it does not matter how long this takes, because when the light finally dawns, the whole thing will open up like a glittery golden magical box.

When I was working with *Minerva Britanna*, I focused on a small number of emblems and hung them up around in the house. I looked at them when I was thinking or eating, I had them beside me when I was working, and I doodled them on paper, just for fun, not as an intentionally magical act. That process let the imagery of the emblems make its way into my subconscious where my mind could ponder it in dreams and in blank waking moments.

Once you have one major "ahha!" moment, which will act as a key, then the whole thing will start to unlock. Once you recognize one image, then you will see all the others, and wonder why you did not see the pattern straightaway, as it is so obvious! This is what I love about these Renaissance magical puzzles: they are so much fun.

The magical knowledge contained within *Minerva Britanna* is not unknown today to magicians, but it does give us an insight into the magical minds of people of its time, and it is part of our magical history. By working with *Minerva Britanna*, whether just as a puzzle or as a visionary magical quest, you will learn more about your magical ancestors from the inside out, as opposed to simply reading about them. And by revealing the origins of certain aspects of, say, nineteenth-century magical thought, it can help us understand why magic today is as it is. It also helps us reach back to a magical time where magicians were a lot closer to faery and Underworld magic than most magicians are today. Nineteenth-century magicians took us away from the land and locked magic in vaults and temples, far away from the trees, the birds, and the Faery Queene. By peering back into the soul of English Renaissance magic through *Minerva Britanna*, we can recover that wildness in our magical practice, and bring back to our work some of the love of playfulness and puzzles... and the shadow of the Faery Queene.

Josephine McCarthy, May 2017

References

The Emblem, by John Manning.

Triangular Numbers in Henry Peacham's Minerva Britanna: A Study in Jacobean Literary Form, by Dr Roger Stritmatter.

Student records, Trinity College, Cambridge University.

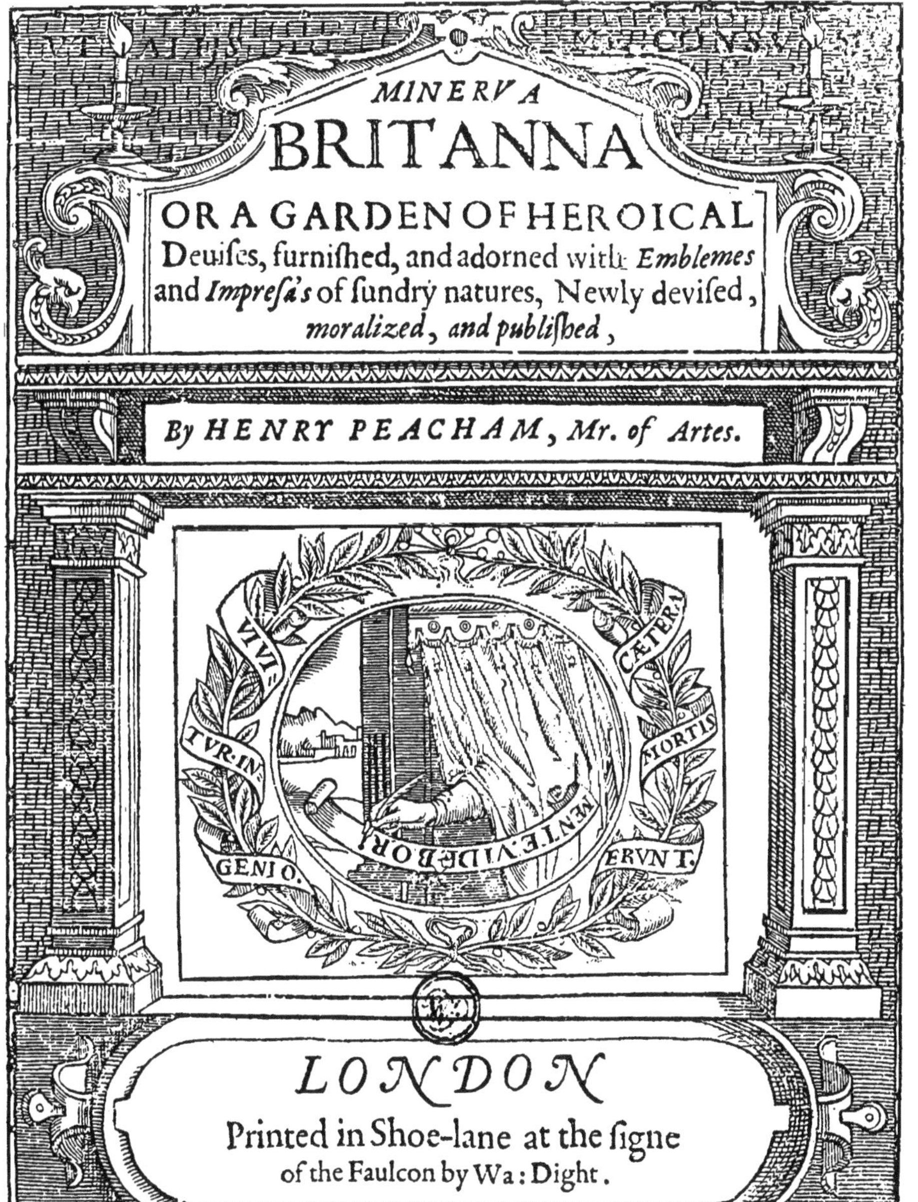
MINERVA
BRITANNA
OR A GARDEN OF HEROICAL
Deuiſes, furniſhed, and adorned with Emblemes
and Impreſa's of ſundry natures, Newly deviſed,
moralized, and publiſhed,
By HENRY PEACHAM, Mr. of Artes.
VIVI
TVR·IN·
GENIO.
CÆTERA
MORTIS
ERVNT.
MENTE·VIDEBORI
LONDON
Printed in Shoe-lane at the ſigne
of the Faulcon by Wa: Dight.

ICH DIEN. *i.* (*Germanicè*,) Servio.

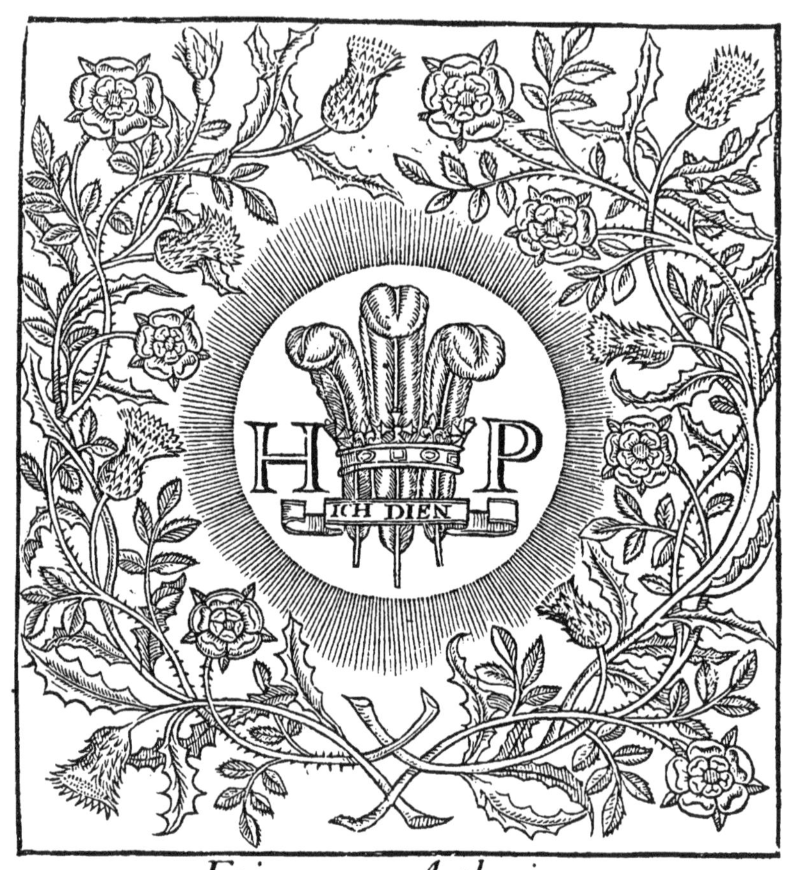

Epigramma Authoris.

Se dicit Servum modo patre superstite Princeps,
Primus at Imperio Servus (b) HIC, INDE *regit.*

cſ. 4. 1. ICHDIEN grammma.

TO THE RIGHT HIGH AND MIGHTIE HENRIE, ELDEST SONNE OF our Soveraigne Lord the KING, Prince of Wales, *DVKE of CORNWALL and ROTHSAY and Knight of the moſt noble order of the GARTER.*

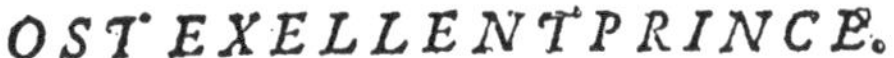

M*OST EXELLENT PRINCE.*
Hauing by more then ordinarie ſignes, taſted heeretofore of your gratious favour: and evidently knowen your *Princely* and *Generous* inclination, to all good Learning and excellencie. I am emboldened once againe, to offer vp at the Altar of your gratious acceptance theſe mine *Emblemes*: a weake (I confeſſe,) and a worthleſſe Sacrifice, though an aſſured pledge, of that Zeale and Duetie, I ſhall for ever moſt Religiouſlie owe vnto your Highnes: ſhewing herein rather a will to deſire, then worth to deſerue, ſo peereleſſe a patronage. Howſoever the world ſhall eſteeme them in regard of their rude and homely attire, for the moſt part they are Roially diſcended, and repaire into your owne boſome (farre from the reach of Envie) for their protection. For in truth they are of right your owne, and no other then the ſubſtance of thoſe Divine Inſtructions, his *Maieſtie* your Royall *Father* præſcribed vnto you, your guide (as that golden branch to *ÆNEAS,*) to a vertuous & true hap- Æneid·6.
py life. It is now two yeares ſince I preſẽted vnto your Highnes ſome of them, then done by me into Latine verſe, with their pictures drawen and limned by mine owne hand in their liuely coulours; wherein, as neere as I could, I obſerued the *Method* of his *Maieſties* BASILICON DORON, but by reaſon of the great number I had ſince that, newly invented: with ſome others collected, (tieng my invention to no one

 Subiect

Subiect as before) I am here conſtrained aſwell of Neceſſitie as for varietie ſake, to intermixe (as it were *promiſcue*) one with the other in one entire volume, the rather becauſe of their affinitie & end, which is one and the ſelfe ſame, that is, the faſhioning of a vertuous minde. I dare not diſcourſe at large vnto your Highnes, of the manifold Vſe, Nature, Libertie, and ever eſteemed exellencie of this kind of *Poeſie*: it being the rareſt, and of all others the moſt ingenious, and wherein, the greateſt *Princes* of the world, many times haue moſt happily exerciſed their Invention: becauſe I doubt not, but your Highnes already knoweth whatſoever I might ſpeak herein. Onely what I haue done, I moſt humbly offer vp the ſame vnto your gratious view, and protection. Deſiring of *GOD* to beautifie and enrich your moſt hopefull & Heroique minde, with the divineſt giftes of his grace, and knowledge, heartily wiſhing, there were any thing in me, worthy of the leaſt favour, and reſpect of ſo exellent a *Prince*.

To your Highnes,

The moſt ſincerely and affectionately devoted

in all dutie and ſervice.

HENRY PEACHAM.

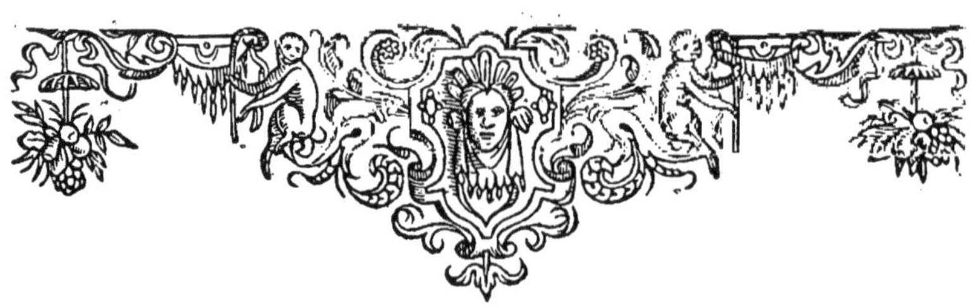

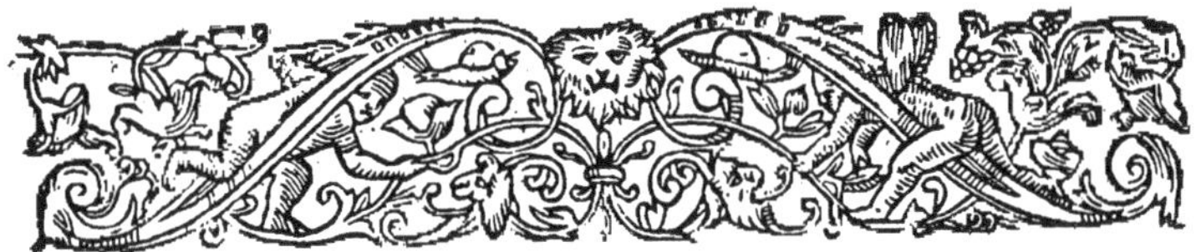

To the Reader.

I haue heere (kind Reader) ſent abroad vnto thy view, this volume of *Emblemes*, whether for greatnes of the chardge, or that the Invention is not ordinarie: a Subiect very rare. For except the collections of Maſter *Whitney*, and the tranſlations of ſome one or two elſe beſide, I know not an *Engliſhman* in our age, that hath publiſhed any worke of this kind: they being (*I* doubt not) as ingenious, and happy in their invention, as the beſt French or Italian of them all. Hence perhaps they terme vs *Tramontani Sempii*, Simple and of dull conceipt, when the fault is neither in the Climate, nor as they would haue it, in the conſtitution of our bodies, but truely in the cold & frozen reſpect of Learning, and artes, generally amongſt vs: comming far ſhorte of them in the iuſt valewing of well deſeruing qualities. To begin at the foote of their *Alpes*, and ſo diſcend by *Germanie* (which *Bodine* truly termeth *officinam hominum*, a ſhoppe of abſolute men for all Artes) how ſhe hath excelled in this, as in all other rare Invention, witneſſe the many volumes ſhe hath ſent vs over of this Subiect: With what excellent Bodies, and *Motto's*, haue the *Netherlandes* eſpecially *Holland*, and *Zealand*, vpon ſundry occaſions (as the recoverie of their Libertie, the overthrow in *eighty eight*, and the like) commended their Invention to the world? as we finde in *Meteranus*, and others. I ſhould ſeeme partiall, if I ſhould lay to your view, the many and almoſt vnimitable *Impreſa's* of our owne Countrie: as thoſe of *Edward* the black Prince, *Henry* the fourth, *Henry* the ſeuenth, *Henry* the eight, Sir *Thomas Moore*, the Lord *Cromwell*, & of later times, thoſe done by Sir *Phillip Sydney*, and others. Nor were it needefull ſince their Memory is freſh, and many of their ſheildes yet ſcarce drie in the world. Who hath ever ſeene more wittie, proper, & ſignificant deviſes, then thoſe of *Scotland*? (to omit more auntient times) as that of *King James* the third, deviſing for himſelfe (to expreſſe the care he had of his country and People) a *Hen* ſitting over her *Chickens*, with the word *Non dormit qui cuſtodit*: as alſo of *Iames* the fowrth, taking to himſelfe a bifront, or double face, plac't vpon the top of a Columne: the heades crowned with *Laurell*, the word *Vtrumque*: meaning (as it it is thought) he would constantly, and advisedly like *Ianus*, obserue the proceedings aswell of the *French* as the *English*, holding them both at that time in Ielousie. Many and very excellent haue I seene of his *Maiesties* owne Invention, who hath taken herein in his yonger years great delight, and pleasure, by which thou maiest see, that we are not so dull as they would imagine vs, nor our Soile so barren as that we neede to borrow from their Sunne-burnt braines, our best Invention. Whereas I haue heere dedicated many *Emblemes* to sundry and great Personages, (yea some to Forraigne Princes,) I haue heerein but imitated the best approued Authours in this kind: as *Alciat*, *Sambucus*, *Iunius*, *Reusnerus*, and others: they being such, as either in regard of their transcendent dignitie, and vertues, deserue of all to be honoured: or others whome for their excellent parts and qualities, I haue ever loued, and esteemed: or lastly some of my private friendes, to whome I haue in particular beene most beholden some way or other. Wherein I trust thou wilt not condemne me, since I haue no other meane then by word to shew a thankfull minde towards them.

It is not my intent here (which I might well doe) to discourse at large of the Nature and Libertie of *Embleme*, wherein it differeth from the *Impresa*; because heerein I haue beene alreadie prevented by * others. The true vse heereof from time to time onely hath beene, *Vtile dulci miscere*, to feede at once both the minde, and eie, by expressing mistically and doubtfully, our disposition, either to *Loue*, *Hatred*, *Clemencie*, *Iustice*, *Pietie*, our *Victories*, *Missfortunes*, *Griefes*, and the like: which perhaps could not haue beene openly, but to our præiudice revealed. And in truth the bearer heerein doth but as the Travailer, that changeth his Silver into Gold, carry about his affection in a narrow roome, and more safely; the valew rather bettered then abated.

Paulus Iovius. Sambucus. Mr. Sam. Daniell.

Accept I pray thee in good worth, what I haue heere done, not for any hope of reward, or gaine, but onely for thy pleasure, and recreation, Imagining thou art delighted (as I haue ever beene my selfe) with these ever esteemed, honest, and most commendable Devises.

Thine assuredly,

HENRY PEACHAM.

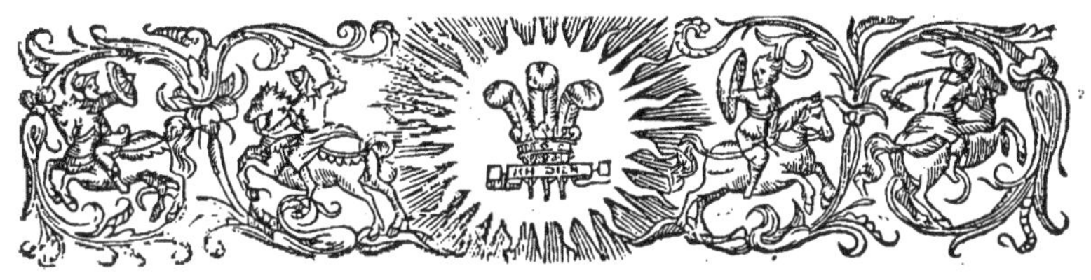

AD AVGVSTISSIMVM ET LONGE NOBILISSIMVM HENRICVM WALLIÆ PRINCIPEM.

Carmen Panegyricum.

Quæ damus iſta novis excuſa *EMBLEMATA* formis,
(Docta ſonare prius numeris ſua verba Latinis;)
Accipe quo ſoleas vultu, votiſq; ſecundis
Annue, parva licet, nec ſint tè Principe digna.
Cum rabidus latê torreret *SIRIVS* arva,
Flavaque anhelantis premeret Sol terga *LEONIS*,
Fronde ſub vmbroſa patulæ requievimus vlmi,
Ad ripas *GRENOVICA* tuas; (vbi *THAMESIS* vnda
Alluit *ANGLIGENVM* regalia tecta Monarchæ.)
Hic vbi ſollicita dum plurima mente revolvo,
Adſtitit inſomni corâm pulcherrima Virgo,
Tecta caput galea, gemmis auroque nitente:
Pone ſuas diffuſa comas, clypeusque ſiniſtrâ,
GORGONIS oſtendens argenteus ora *MEDVSÆ*:
Vndique fraxineam dum dextra viriliter haſtam
Torquet, et incerto circûm aëra verberat ictu.
Obſtupui, et gelidus tremor inde per oſſa cucurrit,
Cum Dea facunda extempló ſic ora reſolvit.
Pone metum Vates, animos timor vrget inertes,
Conſilijque venit ſani notiſſimus hoſtis:
Hinc citus exurgas et ſummi Principis Aulam
I pete, qua ſilvas Nymphæ coluêre virentes:
Qua *DRYADVM* ſedes *THAMESIDOS* vnda ſalutat,
Turrigerumque caput iactat *RICHMVNDIA* cœlo.

Eſt

Est *HENRICVS* ibi, quo non clementior alter,
Quoque Deus nostro dederit nil dulcius ævo;
Aemulus Herôum veterum ac virtutis avîtæ;
(Et mea siquid habent vnquam præsagia veri)
PIERIDVM pater, et doctis decus omne futurus.
Excipiet longos hic læta fronte labores,
Aspice vt huic desint provecti Iudicis ora,
Nec sulcat faciem minitantis ruga Tyranni:
Candor inest vultu placidus, mens concolor isti.
Insuper invitet te Bibliothêca referta,
Artibus omnigenis *MVSÆ* quam struxit Asylum:
Namque feros toto compescuit orbe tumultus
Candida *PAX*, cœlo lætis invecta triumphis.
Non furit indomitus *MARS* ferro et cæde nefanda,
Buccina non orbis exosaque matribus arma;
Infestant nostras subitis terroribus oras.
Iam posuêre *NOTI* immites, creberque procellis
AFRICVS, et *BOREAS* solito sunt carcere vincti:
Occidui spirant *ZEPHYRI*, nunc omnia Tellus
Parturit, atque novo rident animalia Vere.
Dum Nymphæ ducunt circûm per opaca choreas,
Et Rosa verna viret, silvis dum mille sonoras,
Gutture multiplici renovat *PHILOMELA* querelas:
Ad gelidos fontes, vel forte legaris in vmbra,
Gratior aut hospes sis (post convivia) mensæ.
Vix ego servo librum, properantem visere tecta
Regia, et *HENRICI* notos pietate Penâtes.
Iste tibi veniat modo qualiscunque libellus,
Inconcinna, levis, male culta, incompta *MINERVA*,
Hanc precor excipias placidê, (Dignissime *PRINCEPS*.)
Maiori interea nitetur carmine Musa,
(Pone legens rerum vestigia lata tuarum)
Vt magnum resonent *GANGETICA* littora nomen;
b Arthurum. Et reducem (b) *HEROEM* horrescant grassantia latê,
(Sacrilege *ACHMETES*) olim tua castra *BRITANNVM*,
Cum tua non tantum tibi serviet vltima *THVLE*

Vaticinor,

Vaticinor; toto regnabis latiús orbe,
Et reditura tuis sunt aurea sêcla *BRITANNIS*.
Tu vero interea vive, (Augustissime *PRINCEPS*,)
Ducat et ad seros *CLOTHO* tua fila nepôtes:
Vt tua te longum, *BRITANNIA* læta fruatur,
Immensumque tuis repleas virtutibus orbem.

HENRICVS PEACHAMVS.

AD D. HENRICVM PEACHAMVM DE SVA MINERVA.

Prodiit ex cerebro *IOVIS*, alma *MINERVA* profundo;
  Vt quondam cecinit *PINDARVS* ore fluens.
Prodiit ast ictu *VVLCANI* emissa securi:
  Dum caput *ÆGIOCHI* percutit ille *IOVIS*.
Prodiit e cœlo *RHODIIS* dum depluit aurum,
  Aureus est in quo nata *MINERVA* dies;
Prodiit et cataphracta: caput bene casside tecta,
  AEgide tuta sua, cuspide tuta sua.

Fabulæ applicatio.

Est *PEACHAME*, *IOVIS* cerebrum tibi, prodiit illinc
  Hic liber, ingenii vera *MINERVA* tui.
Singula sunt in eo quamvis extempore nata,
  VVLCANI liber hic totus habebat opem,
De summo (*PEACHAME*) polo, tibi depluet aurum,
  Illico et incipient, aurea secla tibi.
Armatur galeâ, clypeo, ense, *MINERVA BRITANNA*,
  Et contra *MOMOS*, est ea tuta satis.

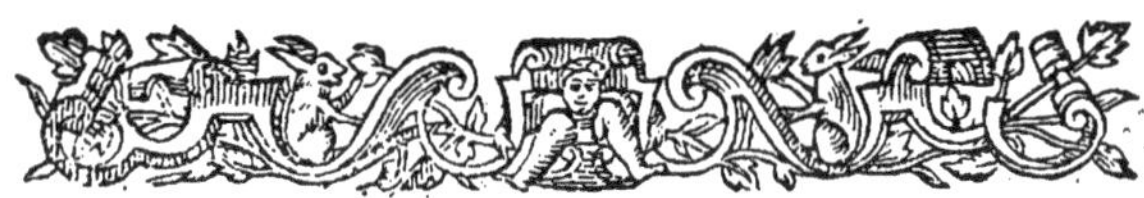

Ex puris Iambis. Ad eundem.

Iniquus æstimator ille ducitur,
Suo metitur omne qui modo ac pede;
Sapitque perparum ille, cui nihil sapit,
Nisi quod approbatur a sua nota.
At æquus ille, quisquis addit ipsius
Opinioni, acutioris arbitrî
Probationem, et acre testimonium,
Et eius, et suis videns ocellulis.

Peritiorum amica testimonia
Habes, labore de tuo probissimo;
Nec illa pauca, laude te ferentium
Ad astra, sicut hoc meretur inclitum
Opus. Mihi nec est opus quid amplius
Loqui, quasi adderem mari meas aquas;
Tamen quod ipse postulas, ego libens
Eos sequor, meumque iungo calculum.

PECHAME perge fausto vt incipis pede
Et ede plura, lividumque *ZOILVM*,
Malumque virus huius invidentiæ
Teruntio valeto, cuncta qui potest,
Placere non potest ei, ipse *IVPITER*;
Nihil morare candidum lapillulum,
Nigrumque fæcis infimæ, places quibus
Sat est placere, doctioribus viris.

THO: HARDINGVS.

IN CLARISSIMI VIRI D. HENRICI PEACHAMI POETAE ANGLI CANTABRIGIENSIS

Minervam Britannam.

Nendo tulit palmam de stultâ PALLAS Arachnê
Ingenij, cum lis inter utramque foret:
Nec satis. offensam facto illam habuisse MINERVAM
Legimus, et pœnas inde dedisse Deæ.
Tela tua est opus hoc ipsâ vel PALLADE dignum
Ingenio.

IN MINERVAM AVTHORIS.

Ingenio, et doctæ facta labore manus
Quam culpare velit quisquis, vel vincere certet,
Fata feret stolidæ MOMVS araneolæ.

Hannibal Vrsinus
Neapolitanus.

SOPRA LA MINERVA BRITANNA DEL SIGr: HENRICO PEACHAMO.

ODE.

Tosto ch' al mondo apparse
Questa PALLA nouella,
Fulminò d' ira, ed' arse
GIOVE d' invidia, e sdegno.
Tremò la terra, e lo stellante regno.

Stupido APOLLO fisse
Le luci riverente
Nel Padre, e così disse
Mentre la terra lieta
Al bel lume di lui, tornò quieta.

Esposto hà fuor dal seno
** La BRITANNA GIVNONE*
Parto: non gia terreno;
Mà quel novello MARTE
*Promesso al mondo in non *mentite carte.*

* ANNA Regina,

* Gildam et Merlinum fortasse intelligit.

Da vn tronco DANO altiero,
Fiorito è 'l PRENCE HENRICO
Ritratto illustre, et vero
D' ARTV. cui sorte accerba
Tolse quello; chi à questi il Ciel riserba,

Visto 'l

ODE.

Visto' l novello parto,
Illuminar la terra:
Invido dal ciel parto,
Bramando dar in luce
Altro parto chi servi al novo Duce.

Dal capo di PEACHAMO,
Lieto discopro al mondo
Quel che cotanto bramo,
Che quegli vsci d' ANNA
Questi produce MINERVA BRITANNA

Giovan: Batista Casella.

AV TRES-EXCELLENT ET TRES-DOCTE POETE MONS[R]. HENRY PEACHAM.

SONNET.

On cognoit des grands Dieux ou l'aise ou la doleur,
A ces pourtraicts astres, que le Ciel nous figure:
Et leurs fils, ces Herôs de leur noble valeur,
En leurs riches blasons tousiours ont quelque Augure.
Tel fust l'ancien devis, qui premier fust parleur
Des Misteres plus beaux, la voix et l'escriture,
Luy servoient cõme aux Dieux, d'un servile MERCVRE
Truchemens à qui manque et le vray sens et l'heur.
PEACHAM, ce beau devis est ton choix, et ta Muse;
Les points Hebreux, le traicts dont le MEMPHITIQVE vse,
Ains Diue mesme, et le Ciel, t'apprend ce stile vieux
Que tu peux bien nommer, la MINERVE BRETONNE;
Car par dessus la Grecque, on luy doibt Couronne;
Si le filer n'est plus, que le scavoir de Dieux.

N. M. Fortnaius.

VPON

VPON THE AVTHOVR AND HIS MINERVA.

PALLAS thou hast a second champion bred,
As great in Artes, as was stout DIOMED
In Armes; that gainst enraged MARS could stand,
And dar'd to wound faire VENVS in the hand:
The ARGIVE fleete his sole Arme could defend,
And with the Gods he durst alone contend;
All this thy influence gaue, and more desired,
Like power thou hast into this braine inspired:
Thy champion too, whose Artes are fam'd as farre,
As was TYDIDES for his deedes of warre.
We know thou art MINERVA that alike
Hold'st Artes and Armes, canst speake as well as strike.

Tho: Heywood.

VPON THE AVTHOVR AND HIS MINERVA.

All eies behold, and yet not all alike,
Effects, and defects, both are in the eie,
As when an obiect gainst the eie doth strike,
Th' imagination straightwaies doth implie
Shapes, or what else the obiect doth present,
Weaker or stronger, as the sight is bent.

Within the minde two eies there are haue sight,
To iudge of thinges interiour hauing sence;
Foresight, and Insight, Iudgment makes them bright,
And most perspicuous through intelligence.
Foresight, foreseeth harmes, that may ensue:
Insight, doth yeild to reason what is due.

VPON THE AVTHOVR.

Then let not men deeme all with corp'rall ei'ne,
Eies may deluded be by falſe illuſions:
Eies may be partiall, eieſight may decline
By weakenes, age, or by abuſions.
Pride, envie, folly, may the ſight pervert,
And make the eie tranſgreſſe againſt the heart.

VVith outward ei'ne firſt view, and marke this booke,
Variety of obiects much will pleaſe;
VVith inward ei'ne then on the matter looke,
Foreſee the Authours care, and little eaſe
T'invent, t'imprint, and publiſh for delight,
And for reward but craues your good inſight.

Peacham my friend, I muſt confeſſe to thee,
My Inſight is but weake; ſuch as it is,
I verdict thus, no better worke I ſee
Of this ſame kinde, nothing I finde amiſſe,
If any fault there be, it is not thine,
The fault ſhall reſt in mens imperfect ei'ne.

William Segar Garter.. Principall king of Armes.

TO MASTER HENRY PEACHAM. A VISION VPON THIS HIS MINERVA.

Me thought I ſaw in dead of ſilent night
A goodly Citie all to cinders turned,
Vpon whoſe ruines ſate a Nymphe in white,
Rending her haire of wiery gold, who mourned
Or for the fall of that faire Citie burned,
  Or ſome deare Loue, whoſe death ſo made her ſad;
  That ſince no ioye in worldly thing ſhe had.

This was that *GENIVS* of that auntient *TROY*,
In her owne aſhes buried long agoe:
So grieu'd to ſee that *BRITAINE* ſhould enioy
Her *PALLAS*, whom ſhe held and honour'd ſo:
And now no litle memorie could ſhow
  To eternize her, ſince ſhe did infuſe,
  Her Enthean ſoule, into this Engliſh Muſe.

E. S.

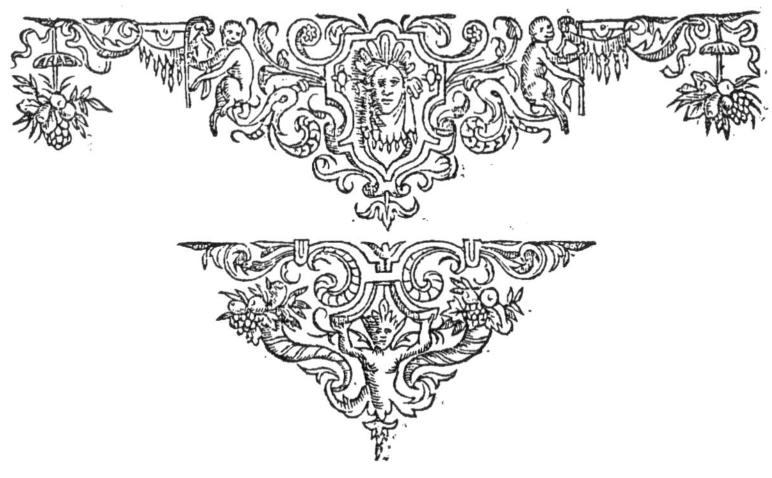

To my dread Soveraigne IAMES, *King of great* BRITAINE. *&c.*

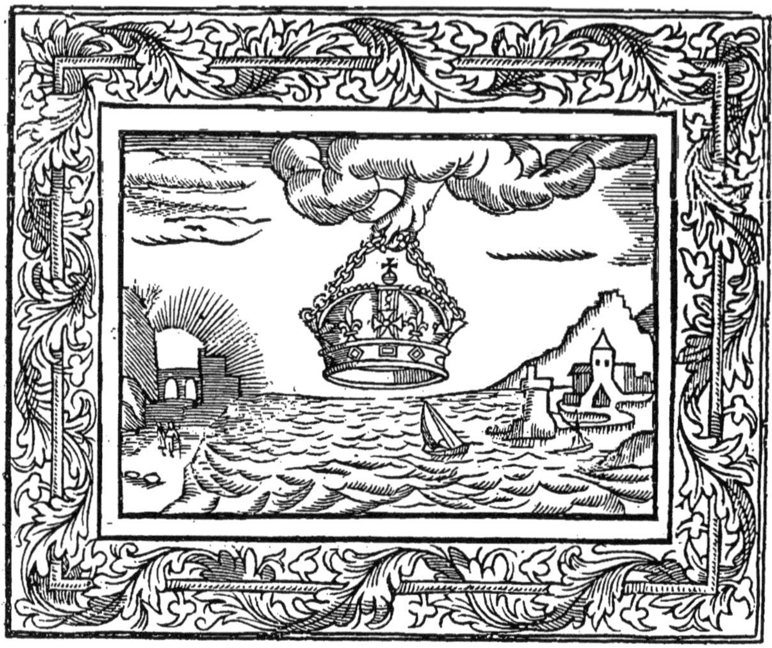

A SECRET arme out stretched from the skie,
In double chaine a Diadem doth hold:
Whose circlet boundes, the greater BRITANNIE,
From conquered FRAVNCE, to * THVLE sung of old:
Great IAMES, whose name beyond the INDE is told:
To GOD obliged so by two-fold band,
As borne a man, and Monarch of this land.

* Tibi serviet ultima Thvle, Virgil: THVLEM procul Axe remotam. Claudian. Schetland. et nautis nostris hodie Thilensel.

Thus since on heauen, thou wholly dost depend:
And from * aboue thy Crowne, and being hast:
With malice vile, in vaine doth man intend,
T'vnloose the knot that GOD hath link't so fast:
Who shoot's at * heaven, the arrow downe at last
Lightes on his head: and vengeance fall on them,
That make their marke, the Soveraigne Diadem.

Διοτρεφέες βασιλῆες. Homer.

Basil: Doron. lib. 1. pag. 2.

Nubibus en duplici vinctum Diadema catena,
Quod procul a nostro sustinet orbe manus:

Non alia te lege Deus (IACOBE) ligavit,
Quem regere imperio, fecit, et esse virum.

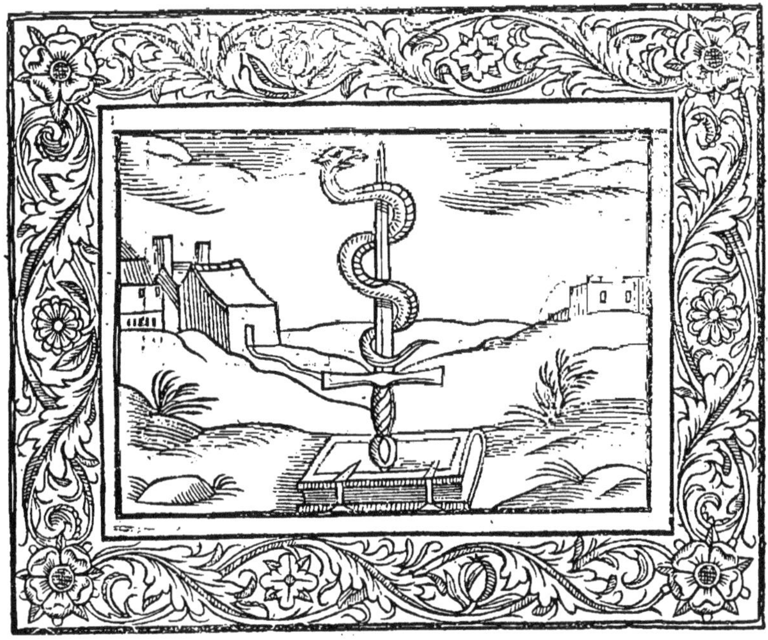

A POYSONOVS Serpent wreathed vp around
In ſcalie boughtes, a ſharpe two edged Sword,
Supported by a booke vpon the ground,
Is worldly wiſedome grounded on GODS word,
The which vnleſſe our proiects doth ſuſtaine,
Our plot is nought, and beſt deviſes vaine.

What ever then thou hap to take in hand,
In formoſt place, the feare of GOD preferre,
* Elſe, like the Foole thou buildeſt on the ſand,
By this (the *Lesbian* * ſtone) thou canſt not erre,
Which who ſo doth, his * firſt foundation lay,
Contriues a worke that never ſhall decay.

*Firmamentum eſt Dominus timentibus eum. Pſalm: 24.

* Ariſtot: in Ethicis.

* Conſiliorū gubernaculum lex divina ſit. Ciprian in Epiſtolis.

Squammiger in gyros gladio ſe colligit anguis,
Naturam ſignant quæ POLITIA tuam;
Effera Iuſtitia eſt, Prudentia vana SOLONIS,
Hæc niſi ſuſtentent Biblia ſacra DEI.

Baſili: Doron. lib: 1. pag: 3.

Timor igitur DEI ſolus eſt, qui cuſtodit hominum inter ſe ſocietatem, per quem vita ipſa ſuſtinetur, munitur, gubernatur. &c.

Lactantius de Ira divina. Cap 21.

Cui cedet.

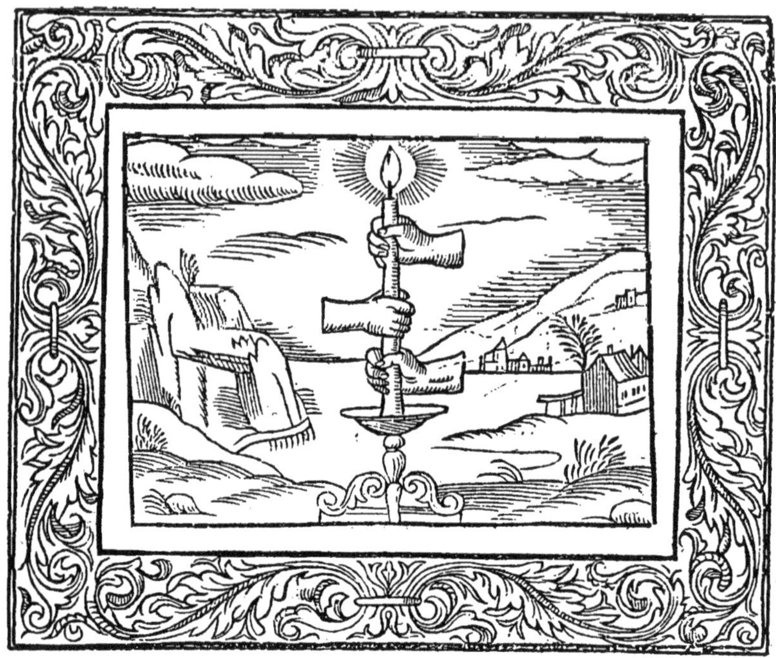

Two handes togeither heere with griping hold,
And all their force, doe ſtriue to take away
This burning Lampe, and Candleſtick of Gold,
Whoſe light ſhall burne in ſpite of Hell for ay:
And brighter then the beames of PHOEBVS ſhine,
For tis the Truth ſo holy and divine.

Which foule Ambition hath ſo often vext,
And ſwelling pride of Prælates put in doubt,
With Covetuouſnes that greedie Monſter next,
That long I feare me ſince it had bene out,
Did not thy hand (deare Saviour) from aboue
Defend it ſo, that it might never moue.

Quoties hominibus præeſſe deſidero, toties Deo meo præire contendo. Auguſt: ſuper Pſalm:

Baſil: Doron. lib: 2: pag: 38.

Perdita Avarities, et dira Superbia, Peſtis
Chriſtiadum infœlix, Ambitioque ſimul:
Certatim vt tentent extinguere lampada verbi,
Ni tua ſuccurrat (CHRISTE miſerte) manus.

Gregor: Moral: 26.

Summus locus bene regitur cum is qui præeſt, vitiis potius quam fratribus dominatur.

Omnis adeundi honoris eccleſiaſtici abſcinderetur ambitio, ſi ſe iudicandos, potius quam iudicaturos hi qui præeſſe volunt populis cogitarent.

Origen: ſuper Epiſt: ad Roman:

Nuſquam

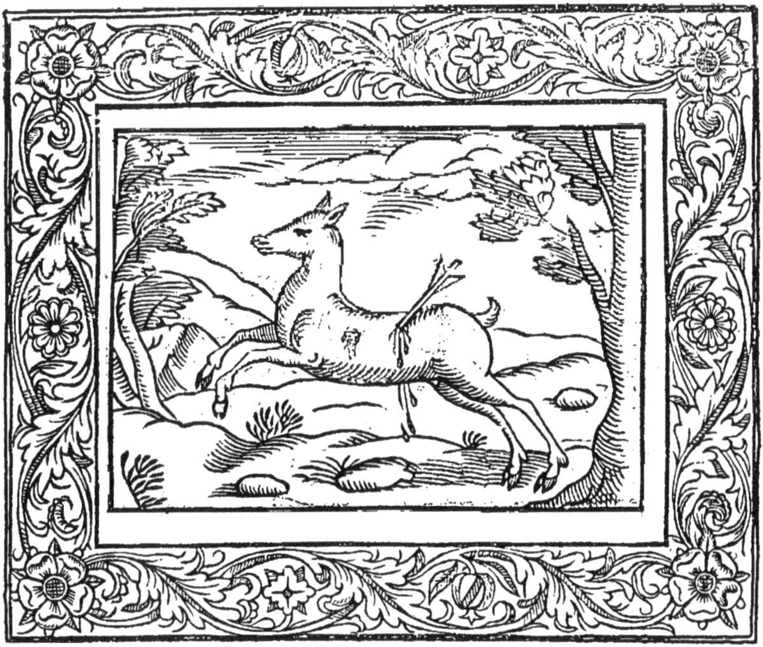

The silly Hind among the thickets greene,
While nought mistrusting did at safetie goe,
His mortall wound receiu'd with arrow keene
Sent singing from a Sheepeheard's secret bowe;
And deadly peirc'd, can in no place abide,
But runnes about with arrow in her side.

So oft we see the man whome Conscience bad
Doth inwardly with deadly torture wound,
From * place to place to range with Furie mad,
And seeke his ease by shifting of his ground
The meane neglecting which might heale the sinne,
* That howerly denckles more and more within.

* Mala conscientia in solitudine anxia, et sollicita est. Seneca Epist: 14.

* Perfecto demũ scelere magnitudo eius intelligitur. Tacitus 14.

Dictæus volucri quam fixit arundine pastor
Cerva fugit, nullis convalitura locis;
Conscia mens sceleris quem torquet, vbique pererrat,
Vulnere neglecto quod miser intus alit.

Basil: Doron. lib: 1. pag: 15.

Tranquillitate conscientiæ nil beatius excogitari potest.

Augustin: 21. de civitate DEI.

Conscientia affectuum corrector et animi pædagogus.

Origen.

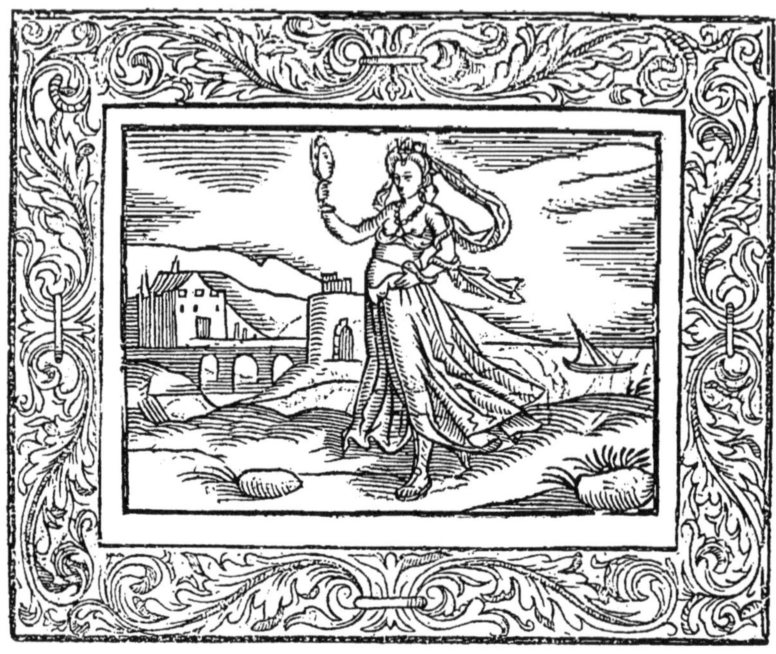

Vide Alciatum. Embl: 69.

A *VIRGINS face with Robes of light aray,*
Why hath (Selfe-loue) our Poets thee aßign'd?
Philaut: Loue should be young, and fresh as merry MAY,
Such clothing best agreeth with my mind.
What meanes that poisonous Serpent in thy hand?
Philaut: My bane I breed, by this you vnderstand.

I'th other hand say why that looking glasse?
Since in thee no deformitie I find,
Philaut: Know how in Pride Selfe-loue doth most surpasse,
And still is in her Imperfections blind:
And saue her owne devises * doth condemne,
All others labours, in respect of them.

* Quod volumus sanctum est. Augustin: contra Cresconium Grammat:

Cur Virgo incedis Philautia? *PHILA:* Virginis ora
Malit amor. *Serpens quid sinuosa manu?*
Philaut: Pectore virus alo. *Speculum sed consulis.* *PHI:* inde
Cætera dedignor, dum mea sola placent.

Basili: Doron. lib: 2. pag: 65.

Humanæ

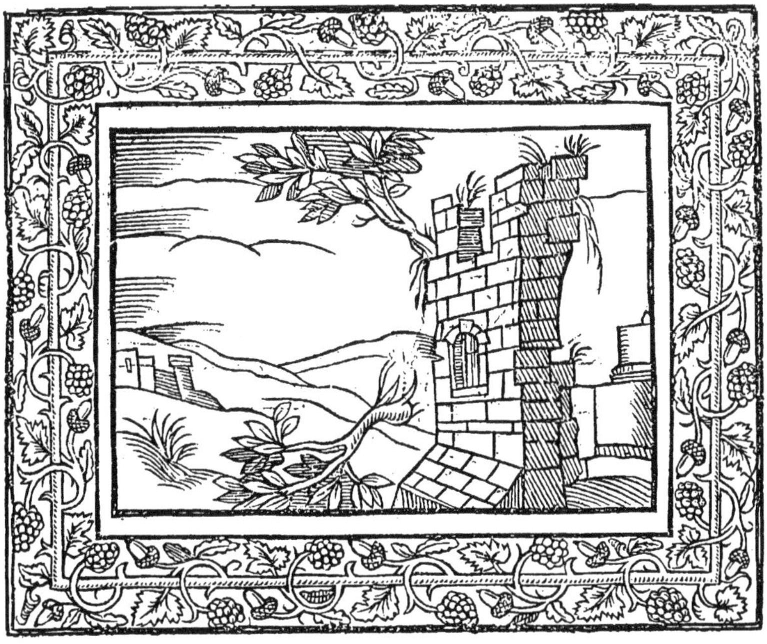

AT laſt my braunch doth wither and decay,
And with the ruine downe my ſelfe doe fall,
Whoſe pride did loath on ſurer ground to ſtay,
But needes would raigne, as KING vpon the wall,
To overlooke in ſcorne the ſhrubs below,
That did (I find) in greater ſafetie growe.

Omnis plantatio quam non plãtaverit pater meus cœleſtis, eradicabitur. Math: 15.

By this ſame tree, are all Traditions ment,
And what elſe hammer'd out of humane braine,
That on the Rocke, to reſt are not content,
But puffed vp with pride, and glory vaine;
Vnto their ſhame, doe moulder downe, and fall,
As doth this Elder growing on the wall.

Si ad divinæ traditionis caput, et originem revertamur, ceſſat õnis error humanus. Ciprian ad Pompeium.

Spreta cado tandem lapidum compâge ſoluta
Nec terræ ramos rebar egere meos:
Sic freta elanguent humano cuncta cerêbro,
Vt ſtabilis fugiant fœdera firma DEI.

Baſili: Doron.

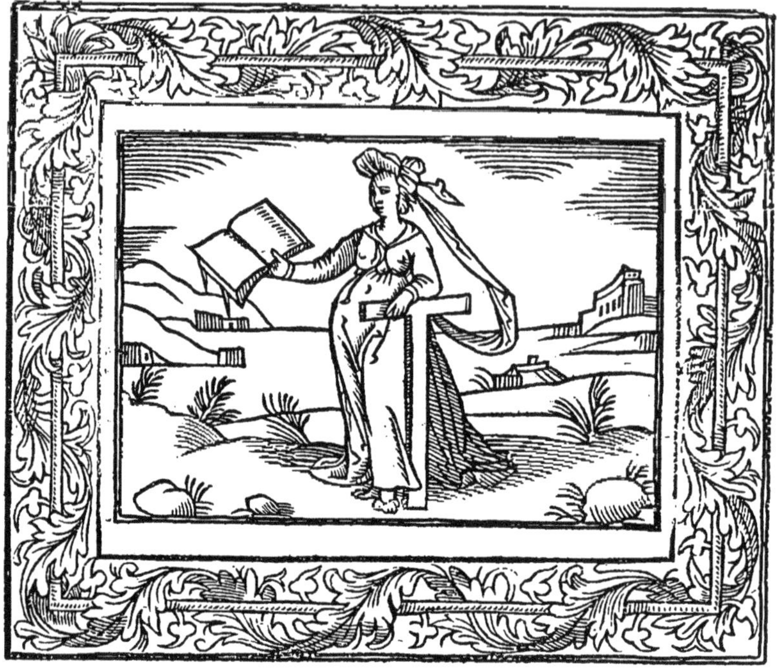

My hope is heauen, the crosse on earth my rest,
The foode that feedes me is my Saviours bloud,
My name is FAITH to all I doe protest,
What I beleeue is Catholique and good,
And as my Saviour strictly doth commaund,
My good * I doe with close and hidden hand.

* Tunc veraciter fideles sumus, si quod verbis promittimus, operibus adimplemus. Gregor: Homil: 29.

Nor Heresie, nor Schisme, I doe maintaine,
But as CHRIST's coate so my beliefe is one,
I hate all fancies forg'd of humane braine,
I let contention and vaine strifes alone;
If ought I neede I craue it from aboue,
And liue with all in Charitie and Loue.

Basil: Doron. lib: 1. pag: 11.

Crux mihi grata quies, sola et fiducia, cœlo
Me terris lactant vulnera (CHRISTE) tua:

Sancta Fides dicor, cunctis mea dogmata pando
Abdo sed occulte Religionis opus.

Titus. 3. Curent bonis operibus præesse qui credunt Deo.

Bernar: in Cant Serm: 24.

Mors fidei est separatio charitatis, credis in Christum? fac Christi opera vt vivat fides tua.

Nec

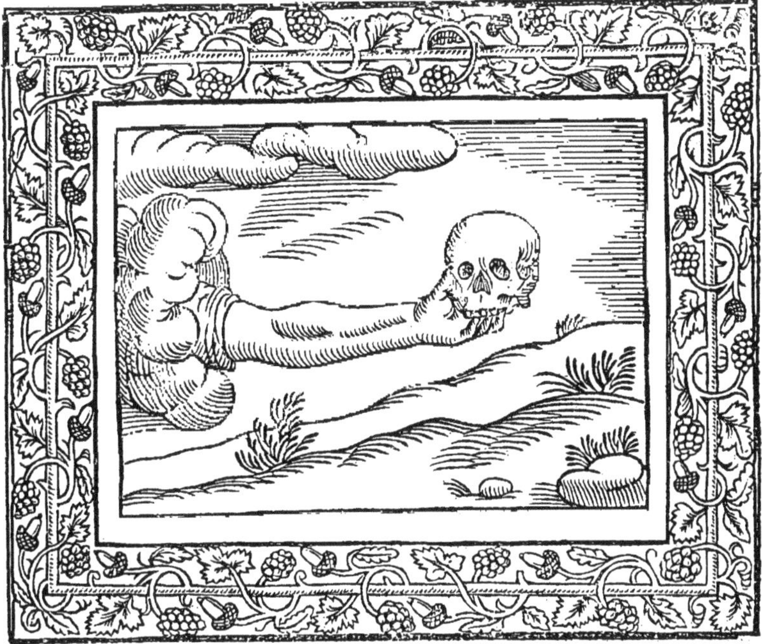

The Æthiopian Princes at their feaſtes,
Did vſe amid their cates, and coſtly cheere
A deadmans head, to place before their gueſtes,
That it in minde might put them what they were:
And PHILLIP dayly cauſed one to ſay,
Oh King remember that thou art but clay.

If Pagans could bethinke them of their end,
And make ſuch vſe of their mortalitie,
With greater hope their courſe let chriſtians bend,
Vnto the haven of heavens fœlicitie;
And ſo to liue while heere we drawe this breath,
We haue no cauſe to feare, or wiſh for death.

Perge tuo laute genio indulgere PHILIPPE,
Imperium cernis quam brevis hora manet:
Non properans timeo lethum mens conſcia recti
Inculcat quovis tempore CHRISTE veni.

Sed hoc meditatum ab adoleſcentia eſſe debet, mortem vt negligamus, ſine qua meditatione, tranquillo eſſe animo nemo poteſt.

Memorare noviſſima et non peccabis in eternum. Eccleſiaſt. 7.

Timor futuræ mortis quaſi clavis carnis omnes motus ſuperbiæ ligno crucis affigit. Aug: lib: 2 de doct: chriſtiana.

Baſil: Doron. lib: 1. pag: 17.

Mortem optare malum timere peius. Seneca in Oedipo.

Cicero in lib: de ſenectute.

Pſalmi

To the right Reverend Father in GOD, IOHN *Bishop of London.*

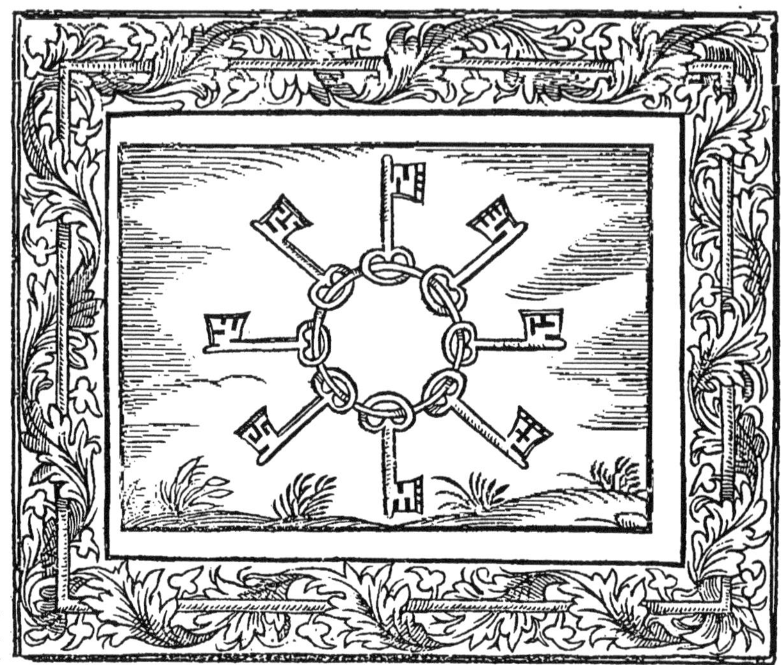

Basilic: Doron. lib: 1. pag: 11.

* Liber omnis Psalmorum similis est vrbi pulchræ, atque magnæ, cui ædes cõplures diversæque sint, quarum fores propriis clavibus diversisque claudantur, quæ cum in vnum locum cõgestæ permixtæque sint. &c Hilar: in prolog: psalmor explanat

TO sundry keies doth * HILARIE compare
The holy Psalmes of that prophetique King,
Cause in their Natures so dispos'd they are,
That as it were, by sundry dores they bring,
The soule of man, opprest with deadly sinne,
Vnto the Throne, where he may mercy winne.

οἱ μὲν ἐν διηγήματι λεγόμενοι, οἱ δὲ ἐν παραινέσει. οἱ δὲ ἐν προφητείᾳ. οἱ δὲ ὡς ἐν εὐχῇ. οἱ δὲ ὡς [ἐν] ἐξομολογήσει. Athanasius tomo primo in Epist: ad Marcellinum de interpreta: psalmorum.

For wouldst thou in thy Saviour * still reioyce,
Or for thy sinnes, with teares lament and pray,
Or sing his praises with thy heart and voice,
Or for his mercies giue him thankes alway?
Set DAVIDS Psalmes, a mirrour to thy mind,
But with his Zeale, and heavenly spirit ioin'd.

Clavibus innexis hymnos HILARIVS aptat,
Iessæi cecinit quos pia Musa senis,

Et vere, innumeros aditus hi quippe recludant
Mens quibus ætherei pulsat Asyla DEI.

Prius

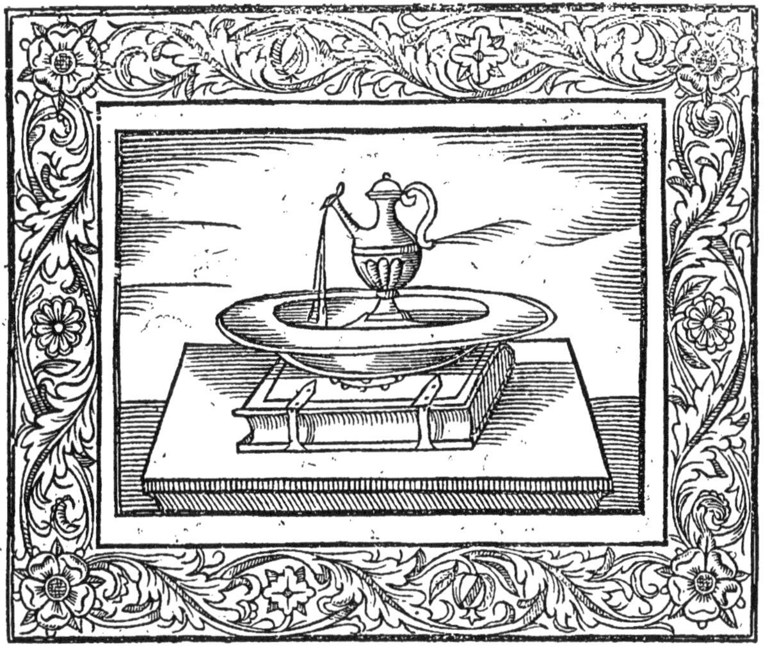

WHO takes in hand to turne this ſacred booke,
And heavenly wiſedome, doth from hence require,
His handes be cleane, I wiſh him firſt to looke:
No Dog or Swine, that walloweth in the mire, Διὶ λείβειν χερ-σὶν ἀνίπτοις. Heſiod:
Let dare to come, this pretious Iewell nigh,
The foe to filth, and all impuritie.

But if thou needes wilt launch into this ſea,
Where Lambes may wade, and Elephants may ſwimme,
Caſt all vncleane affections away,
And firſt with heartie prayer call on him,
Whoſe holy Spirit muſt guide thee in the ſence,
A thouſand times elſe better thou wert thence.

Sacra tuis manibus quicunque volumina verſas
Sordibus immunis quære ſalutis iter: Baſil: Doron. lib: 1. pag: 10.
Quoque volutaras carnis prius exue cœnum,
Aut Sus conſilium linque lutoſa DEI.

Veluti in coronis flores eſſe puros et ſuaves, niſi pura ſit et caſta manus contexens: ſic non ſatis eſt vt in ſacrarum literarum lectione verba ſint ſancta et pia niſi pura etiam ac ſanctiſſima mente hæc legantur, ac animo concipiantur. Tuitienſis.

* Ad Divos caſte adeunto. * Cicero.

To the High and mightie *IAMES*, King of greate Britaine,

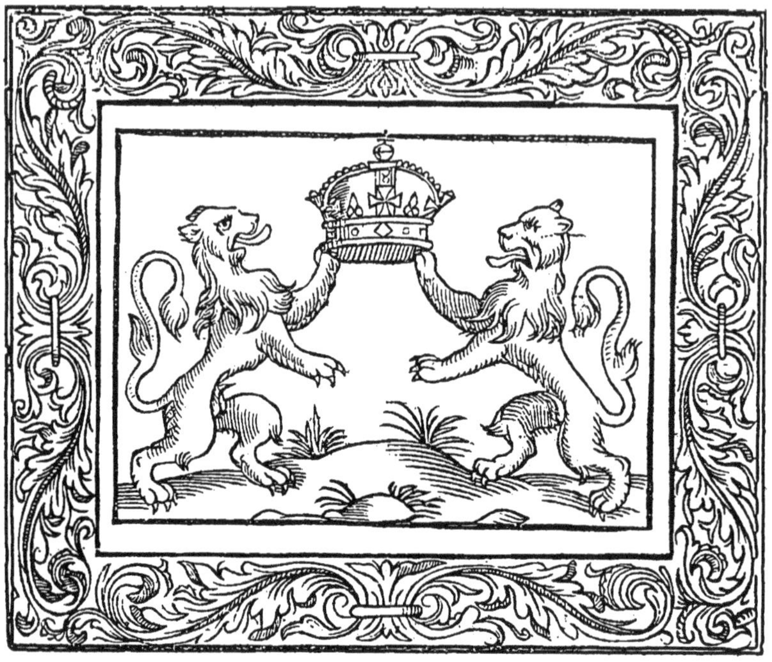

TWOO Lions ſtout the Diadem vphold,
Of famous Britaine, in their armed pawes:
Scilicet Anglicus et Scoticus.
The one is Red, the other is of Gold,
And one their Prince, their ſea, their land and lawes;
Their loue, their league: whereby they ſtill agree,
In concord firme, and friendly amitie.

BELLONA henceforth bounde in Iron bandes,
Shall kiſſe the foote of mild triumphant PEACE,
Nor Trumpets ſterne, be heard within their landes;
Envie ſhall pine, and all old grudges ceaſe:
Braue Lions, ſince, your quarrell's lai'd aſide,
On common foe, let now your force be tri'de.

Vnum ſuſtentant gemini Diadema Leones,
Concordes vno Principe, mente, fide.

Fœdere iunguntur ſimili, cœloque, ſaloque,
Nata quibus Pax hæc inviolanda manet.

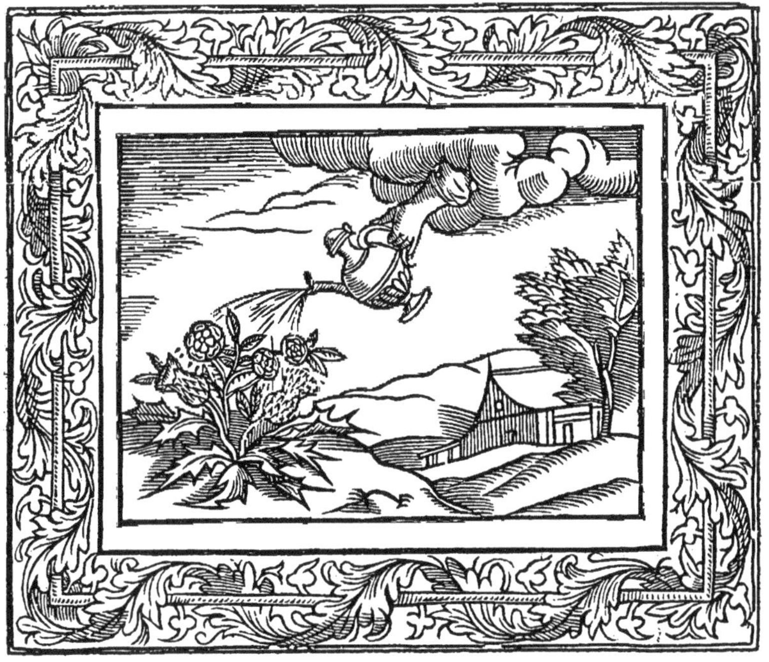

THE Thiſtle arm'd with vengeaunce for his foe,
And here the Roſe, faire CYTHERAEAS flower;
Together in perpetuall league doe growe,
On whome the Heavens doe all their favours power;
" For what * th' Almighties holy hand doth plant,
" Can neither coſt, or carefull keeping want. * 1. Cor 3. 6.

Magnifique PRINCE, the ſplendour of whoſe face,
Like brighteſt PHOEBVS vertue doth reviue;
And farre away, light-loathing vice doth chaſe,
Theſe be thy Realmes; that vnder thee doe thriue,
And which vnite, GODS providence doth bleſſe,
With peace, with plentie, and all happines.

Terror hic hoſtilis, Cypriæ ſacra illa puellæ,
Carduus vnanimes, et roſa verna virent.
Quæ gelidus cœlo fœcundans imber ab alto
Omina dat regnis (summe Monarcha) tuis.

13 TO THE THRICE-VERTVOVS, AND FAIREST OF QVEENES, ANNE QVEENE OF GREAT BRITAINE:

Anagramma D: Gul: Fouleri.

In ANNA regnantium arbor.
ANNA *Britannorum Regina*.

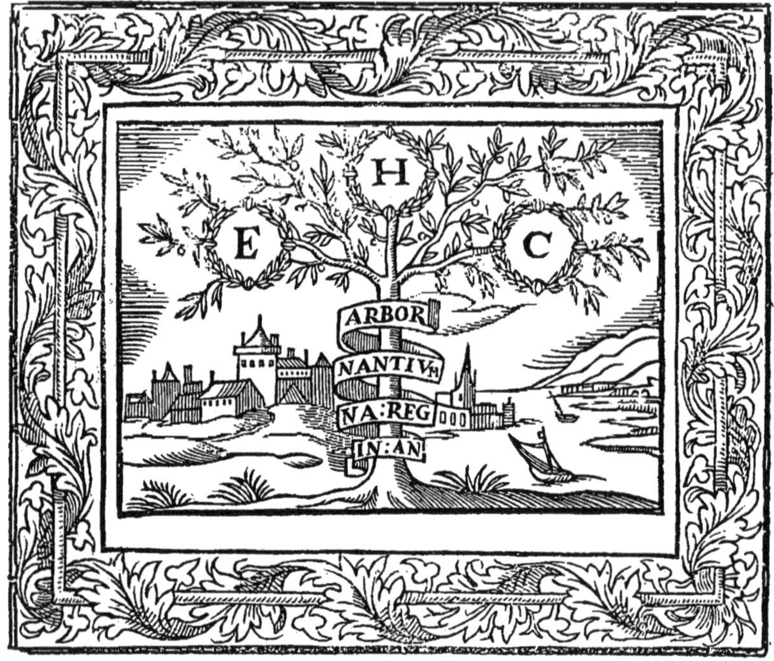

AN Oliue.lo, with braunches faire dispred,
Whose top doth seeme to peirce the azure skie,
Much seeming to disdaine, with loftie head
The Cedar, and those Pines of THESSALIE,
Fairest of Queenes, thou art thy selfe the Tree,
The fruite * thy children, hopefull Princes three.

Which thus I ghesse, shall with their outstretcht armes,
In time o'respread Europa's continent,
* To shield and shade, the innocent from harmes,
But overtop the proud and insolent:
Remaining, raigning, in their glories greene,
While man on earth, or Moone in heauen is seene.

* Non classes, non Legiones, perinde firma imperii munimenta quam numerum liberorum. Tacitus. 4. Hist:

* parcere subiectis. &c.

Fatum

To the most excellent Princesse ELIZABETH, onely Daughter to our Soveraigne Lord King IAMES, King of great BRITAINE.

ELISABETHA Steuarta. *Has Artes beata velit.* Anagramma.

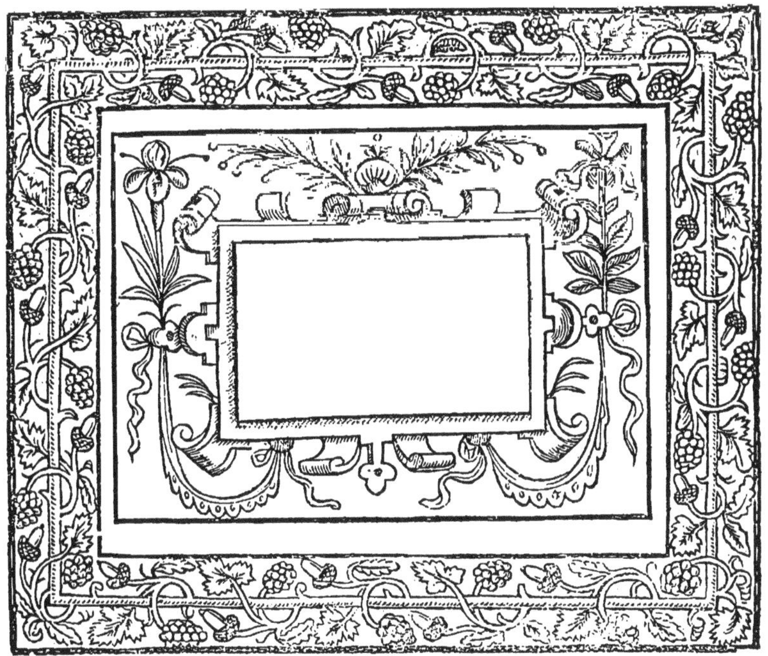

FAIRE Princesse, great, religious, modest, wise,
By birth, by zeale, behauiour, iudgment sound,
By whose faire arme, my Muse did first arise,
That crept before full lowly on the ground,
And durst not yet from her darke shade aspire,
Till thou sweete Sunne, didst helpe to raise her higher.

Thus since by thee, shee hath her life and sappe,
And findes her growth by thy deere cherishent,
In thy faire eie consistes her future hap:
Heere write her fate, her date, her banishment,
Or may she that day-lasting Lillie be,
Or * SOLI-SEQVIVM e're to follow thee.

* The flower of the Sunne (some take it for the Marigold) continually following the same.

To the moſt Chriſtian King LOVIS, *XIII. King of* FRAVNCE *and* NAVARRE.

Anagram: Henr. IIII. occiſi a ſceleſtiſſimo illo Ravillac. G. F.

Henricus IV Galliarum Rex.
In Herum exurgis Ravillac.

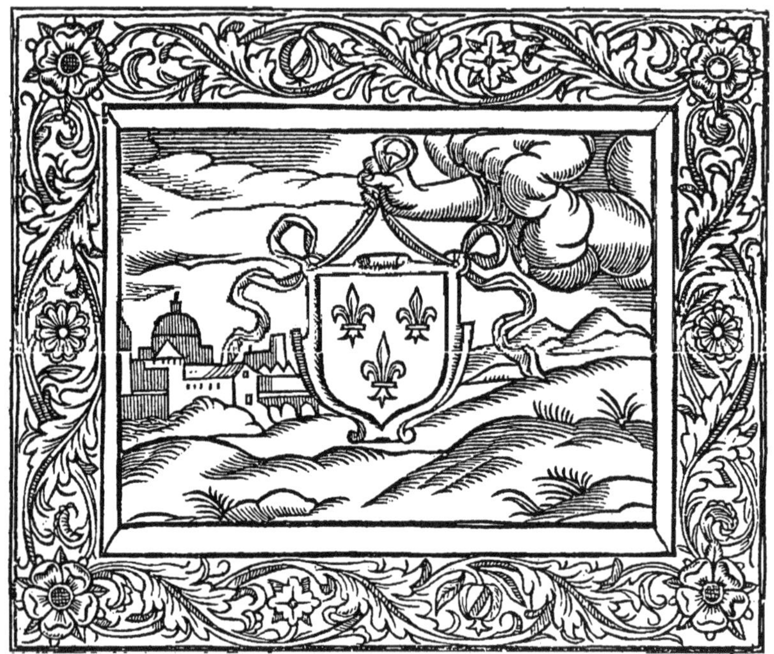

MOST Chriſtian King, if yet haſt turn'd away,
Thoſe kindly rivers, from thy royall eies
For Fathers loſſe, this little view I pray
Our Muſe reſerues from his late Exequies:
The leaſt of littles, yea though leſſe it be,
It's thine, and ſigne, of her loues loyaltie.

Which, whereſoe're preſented to thy view,
(For all thinges teach vs) thinke a heavenly mind
Is meant vnto thee, by that cullour Blew,
The Gold, the golden plentie thou doſt find;
The number of thy * Heaven-ſent Lillies, three,
Is concord's ground, the ſweeteſt harmonie.

* Tria lilia cœlitus delata. S: Clithoveo.

Vnita

To the high and mightie PHILLIP *King of Spaine &c.*

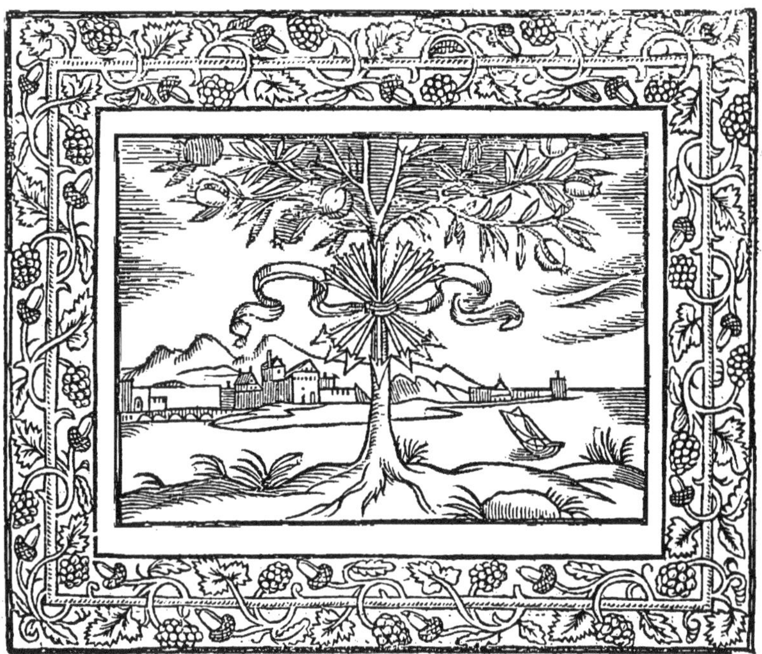

TO you great Prince, ſtrong ſtay, and powerfull prop
Of Chriſtian ſtate, who by thy feared might,
And reſtles care; the ſame ſupporteſt vp;
From neighbour MAHOVNDS vndermining ſpight;
From thy GADE's pillars, to the weſt as farre,
As THETIS leades vs to the Southerne ſtarre.

I offer vp theſe Arrowes, with the Tree
Of thy * Grenade, the Symbole long agoe
Of great FERNANDO's famous *victorie,
What Time he gaue the MOORES their overthrow:
Though here it may impart, the fruite that ſpringes
By Peace and concord of all Chriſtian Kinges.

* In the time of King HENRY the 7. in memory of which battaile wonne by Archerie, the ſheafe of Arrowes is yet giuen on the Spaniſh coine.

TO

TO THE MOST RENOWNED, AND Hopefull, HENRIE Prince of VVALES, &c.

Anagramma Authoris.

Βρεταννίας στέφαρει.

HENRICVS Walliæ Princeps.

Par Achillis, Puer vne vinces.

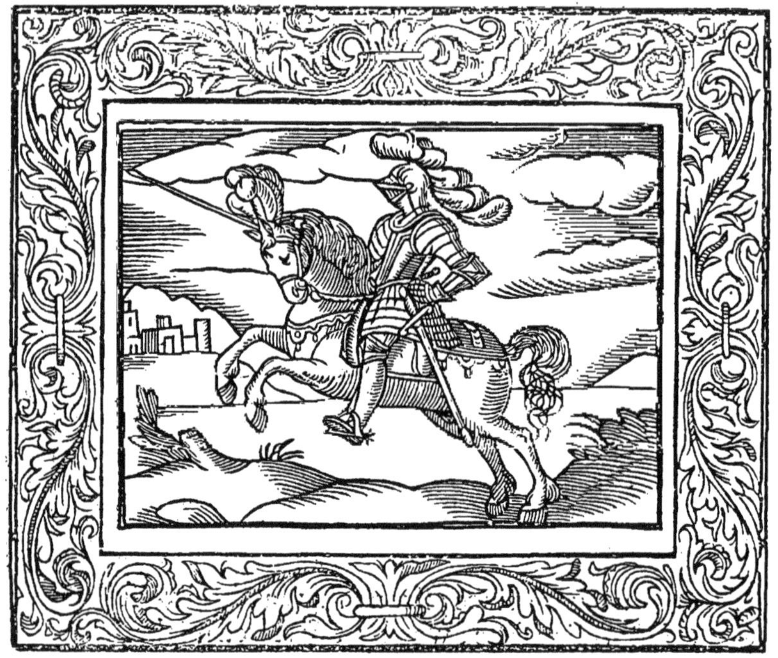

THVS, thus young HENRY, like Macedo's ſonne,
Ought'ſt thou in armes before thy people ſhine.
A prodigie for foes to gaze vpon,
But ſtill a glorious Load-ſtarre vnto thine:
Or ſecond PHOEBVS whoſe all piercing ray,
Shall cheare our heartes, and chaſe our feares away.

* Plutarch in Alexandro.

That (once as *PHILLIP) IAMES may ſay of thee,
Thy BRITAINE ſcarcely could thy courage hold,
That whether TVRKE, SPAINE, FRAVNCE, or ITALIE,
The RED-SHANKE, or the IRISH Rebell bold,

Baſil: Doron.

Shall rouze thee vp, thy Trophees may be more,
Then all the HENRIES euer liu'd before.

Macte tua virtute decus, ſpes alma BRITANNVM
Alter ALEXANDER conſpiciende tuis:
Provocet Hiſpanus, ſeu Turca, rebellis Hibernus
Herulus a tergo ſive laceſſat inops.

E corpore

TO THE RIGHT NOBLE, AND MOST TOWARDLY YOVNG PRINCE, *CHARLES* DVKE OF *YORKE*.

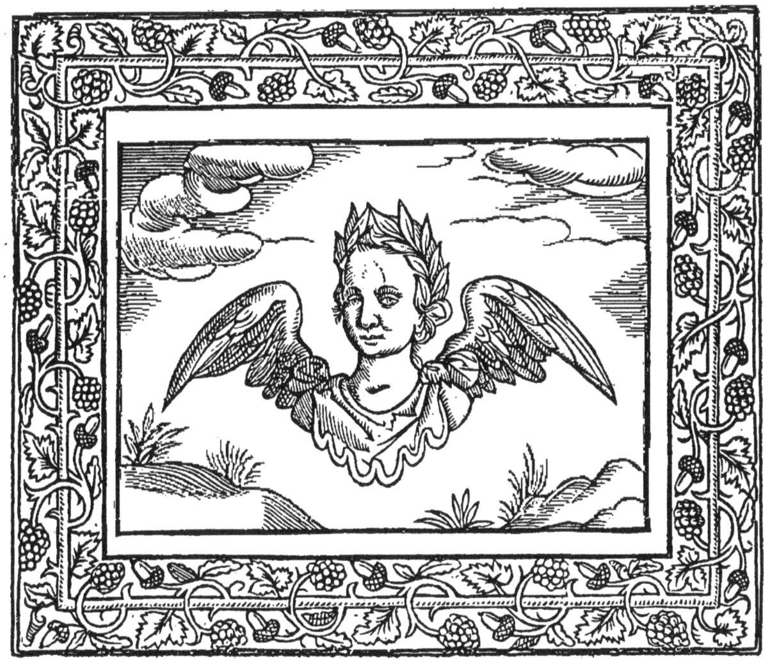

SWEETE Duke, that bear'ſt thy Fathers Image right
Aſwell in * bodie, as thy towardly mind;
Within whoſe cheeke * me thinkes in Red and white
Appeare the Roſes yet againe conioind;
Where, howſoe're their warres appeaſed be,
Each, ſtriues with each, for Soveraignitie.

Since Nature then in her faire-Angell mould,
Hath framd thy bodie, ſhew'd her beſt of art:
Oh let thy mind the * faireſt virtues hold,
Which are the beautie of thy better part:
And which, (braue CHARLES) ſhall make vs * loue thee more,
Then all thy ſtate we outwardly adore.

videtur mihi Venus quæpiam, ac gratia concomitari principem. Xenoph: in Hier:

* Et divitiarum, et formæ gloria, fluxa atque fragilis eſt, virtus clara æternaque habetur. Saluſt: Cat:

Ὡς ἡδὺ κάλλος ὅταν ἔχει νοῦν σώφρονα. Menander.

 TO THE RIGHT HONOVRABLE ROBERT, EARLE OF SALISBVRIE, AND LORD HIGH TREASORER OF ENGLAND, &c.

Anagramma Authoris.

ROBERTVS CAECILIVS.

Is cœlebs, Vrit cura.

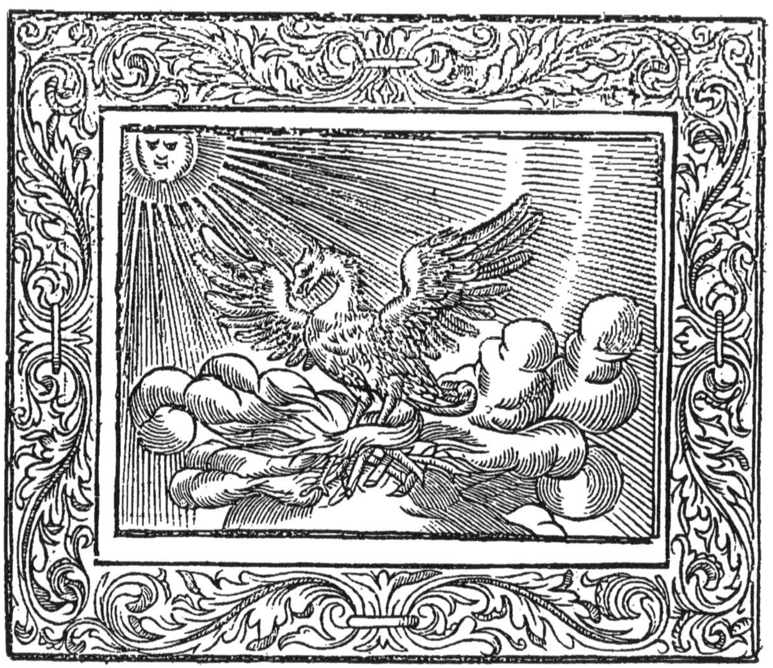

TH' Arabian PHOENIX heere, of golden plumes,
And bicie brest, vpon a sacred pile
Of sweetest odors, thus himselfe consumes;
By force of PHOEBVS fiery beames, the while,
From foorth the ashes of the former dead,
A faire, or fairer, by and by is bred.

You, you (Great Lord) this wondrous PHOENIX are,
Who wast your selfe in Zeale, and whot desire;
Of Countries good, till in the end * your care
Shall worke your end, as doth this PHOENIX fire.
But while you are consuming in the same,
You breede a second, your immortall Fame.

* Alia ex aliis cura fatigat, vexat animos, noua tempestas. Seneca.

To the Right Honourable and my singuler good Lord HENRY HOVVARD *Earle of Northhampton, Lord Privie Seale. &c.*

HENRICVS HOVVARDVS Comes Northamptoniensis.
Pius, Castus huic mentis honor, mere honorandus.

Anagramma Authoris.

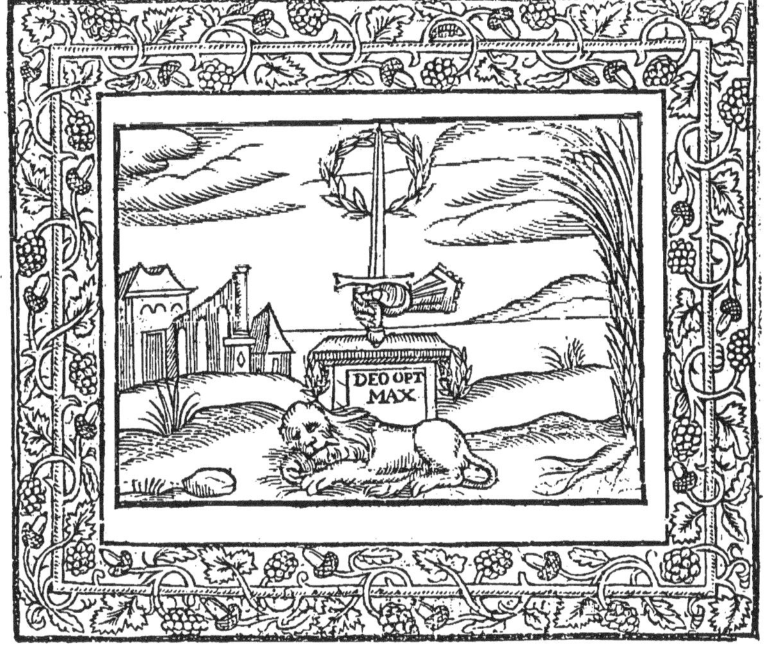

A SNOW WHITE Lion by an Altar sleepes,
(Whereon of Virtue are the Symboles plac't,)
Which day and night, full carefully he keepes,
Least that so sacred thing mought be defac't
By Time, or Envie, who not farre away,
Doe lurke to bring the same vnto decay.

Great Lord, by th' Altar Pietie is ment,
Thus, wherevpon is virtue seated sure:
Which thou protectest with deare cherishment;
And dost thy best, their safetie to procure
By howerly care, as doth this Lion white
Tipe of thy mildnes, and thy feared might,

To the right truely Noble, and most Honourable Lord VVILLIAM, *Earle of Penbrooke.*

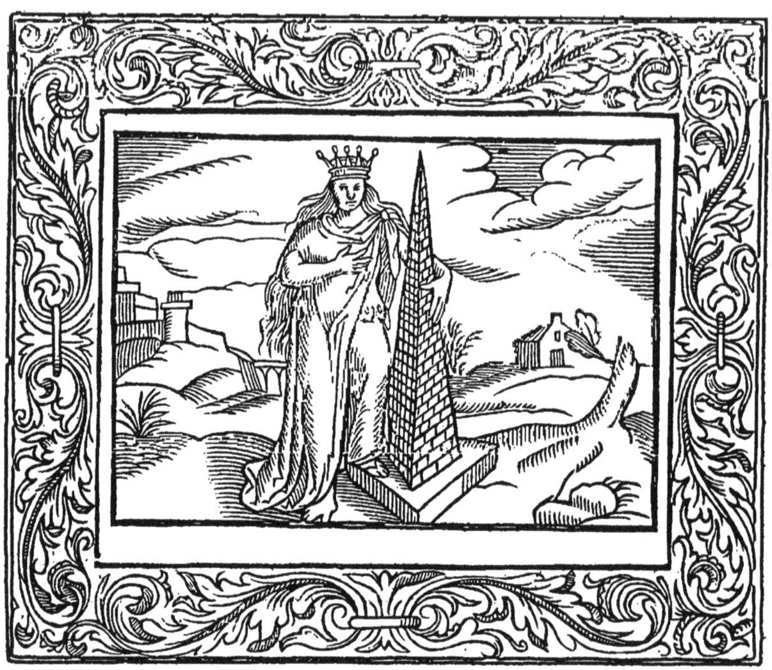

In med: Adriani Imp:

A LADIE faire, who with Maiestique grace,
Supportes a huge, and stately Pyramis.
(Such as th'old Monarches long agoe did place,
By NILVS bankes, to keepe their memories;)
Whose brow (with all the orient Pearles beset,)
Begirte's a rich and pretious Coronet.

Shee Glorie is of Princes, as I find
Describ'd in Moneies, and in Meddailes old;
Those Gemmes are glorious proiectes of the mind,
Adorning more their Roiall heades, then Gold.
The Pyramis the worldes great wonderment,
Is of their fame, some * lasting Moniment.

* Ingenii præclara facinora sicut Anima Immortalia sunt. Salust:

Ovid: ad Liviam.

Facta Ducis vivent operosaque gloria rerum
Hæc manet hæc avidos effugit vna rogos.

Ragione

To the right Honourable Sir IVLIVS CAESAR, *Knight.*

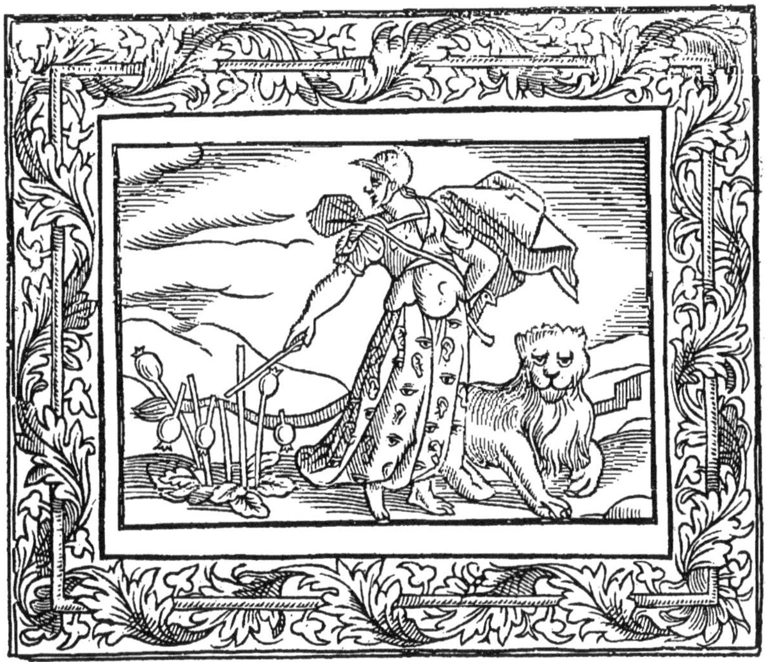

WHO sits at sterne of Common wealth, and state
Of's chardge and office heere may take a view,
And see what daungers howerly must ainate,
His ATLAS-burden, and what cares accrew
At once, so that he had * enough to beare,
Though HERCVLES, or BRIAREVS he were.

He must be strongly arm'd against his foes
Without, within, with hidden Patience:
Be seru'd with * eies, and listening eares of those,
Who from all partes can giue intelligence
To gall his foe, or timely to prevent
At home his malice, and intendiment.

That wand is signe of high Authoritie,
* The Poppie heads, that wisdome would betime,
* Cut of ranke weedes, by might, or pollicie,
As mought molest, or over-proudly clime:
The Lion warnes, no thought to harbour base,
The Booke, how lawes must giue his proiectes place.

* Princeps sua scientia non potest cuncta complecti. Tacitus Annal: 3. Nec vnus mentem molis tantæ esse capacem. Annal: 1.

* πολλοὶ βασιλέως ὀφθαλμοὶ καὶ πολλὰ ὦτα. Xenophon. in Pædia. Cyri.

* Rex velut deliberabundus in hortum ædium transit &c. Livi: lib: primo Decad: 1.

* Ne patiatur hebescere aciem suæ authoritatis. Tacitus Annal: 1.

To the right Honourable, and most noble Lord, HENRY, *Earle of Southampton.*

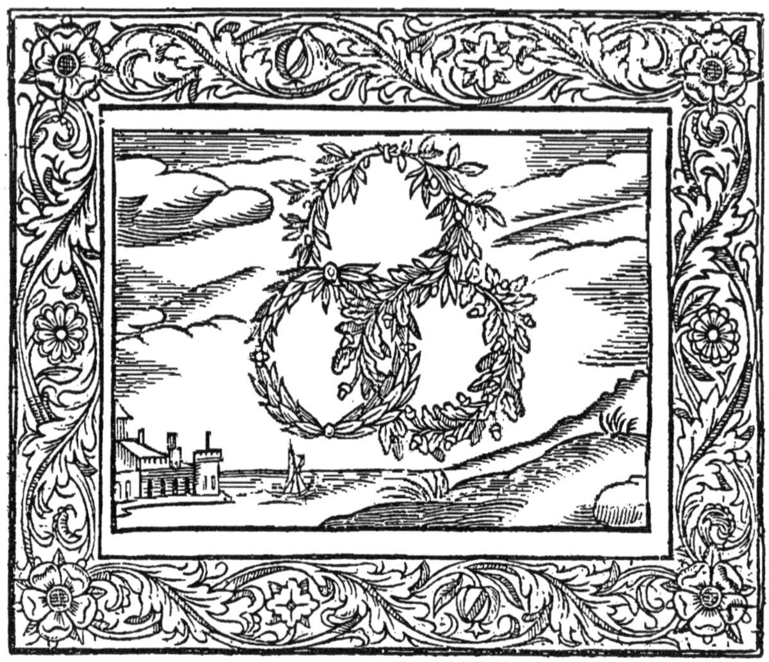

THREE Girlondes once, COLONNA did devize
For his Impresa, each in other ioin'd;
The first of OLIVE, due vnto the wise,
The learned brow, the LAVREL greene to bind:
The OKEN was his due aboue the rest,
Who had deserued in the Battaile best.

Cesar Ripa in Iconol:

His meaning was, his mind he would apply
By due desert, to challenge each, his prize:
And rather choose a thousand times to die,
Then not be learned, valiant, and wise.
How fewe alas, doe now adaies we finde,
(Great Lord) that beare, thy truely noble mind.

Merenti

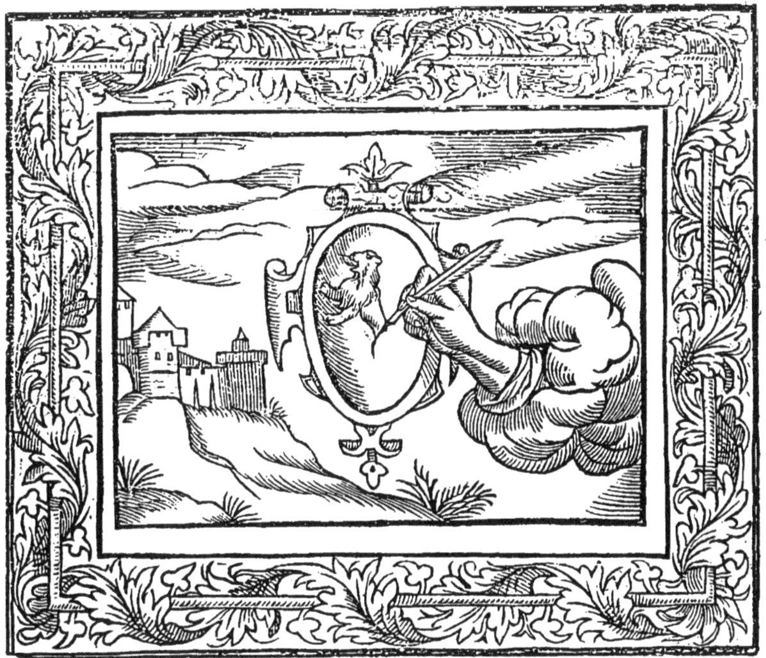

WHEN Troian youth went out into the field,
With courage bold, againſt the Greekes to fight;
With * naked Sword they marched, and their Shield
Devoide of charge, ſaue only painted white:
Herein the Captaine with his hand did write,
(The Battaile done,) ſome Enſigne of his fame,
Who had by valour, beſt deſeru'd the ſame.

Oh Age of Iuſtice, yet vnlike to this
Wherein wee liue, where MOME and MIDAS ſhare
* In vertues merit, and th' inglorious is
Allow'd the place ſometimes in Honours chaire,
Wherein Armes, ill, but worſer, Artes doe fare,
Times haſt, be gone, with all the ſpeede ye may,
That thus we liu'd, no after Age may ſay.

* Enſe levis nudo parmaque inglo-rius alba. Virg: AEneid:

* Virtutis Honos vberrimum ali-mentum. Valer: Max: de inſtitutis antiquis.

Fœlicitas

To my Honourable Lord OLIVER *Lord Saint* IOHN *of Bletnesho.*

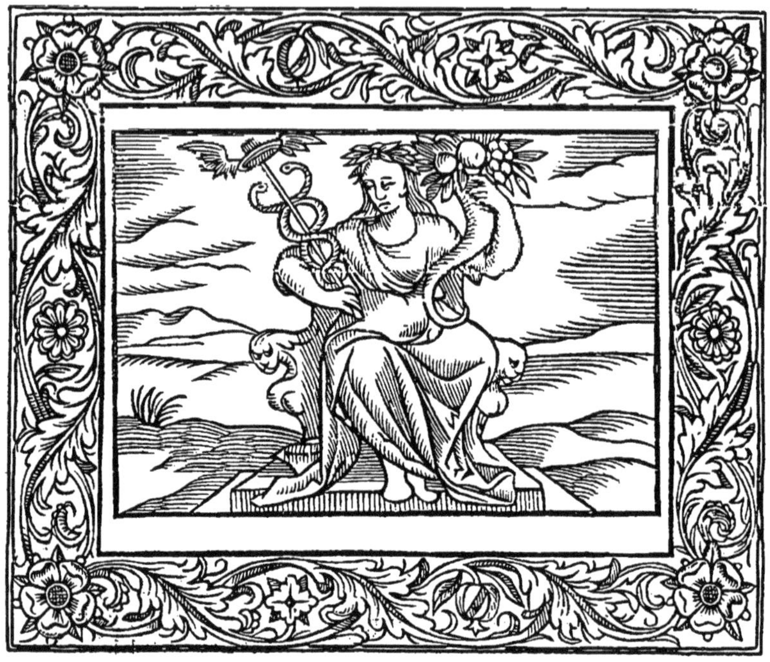

Iulia Mammea.

FOELICITIE by IVLIA once devis'd
This shape doth beare, a Ladie louely bright
With Mercuries Caduceus, enthroniz'd,
Her golden haire with flowery girlonds dight:
The horne of plentie, th'other hand doth hold
With all the fruites, and dainties may be told.

For why? content, she raigneth like a Queene;
Richest in Quiet, and the Muses skill,
Without the which, wee most vnhappie beene
The * plentie that her horned cup doth fill;
Our labours fruite, the which when we possesse
Wee haue attaind our worldly happines.

* Quæ (tamen) alia res civiles peperit furores quam nimia fœlicitas. Flo: 3. Cap: 12.

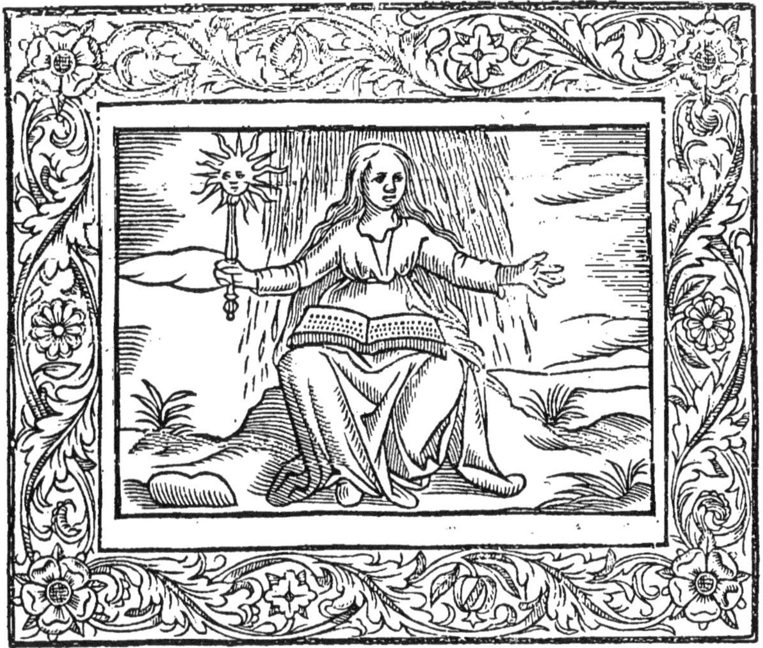

HEERE Learning ſits, a comely Dame in yeares;
Vpon whoſe head, a heavenly dew doth fall:
Within her lap, an opened booke appeares:
Her right hand ſhewes, a ſunne that ſhines to all;
* Blind Ignorance, expelling with that * light:
The Scepter ſhewes, her power and ſoveraigne might.

Her out * ſpread Armes, and booke her readines,
T' imbrace all men, and entertaine their loue:
The ſhower, thoſe ſacred graces doth expreſſe
By Science, that do flow from heaven aboue.
Her age declares the ſtudie, and the paine;
Of many yeares, ere we our knowledge gaine.

* Exempla omnia iacerent in tenebris niſi literarum lumen Hiſtoriæ accederet. Cicero. pro Archia Poeta.

* Studiis ac literis res ſecundæ ornantur adverſæ iuvantur: Cic: ad Luceium Epiſt. 5 famil: vide plura in orat: pro Archia poeta.

Via ad Deum eſt Scientia quæ ad inſtitutionem recte et honeſte vivendi pertinet.

Hugo.

TO the honourable Lord, the L: Harrington.

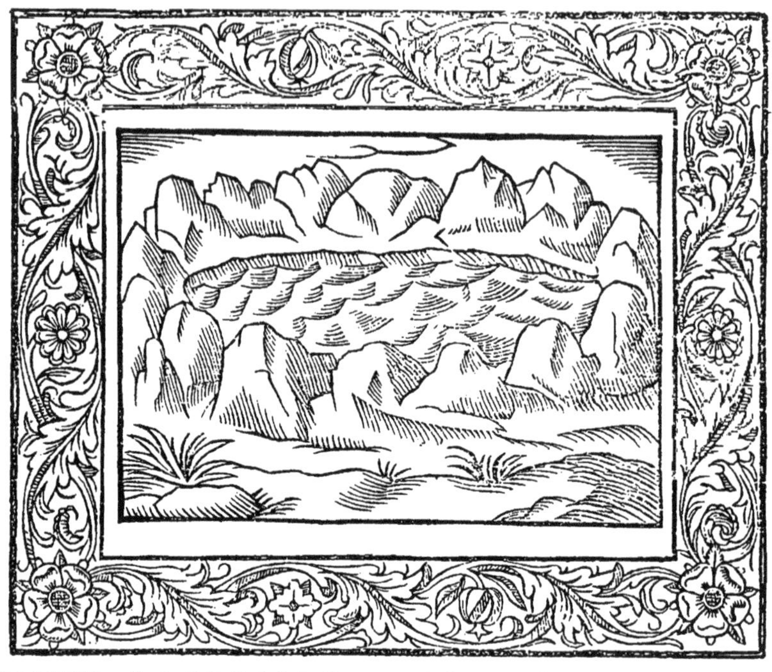

D: Philippi Sydnæi.

THE CASPIAN Sea, as Hiſtories do ſhow,
(Whome Rocky Shores, on every ſide ſurround,)
Was never ſeene by man, to ebbe and flow:
But ſtill abides the ſame, within his bound;
That drought no whit, diminiſheth his ſtore,
Nor neighbour ſtreames, augment his greatnes more.

Thus ſhould we beare, one and the ſelfe-ſame ſaile,
In what ere fortune, pleaſeth God to ſend,
In mid'ſt of trouble, not of courage faile,
Nor be to proude, when fortune is our frend:
And in all honeſt actes, we take in hand,
Thus conſtant, in our reſolutions ſtand.

Statius 5 ſilvar: 1.

Nec tamen hic mutata quies, probitaſve ſecundis
Intumuit, tenor idem animo, moreſq; modeſti
Fortuna creſcente manent.----

His

TO the honourable the Lord Wootton.

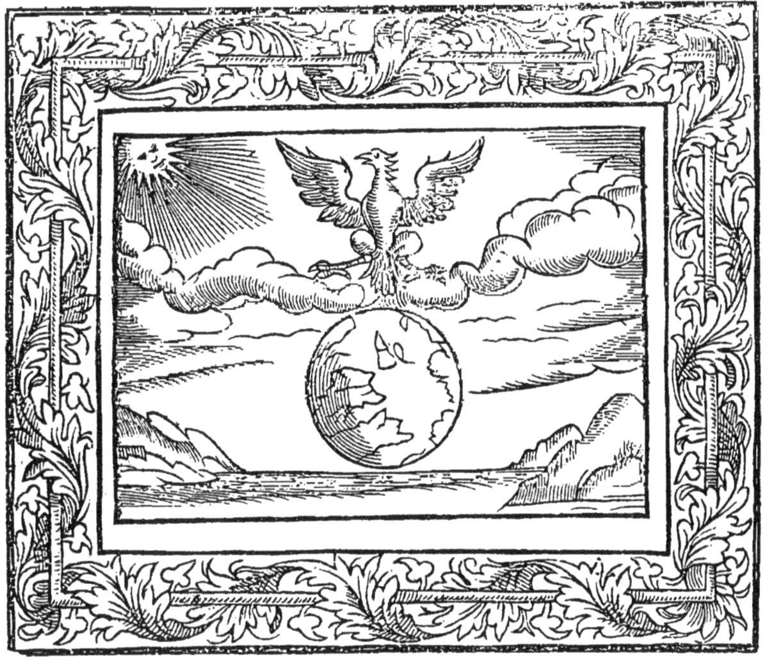

YEE Nobleſt ſprightes, that with the bird of IOVE,
Haue learnt to leaue, and loath, this baſer earth,
And mount, by your inſpired thoughtes aboue,
* To heaven-ward, home-ward, whence you had your birth:
Take to you this, that Monarches may envie,
Your heartes content, and high fœlicitie.

You, you, that over-looke the cloudes of care,
And ſmile to ſee a multitude of Antes,
Vppon this circle, ſtriuing here and there,
For THINE and MINE, yet pine amid their wantes;
While yee your ſelues, ſit as ſpectators free,
From action, in their follies tragædie.

* Virtus reclu-dens immeritis mori Cœlum, negata tentat iter via Cœtusque vulgares, et vdam ſpernit humum fugiente penna: Horat: 3 carm: ode. 2.

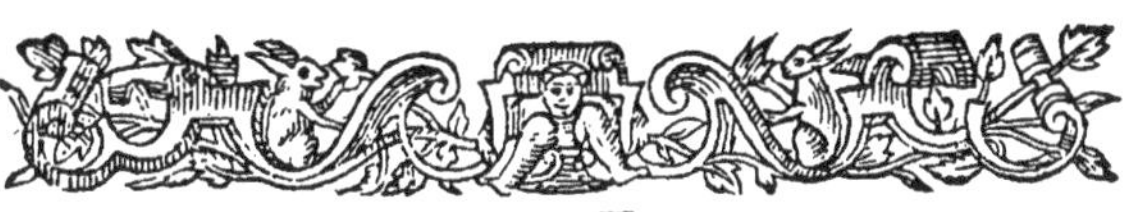

To the Honourable Sir EDVVARD COKE, Lord cheife Iuſtice of the common Pleas.

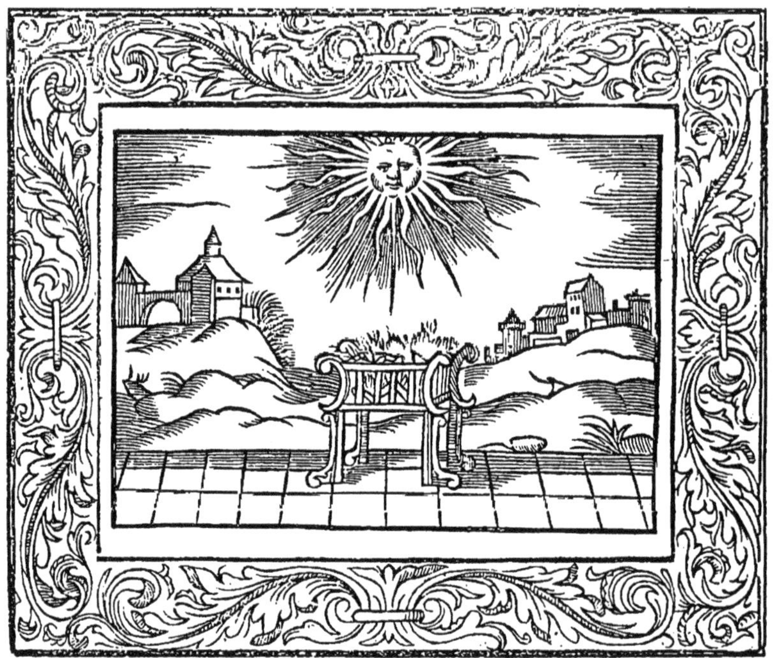

THE fiery Coales, that in the ſilent night,
(When vaile of darknes, all had overſpred)
With glowing heate, about did giue their light,
Since glorious PHOEBVS hath diſcovered
Doe looſe foorthwith their ſplendor, at his ſight:
And of themſelues, doe fall to Cinders quite.

So * traiterous proiectes, while they lie obſcure,
They cloſely feede the plotter, with their light,
Who thinkes within, he hath the matter ſure,
Not dreaming how, the Truth that ſhineth bright;
Will ſoone reveale the ſecret of his thought;
And bring his ripeſt practiſes to nought.

* Iudices iſtis dã tor qui ſacrilegis ſolent.

Nulla eſſe poteſt in tanti ſceleris immanitate punienda crudelitas.
Cicero. 4. in Catilin.

Rex

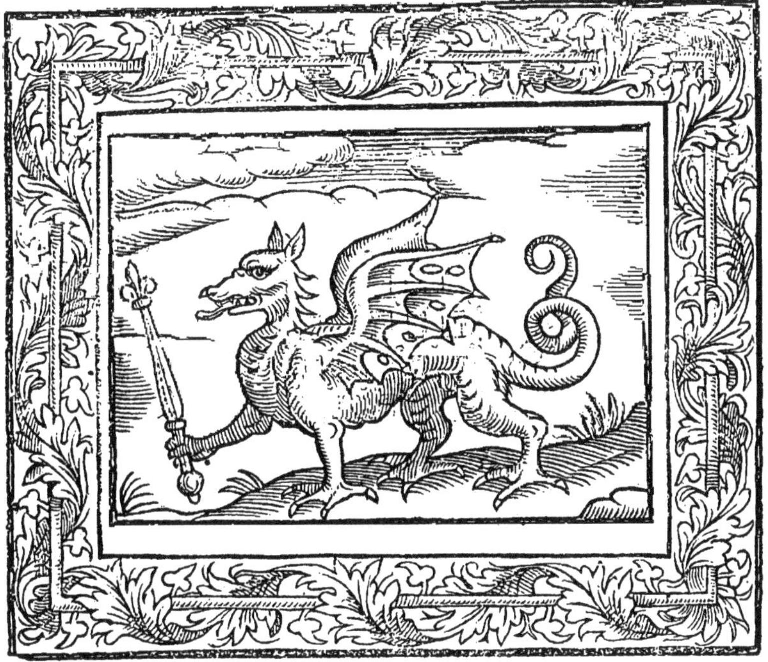

A DRAGON lo, a Scepter graſping faſt
Within his paw: doth ſhew a King ſhould be
Like Æſculapius, ev'er watchfull plac't; Metam: 15.
Amongſt his ſubiects, and with skill to ſee,
To what ill humors, of th'infectious mind.
The multitude, are moſt of all inclind.

And when he findes corruption to abound,
In that Huge body, of all vices ill,
To purge betimes, or elſe to * launch the wound,
Leaſt more, and more, it ranckles inward ſtill:
Or when he would, it bring to former ſtate,
Paſt all recure, his phiſick comes to late.

* Immedicabile vulnus enſe reſecandum eſt ne pars ſincera trahatur. Ovid.

Quæ mala contraxit populus contagia morum,
Ne pigeat medica tot reſecâſſe manu:
(Et Reges olim iuvit medicina) venenis,
Hinc citus occurras quæ valuêre mora.

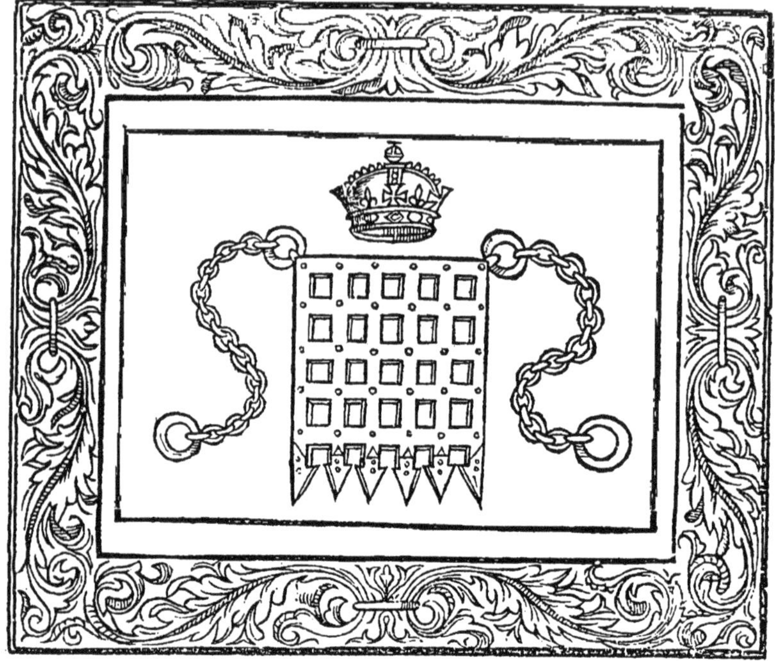

WHILE deadly foes, their engines haue prepard;
with furie fierce, to batter downe the walles,
My dutie is the Citie gate to guard,
And to rebate their Rammes, and fierie balls:
So that if firmely, I do ſtand without,
Within the other, neede no daunger doubt

Dread Soveraigne *IAMES*, whoſe puiſſant name to heare,
The Turke may tremble, and the Traitor pine:
Belou'd of all thy people, farre and neere:
Bee thou, as this Port-cullies, vnto thine,
Defend without, and thou within ſhalt ſee,
A thouſand thouſand, liue and die with thee.

Obſeſſis ut opem certo munimine præſtem,
Quæ non ſuſtineo damna creata mihi.
Sis cataracta tuis (animoſe Monarcha) Britannis,
Intus et invenies pectora firma tibi.

Si ſtatus Imperii, aut ſalus provinciarum
in diſcrimen vertatur, debebit (Princeps) in acie ſtare. Tacit: 4. Hiſt.

Dies

TO the worthie Ladie the L: E: W.

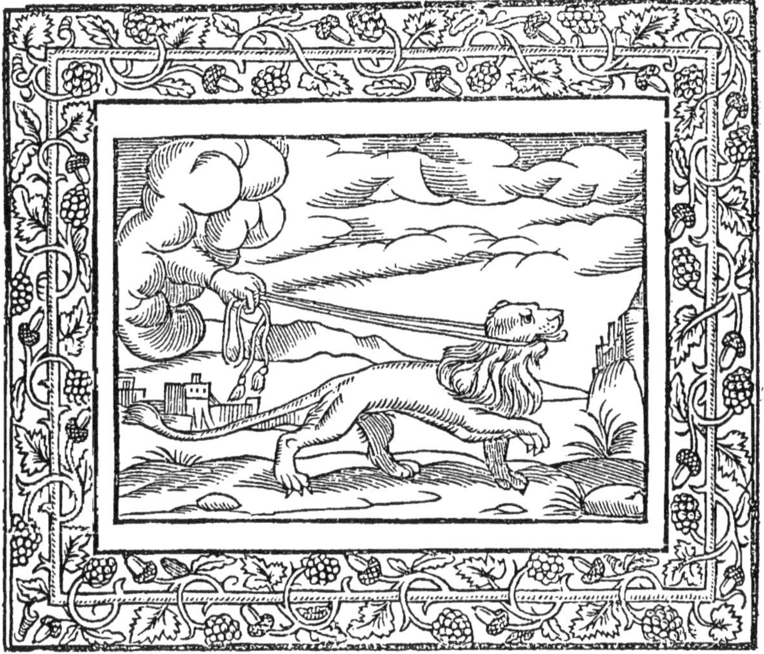

THE feirceſt natures; whome in youthfull prime,
Nor counſel good, nor reaſons rule, could tame,
Are by their owne experience, and in time;
To order brought, and * taught themſelves to frame,
To honeſt courſes, and to loath the waies;
So well they liked, in their youthfull daies.

Why then diſpaire yee Madame, of your ſonne,
Whoſe wit, as in the ſappe, doth but abound:
* Theſe braunches prun'd, that over rancklie runne,
You'le find in time, the bodie inward ſound:
When Dullard ſprightes, like fenny flagges belowe,
Or fruictles beene, or rot while they do grow.

Eximit ipſa dies omnes de corpore mendas,
Quodq; fuit vitium, deſinit eſse, mora.

* Ingenia noſtra vt nobiles et generoſi equi, melius facili frœno reguntur: Seneca de clementia.

* Vellem in adoleſcente quod amputem. Cicero 1 de oratore.

Ovid: 2. de arte amandi.

Labor

TO the most Honorable Lord, the L: Dingwell.

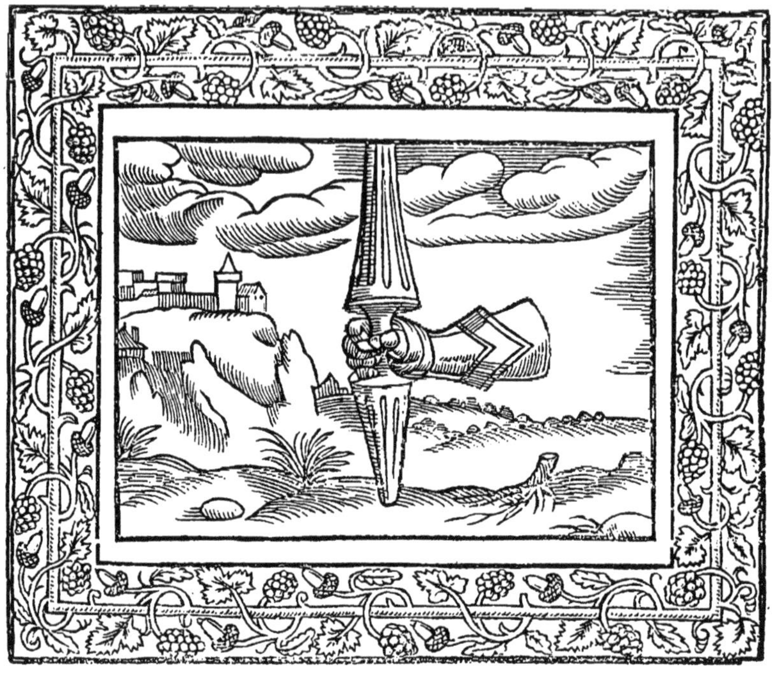

Hugonis Capeti Symbolum.

WHO thirsteth after Honor, and renowne,
By valiant act, or lasting worke of wit:
In vaine he doth expect, her glorious crowne,
Except by labor, he atcheiveth it;
And sweatie brow, for never merit may,
To drousie sloath, impart her living bay.

* primus sumpsisse labores-primus iter sumpsisse pedes. Sil: 1.

* Ipse manu sua pila gerés praecedit anheli militis orapedes mõstrat tolerare laborem, non iubet. Lucan de Catone.

Munditias mulieribus laborem viris convenire. Marius apud Salustium.

* *HAMILCARS* sonne, hence shall thy glory liue,
Who or'e the Alpes, didst foremost lead the way,
With Cæsars eeke, that would the onset giue,
* And first on foote, the deepest foor ds assay:
"* Let Carpet Knightes, of Ladies favours boast,
" The manly hart, brave Action loveth most.

Disce puer virtutem ex me verumq; laborem
Fortunam ex aliis: nunc te mea dextera bello
Defensum dabit, et magna inter praemia ducet,

Virgil AEneid: 2

Ex

To the most iudicious, and learned, Sir FRANCIS BACON, Knight.

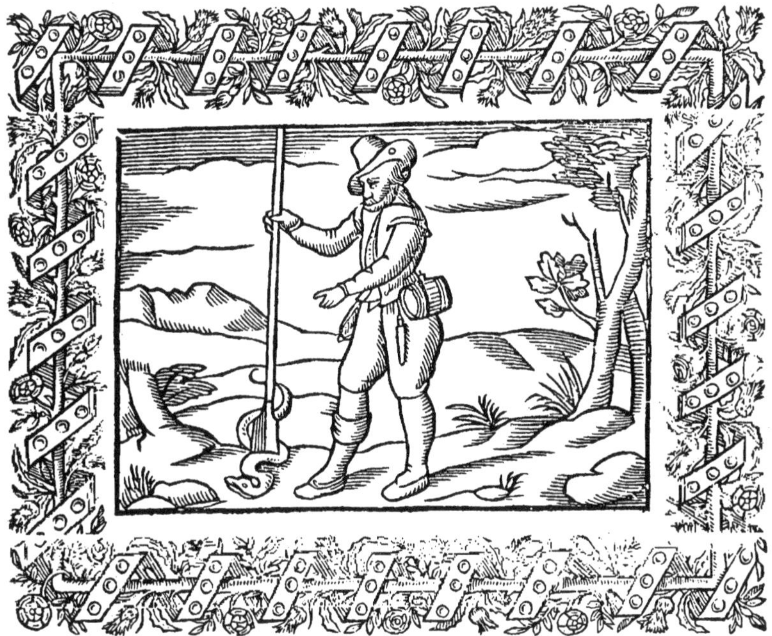

THE Viper here, that stung the sheepheard swaine,
(While careles of himselfe asleepe he lay,)
With Hysope caught, is cut by him in twaine,
Her fat might take, the poison quite away,
And heale his wound, that wonder tis to see,
Such soveraigne helpe, should in a Serpent be.

By this same Leach, is meant the virtuous King,
Who can with cunning, out of manners ill,
Make wholesome lawes, * and take away the sting,
Wherewith foule vice, doth greeue the virtuous still:
Or can prevent, by quicke and wise foresight,
Infection ere, it gathers further might.

* vitiorum emendatricem legem esse oportet Cic: 1 de legibus.

Salus Civitatis in legibus. Arist:

Asia venenato pupugit quem vipera morsu,
Dux Gregis antidotum læsus ab hoste petit:
Vipereis iridem leges ex moribus aptas
Doctus Apollinca conficit arte SOLON.

vitiis quæ plurima menti
Fœmineæ natura dedit humana malignas
Cura dedit leges, et quod natura remittit
Invida iura negant &c.

Ovid Metamor: lib 10.

Anagramma Authoris.

Est hac almus honor.

Thomas Chalonerus.

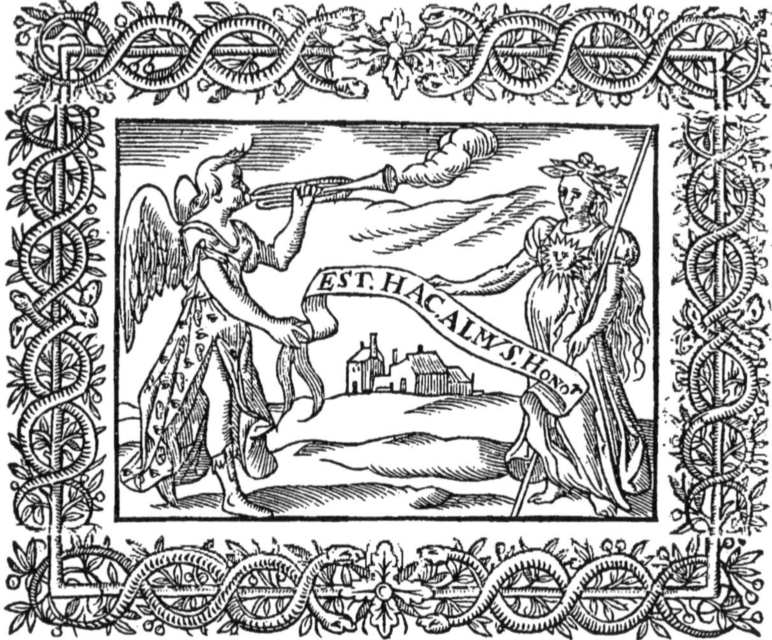

HEERE Virtue standes, and doth impart a scroule,
To living fame, to publish farre and neere:
The man whose name, she did within enroule,
And kept to view, vnseene this many yeare,
That erst me thought, she seemed to envie,
The world his worth, his fame, and memorie.

But since she sees, the Muse is left forlorne,
And fortune fawning, on the worthles wight,
And eke her selfe, not cherisht as beforne.
She bringes Mœcenas once againe to light:
The man (if any else) a frend to Artes,
And good rewarder, of all best desertes.

To the right worſhipfull Sir DAVID MVRRAY *Knight.*

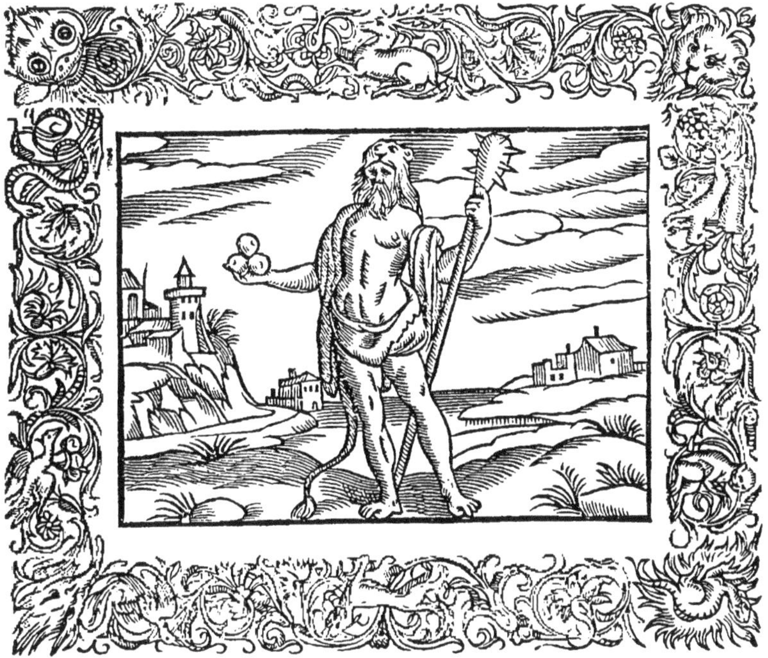

THVS *HERCVLES*, the Romanes did deviſe,
And in their Temples, him a place aſſignd:
To repreſent vnto the peoples eies,
The image of, th' Heroique virtuous mind:
Who like *ALCIDES*, to her laſting praiſe,
In action ſtill, delightes to ſpend her dayes.

Within whoſe hand, three apples are of gold,
The ſame which from th' Heſperides he fetcht,
Theſe are the three Heroique vertues old,
The Lions skinne, about his ſhoulders ſtretcht,
Notes fortitude, his Clubbe the crabbed paine,
To braue atcheiuements, ere we can attaine.

Virtus hominis proprium bonum Tacitus. lib: 4.

1. Moderation of anger.

2. Contempt of pleaſure.

3. Abſtinence from covetouſnes.

Mecum honor et laudes, et læto gloria vultu,
Et decus, et niveis Victoria concolor alis:
Me cinctus Lauro perducit ad aſtra triumphus,
Caſta mihi domus, et celſo ſtant colle penates.

Silius Ital: lib 15 Virtus loquitur

Sic

Ad generosissimum et opt: spei iuvenem NobilemD.C.M. in Italiam nuperrime profectum.

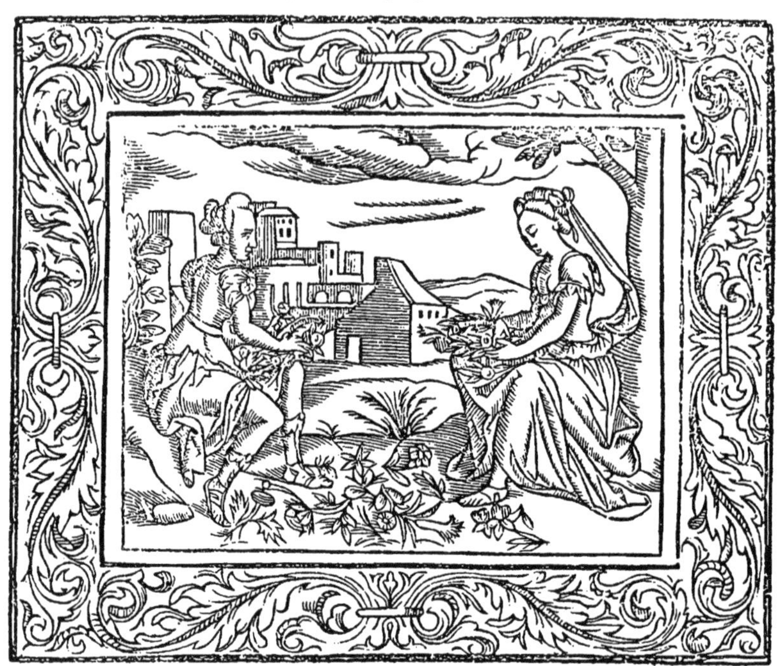

THE Spartan virgines, ere they had composed;
Theire Girlonds, of the fairest flowers to sight:
The wholesom'st herbes, they heere withall inclosed,
And so their heades, full iollily they dight,
In memorie of that same leach they wright:
Who first brought simples, and their vse to light.

So ye braue Lord, who like the heavenly Sphære,
Delight in motion, and aboute to roame:
Must learne to mixe in travaile farre and neere,
With pleasure profite, that returning home;
Your skill, and Iudgment, more may make you knowen;
Then your French suite, or locke so largly growen.

Lips: in Epist: ad Lanoium.

For who's he, that's not ravisht with delight,
Farre Countries, Courtes, and Cities, straung tosee;

To

To haue old *Rome*, preſented to his ſight:
Troy-walls, or Virgils ſweete *Parthenope*.
* Yet nothing worth, vnles ye herewith find,
The fruites of skill, and bettering of your mind.

Congreſſus ſapiētum confert prudentiam non montes aut maria. Eraſmus.

Omnis peregrinatio obſcura et ſordida eſt iis, quorum induſtria in patria poteſt eſſe celebris. Cicero ad cælium. Epiſt.

Tandem divulganda.

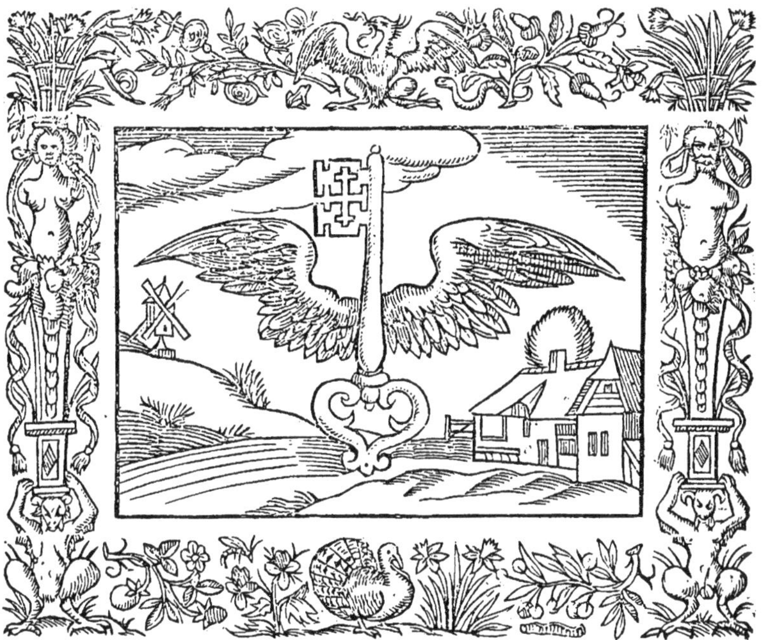

THE waightie counſels, and affaires of ſtate,
The wiſer mannadge, with ſuch cunning skill,
* Though long lockt vp, at laſt abide the fate,
Of common cenſure, either good or ill:
And greateſt ſecrets, though they hidden lie,
Abroad at laſt, with ſwifteſt wing they flie.

Omnia facta dictaque Principis rumor excipit, nec magis ei quā ſoli latere contigit. Seneca de Clementia.

To the right worſhipfull and my ſinguler good frend Mr: ADAM NEWTON Secretarie to Prince Henry.

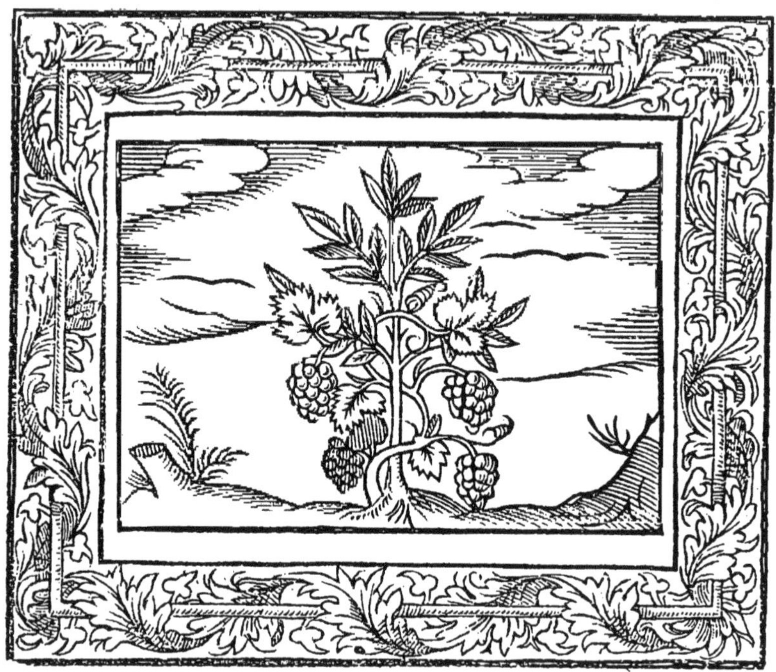

THE Laurel ioyned to the fruitefull vine,
In frendly league perpetually doe growe,
The Laurell dedicate to wits divine,
The fruite of Bacchus that in cluſters growe,
Are ſuch as doe enioy the world at will,
And ſwimme in wealth, yet want the muſes skill.

* Studia recipiunt ſpiritum et ſanguinem ſub te Plin: in panegyr.

(ita) temporibus tuis dicendis non deerunt ingenia Tacitus 1 Annal:

Omnis ratio et inſtitutio vitæ adiumenta hominum deſiderat. Cicero in offic:

This frendſhip ſhould inviolate remaine,
The * rich with Bountie ſhould rewarde the Artes,
The living muſe ſhould gratefully againe,
Adorne Mœcenas with her learned partes:
And when his branch is drie, and withered ſeene,
By her ſupport, preſerue him alway greene.

To the right worshipfull Sir DAVID FOVLIS *Knight.*

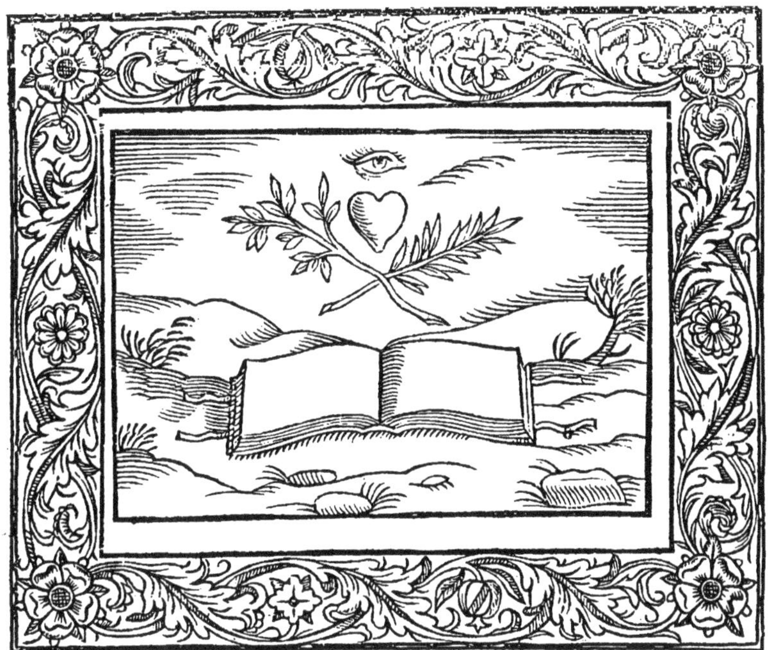

THE meanes of wisedome, heere a booke is seene,
 Sometime the glory of great Salomon,
A Cedar branch, with Hysope knotted greene,
The heart and eie withall, plac'd herevpon:
 For from the Cedar saith the Text he knew,
 Vnto the Hysope, all that ever grew.

The eie and heart, doe shew that Princes must,
In weightiest matters, and affaires of state,
Not vnto others over rashly trust,
Least with repentance they incurre their hate,
 But with sound iudgment, and * vnpartiall eie,
 Discerne themselues twixt wrong and equitie.

Vis consilij expers mole ruit sua.

* Qualis Poetarum ille Cyclops amisso oculo, talis Princeps cui desit hic oculus Prudentiæ. Lipsius in politic:

Horat: ode 3.

Vicinorum

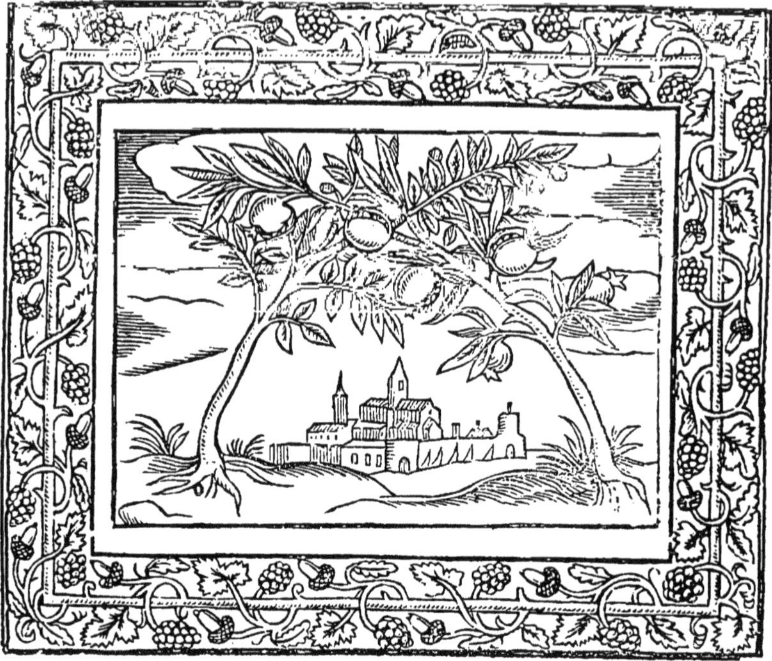

SVCH frendly league, by nature is they ſay;
Betwixt the Mirtle, and Pomegranate tree,
Who, if not planted over-farre away,
They ſeeke each others mutuall amitie:
By open ſignes of Frendſhip, till at laſt,
They one another haue with armes embrac't.

Which doth declare, how * neighbours ſhould vnite
Themſelues together, in all frendly loue;
And not like Tyrants, excerciſe their ſpight,
On one another, when no cauſe doth moue:
But letting quarrels, and old grudges ceaſe,
Be reconcild, to liue, and die, in peace.

* Melior eſt vicinus iuxta, quam frater procul. Proverb.

Ovid 3. Triſt: 4.

Vive ſine Invidia, molleſque inglorius annos
Exige, amicitias et tibi iunge pares.

TO

Edmund Aſhfeild.
I fledd vnſhamed.

Anagramma Authoris.

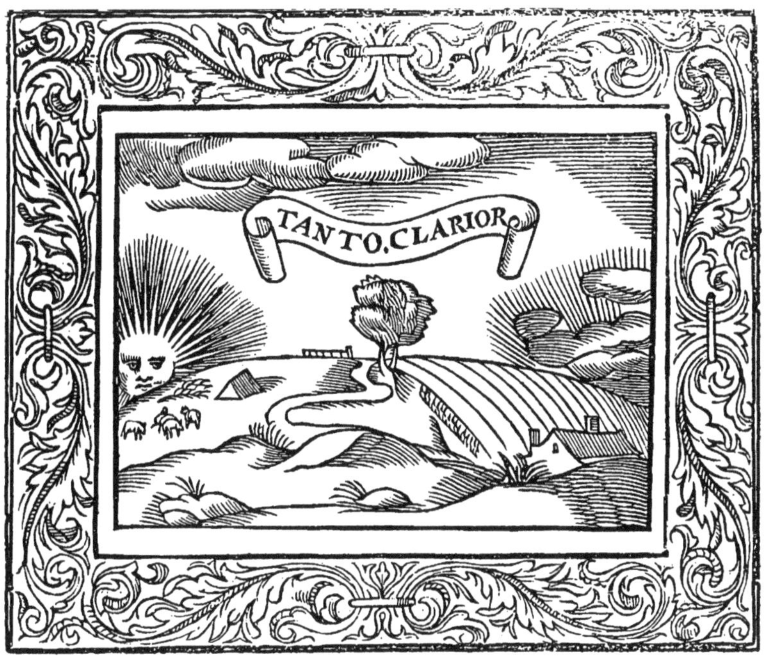

THE clouded Sunne, that weſtward left our ſight,
And for a night, in *THETIS* lap had ſlept,
Againe's return'd, with farre more glorious light,
" To cheere the world, that for his abſence wept:
His beames retaining, vncorrupt and pure,
Although he lay impriſon'd and obſcure.

Noctes rorulentas volo.

* So, Sir, although the cloudes of troubles, had
A while conceald you, from your louing frendes;
You doe appeare at length to make them glad,
And ſo much higher ſtill your name aſcendes,
By how much Envie, ſeeketh to oppreſſe,
And dimme the ſplendor of your Worthines.

* Adverſus virtutem hoc poſſunt calamitates, et damna, et iniuriæ quod adverſus Solem Nebula poteſt: Seneca Epiſt: 113.

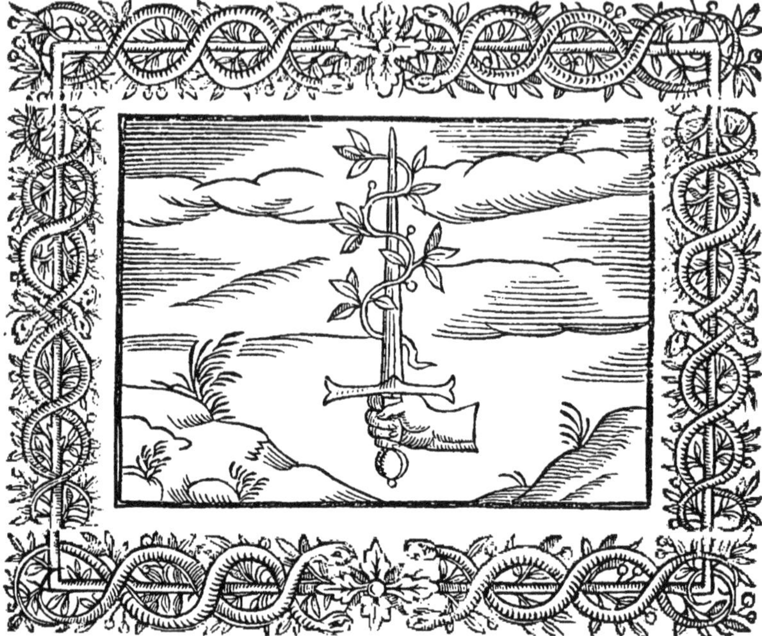

THE vernant Bay, with liuing fame ſhall crowne,
Victorious *Cæſar*, or ſweete *Maro's* brow,
As due reward of Learning, and renowne:
To Iuſtice hand, we do the Sword allow:
For by theſe two, all common-wealthes doe ſtand,
And virtue is * vpheld in every land.

For Honor, Valour drawes her ſword to fight,
* Devoide of feare, or cuts the foamy ſurge:
The Muſe for glorie labours day and night,
To braue attempts, yea this doth cowards vrge:
When Iuſtice ſword, th' inglorious and the baſe,
Vnworthy life, purſues with all diſgrace.

* Nec Domus, nec Reſpublica, ſtare poteſt, ſi in ea nec recte factis prœmia extent vlla, nec ſupplicia peccatis Cicer: de natura Deorum.

* illi æs triplex circa pectus erat Qui fragilem primus pelago commiſit ratem. Horatius.

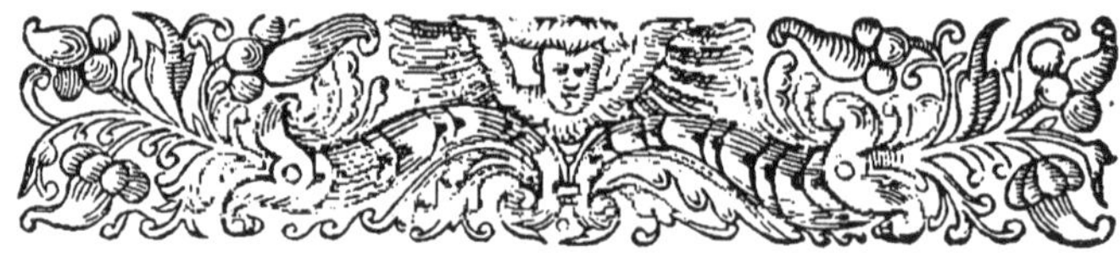

Quia

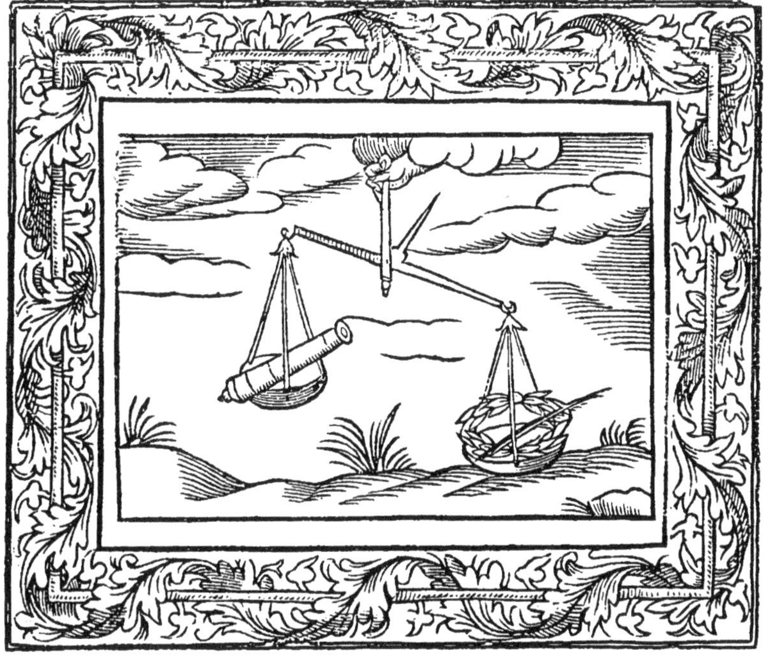

Incerti Authoris.

BEHOLD a hand, extended from the sky;
Doth ſteddilie a peized ballance hold,
The dreadfull Cannon, in one ſcale doth ly,
The Bay ith'other, with a pen of Gold;
Due to the Muſe, and ſuch as learned are,
Th'other Symbole, of th'art Militar.

Though *MARS* defendes the kingdome with his might,
And braues abroad his foe, in glorious armes,
Yet wiſer *PALLAS* guides his arme aright,
And beſt at home preventes all future harmes:
Then pardon * Soveraigne, if the pen and bay,
My better part, the other downe doe wey.

* Regina Eliza-betha. Nam hoc cum pauculis aliis ex illis Haſtiludiorum trophæis in regia pergula adhuc ſervatis deſcripſimus. vt Minerva noſtra non vndique non concinna foret.

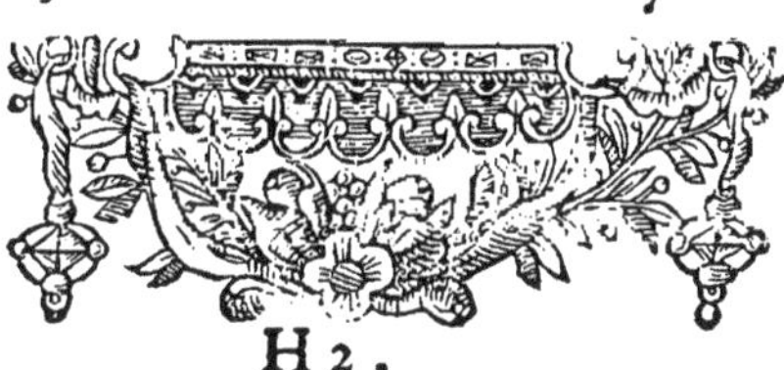

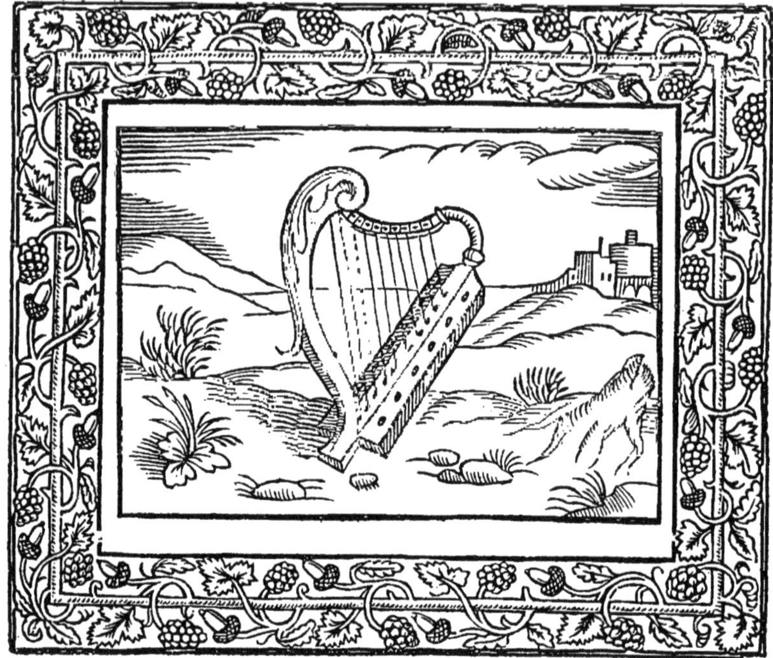

WHILE I lay bathed in my natiue blood,
And yeelded nought saue harsh, & hellish soundes:
And saue from Heauen, I had no hope of good,
Thou pittiedst (Dread Soveraigne) my woundes,
Repair'dst my ruine, and with Ivorie key,
Didst tune my stringes, that slackt or broken lay.

Now since I breathed by thy Roiall hand,
And found my concord, by so smooth a tuch,
I giue the world abroade to vnderstand,
Ne're was the musick of old Orpheus such,
As that I make, by meane (Deare Lord) of thee,
From discord drawne, to sweetest vnitie.

Basil: Doron.

Cum mea nativo squallerent sceptra cruore,
Edoque lugubres vndique fracta modos:
Ipse redux nervos distendis (Phœbe) rebelles,
Et stupet ad nostros Orpheus ipse sonos.

Pœnitentia

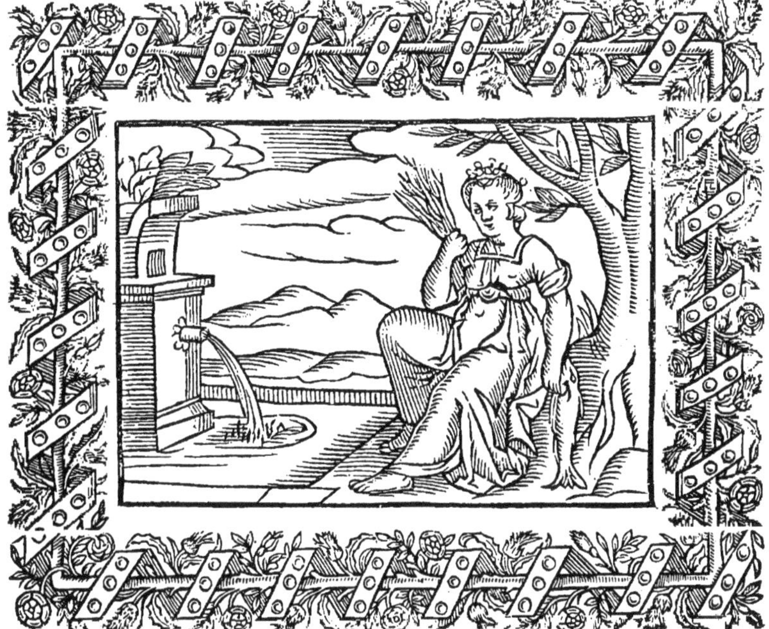

HEERE ſits Repentance, ſolitarie, ſad;
Her ſelfe beholding in a fountaine cleare,
As greeuing for the life, that ſhe hath lad:
One hand a fiſh, the other birch doth beare,
  Wherewith her bodie, ſhe doth oft chaſtize;
  Or faſtes; to curbe her fleſhly enimies.

Septies in die cadet iuſtus et reſurget: impii autem corruent in malum. Proverb: 24.

Her ſolemne cheare, and gazing in the fount,
Denote her anguiſh, and her greife of ſoule,
As often as her life, ſhe doth recount,
Which Conſcience doth, with howerly care enroule,
  The cullor greene, ſhe moſt delightes to weare,
  Tells how her hope, ſhall overcome diſpaire.

Pœnitentia aboleri peccata indubitanter credimus, et in vltimo vitæ ſpiritu ſi admiſſorum pœniteat.

Auguſtin: de Eccleſ: dog: 48.

In tribunal mentis tuæ aſcende contra te, et reum te conſtitue ante te, noli te ponere poſt te, ne Deus te ponat ante te.

Idem in libro de vtilitate agendi pœnitentiam.

Vtile propoſitum eſt ſævas extinguere flammas,
Nec ſervum vitiis pectus habere ſuum.

Ovid: 1 de remedio amoris.

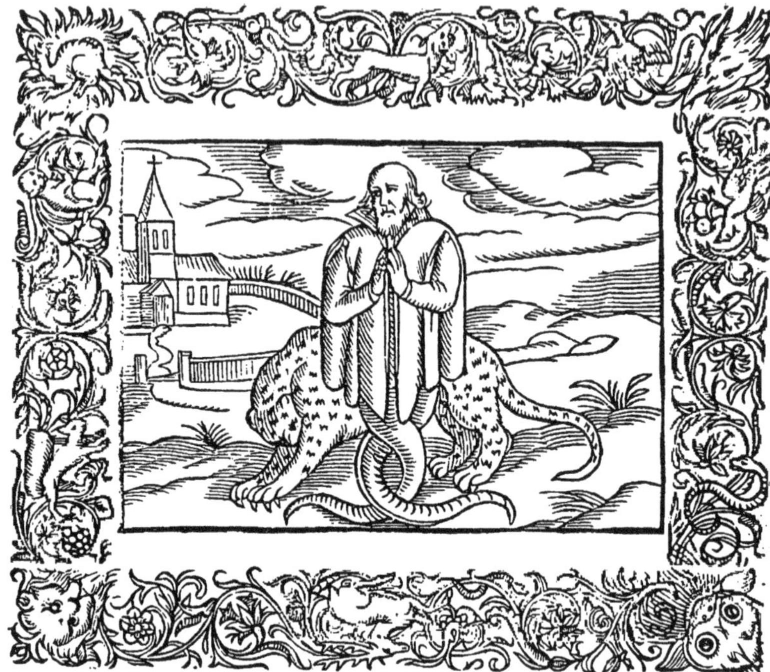

OF simple looke, with countenance demure,
In golden coate, lo heere *DECEITE* doth ſtand,
With eies to heauen vpcaſt, as he were pure,
Or never yet, in knau'ry had a hand,
Whoſe nether partes, reſemble to our ſight
The figure of a fearefull Serpent right.

And by his ſide, a Panther cloſe you ſee,
Who when he cannot eaſily catch his pray,
Doth hide his head, and face, with either knee,
And ſhew his back, with ſpots beſpeckled gay
To other Beaſtes: which while they gaze vpon,
Are vnawares, ſurprized every one.

Iob. 30. Simulatores et callidi provocant Iram Dei
Neque clamabunt cum vincti fuerint, morietur in tempeſtate anima
eorum, et vita eorum inter effœminatos.

Proverb: 4. Abhominatio Domino eſt omnis illuſor.

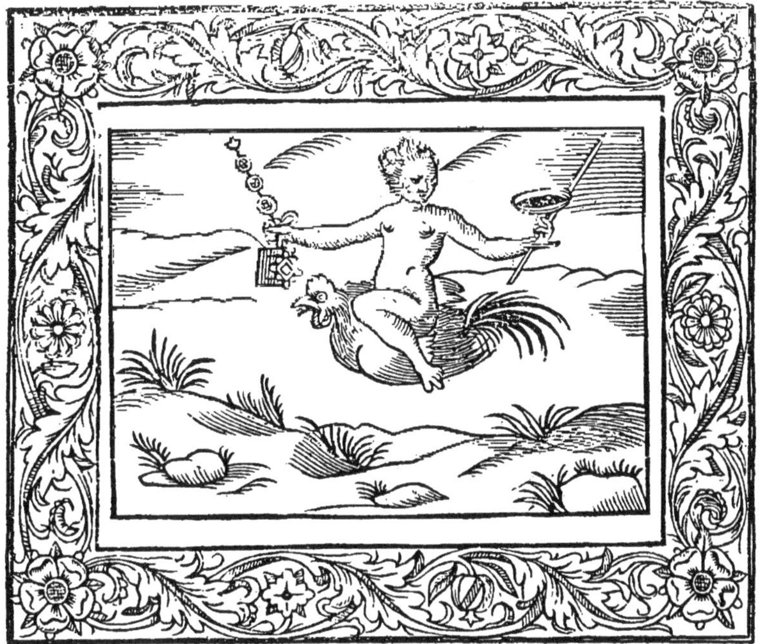

VPON a Cock, heere *Ganimede* doth ſit,
Who erſt rode mounted on *IOVES* Eagles back,
One hand holdes *Circes* wand, and ioind with it,
A cup top-fil'd with poiſon, deadly black:
The other Meddals, of baſe mettals wrought,
With ſundry moneyes, counterfeit and nought.

Theſe be thoſe crimes, abhorr'd of God and man,
Which Iuſtice ſhould correct, with lawes ſevere,
In * *Ganimed*, the foule Sodomitan:
Within the Cock, vile inceſt doth appeare:
Witchcraft, and murder, by that cup and wand,
And by the reſt, falſe coine you vnderſtand.

* O fuge te teneræ puerorum credere turbæ, Nam cauſam iniusti ſemper amoris habent. Tibullus.

Iſta a te puniantur (ô Rex) ne tu pro illis puniaris. Ciprian. de vtilitate Pœnitentiæ.

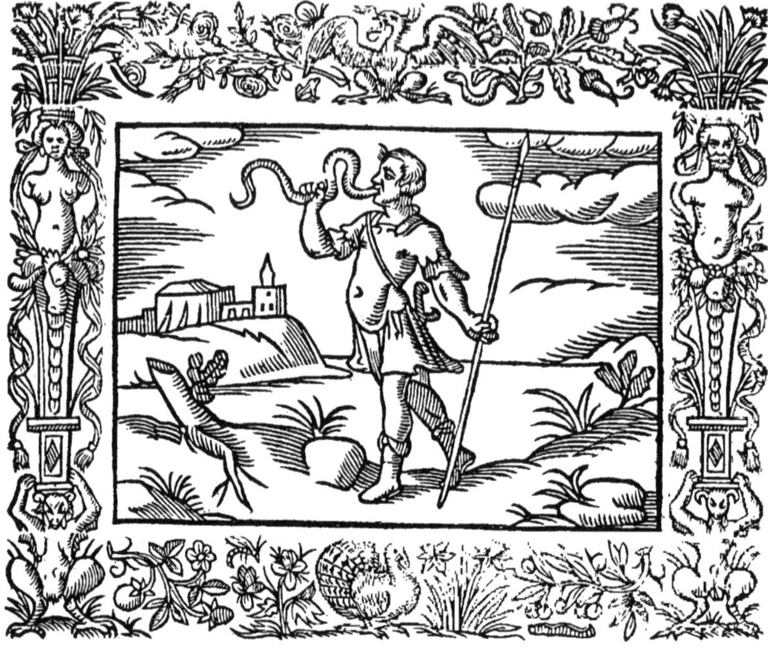

D: Bright in his treatise of melancholie.

A FAMILIE in Libia's said to be,
For prowesse, farre renown'd aboue the rest:
With whome no wholesome diet can agree,
But easilie, all poison they digest:
The Aspe, the Adder, and the vipers broode,
Are said to yeeld their ordinarie foode.

To these infected races, I resemble,
Of Traitors vile, as Gourie and the rest,
To tell whose legend, each good heart may tremble,
While *Psilli-like*, they suck from Mothers brest,
The poison of the sires infected mind,
Transmissing it, to theirs that come behind.

Horatius lib: 4 ode 4.

Fortes creantur fortibus et bonis,
Est in iuvencis, est in Equis patrum
Virtus: nec imbecillem feroces
Progenerant Aquilæ columbam.

Vos

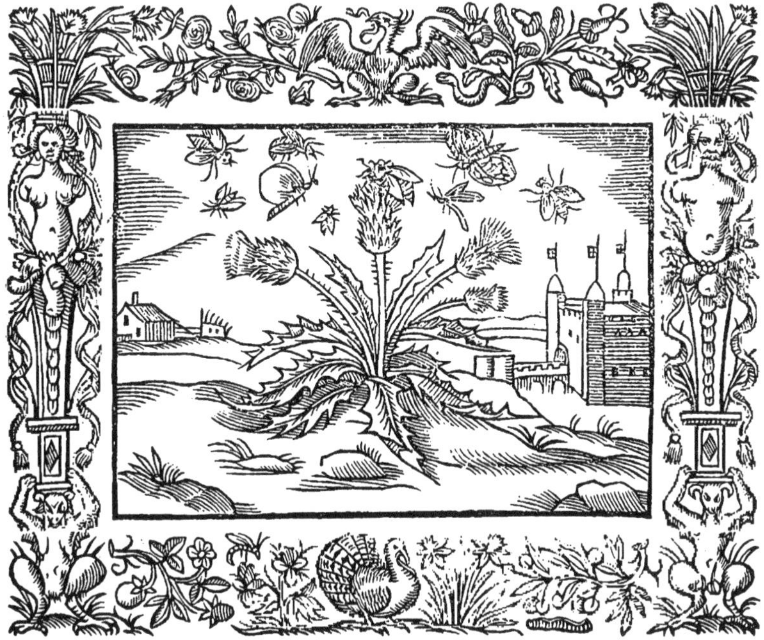

THE painefull Bee, when many a bitter ſhower,
And ſtorme had felt, farre from his hiue away,
To ſeeke the ſweeteſt Hunny-bearing flower,
That might be found and was the pride of May:
Heere lighting on the fair'ſt he mought eſpie,
Is beate by Drones, the waſpe and butterflie.

So men there are ſometimes of good deſert,
Who painfully haue labour'd for the hiue,
Yet muſt they with their merit ſtand apart,
And giue a farre inferior leaue to thriue:
Or be perhaps, (if gotten into grace)
By waſpiſh *Envie*, beaten out of place.

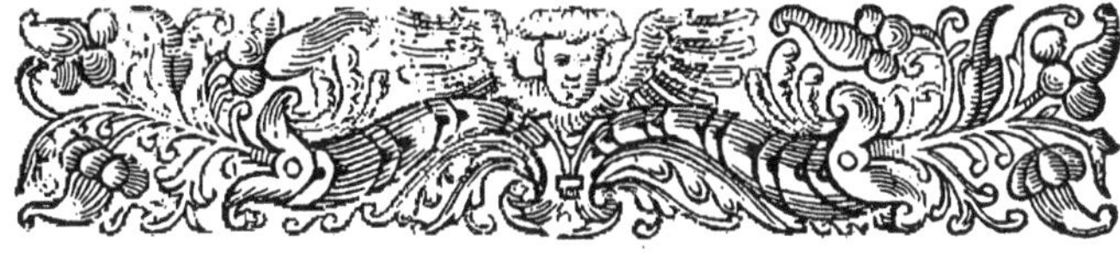

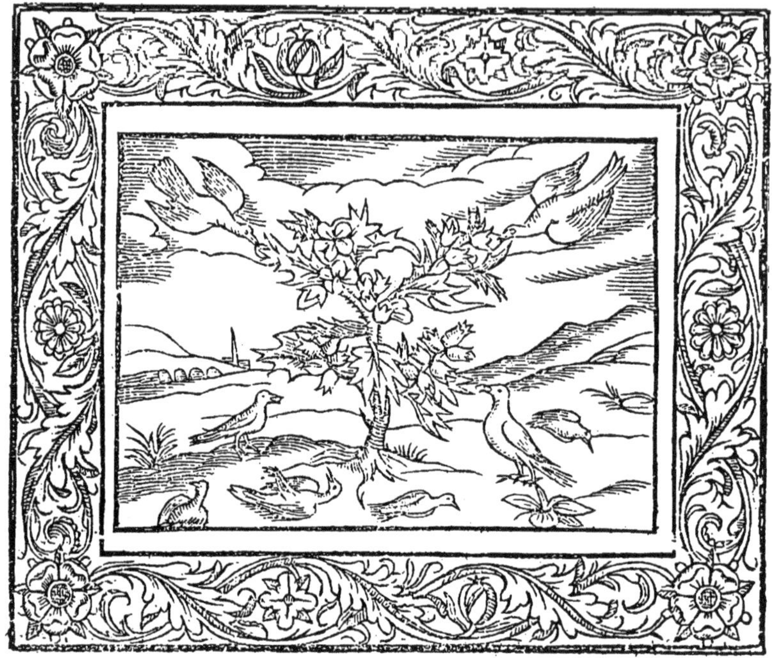

THE Hyoſciame, that about the plaines
Of *Italie*, doth in abundance grow,
Doth beare a flower, wherein a ſeed remaines,
Of Birdes the moſt deſir'd, (as Herballs ſhow:)
Which taſted by them, giddie downe they fall,
And haue no power, to flie away at all.

* Magnæ opes poſſeſſori faſtum et ſupercilium conciliant. Erasmus.

To this ſame fruite, I riches doe compare,
Which though at firſt, with ſweetnes they bewitch:
Within a while, they breede our bane of care,
Or elſe we ſurfet, cloid with overmuch:
Or with their poiſon, * breede out frantique fits:
Or with their loſſe, * bereaue vs of our wits.

* Fœlix qui ſimul opes et mentem habet. Demoſthen: in Olynth.

Sed plures nimia congeſta pecunia cura Strangulat — Iuvenal: Satyr. 10.

Divitiæ inflant animos, ſuperbiam et arrogantiam pariunt, invidiam trahunt, et eouſque mentem alienant, vt fama pecuniæ, nos etiam nocitura delectet.

Seneca de paupertate.

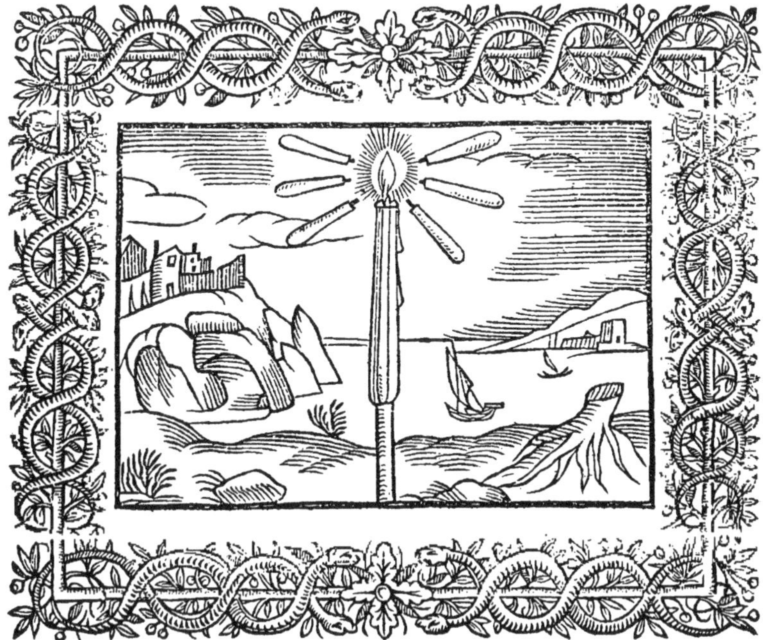

WHO ever doſt a Roiall Scepter ſway,
Or ſit'ſt at ſterne of publique gouerment,
So beare thy ſelfe, that all Inferiors may,
Behold thee as, a bright example ſent;
From God aboue, and cleareſt light to ſhow,
The virtuous pathes, wherein they ought to goe.

Magnum eſt perſonam in Repub: tueri Principis, qui non animis ſolum debet, ſed ocalis ſervire civium. Cic: Philip: 8.

For people, are like buſie Apes inclin'd,
To imitate the Soveraignes manners ſtill,
And to his Actions, frame their varieng mind:
So that he ſtandes, as Torch vpon a hill,
In open view, and ever ſhining bright,
In good or ill, to thouſandes giuing light.

Quo fugis imperii, quiſquis moderaris habênas?
Ceu procul illucens flamma benigna tuis,
Lumina quæ reddas hinc inde imitamina morum
Regis ad exemplum plebs numeroſa rapit.

Baſil: Doron.

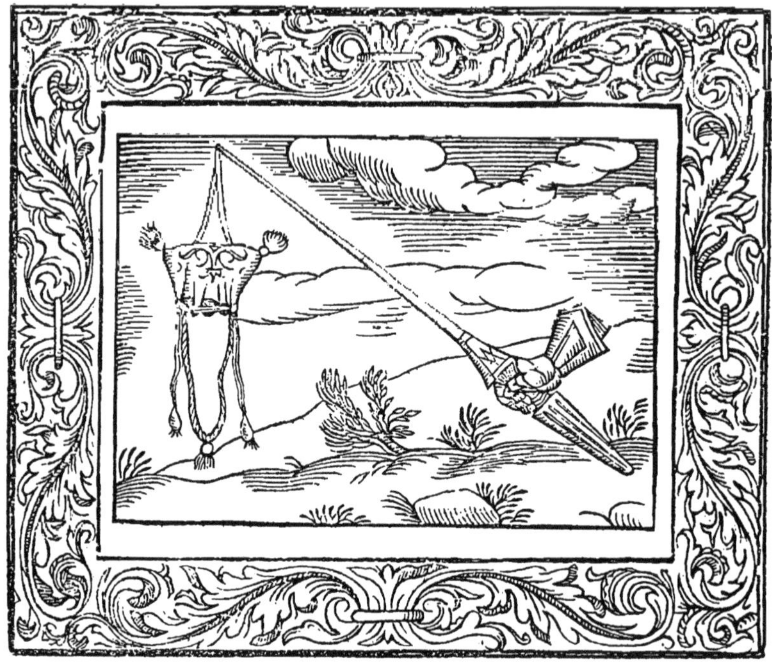

Inter Apotheg: Lycoſthenis.

OF all the vertues, that doe beſt beſeeme;
Heroique valor, and high Maieſtie,
Which ſooner loue, and Honor winne, I deeme,
None may compare, with Liberalitie:
Which well the mightie *ALEXANDER* knew,
As by this *Impreſe* following heere I ſhew.

Melius beneficiis Imperium cuſtoditur quam armis Seneca de brevitate vitæ.

Ere to the charge, he did himſelfe advance,
His purſe by giving he would emptie quite;
And cauſe the ſame be borne vpon a launce,
Throughout the campe, in all the armies ſight:
And heerewithall proclaime, ſee, all is gone,
" We liue in hope, to purchaſe more anon.

" Spes ſupereſt: dictum Alexandri

Cic: 2 de finibus

Liberalitate qui vtuntur, benevolentiam ſibi conciliant, et quod aptiſſimum eſt ad quietè vivendùm caritatem.

In

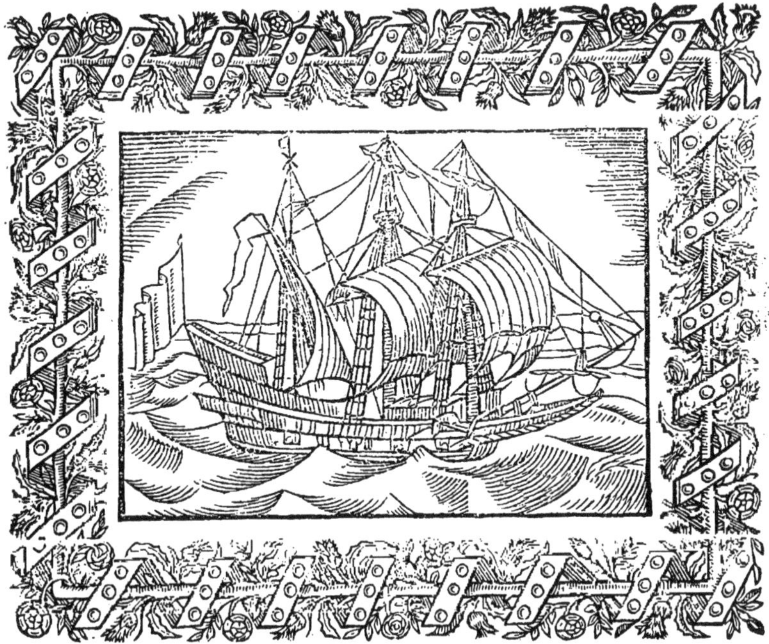

THE Dread-nought Argo, cuts the foaming surge,
Through daungers great, to get the golden prize,
So when our selues, Necessitie doth vrge,
We should avoide ignoble Cowardize,
And vndertake with pleasure, any paine,
Whereby we might our wealth, or honour gaine.

For all in vaine, our partes we keepe within,
Vnlesse we act, or put the same in vre:
Or hope heereafter, Fame our frend to winne,
If can no labour, constantly endure:
Which from aboue, is with aboundance blest,
When slothfull wightes, by nature we detest.

Ipsemet plerunque in opere, in agmine gregario militi mixtus incorrupto Ducis honore: Tacitus 5. Histor:

Facta, non dicta mea vos milites sequi volo. T: Livius lib:

Quibus sudor, pulvis, et alia talia, epulis iucundiora sunt. Salust: Iugurth:

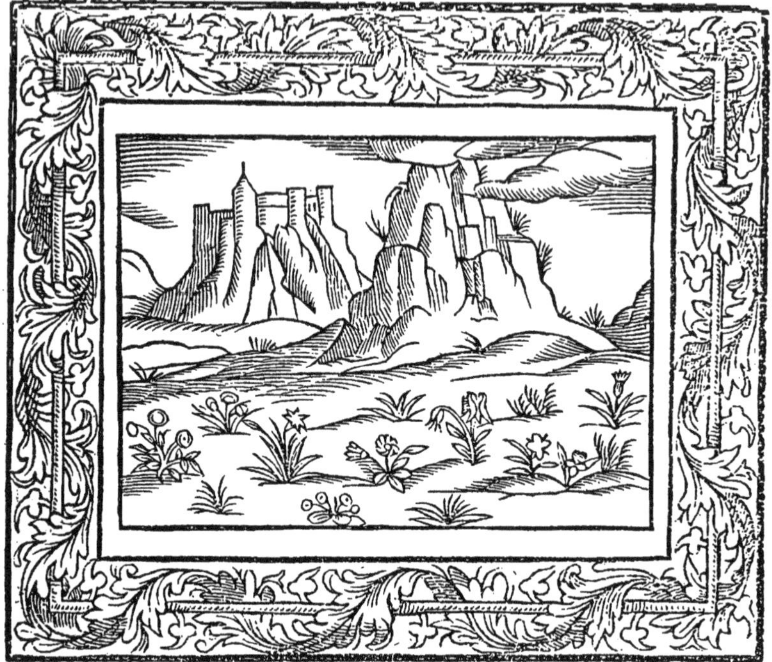

THE Mountaines huge, that ſeeme to check the sky,
And all the world, with greatnes overpeere,
With Heath, or Moſſe, for moſt part barren lie:
When valleis low, doth kindly Phœbus cheere,
And with his heate, in hedge and groue begets,
The virgin-Primroſe, or ſweete Violets.

So God, oft times denies vnto the greate,
The giftes of Nature, or his heavenly grace,
And thoſe that high, in Honor's chaire are ſet,
Doe feele their wantes, when men of meaner place,
Although they lack, the others golden ſpring,
Perhaps are bleſt, aboue the richeſt King,

Humilitas meretur vt homo virtutes occupet, Quia humilibus Deus dat gratiam.
Bernard: in Epiſtola ad Socrum. Servat accepta, quia non requieſcit ſpiritus ſanctus niſi ſuper quietem et humilem.

Candor

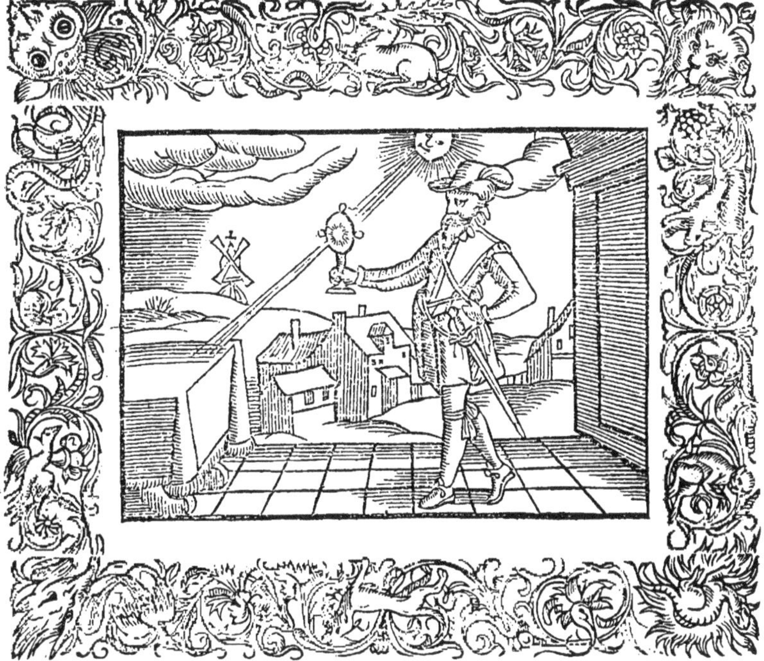

THE burning glaſſe, that moſt doth gather fire,
While *Sirian* Dog doth parch the meddowes greene,
Doth never burne (a thing we much admire)
The cloth, or ſtuffe, that perfect white is ſeene:
But ſoone enflames, all cullors elſe beſide,
The black, the blew, the red, and motley pide.

To this ſame glaſſe, I ſlaunder ſtill compare,
That by degrees, doth ſubtilly gather heate,
And doth not with malicious envie ſpare,
The good, the bad, the little or the greate,
Who though ſhe hath, o're other vertues power,
The conſcience cleere, ſhe never ſhall devoure.

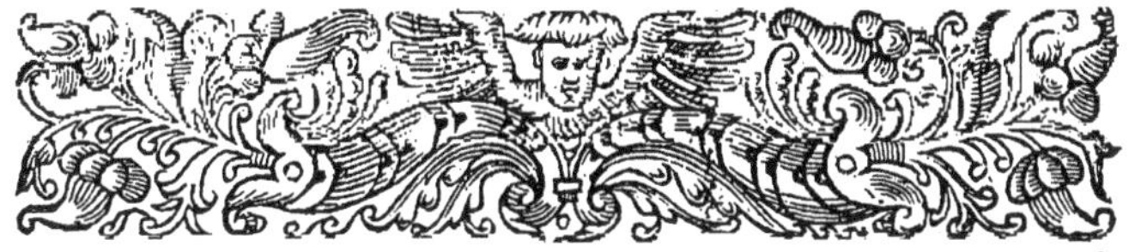

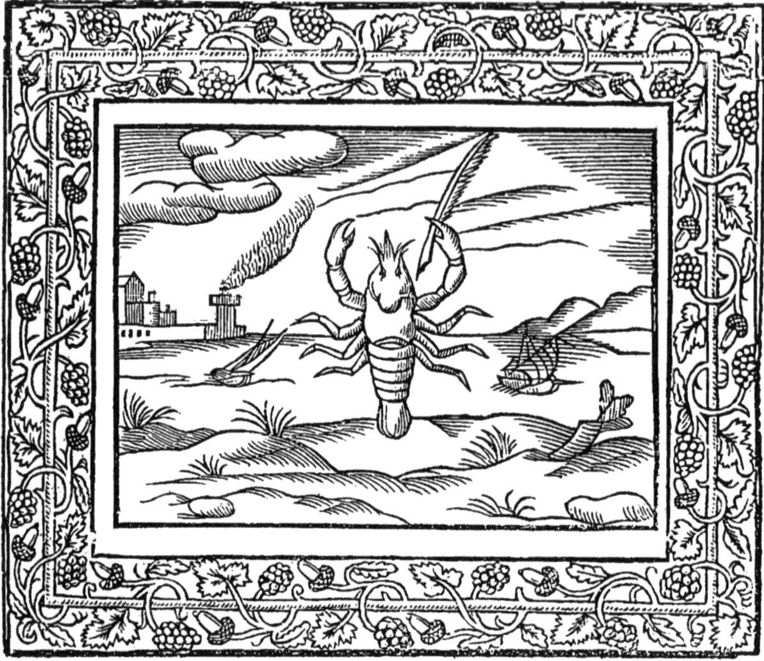

BY worke of wit, who thirſteth after Fame:
And by the Muſe, wouldſt liue a longer day,
What ere thou writ'ſt, ſee carefully the ſame,
Thou oft peruſe, and after pauſe, and ſtay;
Mend what's amiſſe, with *ARGVS* hundred eies,
I meane advice, and Iudgment of the wiſe.

Temeritas præter quam quod ſtulta eſt etiam infœlix. Livius 22.

-nonumque premantur in annum Horatius.

For as in Children, eaſily we behold,
Some neere reſemblance of the mouth, or eie:
Of Parents likenes: ſo our workes vnfold,
Our mindes true Image, to poſteritie.
Beſide, lew'd lines, our loues, and leaſinges vaine
Doe die: when wiſe wordes ever doe remaine.

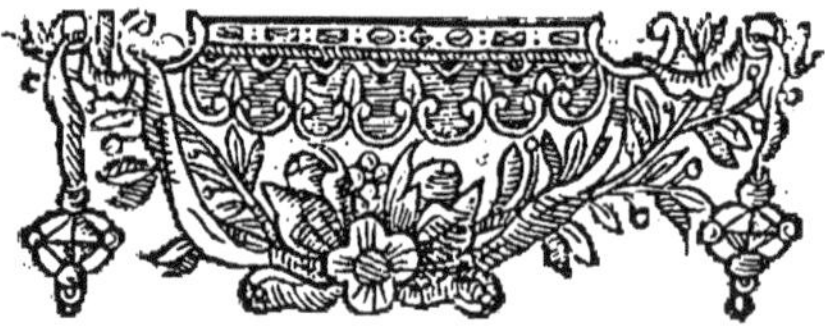

Pulchritudo

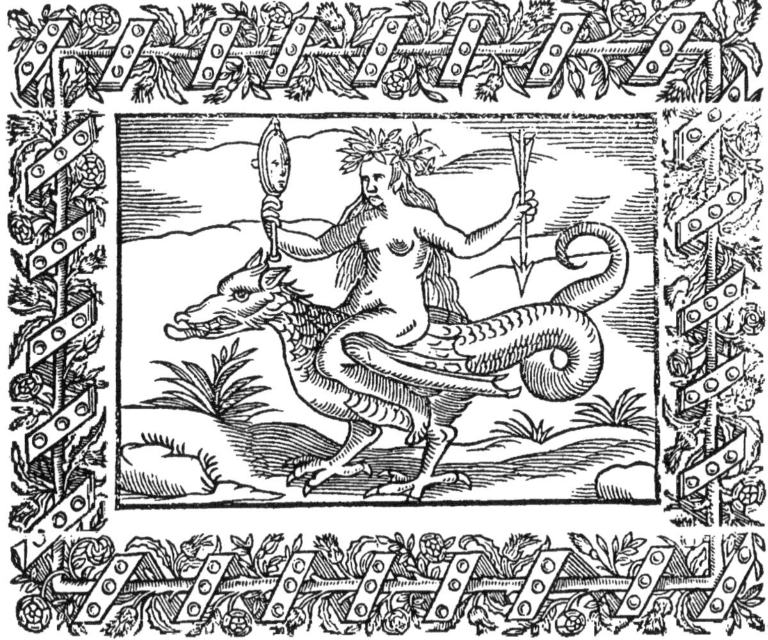

A VIRGIN naked, on a Dragon ſits,
One hand out-ſtretch'd, a chriſtall glaſſe doth ſhow:
The other beares a dart, that deadly hits;
Vpon her head, a garland white as ſnow,
Of * print and Lillies. Beautie moſt deſir'd,
Were I her painter, ſhould be thus attir'd.

* Alba liguſtra cadunt.—

Her nakednes vs tells, ſhe needes no art:
Her glaſſe, how we by ſight are moou'd to loue,
The woundes vnfelt, that's giuen by the Dart
At firſt, (though deadly we it after prooue)
The Dragon notes loues poiſon: and the flowers,
The frailtie (Ladies) of that pride of yours.

Cumq́ue aliquis dicet, fuit hæc formoſa, dolebis;
Et ſpeculum mendax, eſſe querêre tuum.

Ovid: 2. de Arte amandi.

Nec ſemper violæ, nec ſemper Lilia florent:
Et riget amiſſa ſpina relicta roſa.

Idem.

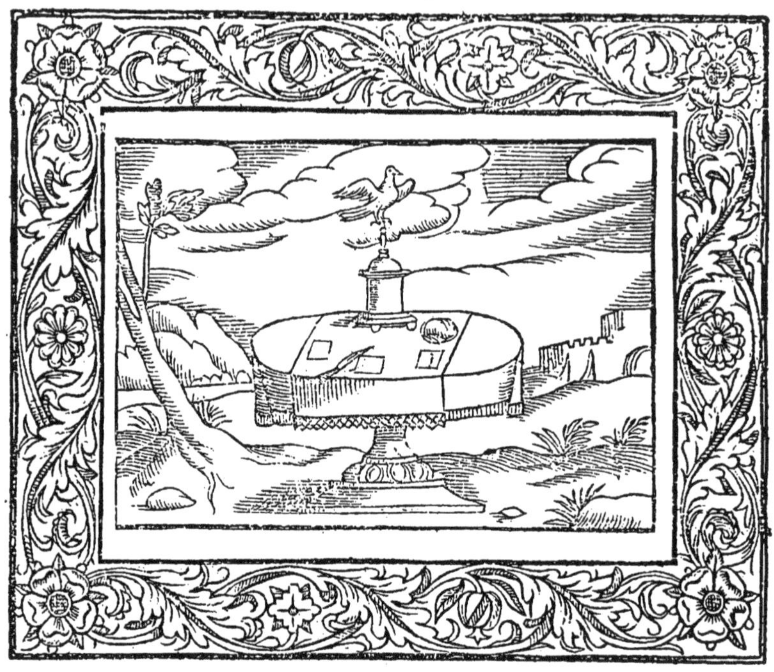

A SILVER Salt, heere on the Table standes,
On which the peace-full Turtle Doue doth sit,
Who at the bord, a * silent tongue commaundes:
The Salt, that we should season still with it
Discourses honest, not with idle tongue,
Speake what we list, to doe another wrong.

* Nec magnæ res sustineri possunt ab eo, cui silere grave est. Curtius lib: 4.

Arist: 4. Ethic.

Some men there are, whose glorie's to depraue,
With ill report, a man behind his back,
And then suppose, their credits best they saue,
With slaunders vile, when they anothers crack:
When wisedome staid, will let such leasinges rest,
And speake even of, her enimie the best.

Imminuunt Dicteria Maiestatem.

Ad vinum diserti. Cicero pro M: Cælio.

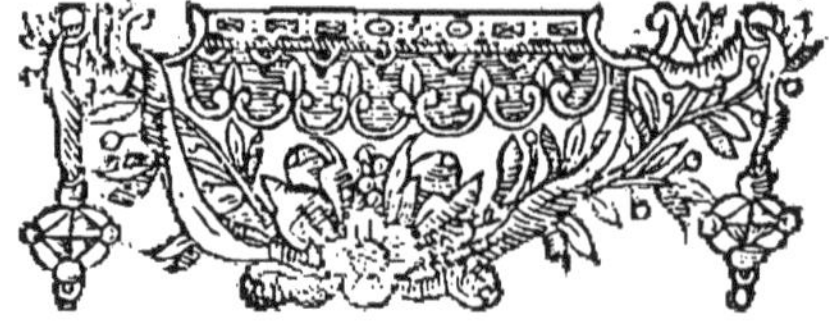

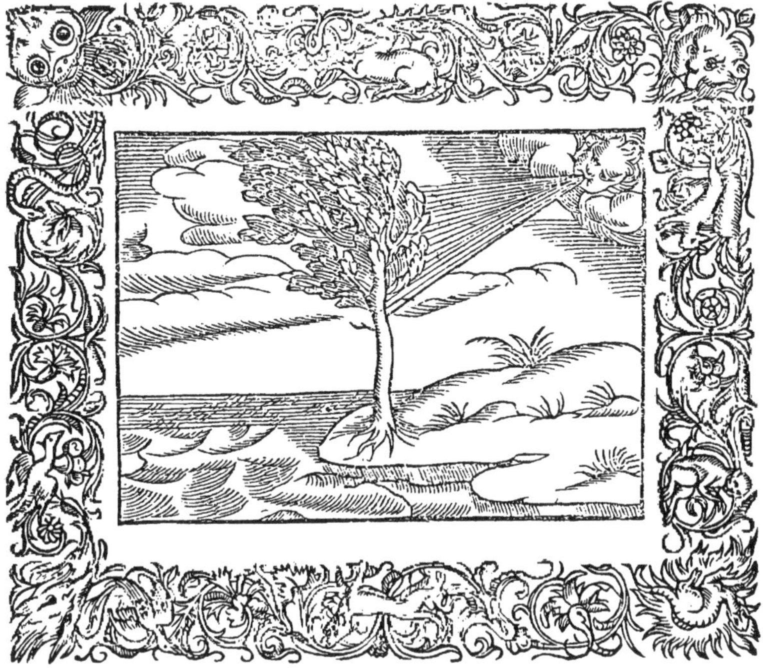

WHO wouldſt diſpend in Happines thy daies,
And lead a life, from cares exempt and free,
See that thy mind, ſtand irremoou'd alwaies,
Through reaſon grounded on firme conſtancie,
For whom opinion doth * vnſtaiedly ſway,
To fortune ſooneſt, ſuch become a pray.

* Maximum indicium malæ mentis fluctuatio. Seneca in proverb:

Ye loftie Pines, that doe ſupport the ſtate
Of common wealthes; and mightie government,
Why ſtoope ye ſoon'ſt, vnto the blaſt of fate,
And fawne on Envie, to your ruine bent:
Be taught by me, to ſcorne your worſer happe,
The waue by Sea, or land the Thunderclap.

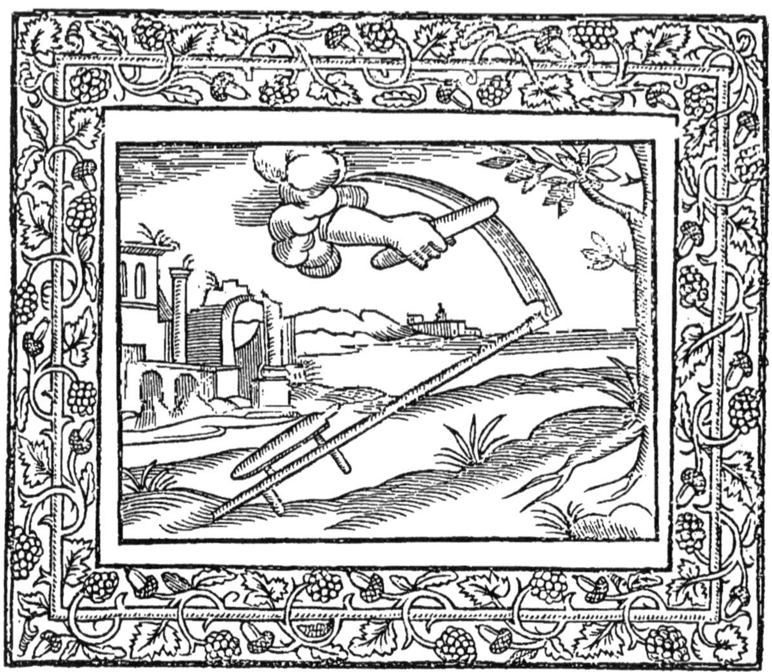

THEY tell me *Tusser*, when thou wert aliue,
And hadst for profit, turned euery stone,
Where ere thou cammest, thou couldst never thriue,
Though heereto best, couldst counsel every one,
As it may in thy Husbundry appeare,
Wherein a fresh, thou liu'st amongst vs heere.

So like thy selfe, a number more are woont,
To sharpen others, with advice of wit,
When they themselues, are like the whetstone blunt,
And little care, to keepe or follow it:
Eeke heere I must, the careles Pastor blame,
That teacheth well, but followes not the same.

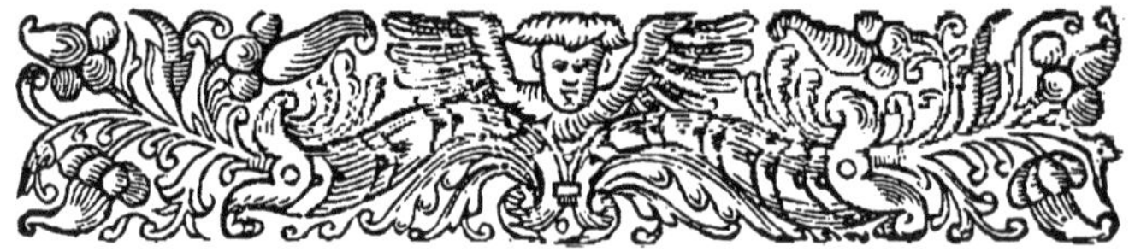

Quicquid

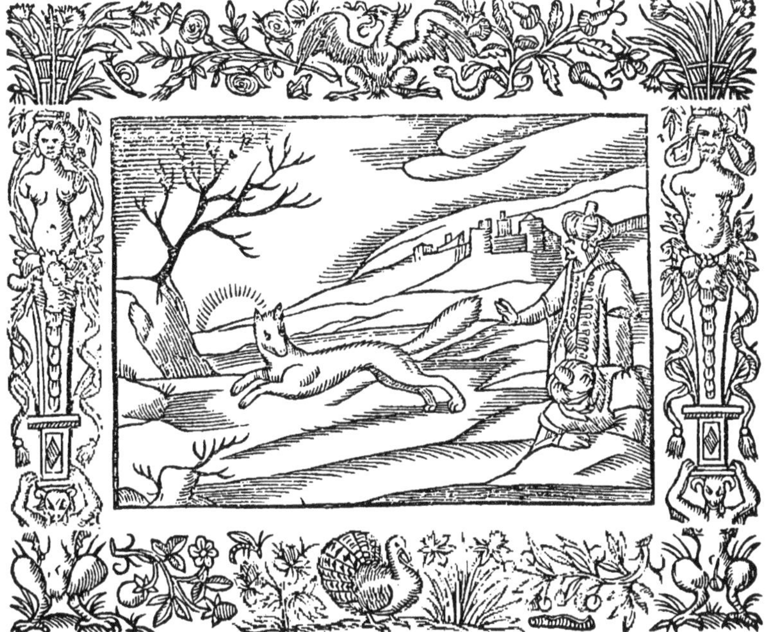

IT was the Custome of the *Thracians* once,
Ere they would ore a frozen river passe,
To take a Fox, and turne him for the Nonce,
Vpon the Ice, to try how thick it was,
Who to the streame, by laieng downe his eare,
Could heare the noise, and know the thicknes there. Plutarch:

Which if he found to tender for his weight,
He back returnd, and thankt them, he would none,
Which sheweth vs of some, the subtile sleight,
Who hazard first, the poore, and weaker one
To serue their turnes, whome God preserueth oft,
When they themselues, within the pit are caught.

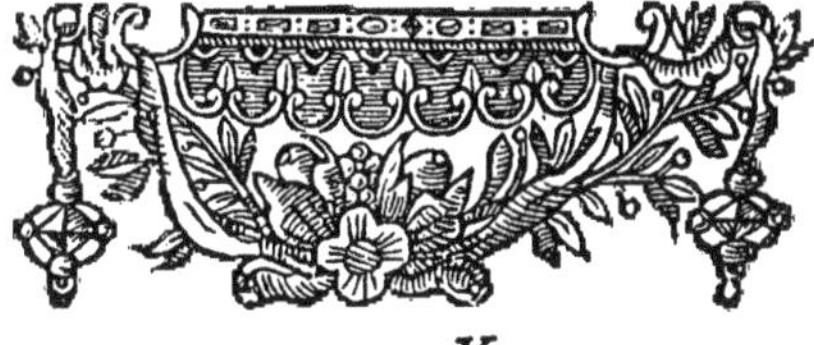

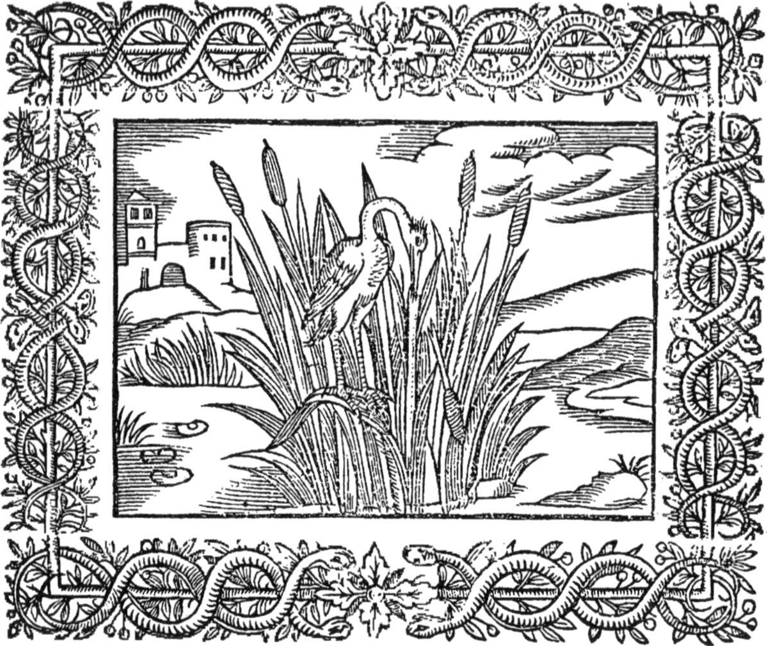

THE Fenny Bitter, that delightes to breede
In thickest sedge, by moore, and river side,
By thrusting low his bill into a reede,
All summer long, at morne and eventide:
Though neere, yet makes farre seeming such a sound,
That oft it doth, the Passenger astound.

This Figure fits, two sorts of people base,
The Coward one, that will with wordes affright,
When dares not looke, true Valor in the face:
The other is, the proude vaine-glorious wight,
Who where he comes, will make a goodly show
Of wit, or wealth, when it is nothing so.

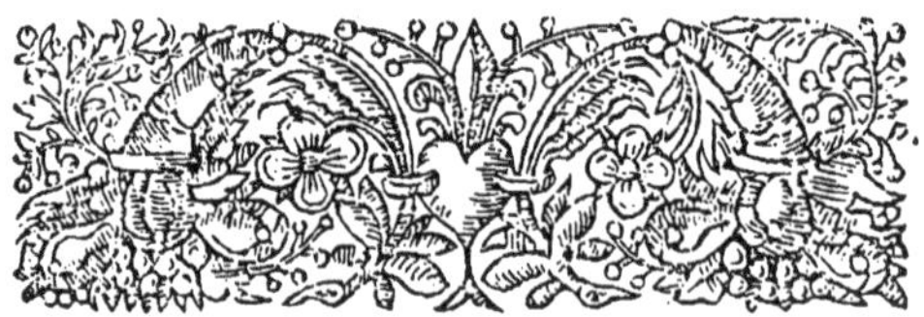

Deos

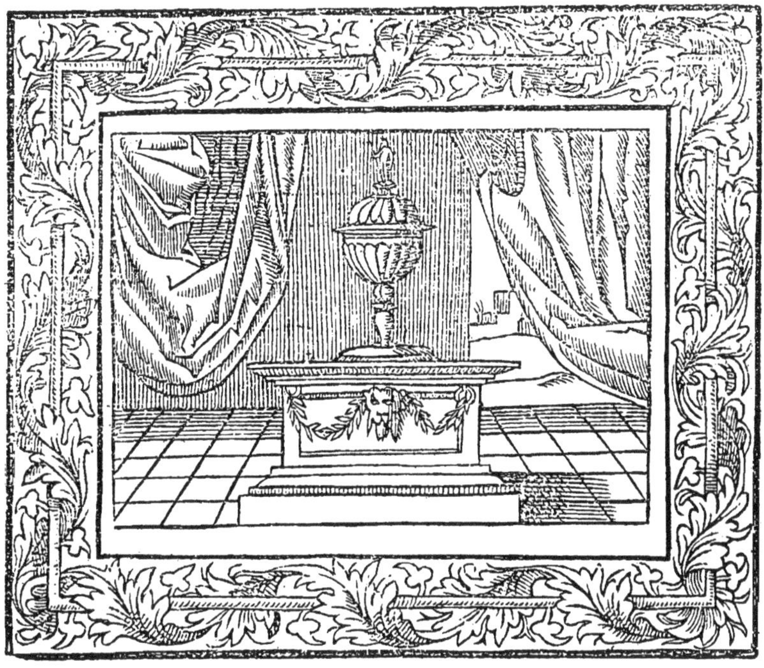

THE Romane Ladies, yearely did present
Their Iewells, and the best attire they wore
To *Delphos*, which were by commandement
Into a Goblet turnd, and plac't before
The *Pythian* God, as offring for the sinne
Of loathed pride, they fear'd they liued in.

Plutarch in Sympos; sap:

A mirror for such wightes, as will allow
Religion, or the church, the least of all,
Nay, from the same purloine they care not how,
Till Church perforce, hath stript them out of all:
This also tells our gallant Dames beside,
No vice offendes the Lord, so much as pride.

Quod in divinis rebus sumas sumptus sapienti lucro est.

Plautus in Milite Glor:

To the right worshipfull, Mr: D: Laifeild, sometimes my Tutor in Trinitie Colledge in Cambridge.

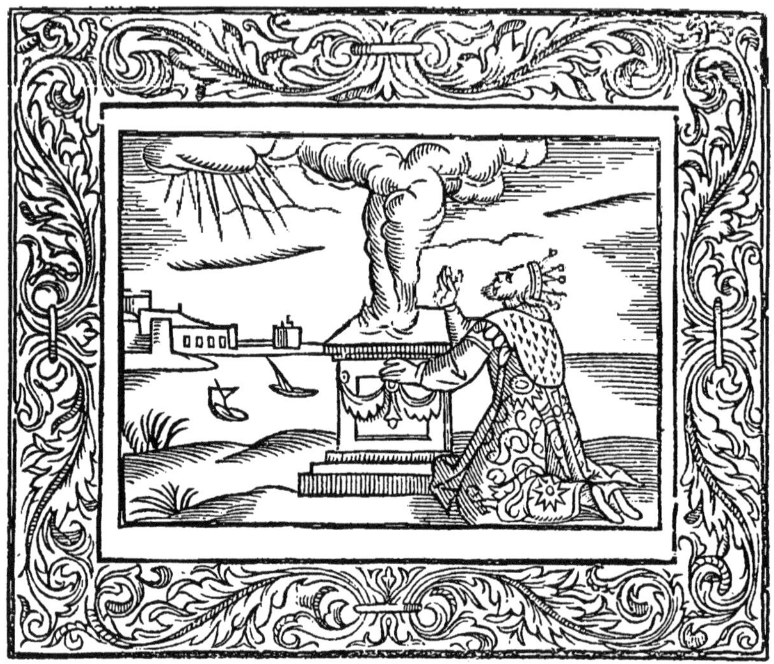

WHEN *Priam* saw his Citie set on fire,
At once and drowned, in his Peoples blood,
To pacifie the heavens enkindled ire,
(Since humane helpe, doth faile to do him good:)
Creusa warnes him to the Altar flie,
Although he were assured there to die.

The case is every christians in distresse,
Who to the Lord, himselfe should recommend,
As who can best the wrongfull cause redresse,
And patiently t' abide, what he shall send:
Fall'n into handes of foes, our freedome thence,
Or glorious death, to crowne our innocence.

Augustin: super Psalm: 74.

Non est quo fugias a Deo irato, nisi ad Deum placatum.

Allah

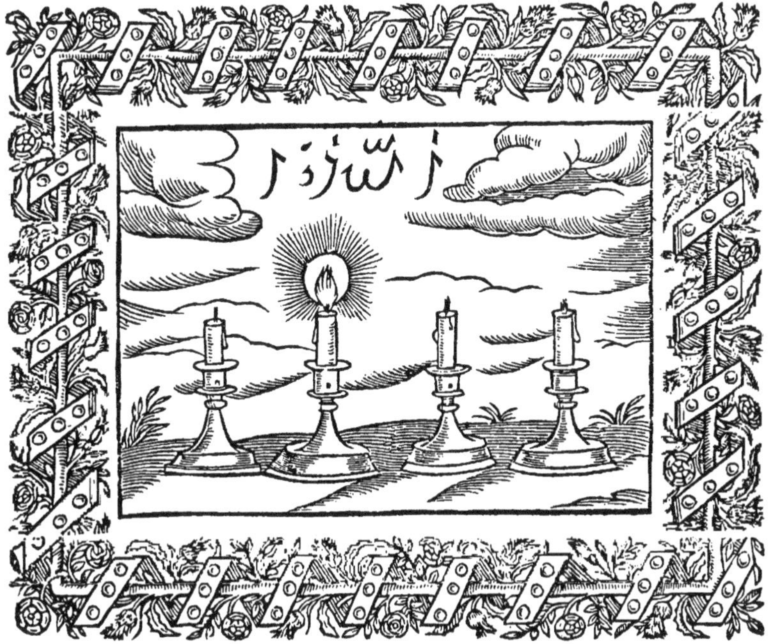

PROVDE Empresse, of the prouder Tyrant mind,
Of *Soliman's* high boundles-swelling thought:
When like the Ocean, boyling with the wind,
Of vaine Ambition, all in vaine he wrought,
To vndermine our Christian happie state,
And drowne her in, a deluge of his hate.

Qui tot armatorum millibus viennam Austriæ patrum memoria obsidebat, fortiter tamen vi et virtute Caroli quinti et Germanorum, re infecta discedere coactus.

But as our God, hath giu'n the Sea his bound:
So (*Pagan*) scatterd he, thy froathy Ire:
And while thou dream'st, of compassing this round,
Thy Snuffe went out, and yet thou want'st no fire:
Not that same which, thy fat Ambition fed,
But that of Hell, that eates thee, liuing-dead.

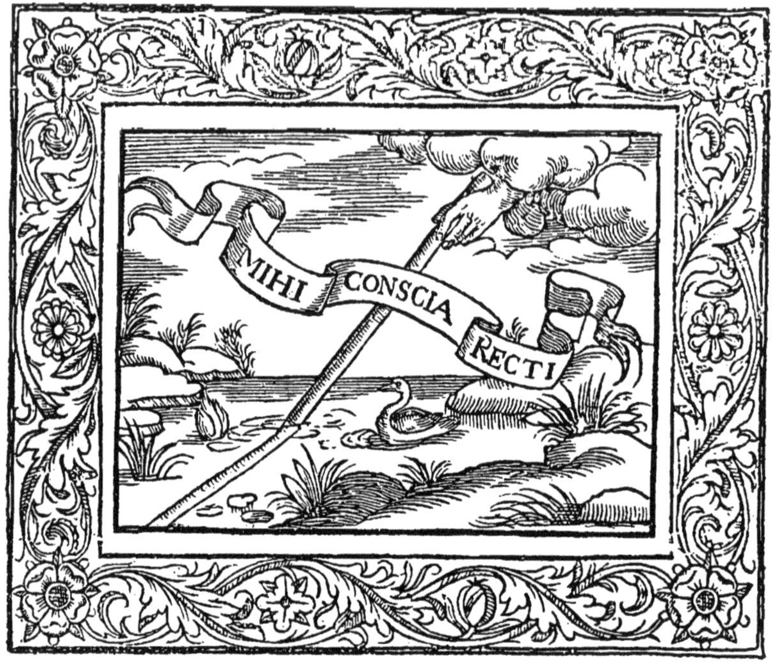

ALTHOVGH the ſtaffe, within the river cleere,
Be ſtraight as Arrow, in the *Perſian* bow:
Yet to the view, it crooked doth appeare,
And one would ſweare, that it indeede were ſo:
So ſoone the Sence deceiu'd, doth iudge amiſſe,
And fooles will blame, whereas none error is.

This ſtaffe doth ſhew, how oft the honeſt mind,
1 Cor: 11. 31. That meaneth well, and is of life vpright,
Is raſhly cenſur'd, by the vulgar blind,
Through vaine *Opinion*: or vile envious ſpite:
But if thou know'ſt, thy * conſcience cleere within,
What others ſay, it matters not a pinne.

* Bona conſcientia quotidie vireſcit, laboribus non affligitur, afficit gaudio viventem, æternumque durat Bernard: in lib: de conſcientia.

Ovid: 1. Faſto:
Conſcia mens vt cuique ſua eſt, ita concipit intra
Pectora, pro facto ſpemque metumque ſuo.

Fit

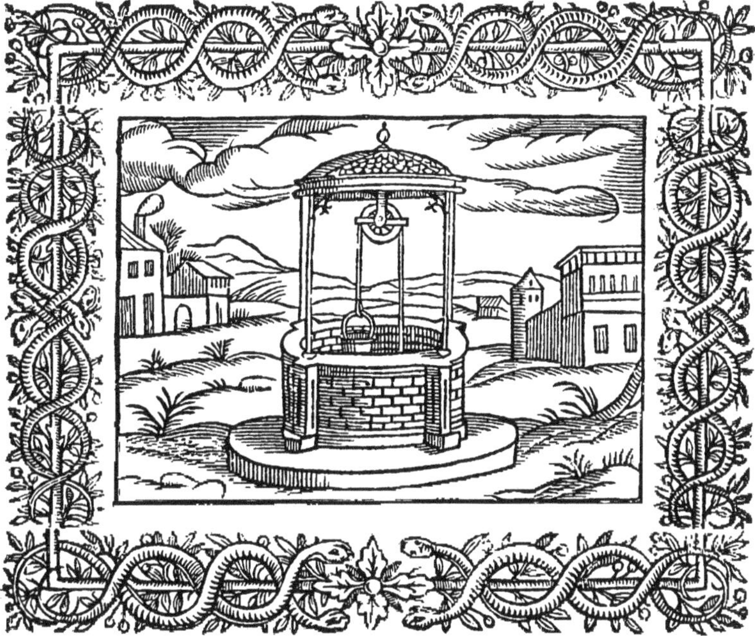

IF that the Well-we draw, and emptie oft:
The water there remaineth ſweete and good:
But ſtanding long, it growes corrupt and naught,
And ſerues no more, by reaſon of the mudde,
  In Summer hot, to coole our inward heate,
  To waſh, to water, or to dreſſe our meate.

So, if we doe not excercife our wit,
By dayly labour, and invention ſtill:
In little time, our ſloth corrupteth it,
With in bred vices, foule and ſtincking ill:
  That both the glories of our life deface,
  And ſtoppe the ſource, and head of heavenly grace.

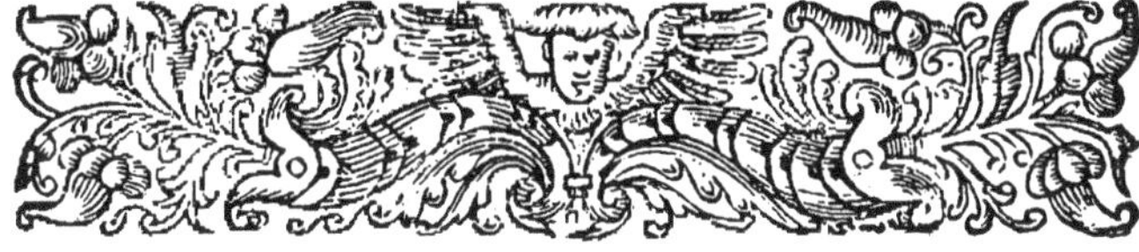

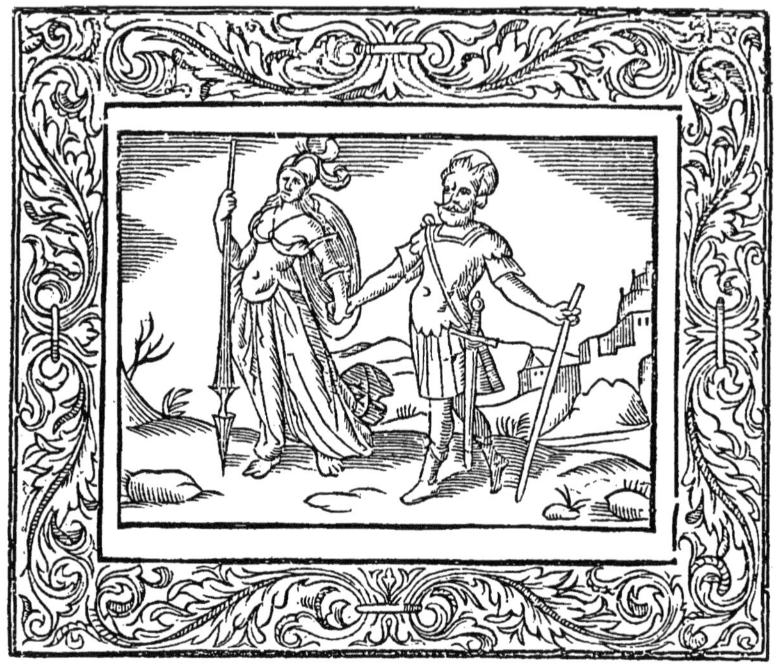

LO *Pallas* heere, with heedefull eie doth leade;
Vliſſes in his travaile farre and neere:
That he aright, might in his Iourney treade,
And ſhunne the traine of Error, every where:
N'ought had *Vliſſes*, ever brought to paſſe,
But this great Goddeſſe, his directreſſe was.

Homer: Odyſs: lib:

Though *Homer* did invent it long agoe,
And we eſteeme it as a fable vaine:
While heere we wander, it doth wiſely ſhow,
With all our actions, *wiſedome* ſhould remaine;
And where we goe, take *Pallas* ſtill along
To guide our feete, our eares, and laviſh tongue.

Wiſedome is only the Princes vertue. Ariſt: 3. politic:

Mens vna ſapiens plures vincit manus.

Euripides.

----Non ſolis viribus æquum
Credere, ſæpe acri potior prudentia dextra.

Valerius Flaccus 3. Argonaut:

In

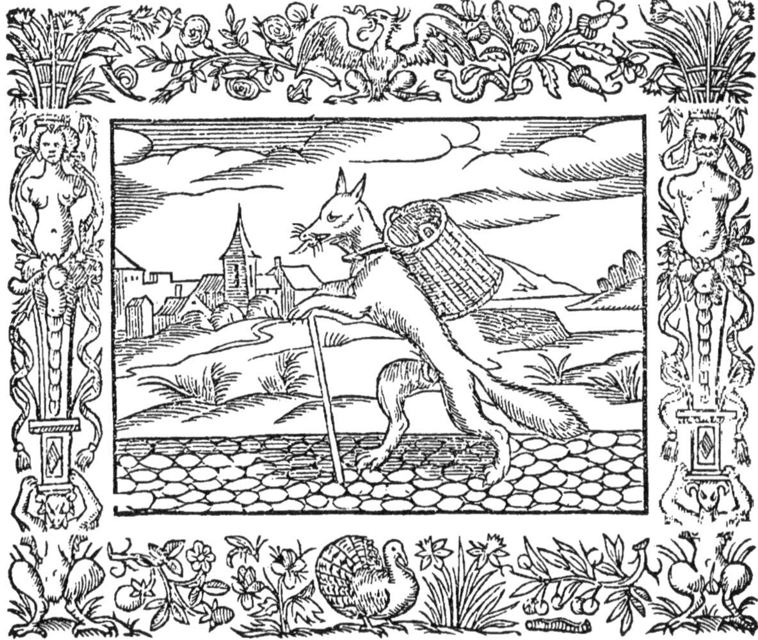

THE Houndes, ſometimes the Fox had put in truſt,
From Towne, to Towne, to beg for their releiſe:
Who was a while in's office very iuſt,
But ſhortly after, proou'd an errant theiſe:
By eating, or embezling, of the beſt,
And caſting to, the ſterued Houndes the reſt.

Of Regnards kind, there is a craftie crew,
Who when at death of frendes, are put in truſt,
Doe robbe the Church, or Infantes of their dew,
Diſpoſing of anothers as they luſt:
Whome being bound, in Conſcience to preſerue,
They ſuffer oft, in open ſtreete to ſterue.

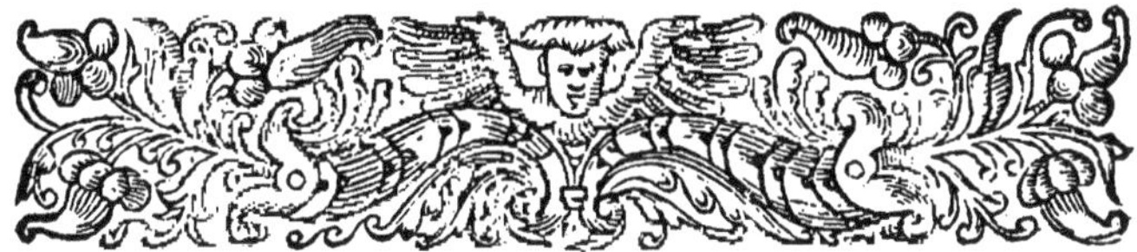

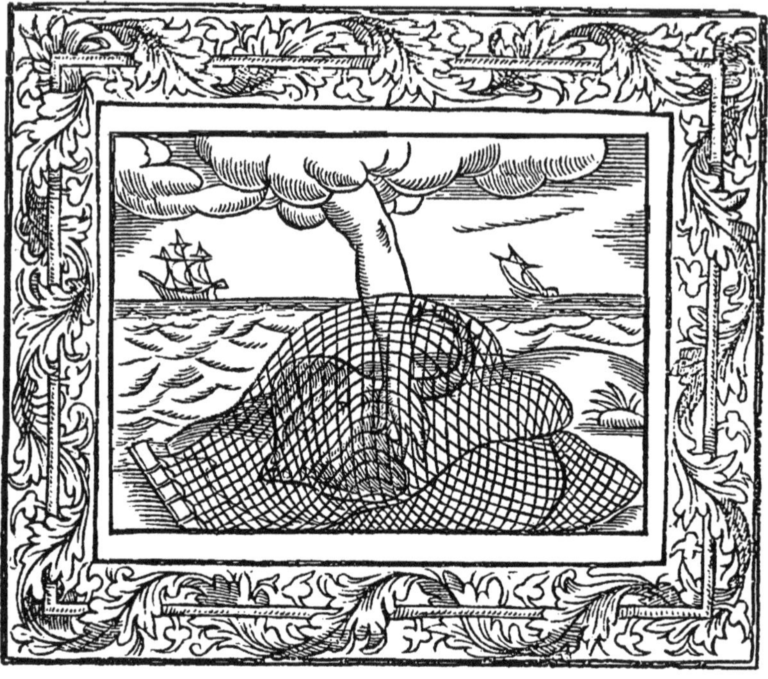

WHO lightly sets his enimie at nought,
And feares him not because he is too weake:
Or that he is thy pray, alreadie caught,
Within such net, he cannot eas'ly breake:
Repents him often, and doth prooue too late,
No foe so dang'rous, as the desperate.

Wherefore saith one, giue passage to his Ire,
Abuse him not with too much insolence:
Least hopeles backe, he doth againe retire,
With Furie arm'd, in stead of Patience:
And prooues the Victor, when with cunning skill,
Thou might'st before, haue rul'd him at thy will.

Ad Sidoniam virginem nobilem.

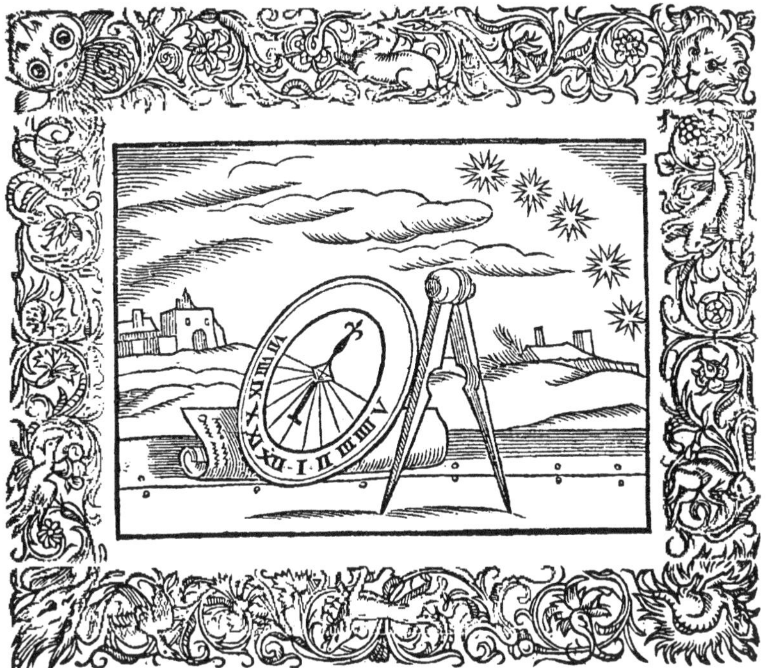

THOV greeu'ſt *Sidonia*, that I thus divide,
My Loue ſo largely, to a ſeverall frend:
While thou, thou think'ſt, remainedſt vneſpi'de:
Or takeſt thy fortune, at the latter end:
And certes who his loue, impartes to all,
Affectes but coldly, nay loues not at all.

With wonder rapt, though much I doe admire
Some Starres for luſtre, and their glories beſt:
You are that Arctick; moſt I doe deſire,
Whereon my hope, hath wholly ſet her reſt:
And who (ſweete Maide,) when others downe do ſlide,
To vnknowne Fate, muſt be my ſureſt guide.

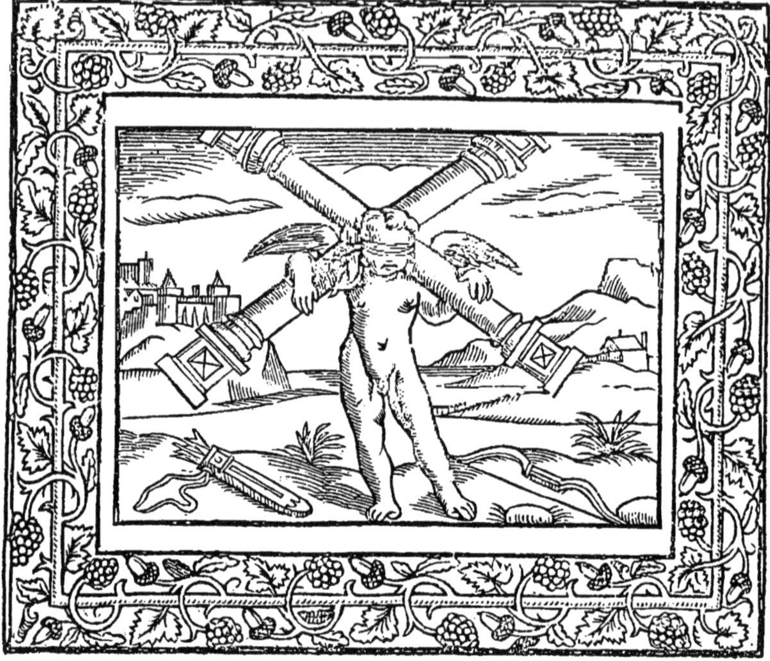

TWO Columnes ſtrong, heere little Loue doth beare,
Vpon his ſhoulders bare: though Lillie white,
Vis magna mentis. Seneca. As if another *Hercules* he were:
And would erect them, in a deepe deſpite,
Of that *Coloſſe*, or *Pharos* fiery bright
Th' *Egyptian* Piles, proude *Mauſoleus* toombe
Spaines Pillars, or great *Traians*, yet in Roome.

Nor may you leſſe imagine *Cupids* might:
Though (Ladies) he, but ſeeme a child in ſhow,
Since hand to hand, himſelfe in ſingle fight,
Hath giuen the great'ſt *Hero'es* their overthrow:
Ne could the wiſeſt man avoide his bow:
Whoſe Trophees, & braue triumphes, were they ſhowne,
Thy Sonne *Alcmena*, never had beene knowne.

Seneca in Medea

Cæcus eſt ignis, ſtimulatus ira
Nec regi curat, patiturve frœnos
Haud timet mortem, cupit ire in ipſos
Obvius enſes.

Ad

Ad amicum ſuum Iohannem Doulandum Muſices peritiſſimum.

Iohannes Doulandus.

Annos ludendo hauſi.

Anagramma Authoris.

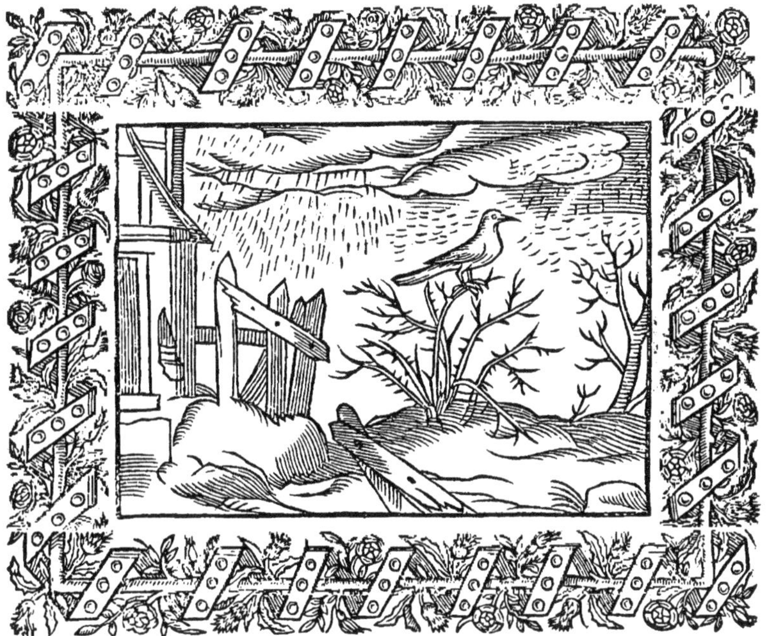

HEERE *Philomel*, in ſilence ſits alone,
In depth of winter, on the bared brier,
Whereas the Roſe, had once her beautie ſhowen;
Which Lordes, and Ladies, did ſo much deſire:
But fruitles now, in winters froſt, and ſnow,
It doth deſpiſ'd, and vnregarded grow,

So ſince (old frend,) thy yeares haue made thee white,
And thou for others, haſt conſum'd thy ſpring,
How few regard thee, whome thou didſt delight,
And farre, and neere, came once to heare thee ſing:
Ingratefull times, and worthles age of ours,
That let's vs pine, when it hath cropt our flowers.

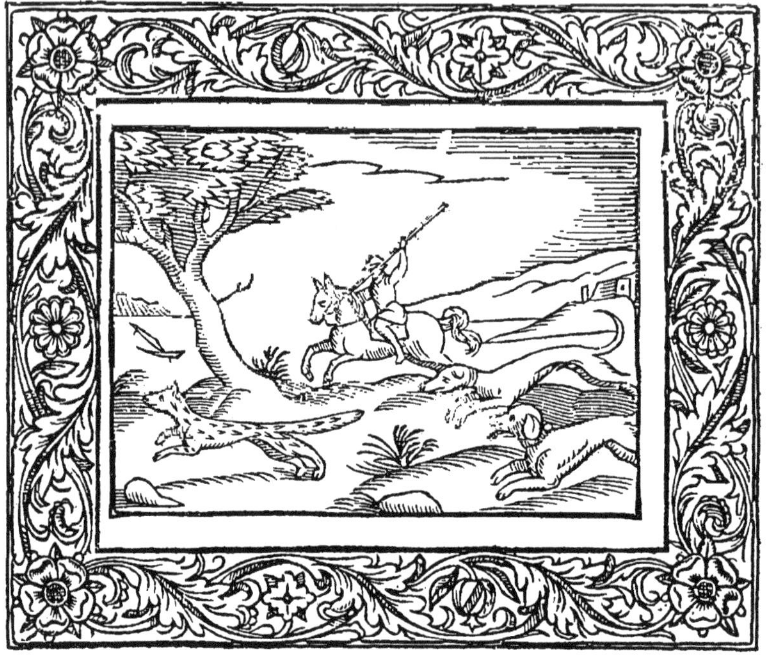

THE *Ermin* heere, whome eager houndes doe chaſe,
And hunters haue, around environ'd in,
(As ſome doe write) will not come neere the place,
That may with dirt, defile his daintie skinne:
But rather chooſeth, then the ſame ſhould ſoile,
Be torne with dogges, or taken with the'toile.

Me thinkes even now, I ſee a number bluſh,
To heare a beaſt, by nature ſhould haue care,
To keepe his skinne, themſelues not care a ruſh,
With how much filth, their mindes beſpotted are:
Great Lordes, and Ladies, turne your coſt and art,
From bodies pride, t' enritch your better part.

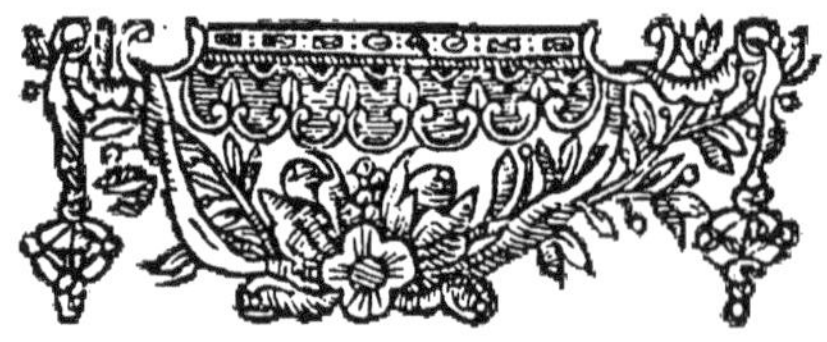

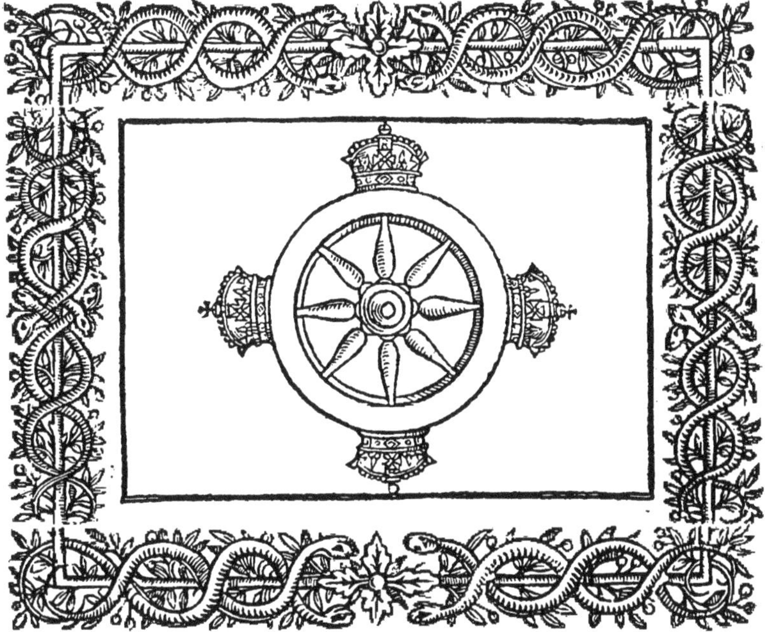

FOWER Captiue Kinges, proud *Sesostris* did tie,
And them compeld his charriot to draw,
Whereof the one, did ever cast his eie
Vnto the wheele: which when the Tirant saw,
And ask'd the cause, the chained King repli'de,
Because heerein, my state I haue espi'de.

For like our selues, the spoke that was on high,
Is to the bottome, in a moment cast,
As fast the lowest, riseth by and by,
All humane thinges, thus find a change at last:
The Tyrant fearing, what his hap might be,
Releas'd their bandes forthwith, and set them free.

Fortunam tuam (Princeps) pressis manibus tene lubrica est nec inuita teneri potest Curt: lib: 7.

Vidi cruentos carcere includi Duces, et impotentis terga plebeia manu scindi Tyranni— Seneca In Herc.

Æstuat ambiguis vita hæc agitata procellis,
Fertque refertque vices sors male fida suas;
Hunc de plebe creat, regnantem deprimit illum:
Vel rota tot casus vna SESOSTRIS habet.

Basil: Doron.

In tranquillissimis rebus interdum existit periculum quod nemo expectat.

Erasmus.

Vita Fortuna regitur, non Sapientia.

Cic: in Tusculan:

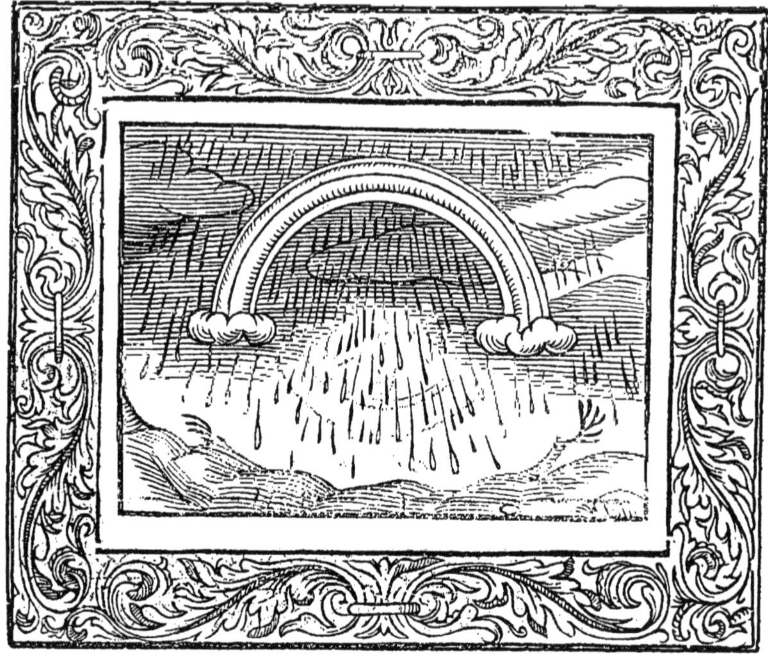

OF orient hew, a Rainebow doth containe,
An hideous ſhower, within her Circlet round,
Reſembling that great puniſhment of raine,
The Lord inflicted when the world was drown'd:
The Rainebow, of his Mercy, heere a ſigne,
Which with his Iuſtice, he doth ever ioine.

For though we howerly, doe the Lord provoke,
By crieng Sinnes, to bring his vengeance downe,
The ſalue he tempers, while he ſtrikes the ſtroke,
And ioines his favor, with a bitter frowne:
To let vs know, that wrath he keepes in ſtore,
And grace for ſuch, as will offend no more.

Quintil: declam: 11. Oh quam difficile hominibus miſereri et ſapere.

---- Peragit tranquilla poteſtas
Claudian: Quod violenta nequit, mandataque fortius vrget
Imperioſa quies ----

Sine

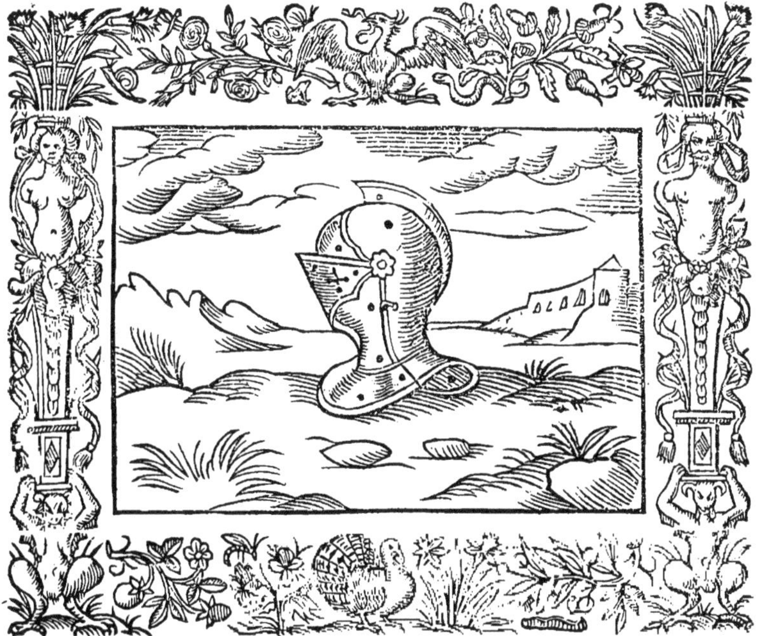

THIS warlick Helme, that naked doth appeare,
Not gold-enchaſed, or with Gemmes beſet,
Yet doth the markes, of many a battaile beare,
With dintes of bullets, there imprinted yet;
No featherie creaſt, or dreaſſing doth deſire,
Which at the Tilts, the vulgar moſt admire.

For beſt deſert, ſtill liueth out of view,
Or ſoone by Envie, is commaunded downe,
* Nor can her heauen-bred ſpirit lowly ſue,
Though t'were to gaine, a kingdome, and a crowne:
Beſide it tells vs, that the valiant heart,
Can liue content, though wanteth his deſert.

* — Emitur ſola virtute poteſtas. Claudian:

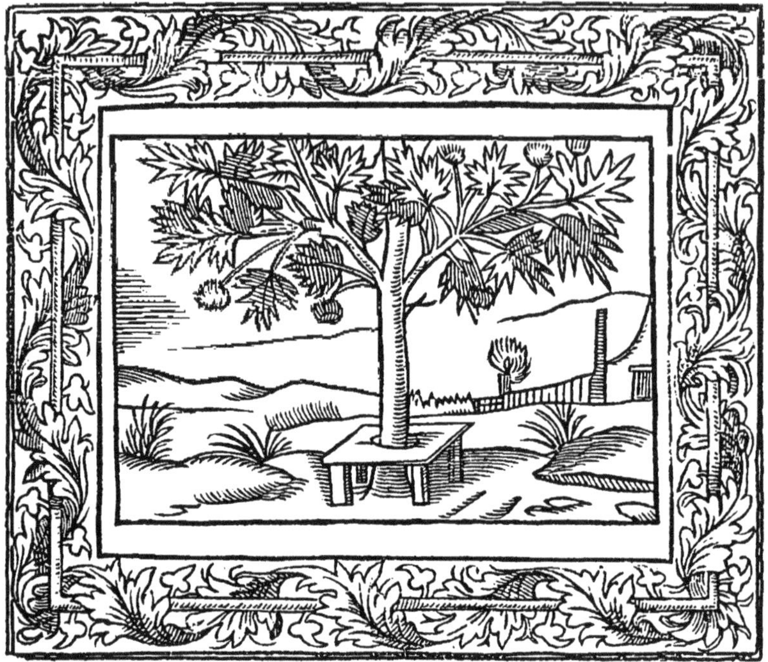

THE *Platane* Tree, that by the bankes of *PO*,
With gentle ſhade refreſheth man and beaſt,
Of other Trees, doth beare the goodlieſt ſhow,
And yet of all, it is the barreneſt:
But Nature though, this tree of fruite bereaues,
It makes amendes, in cooling with the leaues.

This *Platane* Tree, are ſuch as growe aloft,
* Ore-dropping others, with their wealth or might,
And yet, they of themſelues, are barren oft,
Wanting th' endowments, of the meaner wight:
Who many times, in vertue doth excell,
When theſe but haue, the ſhadow, or the ſhell.

* Contemptor animus et ſuperbia commune nobilitatis malum. Saluſt: Iugurth:

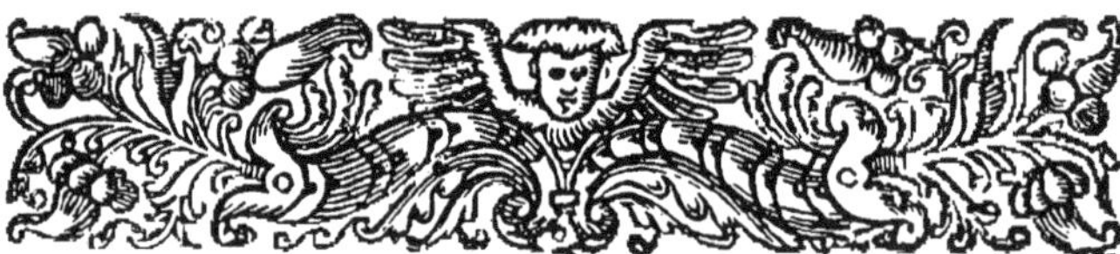

Vita

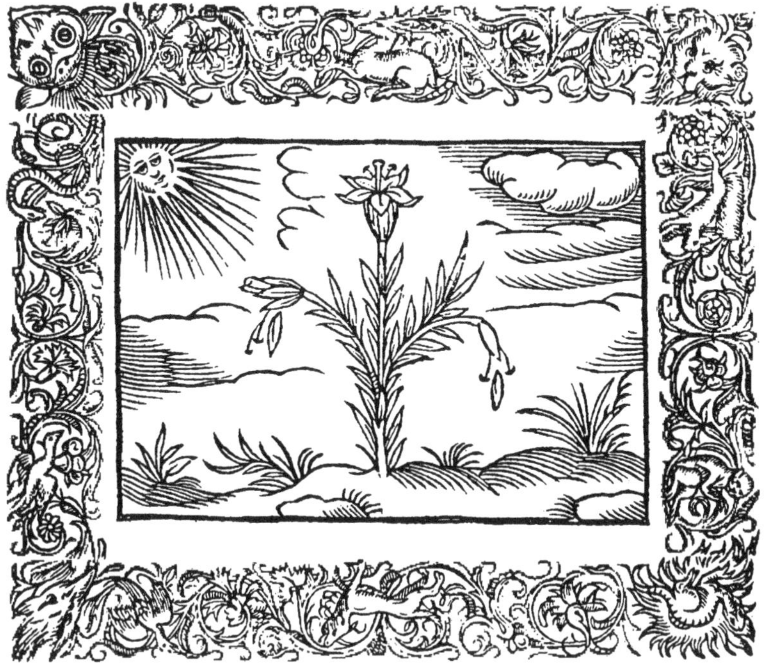

OF all our life, behold the very ſumme,
Which as this flower, continues but a day:
Our youth is morne, our middle age is come
By noone, at night as faſt we doe decay,
As doth this Lillie flowring with the Sunne,
But withered ere, his race be fully runne.

Wherefore our life's reſembled to a ſhippe, Chryſoſtom.
Which paſſeth on, though we doe what we pleaſe,
A ſhade, a flower, that every froſt doth nippe,
A dreame, a froath, a waue vpon the Seas,
Which hath a while his being, till anon,
Some elſe intrude, and hee's forgot and gon.

Cuncta mortalium incerta, quantoque plus adeptus ſis, tanto te magis in lubrico cenſeas. Tacitus 1 Annal.

Brevis est vita, et brevitas ipſa ſemper incerta. Auguſt: de verbis Domini.

Divitiæ

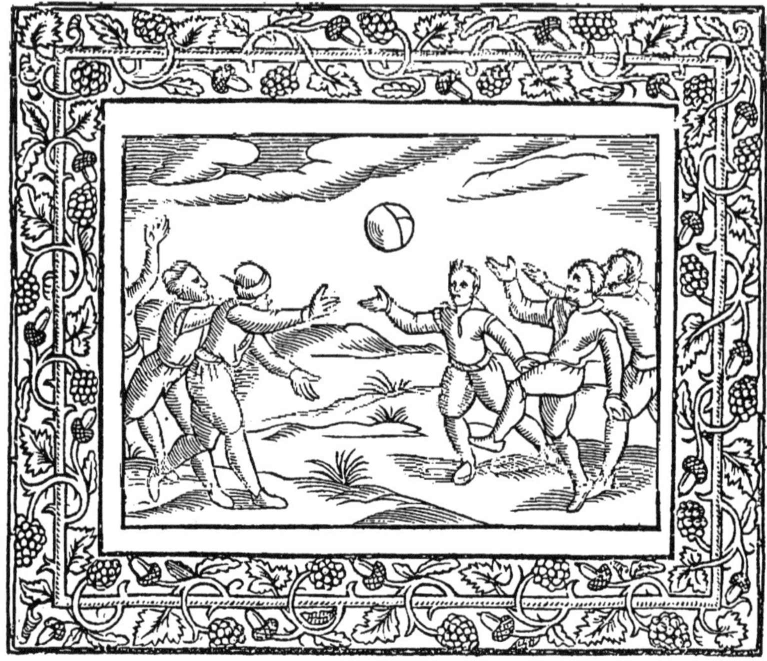

THE country Swaines, at footeball heere are ſeene,
  Which each gapes after, for to get a blow,
The while ſome one, away runnes with it cleane,
It meetes another, at the goale below
  Who never ſtirrd, one catcheth heere a fall,
  And there one's maimd, who never ſaw the ball.

This worldly wealth, * is toſſed too and fro,
At which like Brutes, each ſtriues with might and maine,
To get a kick, by others overthrow,
Heere one's fetch't vp, and there another ſlaine,
  With eager haſt, and then it doth affront
  Some ſtander by, who never thought vpon't.

* Caduca hæc fragilia, puerilibusque conſentanea crepundiis, quæ vires atque opes humanæ vocantur: Valerius lib 6. cap vltimo.

Arbiter

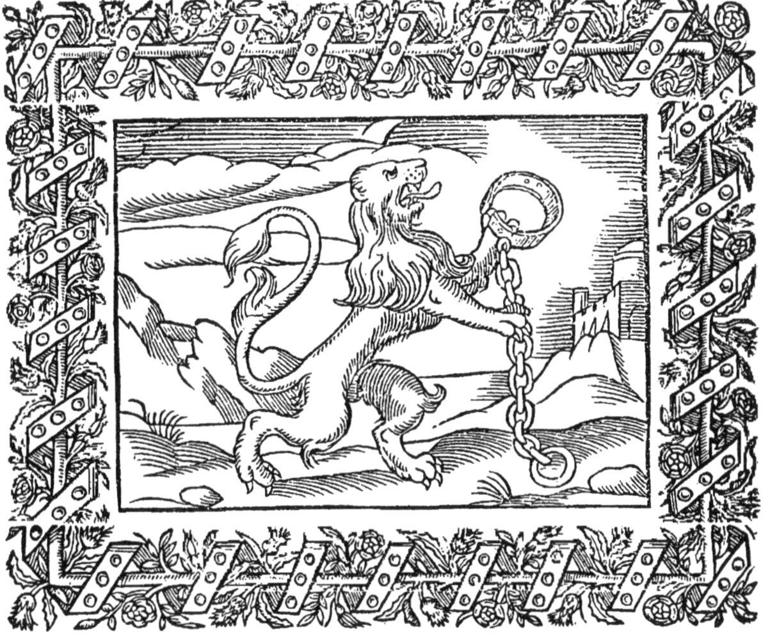

VNTO his life, who lookes with heedie eie,
And labors moſt to keepe a conſcience pure
And doubtes to treade, in errors pathes awrie:
That man is bleſt, and deemed happie ſure:
When vicious perſons, even vnto their graues,
Are lewde affections, and their vices ſlaues.

For as the Lion, that hath ſlipt his band,
Or ſhear'd the chaine, that did his courage hold
Doth not in awe, of churliſh keeper ſtand,
But ſince is waxen, more couragious bold:
The righteous man, ſo from hells bondage free,
Hath heartes content, ioind with his libertie. Baſil: Doron.

Ardua res Cæſar gentes domuiſſe rebelles,
Ferrea Sauromatum et colla dediſſe iugo:
Verius at vincis tua cum vindicta laceſſit,
* Pectora, et hanc poteris ſumère nolle tamen.

* Duo adverſiſſima rectæ menti Celeritas et Ira. Thucidides.

Latius regnes ávidum domandó
Spiritum; quam ſi Lybiam remotis
Gadibus iungas et vterque Pœnus
Serviat vni.

Horat. carm: lib: 2. Ode 2.

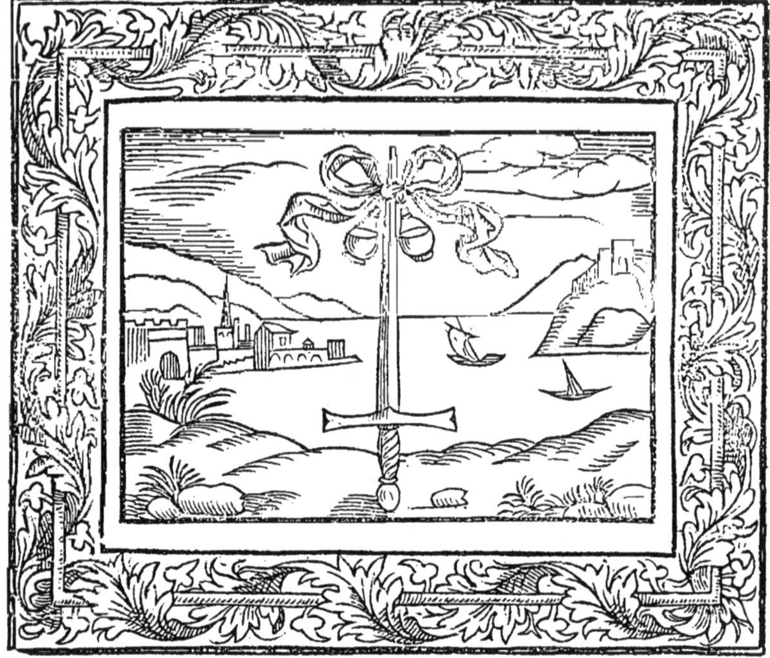

THIS Sword, a Symbole of the Law, doth threate
Perpetuall death, to all of *Adams* race:
But yet th' Almightie, of his mercie greate,
Sendes, after ſentence, pardon of his grace:
For when he found vs, maimed on the ground,
With wine, and oile of grace, he heald the wound.

Our partes it is, ſince by the Law we ſee,
The fearefull ſtate, and daunger we are in,
To doe our beſt, then to his mercie flee,
And new againe, our ſinfull liues begin:
Not truſting to our deedes, and merits vaine,
Since nought but death, doth due to theſe remaine.

Baſil: Doron.

Iuſta licet ſeros Adæ ſub lege nepotes.
Impetat a tergo vindicis Ira Dei,
Vnius hæc præſtat medicamina gratia Chriſti
Vulnere ne pereas quam redivivus habes.

Auguſt: de verbis Apoſt:

Si levis morbus eſſet, medicus non quæreretur, ſi medicus non quæreretur, morbus non finiretur: ideo vbi abundavit peccatum, ſuperabundavit et gratia:

D: Bernard: ſerm ſuper Cant: 54.

Gratia balſamum puriſſimum eſt, et ideo purum, ſolidum et profundum vas requirit:

In

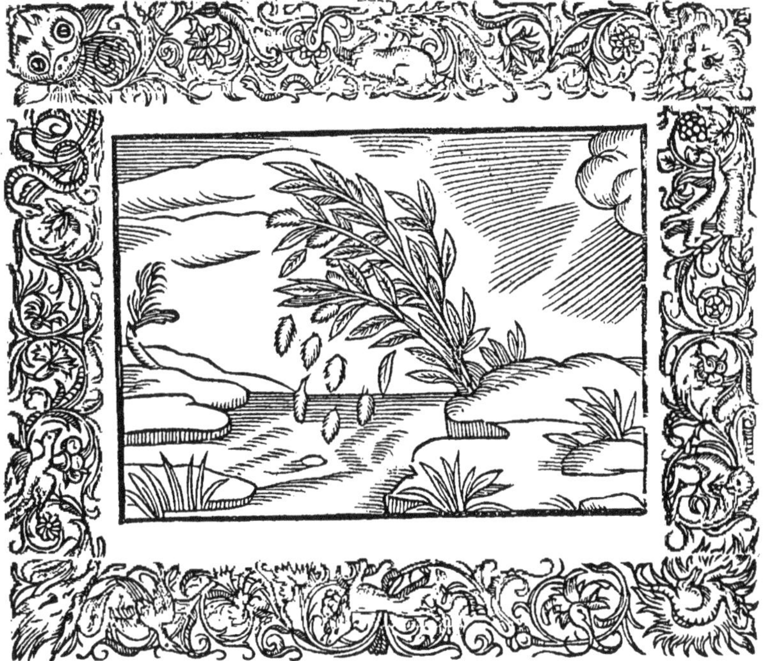

THE watry willow, growing by the ſhore,
Of trees the formoſt, forth her fruite doth ſend,
But laden with her bee-deſired ſtore,
Ere ten daies fully come vnto an end,
Her Palme's ſo ſweete, we lou'd and look't vpon,
With *Boreas* breath, are blowne away and gone.

To this ſame tree, did *Homer* once compare, — Frugi perda.
Such heires as ſtraight, their Patrimonie waſt,
In ri'tous wiſe: and ſuch as Artiſtes are,
Who getting much, doe let it fly as faſt:
Eeke ſuch of wit, or wealth, that make a ſhow,
In ſubſtance when, we find it nothing ſo.

Dilapidare cave nummos ceu neſcius vti — Vrſinus velus
Pelle tamen ſordes, modus optima regula rerum.

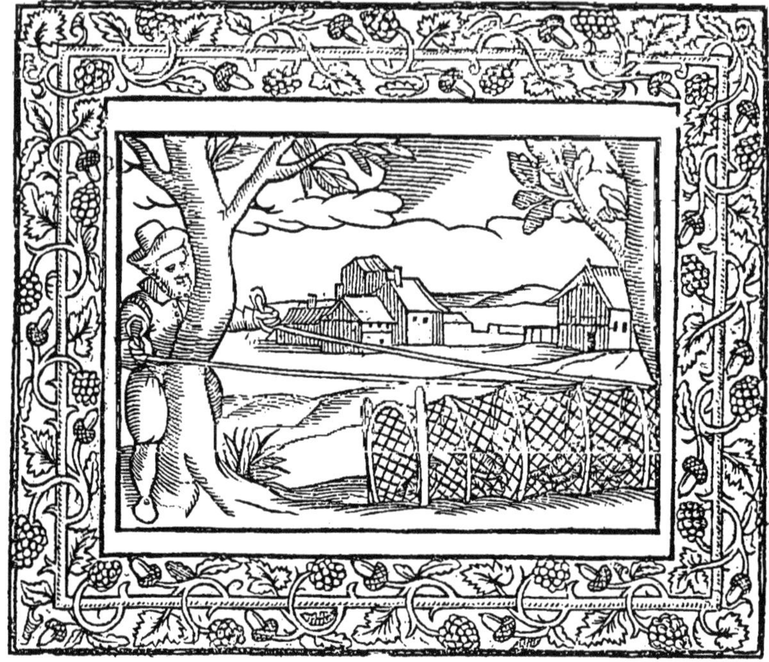

Perdices fœminæ vocem ſequntur. Xenophon.

THE *Partrich* young, in Foulers net ycaught,
Too late the error of their damme repent,
For why? her call them into daunger brought,
And taught at firſt, the heedeles way they went:
Heereby are kinges our common nurſes ment,
When to their luſtes, themſelues become a pray,
And by * example, thouſandes caſt awaie.

Nunquam deceptus eſt princeps niſi qui prius ipſe deceperit. Livi: lib: 4 in panegyr:

* vnius invidia et culpa ab omnibus peccatur. Tacitus Annal 3.

Not heerevpon, as may of moſt be thought,
We ſhould our Prince, like Rebells diſobey,
When they be Tyrants, or with * vices nought,
Do haſten others, and their owne decay:
But to the Lord, like Chriſtians rather pray
For mercie, who hath in his anger ſent
* Such wretches vile, to be our puniſhment.

* Hæc conditio principii vt quicquid faciant præcipere videantur. Quintilia: declamat: 4.

* Tyranni Dei voluntate præſur. Ierem: 27. 8.

Baſil: Doron.

Dum tua qua ducis legimus veſtigia paſſim
Alma parens, capimur præda miſella plagis,
Proh dolor, innocuos quã multos perdis, ab vno
Te, modo diductum principe crimen erit.

In

To the Hon: and most worthy Ladie, E: L:

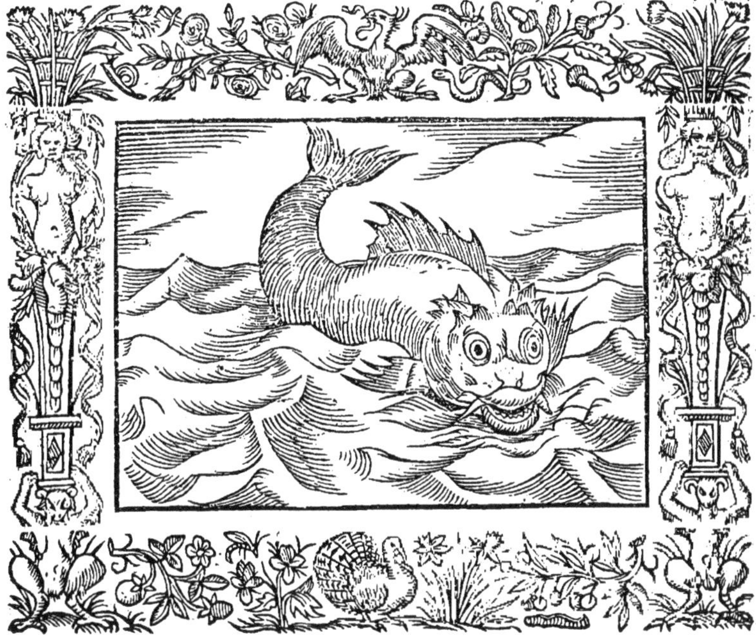

THE frendly *Dolphin*, while within the maine,
At libertie delightes, to sport and play,
Himselfe is fresh, and doth no whit retaine
The brinish saltnes of the boundles Sea
Wherein he liues. Such is the secret skill,
Of Nature working, all thinges at her will.

So you great Ladie, who your time haue spent,
Within that place, where daungers oft abound,
Remaine vntainted of your Element,
And to your praise, yet keepe your honor sound
Diana-like, whose brightnes did excell,
When many starres, within your climate fell.

To the most Honorable and worthie Ladie the Ladie Alicia D:

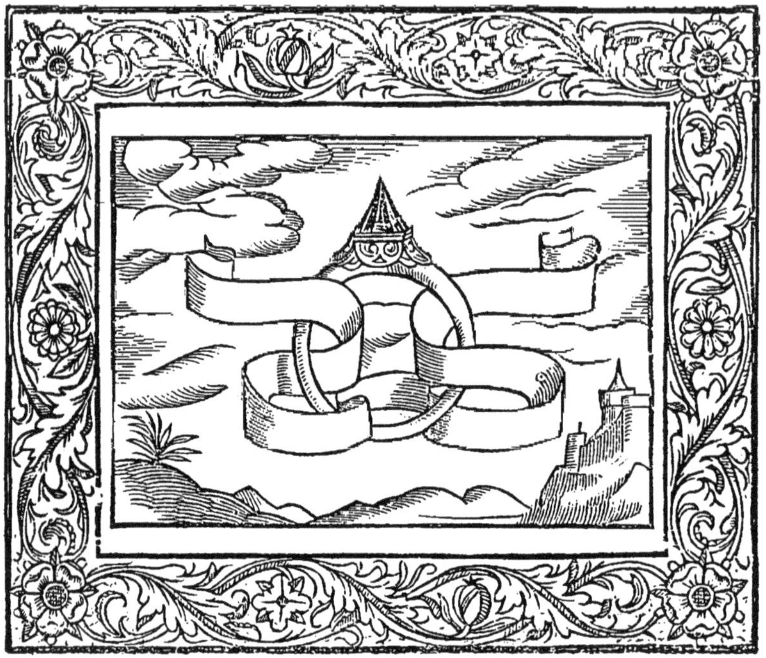

AND ye great Ladie; that are left alone,
To merc'les mercie, of the worldes wide sea,
Behold your faire, though counterfeited stone,
So much you ioi'd in, on your wedding day,
And tooke for true, how after it did prooue,
Vnworthy Iewell, of so worthy loue.

Ah how can man, your sexe (faire Ladies) blame,
Whose brests, are vertues pretious Carcansets,
When he himselfe, first breakes the boundes of shame,
And dearest loue, and loialtie forgets:
Yet heerein happie, ye aboue the rest,
Belou'd of Heauen, and in your children blest.

Paulatim

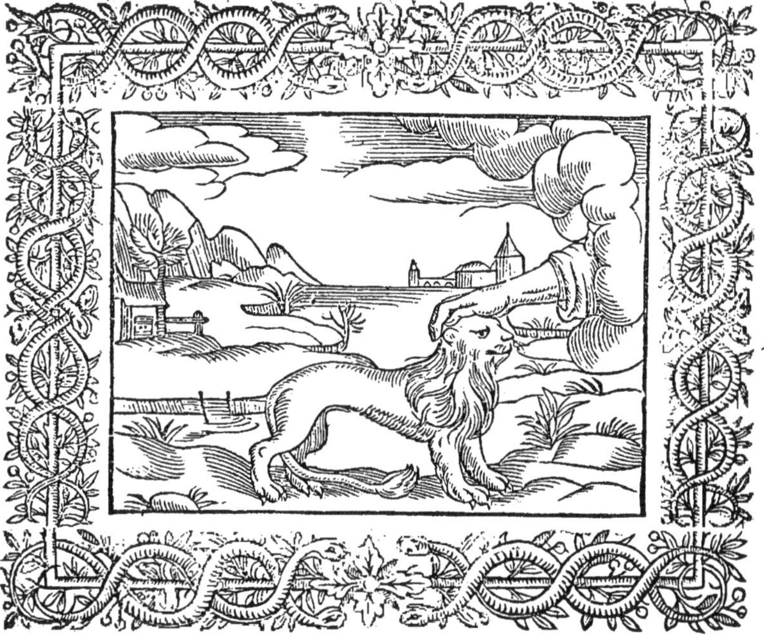

BY violence who tries to turne away,
Strong natures current, from the proper courſe,
To mooue the Earth, he better were aſſay,
Or wreſt from *Ioue*, his thunderbolts perforce,
Bid the Sphæres ſtay, or ioine by art in one,
Our *Thames* with *Tyber*, *Pinde* with *Pelion*.

For nought at all heerein prevailes our might,
With greater force ſhe doth our ſtrength withſtand,
The River ſtopt, " his banke downe-beareth quite,
And ſeldome boughes, are bent with ſtubborne hand:
When gentle vſage, feircenes doth allay,
And bringes in time, the Lion to obay.

" Et ab obice ſævior ibat Ovidi: Metamor:

Sie

To my worſhipfull and kind frend Mr. William Stallenge, ſearcher of the Port of London, and firſt Author of making Silke in our Land.

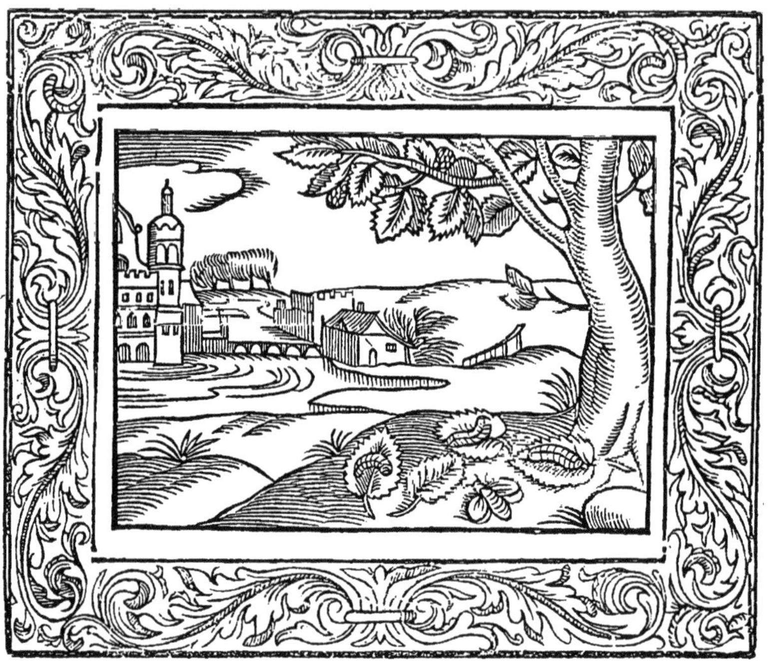

THESE little creatures heere, as white as milke,
That ſhame to ſloth, are buſie at their loome.
All ſummer long in weauing of their their Silke,
Doe make their webs, both winding ſheete and toombe,
Thus to th' ingratefull world, bequeathing all
Their liues haue gotten, at their funerall.

Even ſo the webs, our wits for others weaue,
Even from the higheſt to the meaneſt, worne,
But Siren-like it'h end, our ſelues deceiue,
Who ſpend our time, to ſerue anothers turne:
Or painte a foole, with coate, or cullors gay,
To giue good wordes, or thankes, ſo goe his way.

Tyranni

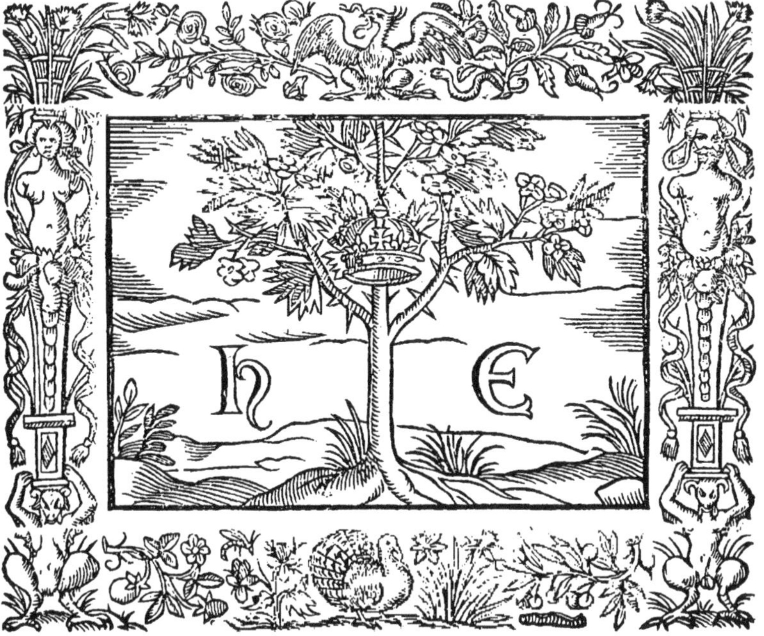

WHEN valiant *Richmond*, gaue the overthrow
T'vſurping *Richard*, at that fatall feild
Of *Boſworth*, as our Hiſtories doe ſhow,
This * Embleme he deviſed for his ſheild,
(For when the battaile, wholly was his owne,
He found his crowne, within a Hawthorne throwne.)

* Paſſim in feneſtris vere regij illius operis apud Weſtmon: invenitur.

Whereat he ſigh'd they ſay, and vttered this,
A * Kingdome eaſeth not, the guiltie mind,
Nor Crowne contents, where inward horror is,
Withall it ſhowes, how I am like to find,
With Honor, and this dignitie I beare,
My part of greiſe, and thornes of heavie care.

* Multæ illi manus tibi vna cervix. Ex dicto Caligulæ.

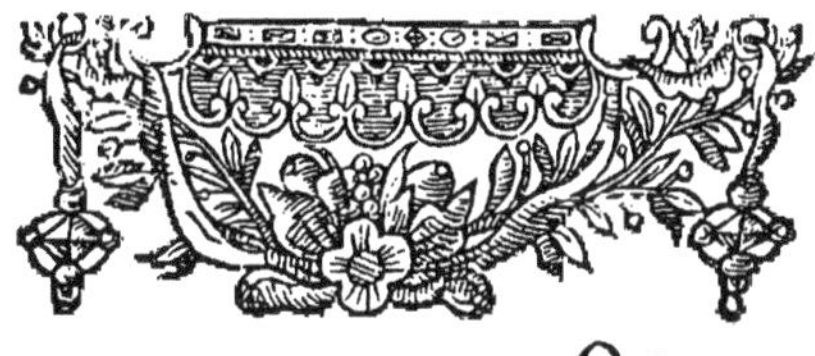

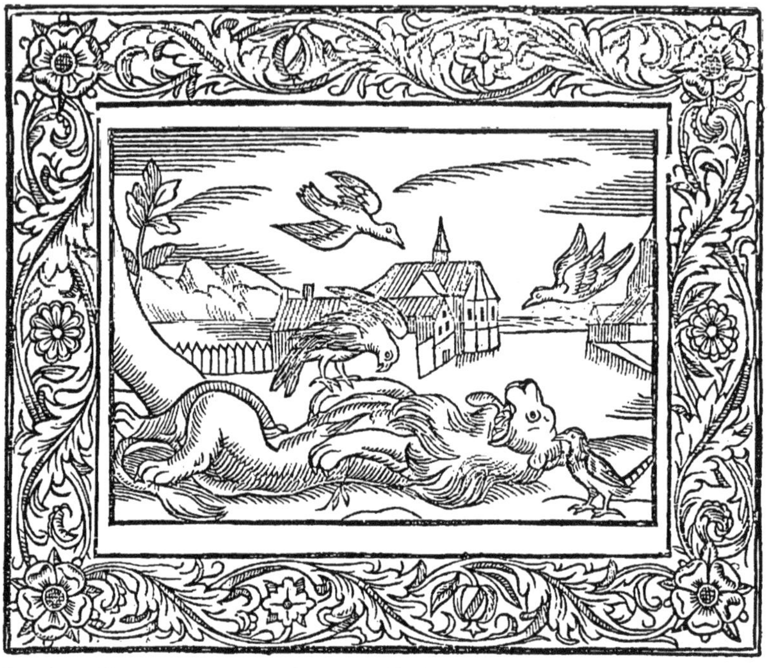

THE *Lion* once, whome all the Beastes did dread,
Doth in a thicket deadly wounded lie,
About whose carkas, yet not fully dead,
Doe flock the *Vultur*, *Puttock*, and the *Pie*,
And where the woundes are greene, and freshly bleede,
They light thereon, and most of all doe feede.

Plutarch: in libello de vtilitate capiẽda ab inimicis.

Such carrion Crowe., thinke thou thine enimie,
Who seldome dare assault thee being sound,
But where he doth thy guiltines espie,
With eager hate, he præies vpon thy wound:
But wisely if thou lead'st thy life vpright,
He leaues thee then with sterued appetite.

Innocentia est puritas animi omnem iniuriæ illationem abhorrens.

Cicero in offic:

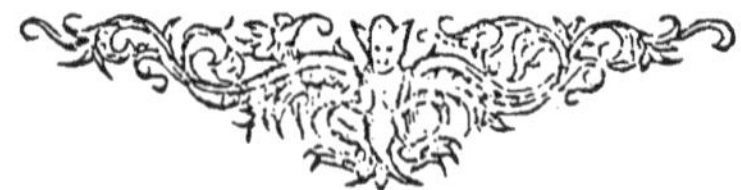

Amor

To my Louing and moſt kind frendes, Mr Chriſtopher Collarde, and Mrs Mabell Collarde his wife, of St Martines in the feildes.

Mabella Colarde.
Bella, alma corde.

Anagramma Authoris.

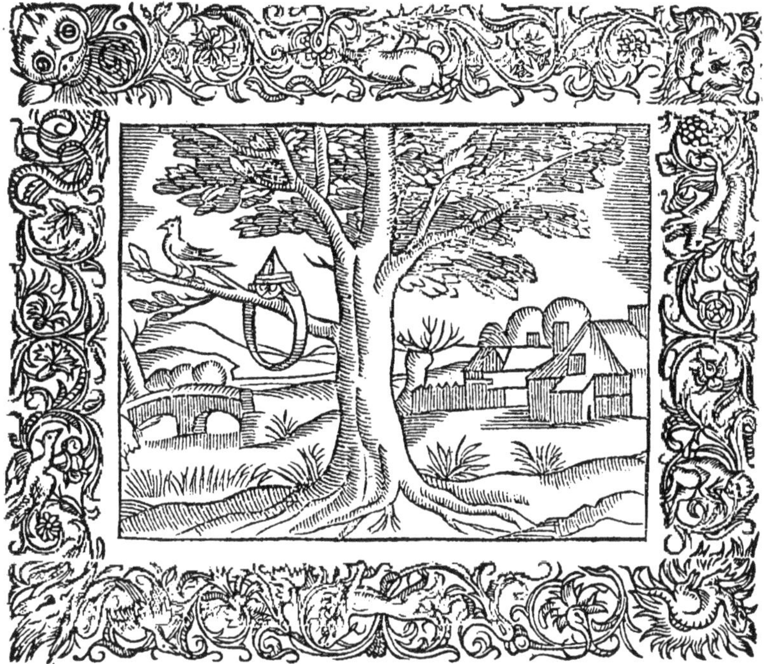

DEAREST of frẽdes, accept this ſmall device,
Wherewith I would your curteſies requite,
But that your loues invaluable price,
Muſt hold me debter, while I view this light,
Nor can my heires, thẽſe papers dead and gone,
Repay the favors for me, you haue done.

A * Turtle heere, vpon an Oliue ſits,
Vpon whoſe branch, depends a Ring of gold,
As beſt the loue of Matrimonie fits,
Thus ever endles, never waxing old,
The branch and bowes, the fruite that from you ſpring,
The Doue your ſelfe, your wife that golden RING.

* Exemplo iunctæ tibi ſint in amore Columbæ: *Propert:* 2. 15.

Aurum rubigine non corrumpitur quocirca in maximo pretio ſemper habebatur.

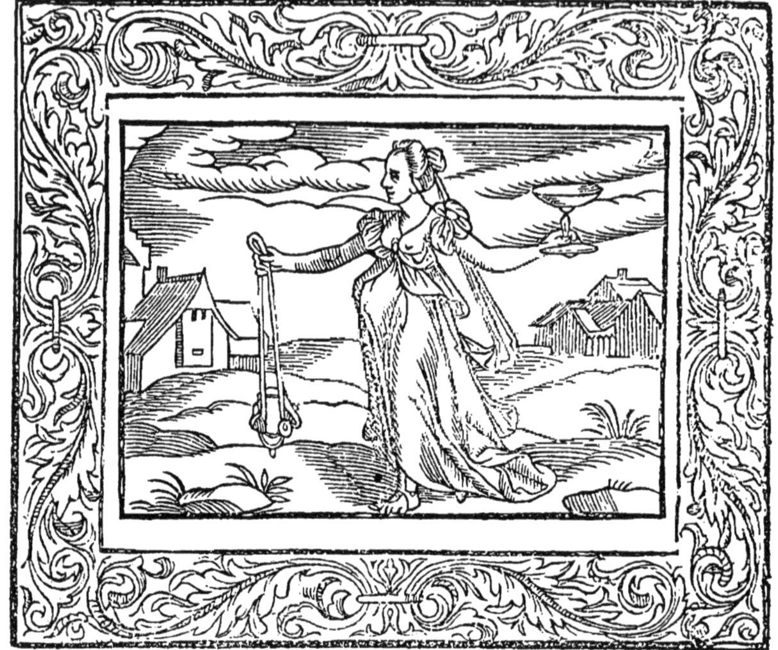

HEERE *Temperance* I ſtand, of virtues, Queene,
Who moderate all humane vaine deſires,
Wherefore a bridle in my hand is ſeene,
To curbe affection, that too farre aſpires:
I'th other hand, that golden cup doth ſhow,
Vnto exceſſe I am a deadly foe.

For when to luſtes, I looſely let the raine,
And yeeld to each ſuggeſting appetite,
Man to his ruine, headlong runnes amaine,
To frendes great greiſe, and enimies delight:
No conqueſt doubtles, may with that compare,
Of our affectes, when we the victors are.

Baſil: Doron.

Quæ rego virtutes placido moderamine cunctas
Affectuſque potens ſum Dea SOPHROSYNE:
Effrænes animi doceo cohibere furores,
Suſtineo, abſtineo, diſplicet omne nimis.

Max: lib 1.

Nihil eſt tam præclarum, tamque magnificum, quod non moderatione temperari debeat.

Servire

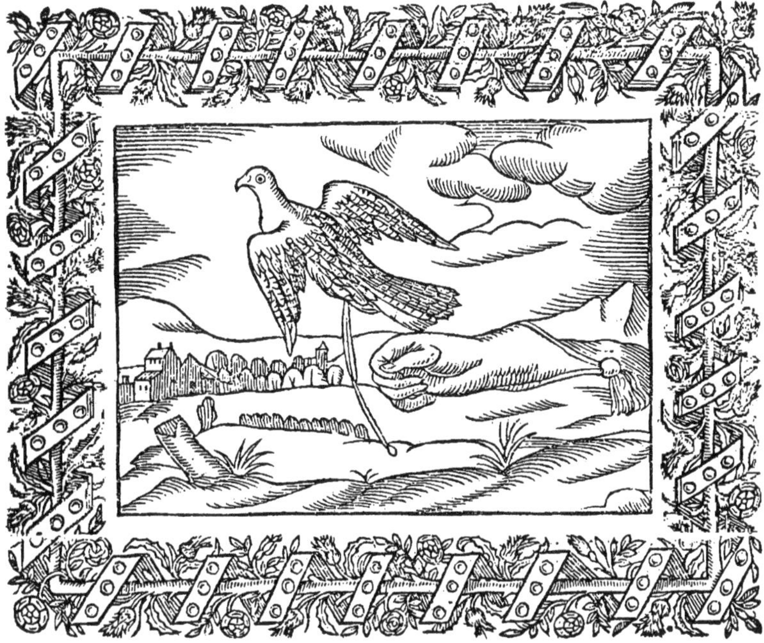

THE Princely *Faulcon*, that hath long beene man'd,
And taught to stoope; vnto the tossed lure,
Is now escaped from his Maisters hand,
And will no more such servitude endure,
But better likes the feilde, and forrestes spray,
And for himselfe, in elder age to pray.

The virtuous mind, and truely noble spright,
Can seldome brooke, in bondage base to serue,
But most doth in his libertie delight,
Still rather choosing, by himselfe to sterue,
Then eate some caterpillar's envied bread,
Or at anothers curtesie be fed.

Species ipsa gratiosi liberti, aut servi dignitatem nullam habere potest. *Cic: ad Q: fratrem Epist: 1. lib: 8.*

Durum, invisum, et grave est, Servitia ferre.

Seneca in Troade Act: 4.

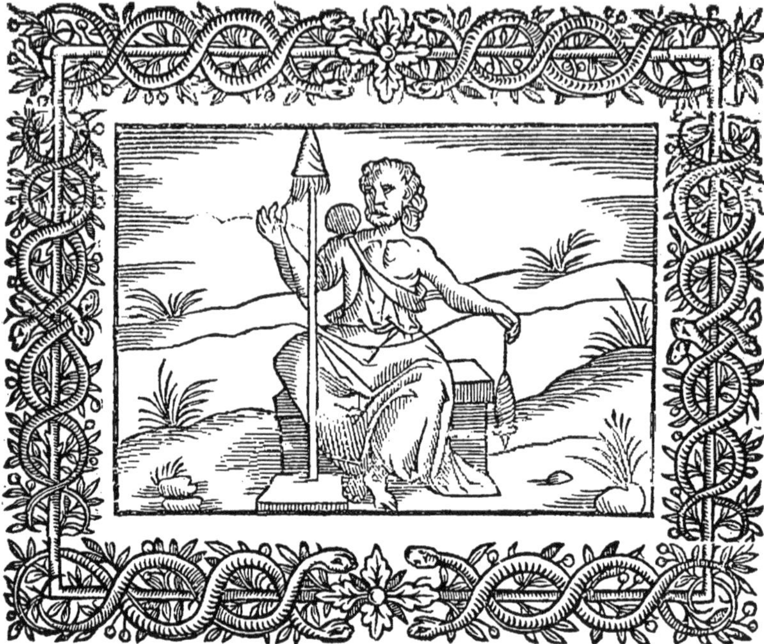

ALCIDES heere, hath throwne his Clubbe away,
And weares a Mantle, for his Lions skinne,
Thus better liking for to passe the day,
With *Omphale*, and with her maides to spinne,
To card, to reele, and doe such daily taske,
What ere it pleased, *Omphale* to aske.

Si temperata accesserit Venus nō alia Dea est adeo gratiosa. *Euripides in Medea.*

That all his conquests wonne him not such Fame,
For which as God, the world did him adore,
As Loues affection, did disgrace and shame
His virtues partes. How many are there more,
Who hauing Honor, and a worthy name,
By actions base, and lewdnes loose the same.

Propert.

Quicquid amor iussit, non est contemnere tutum,
Regnat et in superos ius habet ille Deos.

Vini

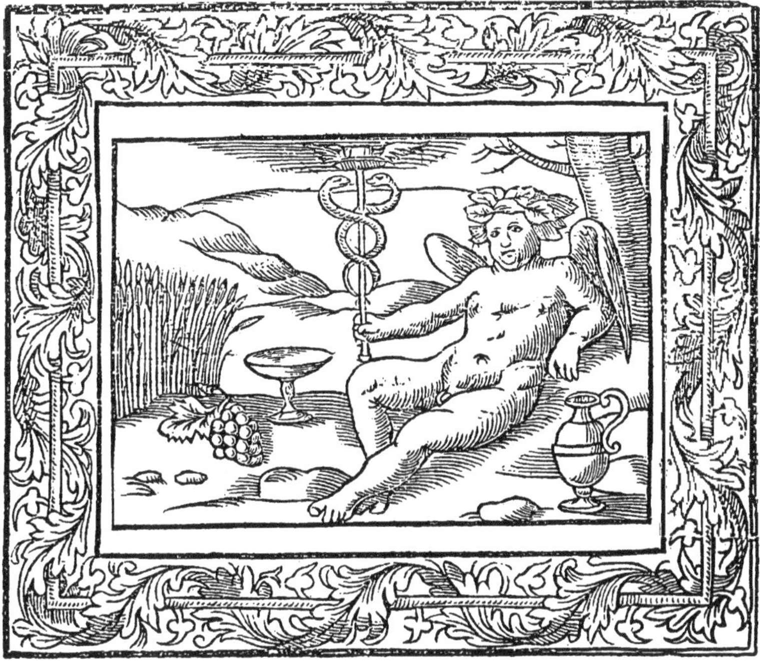

HEERE *Bacchus* winged, midſt his cups doth ſit,
With *Mercuries* Caduceus in his hand,
As God of wine no more, but God of wit,
And Eloquence, which he hath at commaund,
(Since he hath drawne, his bowles and bottles drie,)
Wherewith he ſeemes, to mount aboue the skie.

For when his liquor hath poſſeſſ'd the braine,
The foole himſelfe, the * wiſeſt thinkes to be,
And then ſo giues his laviſh tongue the raine,
You'ld ſweare ye heard another * *Mercurie*,
For lies of Ladies loues, or travailes farre,
His birth, his woundes, or ſervice in the warre.

* Ad vinũ diſerti. *Cic: pro M: Cœlio*

* Fœcundi calices &c.

Honos

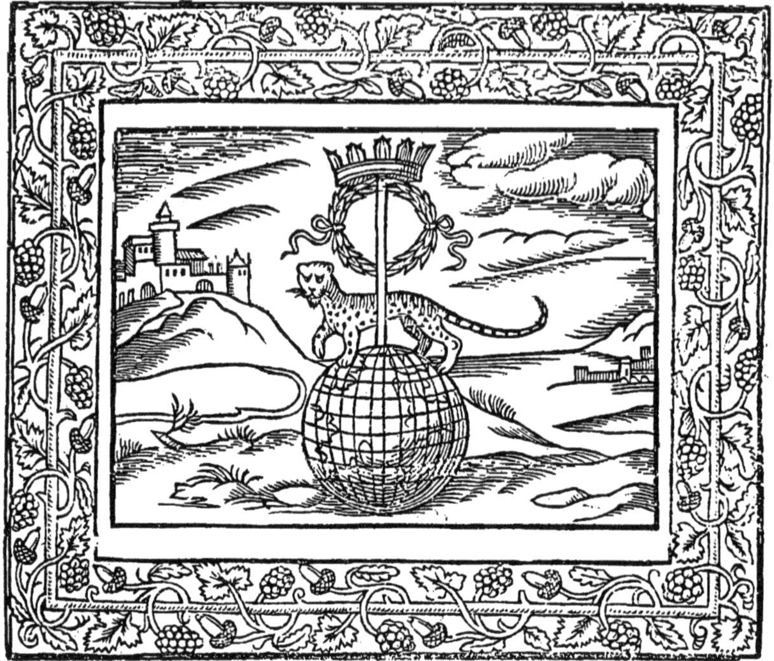

WHO ſeekſt Promotion through iuſt deſert,
And thinkſt by gift, of bodie, or of mind,
To raiſe thy fortune, whoſoere thou art,
This new *Impreſa* take to thee aſſignd,
To warne thee oft, ſuch labour is in vaine,
If heereby thinkſt, thy merit to obtaine.

Fas vbi maxima merces. *Lucan*:

For now the golden time's returned back,
And all's kept vnder, by th' *Athenian* Cat,
Whoſe helpe, and favour, whoſoere doth lack,
May coole his heeles, with *Homer* at the gate:
Such is our age, where virtue's ſcarce regarded,
And artes with armes, muſt wander vnrewarded.

Nũmorum Felis Emb: apud Plutarch: Græci enim (eodẽ teſte) huius effigie ſua numiſmata cudebant.

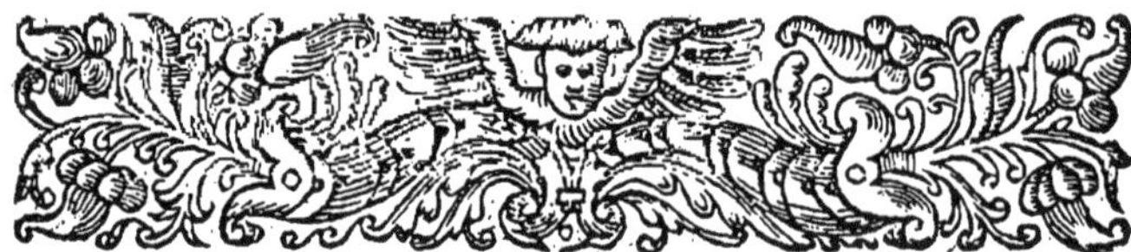

Piorum

To the thrice famous and farre renowned Universitie of Oxford.

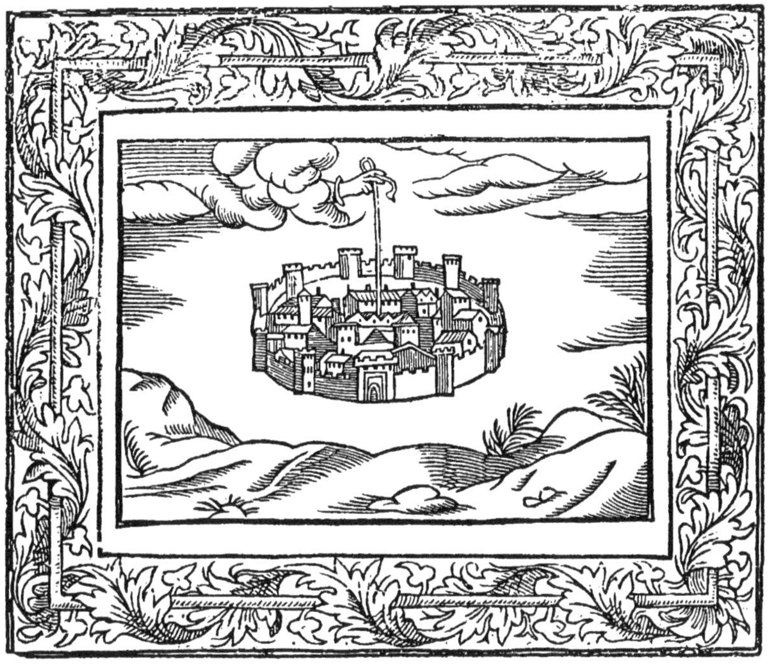

DEARE Sister of my ever-loued * Mother,
From whome this little that I haue I drew,
Ingratefully greate light I cannot smother,
Some lesser sparkes, which I deriu'd from you,
Which first enflam'd to this, my duller spright,
And lent in darke, my Muse her candle light.

* Cambridge and heerein Trinitie Colledge.

Faire Academe, whome Fame and Artes conspire,
To make thee mirror to all mortall eine,
Within our Sphære, that *Europe* may admire,
The gratious Lampe that on thy brow doth shine:
And shewes the TRUTH around by land and sea,
Directing thousandes erring, in their way.

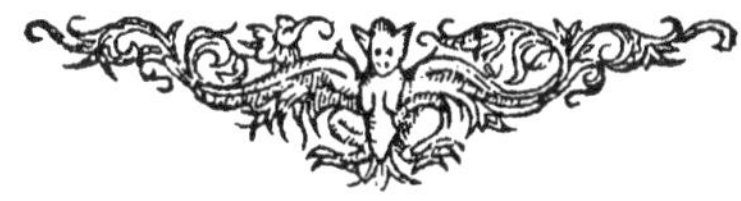

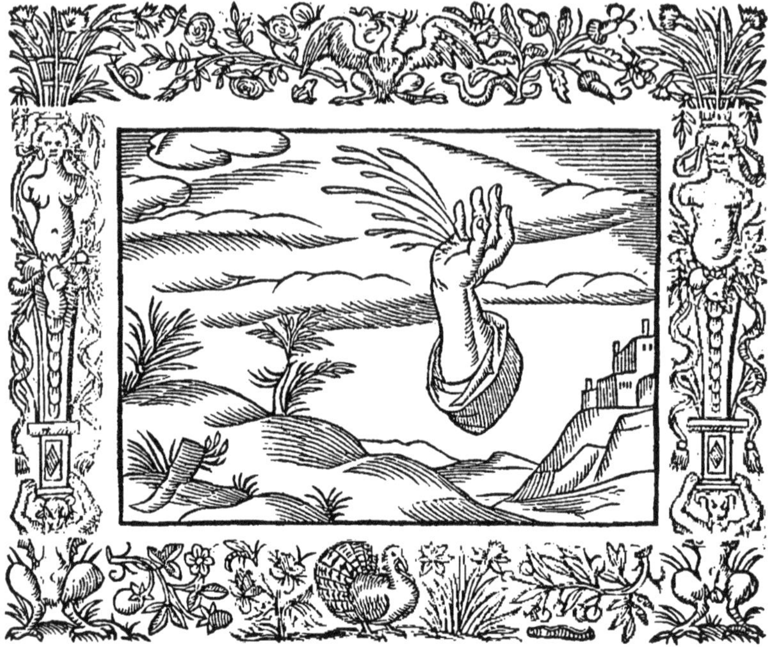

THE *Atheiſt* vile, that Giant-like attemptes,
To bandie faction with Almightie *IOVE*,
And thinkes this fraile worlds priviledge exemptes,
All Faith, and Feare, due vnto heauen aboue:
Vnto his terror, let him heere behold,
What Hiſtories of *IVLIAN* haue told.

For after that he had his Lord defi'de,
And wounded deadly lay in deepe diſpaire,
Thou, *GALILÆAN now or'ecom'ſt*, he cri'de,
Wherewith he caſt his blood into the Aire:
A fit example, for the faithles wight,
And ſuch as in prophanenes doe delight.

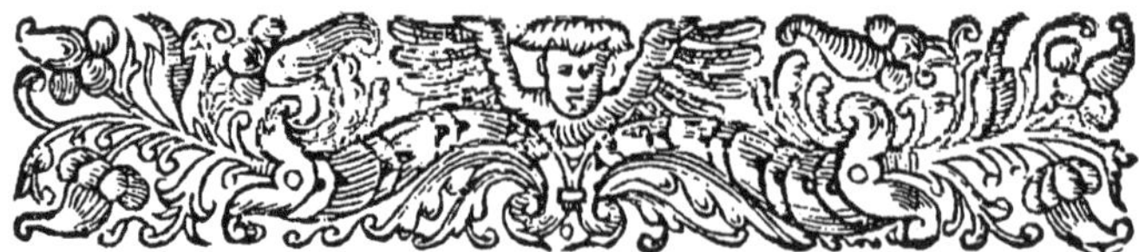

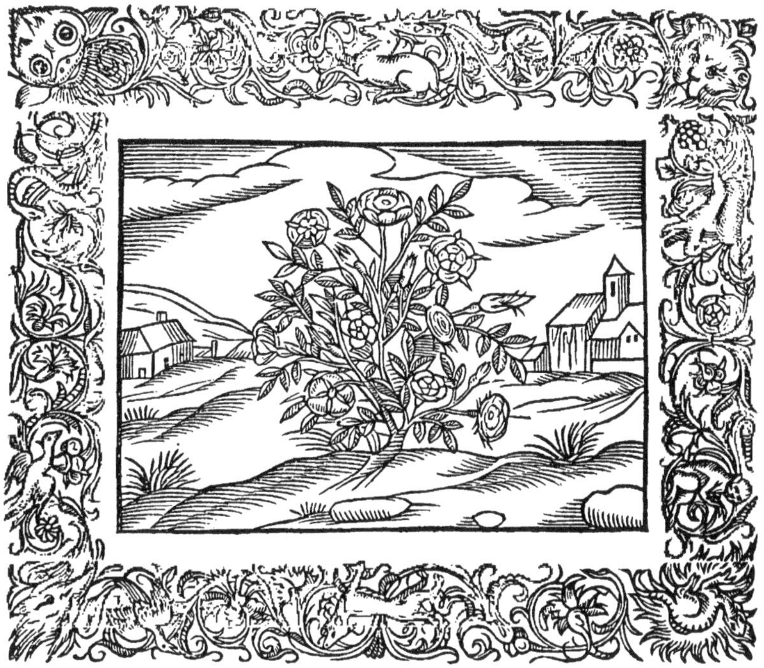

THE *Roses* ſweete, that in the Garden grow,
If that not often dreſt where they abide,
Become as wild as thoſe, we ſee doe blow
In every feild, and hedge-row as we ride:
And though for beautie, once they did excell,
They now haue loſt, both cullor and the ſmell.

So many men, whome Nature hath endu'de,
With rareſt partes, of bodie, or the mind,
Do in themſelues by Sloth, grow rancke and rude,
Not leauing any memorie behind,
Saue that they liued heere, and ſometime were,
* A needeles burthen which the Earth did beare.

* Telluris inutile pondus.

Cernis vt ignavum corrumpant otia corpus
Vt capiant vitium ni moveantur aquæ,
Et mihi ſiquis erat, dicendi carminis vſus
Deficit, eſtque minor factus inerte ſitis.

Ovidius.

Ite nunc fortes vbi celſa magni
Ducit exemplis via, cur inertes
Terga nudatis? Superata tellus
Sidera donat.

Boethius. 4. 7.

MINERVA BRITANNA:

THE SECOND PART

OR A GARDEN OF HEROY-CAL Devices: furnifhed, and adorned with Emblemes, and *Impreſa's* of ſundry natures. Newly deviſed, *moralized, and publiſhed,*

BY HENRY PEACHAM, Mr, of Artes.

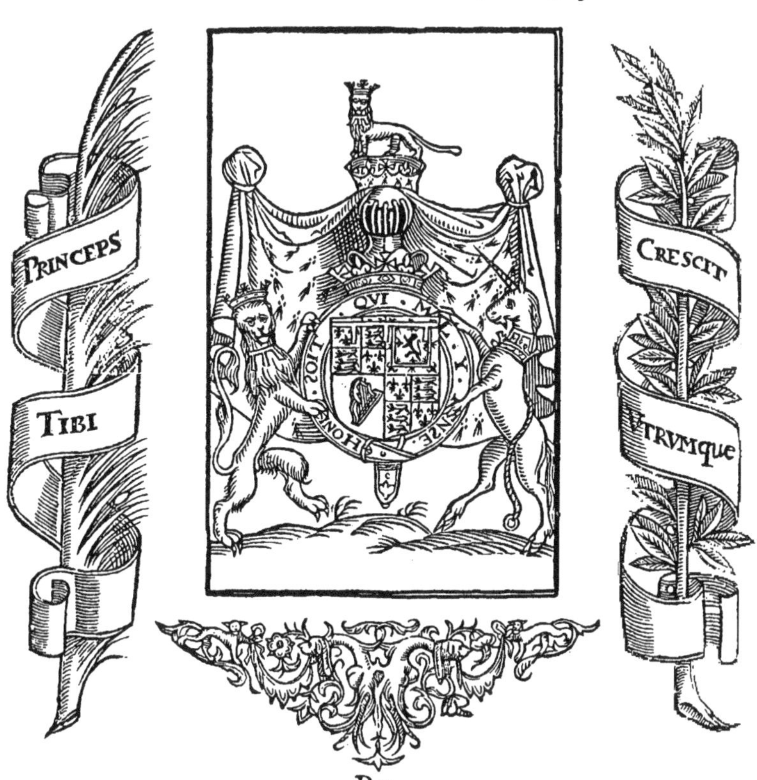

P 3.

The Author to his Muſe.

NOW ſtrike wee Saile, and throw aſide our oare
My wearie Muſe, the worſt is well nie paſt:
And take a while, our pleaſure on the ſhore,
Recounting what wee overcame at laſt:
To what deepe danger were our fortunes caſt:
What Rocks, the greateſt, & unknowen ſhelues,
We dar'd to touch, and yet did ſaue our ſelues.

HENRY, who art both Load-ſtone, and the ſtarre,
Of Heartes and Eies, our wiſhed Loue and Light:
By thee conducted, we arriue thus farre;
That now OPINIONS uttermoſt deſpight,
Nor ENVIE, that the iuſteſt one doth bite,
We doubt at all; but forth into the maine,
With doubled courage, put our ſelues againe

And you great PRINCESSE, through whoſe Chriſtall breſt,
ELIZAS Zeale, and Pietie doe ſhine;
Heire of her Name, and Virtues, that inveſt
You in our Heartes, and Loues immortall ſhrine:
Oh ſend from that pure Maieſtie of thine,
Thoſe beames againe, from whence (as PHOEBVS bright)
Our feeble Muſe, deriues her life and light.

Eeke pardon (PEERES,) that heere my ruder verſe,
Vnto yout worthes, and greatnes dares aſpire;
Or out of courſe, if I your rankes reherſe:
But as i'th Preſence, twixt the Lord and Squire,
(He neere the ſtate, the other by the fire,)
Small difference ſeemes; ſo heere moſt Honor'd traine,
Ye take your lots about your Soveraigne.

And whatſoever EIE ſhalt elſe peruſe,
Theſe ruder lines, devoid of skill and Art;
Reſerue thy good opinion of our Muſe,
That may heereafter worke of worth impart:
And though ſhe taſtes of Countrey and the Cart,
(As that DICTATOR) all'in time ſhe may,
Within the Citie beare a greater ſwey.

CINCINATVS a noble romane, cald from his plough, to the Dictatorſhip.

Illustrissimo et potentissimo Principi ac Domino, D: Mauritio Hessiæ Lantgravio, Comiti in Catzenellen bogen Dietz, Zigenhain, et Nidda &c

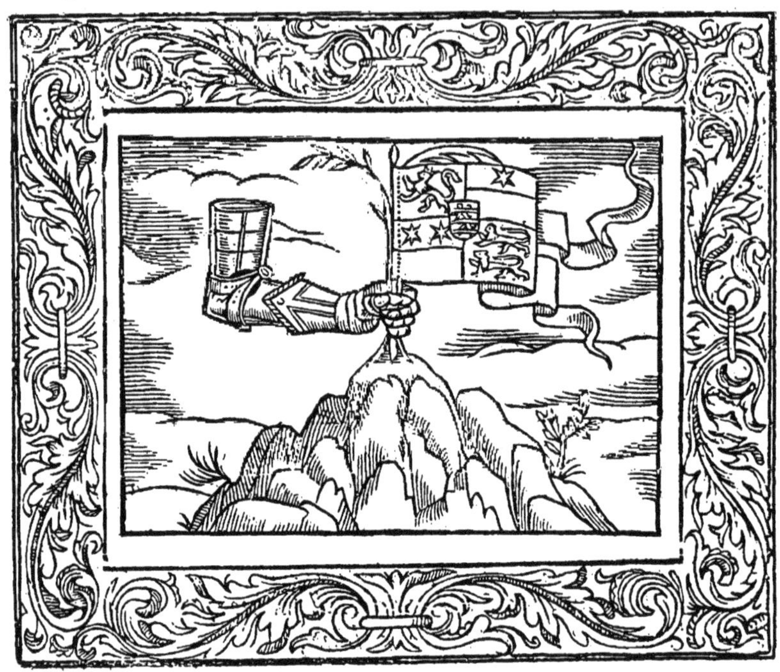

TO you great *Prince*, who little neede be knowne,
By me or by my worthles *Poësie*,
Since those admired virtues of your owne,
Haue made you obiect of the worldes wide eie,
Your bounteous mind, your matchles Pietie,
Your languages, and learning in all artes,
That gaine you millions of remotest heartes.

I consecrate in gentle Muses name
This Monument, and to your memorie,
Which shall outweare the vtmost date of Fame,
And wrestle with the worldes Eternitie:
For as Artes glorie is your *GERMANIE*,
For rar'st invention, and designe of wit,
So ye braue *Maurice* are the pride of it.

This most noble Prince beside his admirable knowledge in all learning, & the languages, hath exellent skill in musick. Mr Douland hath many times shewed me 10 or 12 severall sets of Songes for his Chappel of his owne composing.

Distantia

To the thrice Noble, and exellent Prince: *Ludowick* Duke of *Lennox*.

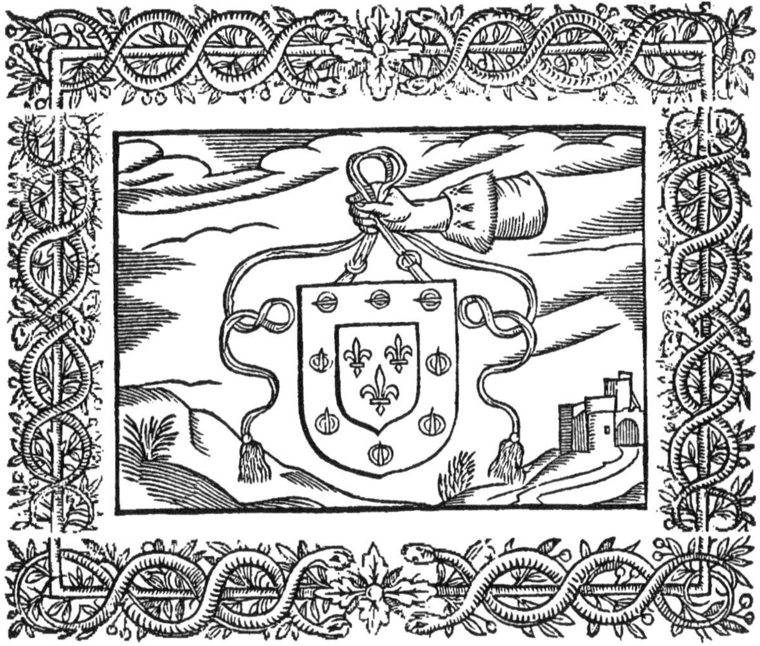

NOR may my Muse greate *Duke*, with prouder saile,
Ore-passe your name, your birth, and best deserts:
But lowly strike, and to these cullors vaile,
That make ye yet belou'd in forrein partes,
In memorie of those disioined heartes:
  Of two great kingdomes, whom your grandsire wrought,
  Till Buckle-like, them both in one he brought.

* Mild *Peace* heerein, to make amendes againe,
Ordaines your daies ye shall dispend in rest,
While *Horror* bound, in hundred-double chaine,
At her faire feete, shall teare her snakie crest,
And *Mars* in vaine, with Trumpet sterne molest
  Our Muse, that shall her loftiest numbers frame,
  To eternize your *STEVVARTS* Roiall name.

* —Pax optima rerum
Quas homini nouisse datum est, pax vna triũphis
Immeritis potior
Silius lib 11.

Quod proavum virtus discordia iunxit in vnum
Regna duo, hæc facto præmia digna tulit:
Cui LVDOVICE vices iterum PAX alma rependens,
Tempora dat rebus DIVA quieta tuis.
Basilic: Dorō.

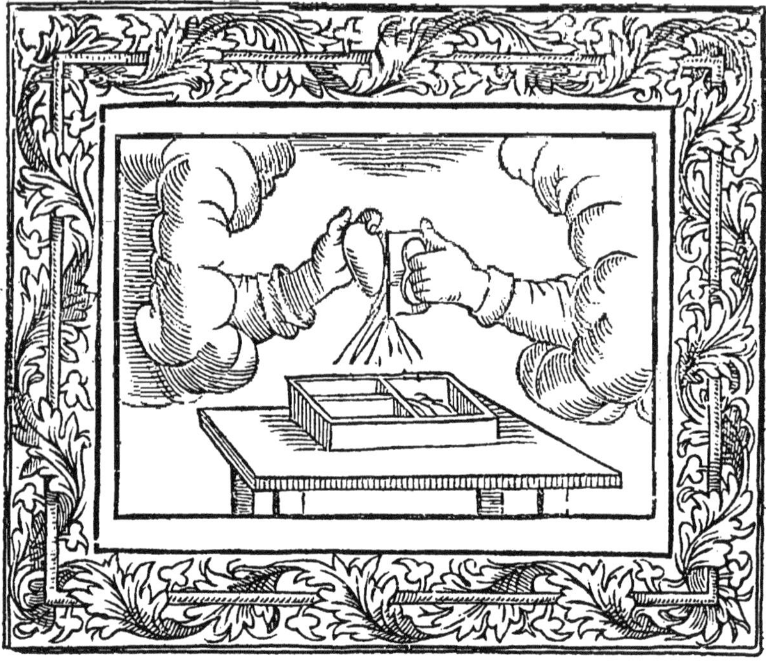

THE *Steele* and *Flint*, doe heere with hardie strokes,
And mutuall hewing, each the other wast:
While vnderneath the open *Tinderboxe*,
Vnto his gaine, consumes them both at last:
And to the backs, when they are spent and worne,
He throwes them by, for he hath seru'd his turne.

So, when the Paisant with his neighbour warres,
They weare awaie themselues, in golden sparkes;
The *Boxe*, are Pettifoggers from their Iarres,
Who walke with Torches, vsher'd by their Clearkes:
While blind by Owle-light, Hoidon stumbling goes,
To seeke his Inne, the *Windmill*, or the *Rose*.

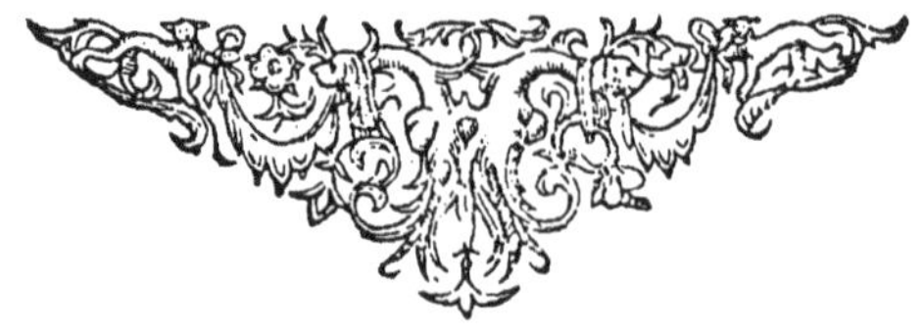

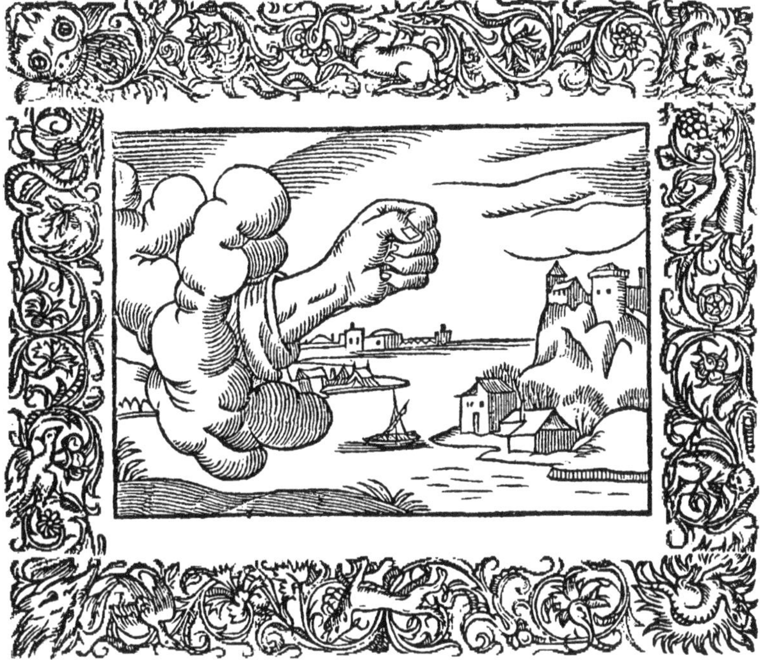

THE hand that gripes, ſo greedily and hard,
What it hath got by long vnlawfull gaine;
Withall for Battaile ready is prepard,
Still to defend, what it doth faſt retaine:
(For wretches ſome, will ſooner ſpend their bloods,
Then ſpare we ſee, one penworth of their goods.)

Of *Avarice*, ſuch is the nature ſtill,
Who hardly can endure, to liue in Peace;
But alwaie preſt, to quarrell, or to kill,
When ſober mindes, from ſuch contention ceaſe:
And ſeeke no more, then quiet and content,
With thoſe good bleſſinges, which the Lord hath ſent.

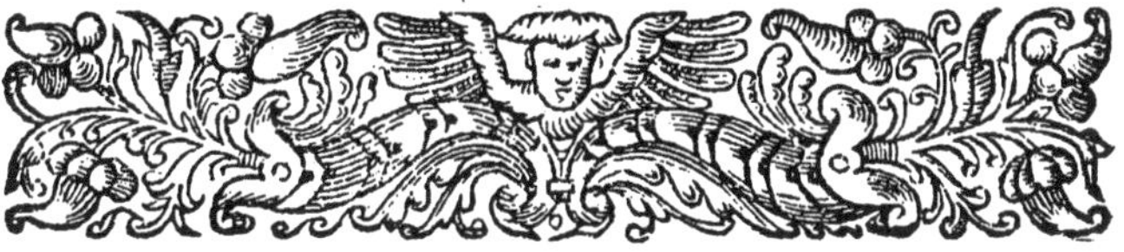

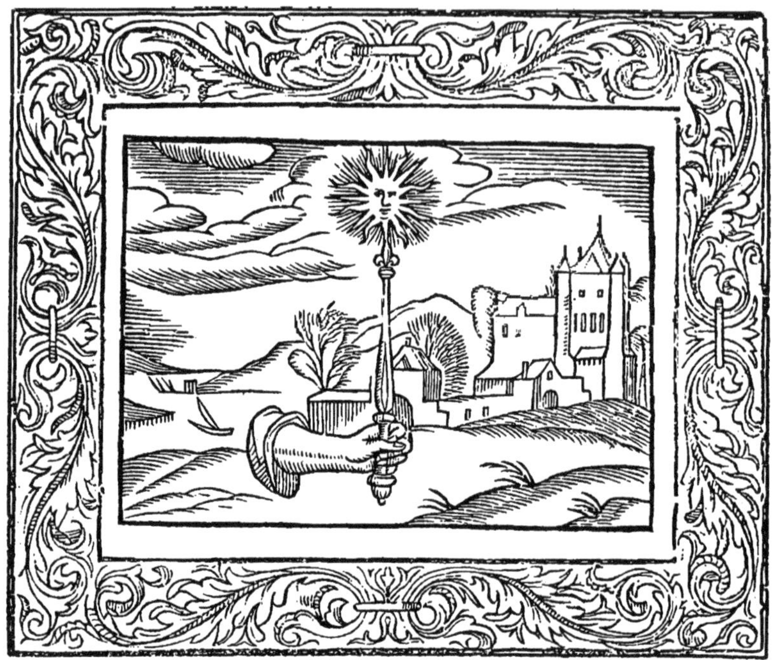

THE glorious Sunne, that cheeres vs with his light,
And giueth life, and growth to every thing:
* Can brooke no peere, to check his soveraigne right,
But onely will remaine, the Heauens sole king:
When lesser starres, that borrow from his light,
Doe keepe their course, in numbers infinite.

* Arduũ semper eodem loci, potentiam et concordiam esse: *Tacitus lib: 4 Annal:*

So fares it with the vulgar that doe goe,
In loue, and mutuall concord most secure,
When *Paritie* procures the overthrow,
Of Monarchies, that else might well endure:
* And like moe Sunnes in skie, portendeth still,
The Princes ruine, or a worser ill.

* Εἰ θέλουσι δύο ἥλιοι &c Si duo Soles velint esse, periculum ne incendio omnia perdantur. *Serinus.*

Tacitus 1. Hist: Et Pacis interest, potestatem omnem ad vnum conferri.

Basilic: Doron.

Nulla ferat cœlo præter sua lumina Titan,
Innumeris gaudent astra minora choris.
Infima plebs hominum melius numerosa vagatur:
Cum maneant Reges invida fata pares.

Non

To my Scholler Mr. HANNIBAL BASKERVILE.

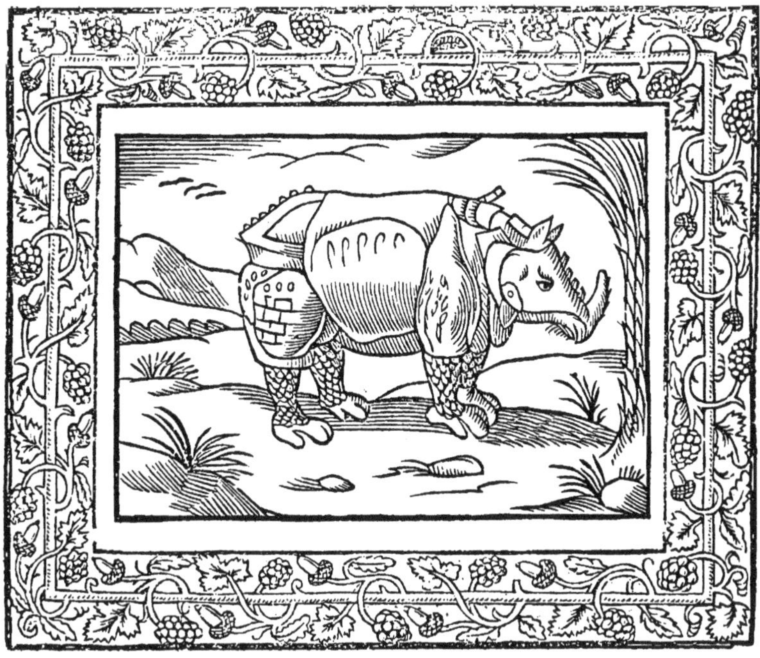

THIS *Indian* beaſt, by Nature armed ſo,
That ſcarce the Steele can peirce his ſcalie ſide:
Aſſaulteth oft the *Elephant* his foe,
And either doth the conqueror abide,
Or by his mightie combatant is ſlaine,
For never vanquiſht, he returnes againe.

So you that muſt encounter Want, and Care,
To overcome your hard, and crabbed skill,
Take courage, and treade vnder foote diſpaire,
For better hap, attendes the vent'rous ſtill:
And ſooner leaue, your bodie in the place,
Then back returne, vnletter'd with diſgrace.

This Embleme was deviſed at firſt by Paulus Iovius.

A Rhinoceros was ſét to Rome by Emanuel king of Portingal who fought with it cõming on land thorough Provence: but by the waie, by hard fortune it was drowned neere Porto Venere: ſeeking a long time to ſaue it ſelfe amóg the Rocks. *Paulus Iovius.*

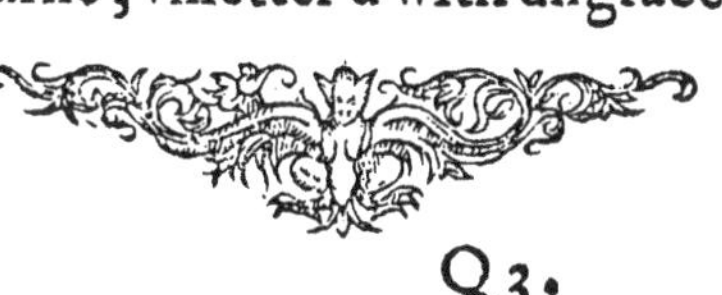

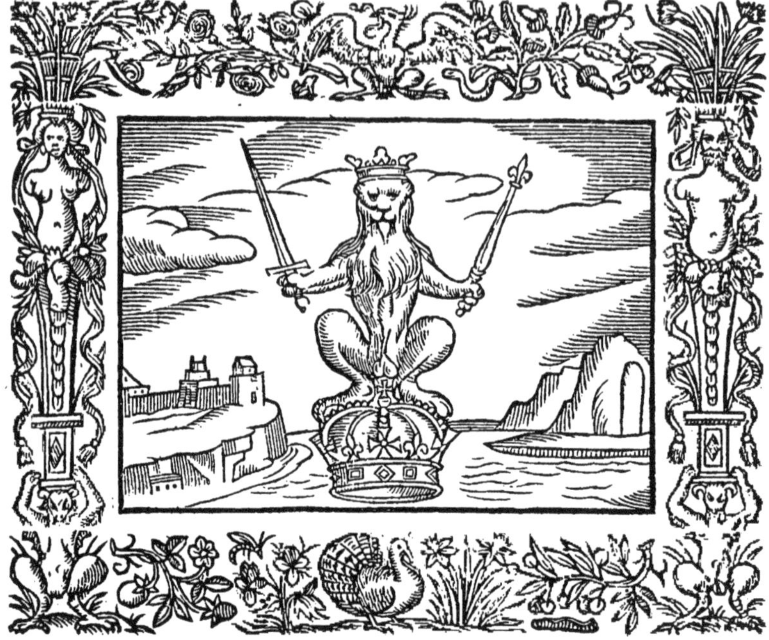

VAINE man who think'ſt, that happines conſiſtes,
In great commaund, and Roiall dignitie;
And Kinges with Scepters hold within their fiſtes,
The perfect ſumme of all Fœlicitie:
No no, their Crownes are lin'd with pricking thorne,
And ſable cares, with crimſon Robes are worne.

Who liſt deſcribe the motion of the Sphære,
Another, ſome rare, beauteous modell draw;
With Eloquence, let him goe charme the eare,
Thy onely art, muſt be to keepe in aw,
And curbe with *Iuſtice*, the vnrulie crew,
To favor skill, and giue the good their due.

Virgil: Æneid: 6.

Excudant alii ſpirantia mollius æra
Credo equidem et vivos ducent de marmore vultus
Orabunt cauſas melius &c.

Ad BRITANNIAM.

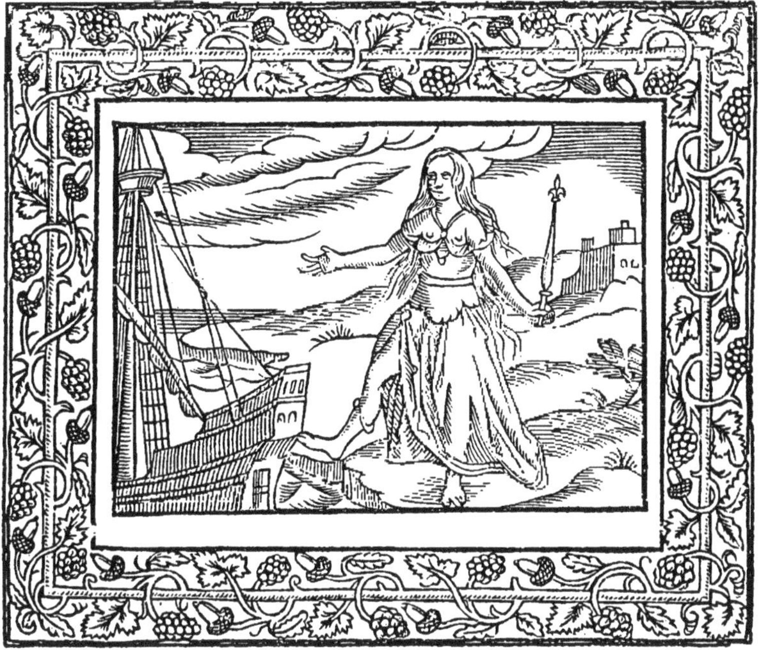

WITH haire diſhevel'd, and in mournefull wiſe,
Who ſpurnes a ſhippe, with Scepter in her hand:
Thus *BRITAINE*'s drawen in old Antiquities,
What time the *Romanes*, overran her land:
Who firſt deviſ'd her, ſitting in this plight,
As then their captiue, and abandon'd quite.

Inter Claudi juris miſmata.

But what can long continue at a ſtay,
To all thinges being, Fates a change decree:
Thrice-famous *Ile*, whome erſt thou didſt obey,
Vſurping *Roome*, ſtandes now in aw of thee:
* And trembles more, to heare thy Soveraignes name,
Then thou her Drummes, when valiant *Cæſar* came.

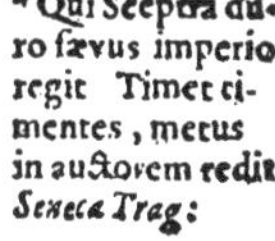
* Qui Sceptra duro ſævus imperio regit Timet timentes, metus in auctorem redit. *Seneca Trag:*

Eo

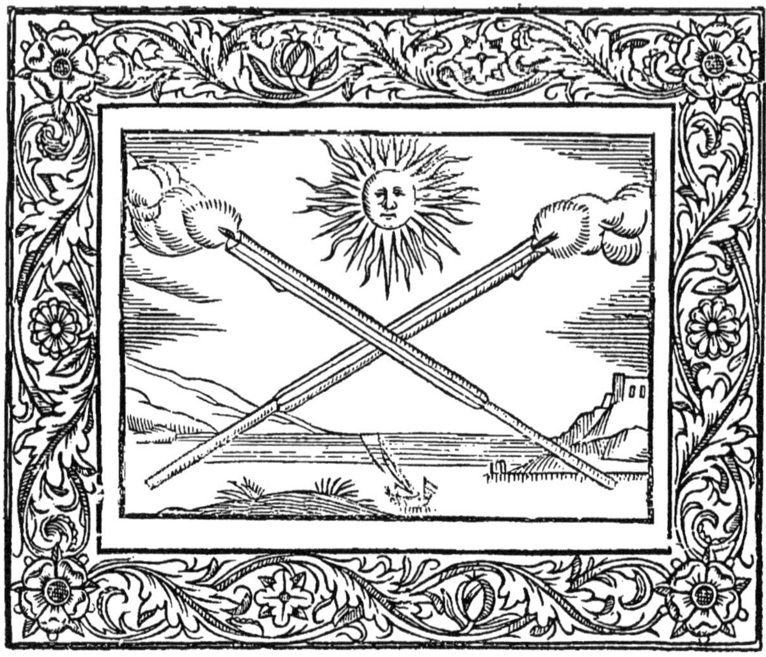

* Compeſcat ſe Humana temeritas, et id quod eſt non quærat, ne illud quod eſt non inveniat: *Auguſtin: de Gent: contra Manic: lib: 1.*

WHY doth vaine man, with * raſh attempt deſire,
To ſearch the depth, of Miſteries divine:
Which like the Sunne vpon his earthy fire,
With glorie inacceſſible do ſhine:
And with the radiant ſplendor of their ray,
Chaſe all conceipted Ignorance away.

Multo facilius invenit ſyderum conditorem humilis pietas, quã ſyderum ordinem ſuperba curioſitas *Idem de Eclipſ: Solis.*

What mortall man might ever comprehend,
Gods ſacred eſſence, and his ſecret will,
Or his ſoules ſubſtance, or could but intend,
Leaſt while to view, this glorious creature ſtill:
* Be wiſe in what the word doth plainely teach,
But meddle not, with thinges aboue thy reach.

* Imo, Deus melius neſciendo ſcitur: *Auguſti. lib: 11 de ord:*

Baſilic: Doron.

Quid volucri tentas humana ſcientia penna
Quærere inacceſſi Myſtica ſacra Dei:
Caligans oculis, obtuſæ et acumine mentis,
Dum petis igniculis alta negata tuis.

Piorum

To the modest and virtuous minded, Mrs. Elizabeth Apsley, attending vpon the most excellent Princesse, the Ladie Elizabeth her grace.

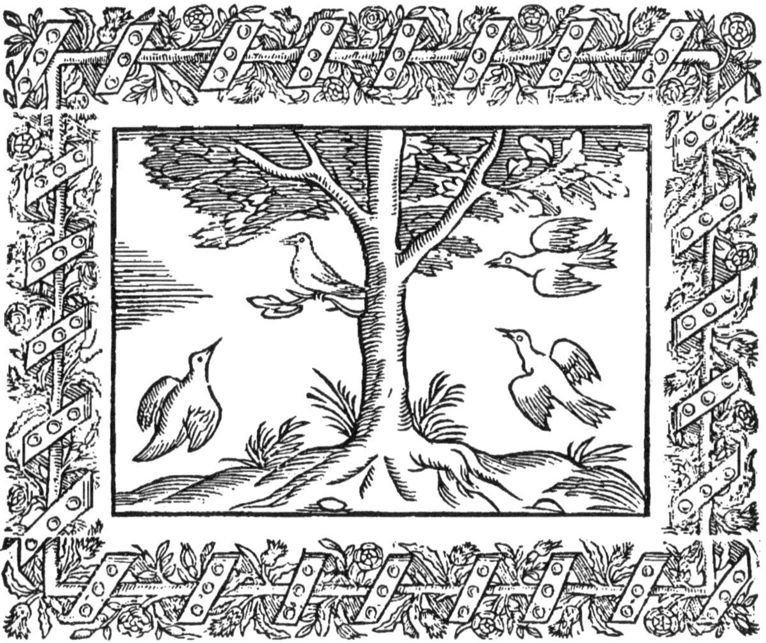

WHILE that the *Mavis*, and the morning *Larke*,
Doe cheerely warble their delicious straines,
The *Turtle* likes the shade, and thickets darke,
And solitarie by herselfe remaines,
Recording in most dolefull wise her woe,
Letting the pleasures, of the season goe.

The godly wight, whome no delight of Sinne,
Doth with vaine pleasure draw: or worldly care,
Esteemeth not, these fleeting Ioies a pinne:
But to the Lord, in private doth repaire,
With quiet Conscience; when the wicked oft,
Are in the mid'st, of all their pleasures caught.

Deus vitam annuntiavi tibi, posuisti lachrymas meas in conspectu tuo. *Psalm: 55.*

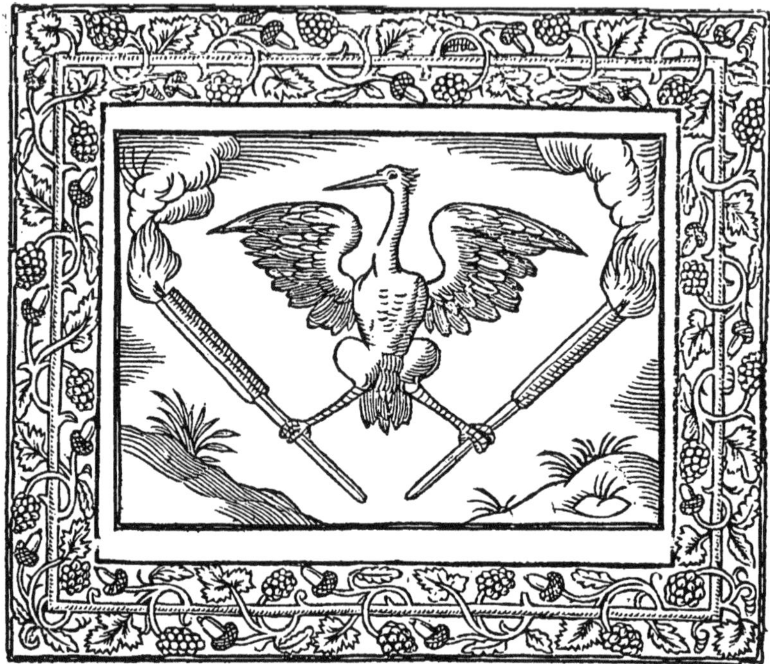

BEHOLD a *Storke*, betweene two Torches plac'd,
Of milkie hew, with winges abroad diſplaide;
In aunchient time, the marke of wedlock chaſt,
Becauſe this Bird, a deadly foe is ſaid
T' Adulterie, and fouleſt foule Inceſt,
The *Veſtal* maide, the fire beſeemeth beſt.

Chaſt *Loue*, the band of everlaſting *Peace*,
The beſt content we haue, while here we liue,
That bleſſeſt Mariage, with thy ſweete encreaſe,
And doſt a pledge, of that coniunction giue
Twixt Soule, and Body, eke the mutual *Loue*,
Betweene the Church, and her ſweete Spouſe aboue.

Horat: 1 carm: 13

Fœlices ter, et amplius,
Quos irrupta tenet copula: nec malis
Divulſis quærimoniis
Suprema citiùs ſolvet amor diē.

In

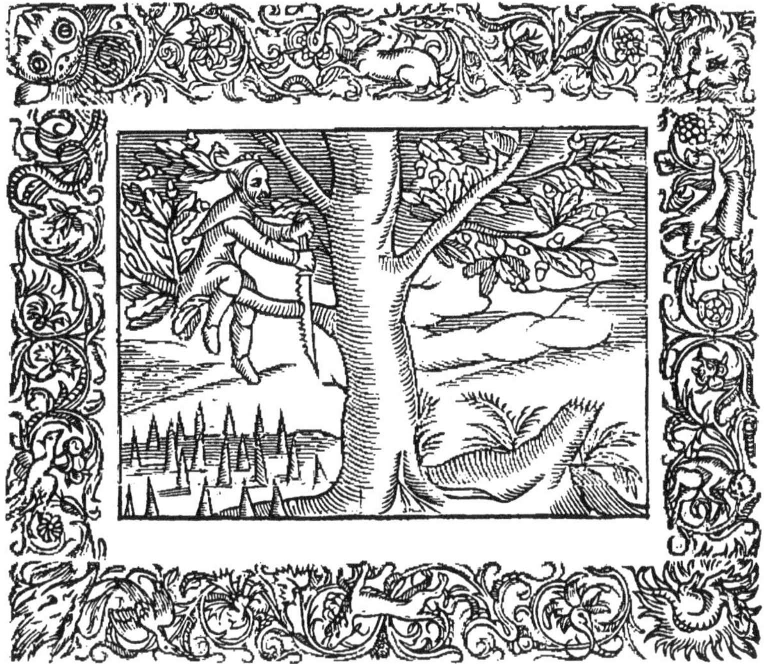

THIS simple Foole, that here bestrides the bow,
And knowing well, the daunger vnderneath,
Yet busilie doth saw the same in two,
Like idle Ape, though to his present death:
Which if he had forborne, and let it grow,
He free from harme, had scapt the pikes below.

To this same Idiot, such we liken may,
Of trustie Frendes as doe not know the vse,
But while they are their props, and onely stay,
Will cut them off, by this, or that abuse;
Or loose their favor, by behaviour ill,
Who otherwise, might haue vpheld them still.

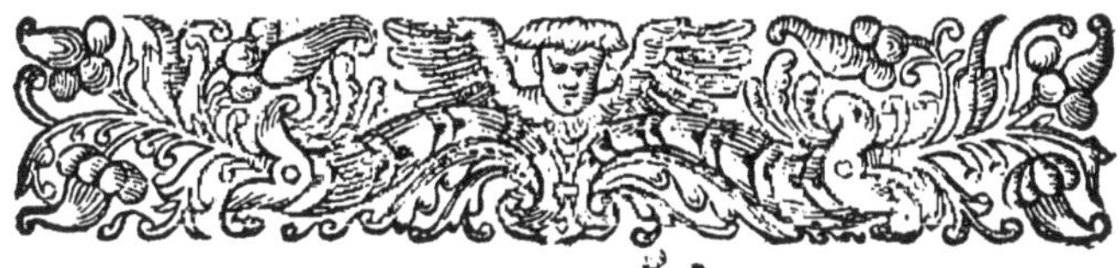

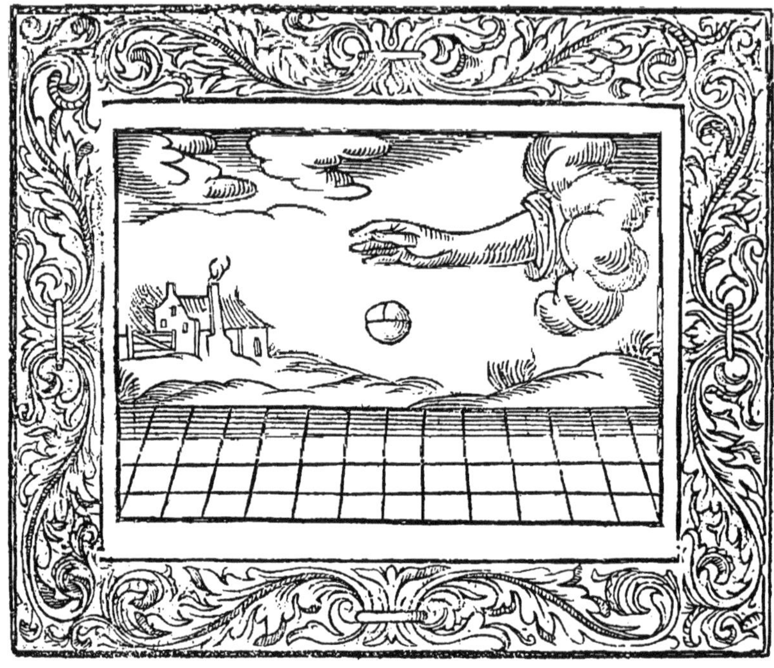

Caroli Vrsini Symbolum Gnome vero mutata.

THE *Tennis-ball*, when strucken to the ground,
With Racket, or the gentle Schoole-boies hand,
With greater force, doth back againe rebound,
His Fate, (though senceles) seeming to withstand:
Yea, at the instant of his forced fall,
With might redoubled, mountes the highest of all.

* Dij nos homines quasi pilas habent. *Plautus*. So the Philosophers haue heretofore sayd.

So when the * Gods aboue, haue struck vs low,
(For men as balls, within their handes are said,)
We cheifly then, should manly courage show,
And not for every trifle be afraid:
For when of *Fortune*, most we stand in feare,
Then *Tyrant-like*, she most will domineere.

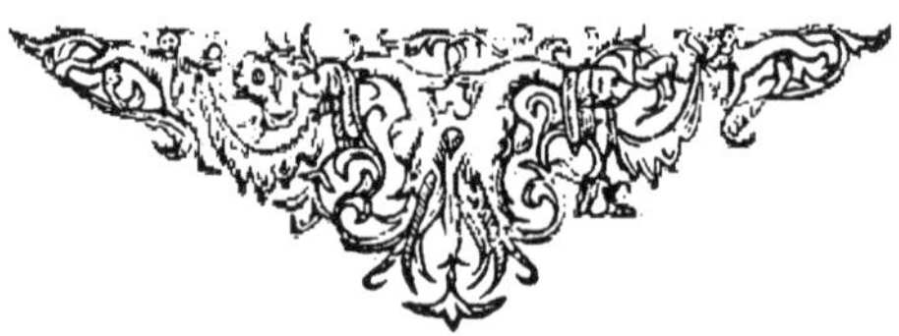

Par

The device of the late Honorable, Earle of Essex.

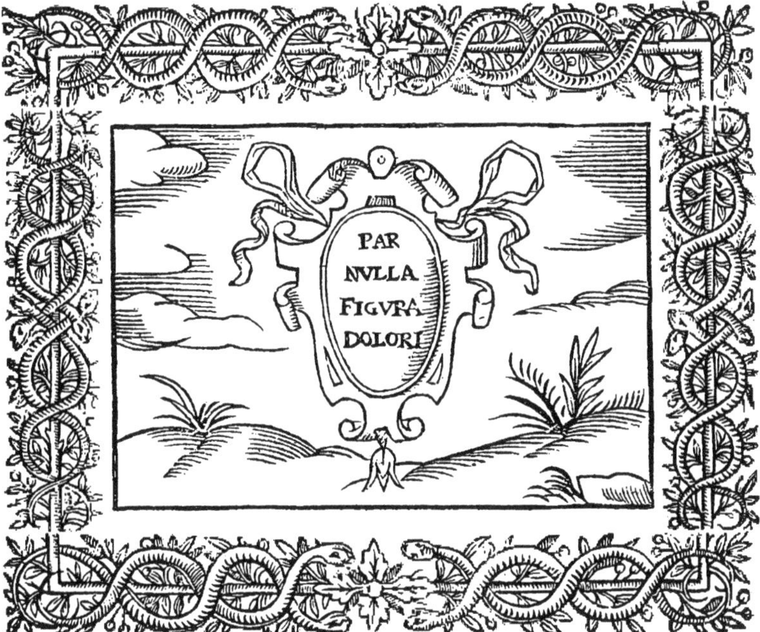

WEE eaſ'ly limme, ſome louely-Virgin face,
And can to life, a Lantſcip repreſent,
Afford to Antiques, each his proper grace,
Or trick out this, or that compartement:
But with the Pencill, who could ere expreſſe,
The face of griefe, and heartie penſiuenes.

For where the minde's with deadly ſorrow wounded,
There no proportion, can effect delight,
For like a *Chaos*, all within's confounded,
Reſembling nothing, ſaue the face of night,
Which in his ſheild, this noble *Earle* did beare,
The laſt *Impreſa*, of his greife, and care.

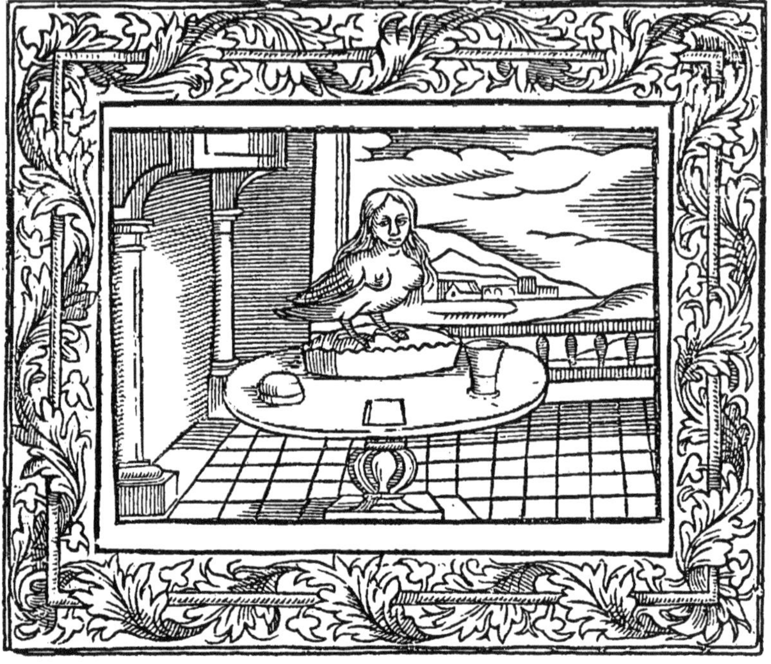

OF Virgins face, with winges, and tallants strong,
Vpon thy table, *PHINEVS* here behold,
Ovid: Metam: lib: 6.
A monstrous *Harpie*, that hath præied long,
Vpon thy meates, while thou art blind, and old,
And at all times, his appetite doth serue,
While vnregarded, thou thy selfe dost sterue.

The Courtes of Kinges, are said to keepe a crew
Of these * still hungry for their private gaine:
The first is he, that carries tales vntrue,
The second, whome base * bribing doth maintaine,
The third and last, the Parasite I find,
Who bites the worst, if Princes will be blind:

* Hirudines ærarii. *Cic: ad Atticum* 1.

* Nihil in penatibus eius sit vænale, aut ambitioni pervium. *Tacitus Annal:* 13.

Insidit dapibus volucris fœdissima Phineu
(Harpyiam vocitant) vngue rapace tuis:
Crimina qui defert, repetundus, Gnato notantur
Vile genus fucos, quos alit Aula suos.

Basilic: Doron.

B: Mantuan: in AEglog:

Est et apud Reges rudis, invida, rustica turba,
Histrio, scurra, quibus virtus odiosa, Pòetas
Mille modis abigunt, vt quando cadavera corvi
Invenere, fugant alias volucresque ferasque.

Salomone

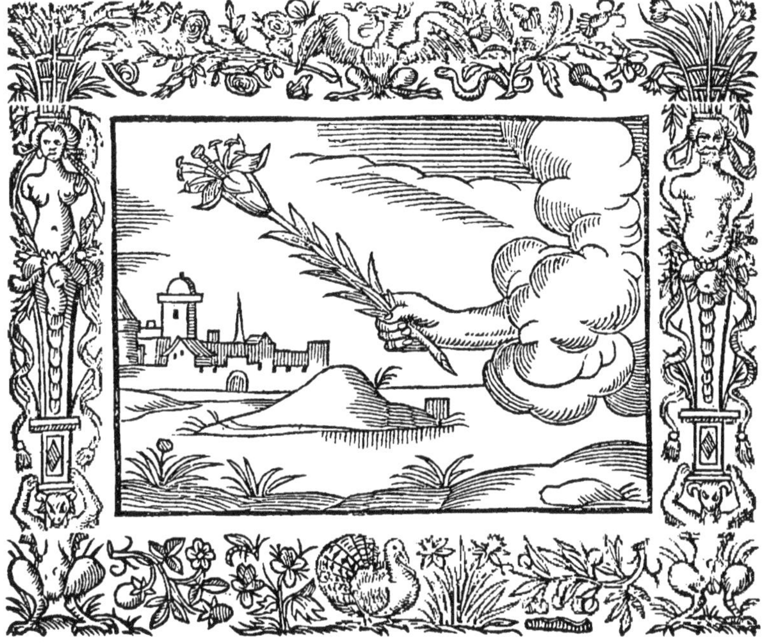

LET Courtly Dames, their coſtly Iewells boaſt,
And *Rhodopis*, in ſilkes and ſattens ſhine;
Behold the *Lillie*, thus devoid of coſt,
In flowery feildes, is clothd by power divine,
In pureſt white, fair'ſt obiect of the eie,
Religions weede, and badge of Chaſtitie.

Math: 6. 24.

Albedo obiectum viſus. *Ariſt.*

Why ſhould ye then as ſlaues to loathed pride,
And frantique fooles, thinke ye are halfe vndone,
When that ye goe not in your cullors pide,
Or want the grace, of neweſt faſhion:
When even the *Lillie*, in glorie doth ſurpaſſe,
The rich, and roiallſt King, that ever was.

Splendida fluctivagos quid iactitat Aula lapillos?
Intumet et Rhodopis bombycis arte levis?
Regibus anteferor, mediis quod veſtit in agris.
Vita oculi candor, virgineumque decus.

Soboles

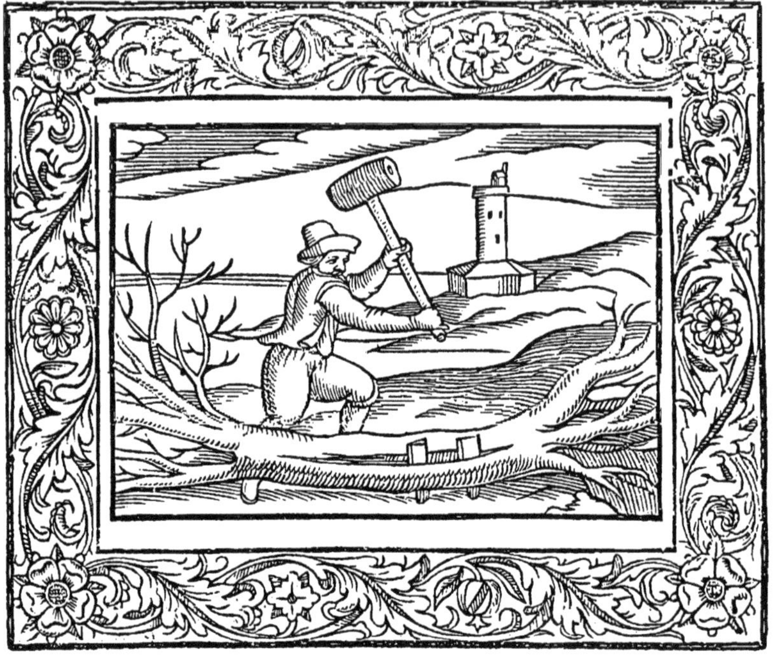

Ex Æsopi fabu:

THE Husbandman, in depth of winter feld,
An aged *Willow*, fewell for to burne,
But wanting wedges, Grandsire was compeld,
To rend with bowes, the bodie for his turne:
And while the *Willow*, now was rent in twaine,
It gaue a grone, and thus seem'd to complaine.

Oh greife, of greifes! that thus I should be torne,
And haue my heart, by those asunder rent,
That are my fruite, and of my bodie borne,
Who for my stay, and comfort, should be sent:
You Parents good, your selues behold in me,
Whose Children wicked, and vngratious be.

Parentes charissimos debemus habere, quod ab his vita, patrimonium, libertas, civitas data est.

Cicero post redit: in Senatum.

Innocentiam

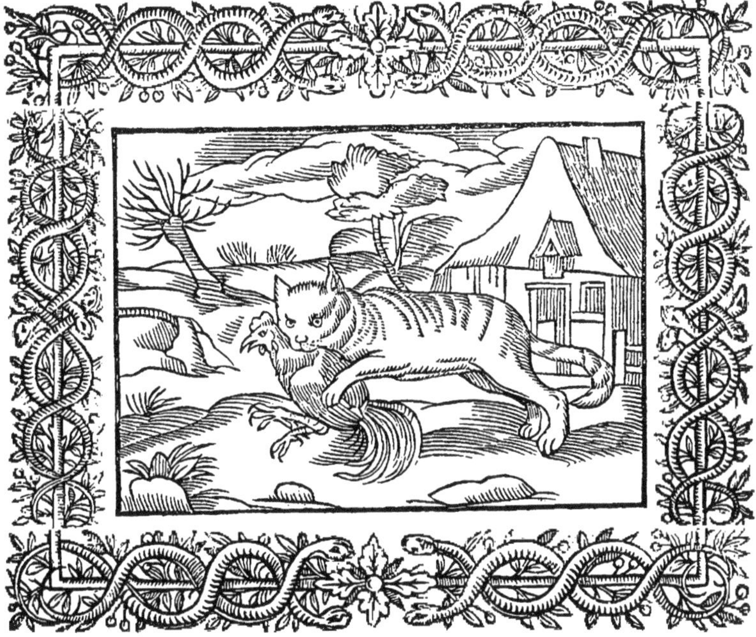

THE *Cat*, the *Cock* held priſoner in her paw,
And ſaid of Birdes, he moſt deſeru'd to die,
For that contrarie vnto Natures Law,
His kindred he abuſ'd inceſtuouſly:
His Mother, Siſters, and a noiſe did keepe,
With crowing ſtill, when others faine would ſleepe.

In his defence, heereto repli'de the *Cock*,
My fault of luſt, is for my maiſters gaine,
I am for crowing, call'd the Plowmans clock,
Whome I awake betime, to daily paine:
No doubt (quoth *Puſſe*,) of reaſons thou haſt ſtore,
But I am faſting, and can heare no more.

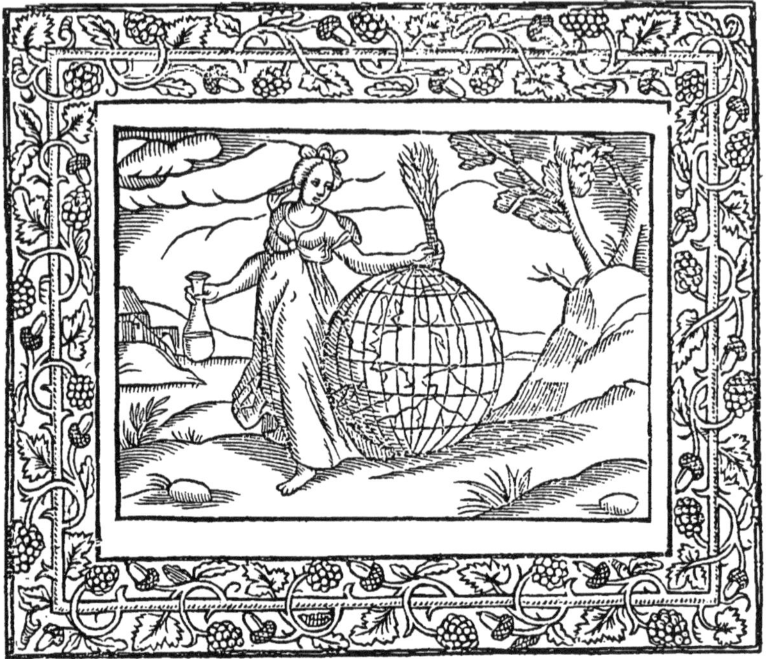

SEE here our humane miſeries in breiſe,
That doe our life, vnto the laſt amate,
And ſawce the ſweete, with feare, and howerly griefe,
Diſeaſing oft, the high, and happieſt ſtate:
A Rod, the world, a Woman, Ages greiſe,
Which fower, the wiſeſt doe account the cheiſe.

His childiſh yeares, the * Rod keepes vnder ſtill,
His youth with Loue, and ſtrong affectes is vext,
That headlong force him, * pliable to ill,
A retchles wife, and worldly cares are next:
And when both youth, and middle age be paſt,
Diſeaſes ſtraunge, doe end him at the laſt.

* Quid prodeſt manum ferulæ minantis
Tot pati pœnas teneris ſub annis
Et metu ſequi Samium bicerni
Tramite callem. *Camp:*

* Cereus in vitium flecti: *Horat:*

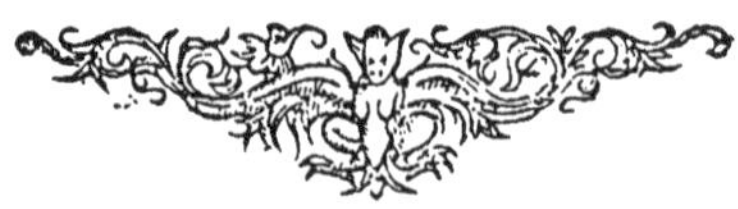

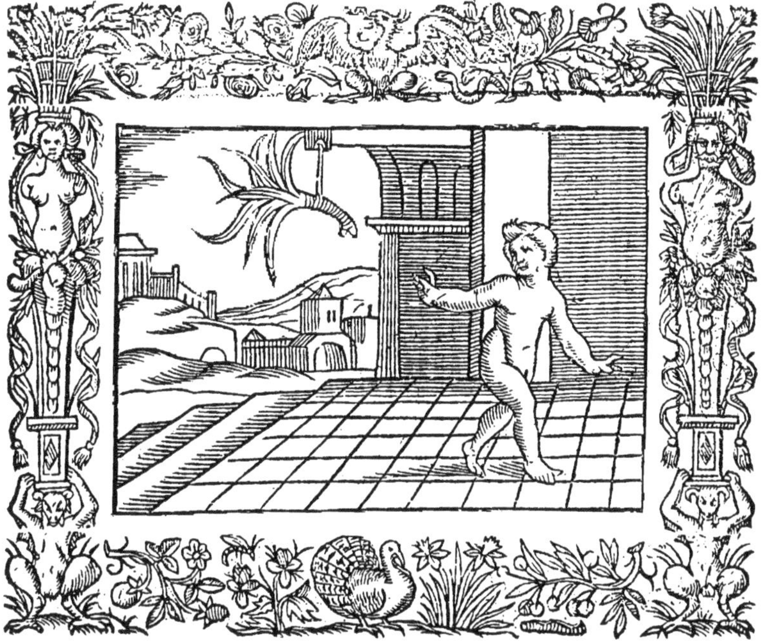

THE * *Semper-vivum*, though from earth remoou'd,
His leafe with flower, are fresh and growing seene,
And many times, as by experience proou'd,
It will abide, in sharpest winter greene,
As faire, and full of life, vnto the view,
As if abroad, in fertil'st soile it grew.

* Some would haue it the Orpine.

So many men, of rarest partes there are,
Who though the world afford them not a foote,
Yet doe they thriue, within the emptie aire,
As well as they, that haue the richest roote:
Yea, when as some, that are vpheld like Hops,
Doe droope, and die, even vnderneath their props.

In murum cadncum inclinantes.

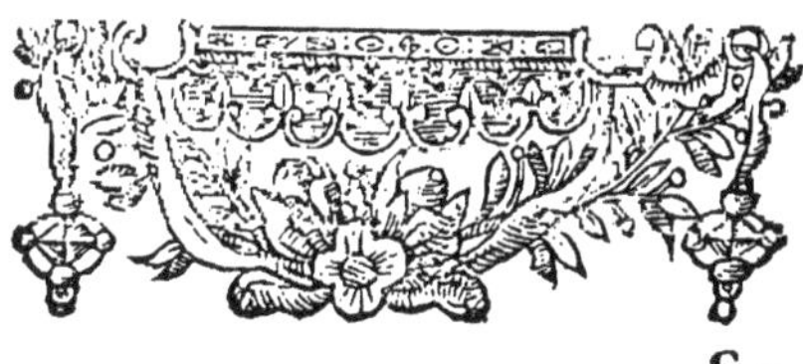

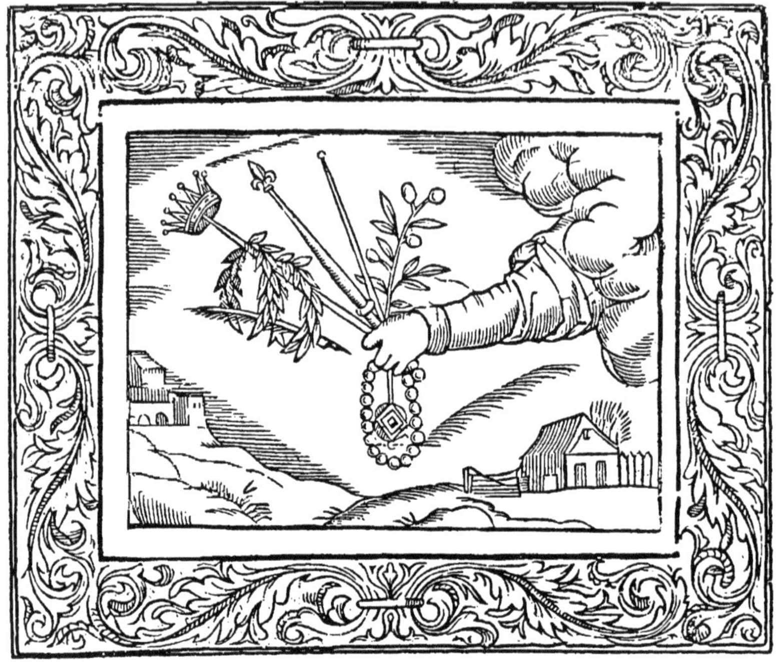

THE ſlothfull man, that loues in idle ſeat,
  And wanton pleaſures, to diſpend his daies:
The Scripture plaine denieth for to eate,
And lawes ſevere, doe puniſh many waies:
  And never Heavens, with their bountie bleſſe,
  The hand addicted vnto Idlenes.

On th'other ſide, when for our ſweatie paine,
To ſale they ſet vs, all the pretious thinges,
The Earth within her boſome, doth containe,
Gemmes, Herbes of virtue, Diadems of Kinges,
  All ſortes of Girlondes, and the Quill of Fame,
  To keepe aliue, the honor of our name.

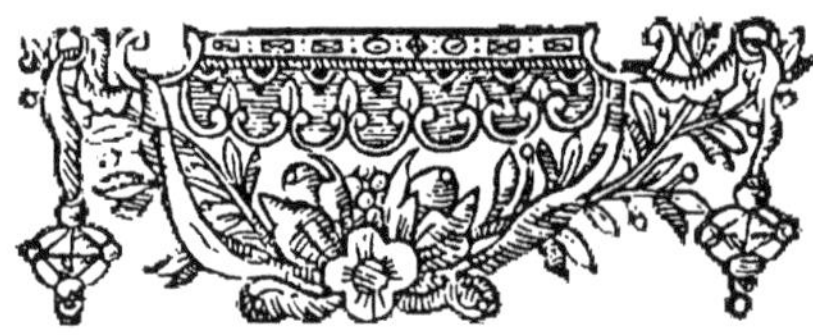

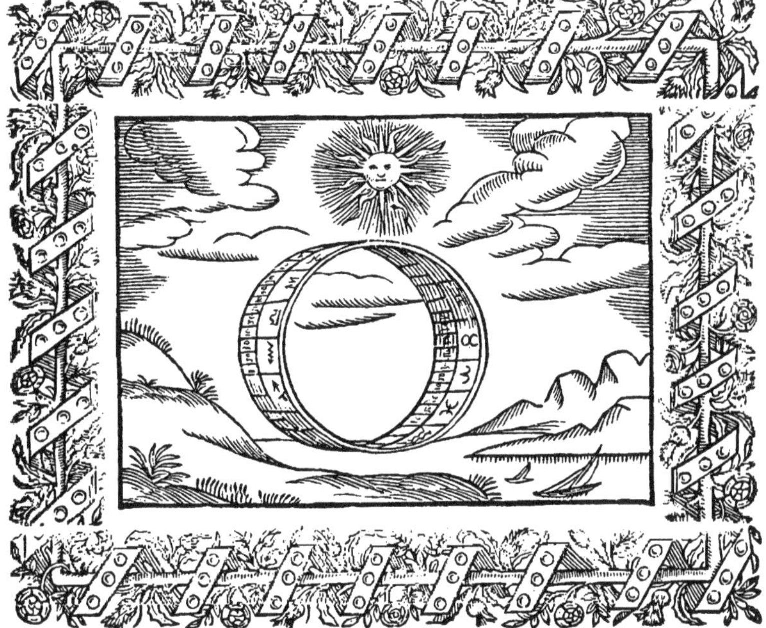

THOVGH life be ſhort, and man doth as the Sunne,
His iourney finiſh, in a little ſpace,
The way is wide, an honeſt courſe to runne,
And great the glories of a virtuous race,
That at the laſt, doe our iuſt labors crowne,
With threefold wreath, *Loue*, *Honor*, and *Renowne*.

Nor can Nights ſhadow, or the *Stygian* deepe,
Conceale faire *Virtue*, from the worldes wide eie,
The more oppreſt, the more ſhe ſtriues to peepe,
And raiſe her *Roſe-bound* golden head on high:
When Epicures, the wretch, and worldly ſlaue,
Shall rot in ſhame, aliue, and in the graue.

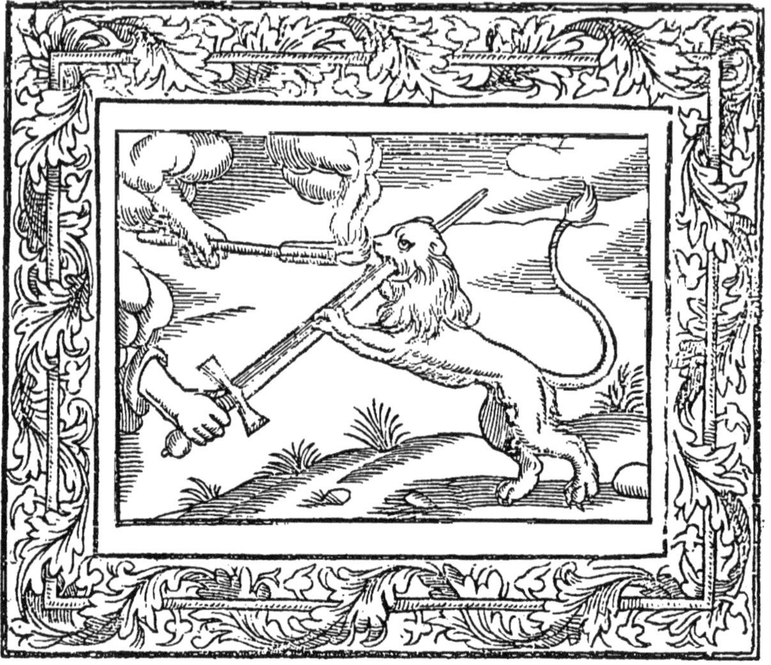

THE valiant heart, that feeles the vtmost ſpight,
Of envious Fortune, who with Sword and fire,
Awaites his ruine, with redoubled might,
Takes courage to him, and abates her ire,
By reſolution, and a conſtant mind,
To deede of virtue, evermore inclin'd.

Whoſe ſp'rite, a ſparke of heavens immortall fire,
Inglorious Sloth, may not in embers keepe,
But ſpite of hell, it will at length aſpire,
And even by ſtrawes, for want of fewell creepe:
When fearefull natures, and the mind vnſound,
At every blaſt, is beaten to the ground.

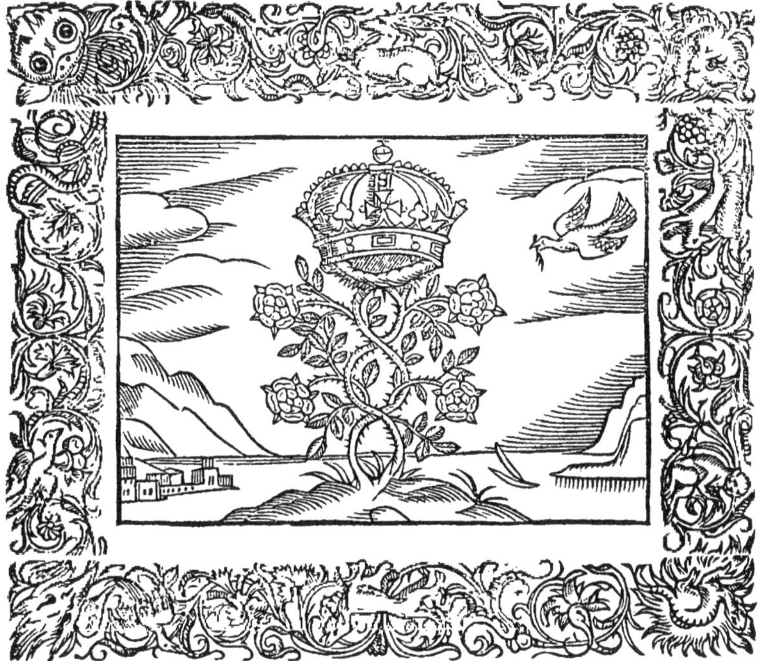

SWEETE Bird, who taught thee here to build thy nest?
(In greater saf'tie then *MEDEA*'s shrine,)
Did Hap, or that thou knew'st a Crowne the best,
From iniurie to shelter thee and thine?
How much I did thy happines envie,
When first I saw thee singing, hither flie.

Your glories Type, even so ye sacred Kinges,
In highest place, the weaker one to sheild,
Thus vnder that sweete shadow of your winges,
Best loues the Artes, and Innocence to build:
And thus my Muse, that never saf'tie knew,
With weary wing, great *HENRIE* flies to you.

To the Honorable, Sir Thomas Ridgewaie, Knight, and Baronet: Treaſurer at warres in Ireland, and one of his Maieſties Privie Counſell there &c.

Anagramma.

Thomas Ridgewaie.
Mihi gravato Deus.

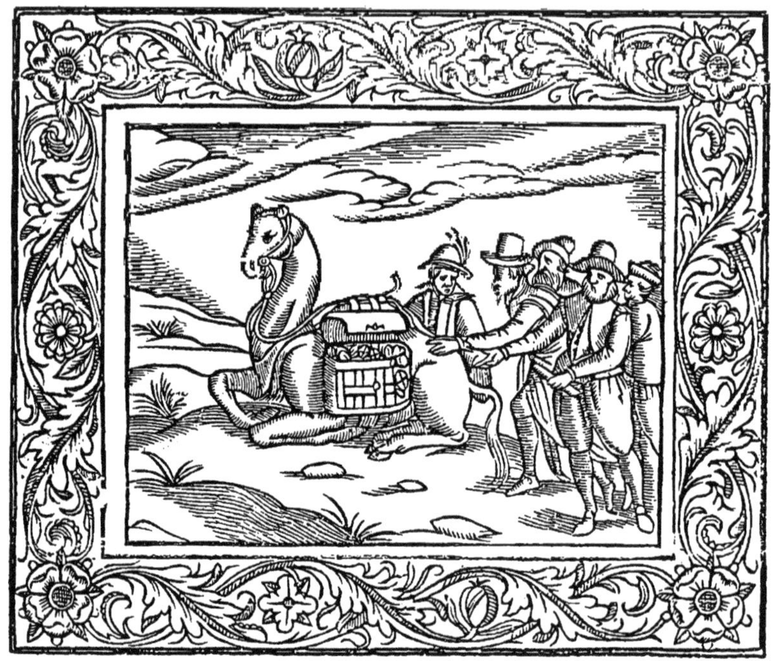

THE *Camell* ſtrong, with burthen great oppreſt,
Is forc'd to yeeld vnto his loade at laſt,
And while he toiles, himſelfe enioies the leaſt,
Of all the wealth, that on his back is caſt:
For why? he muſt the ſame, to thoſe impart,
Whoſe due it is, by Fortune, or deſert.

So honor'd Sir, you, as your *Camell*, beare
A Treaſures charge, that pulls you on your knee,
And though that thouſandes, aske it here, and there,
To thoſe that ought, and beſt deſeruing be,
You only giue, their wages, and their due,
The while the care, and perill lies on you.

Melancholia

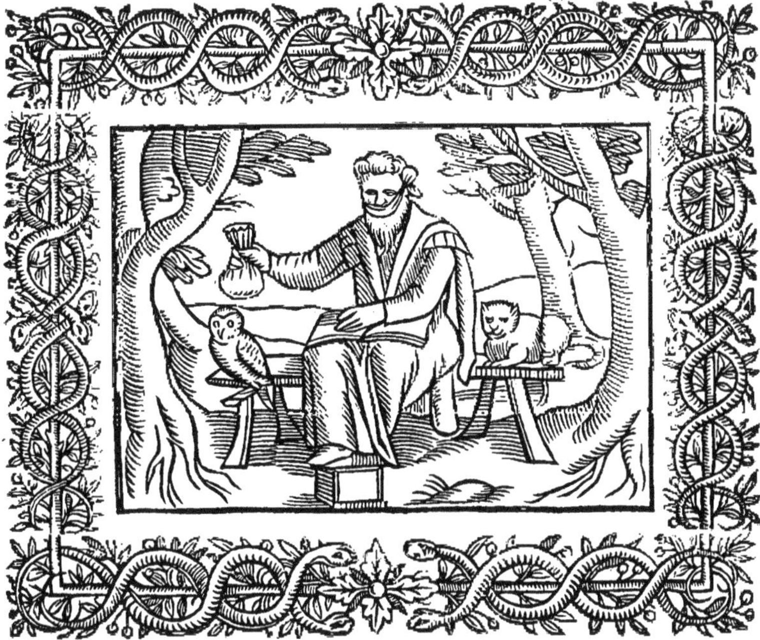

HEERE *Melancholly* muſing in his fits,
Pale viſag'd, of complexion cold and drie,
All ſolitarie, at his ſtudie ſits,
Within a wood, devoid of companie:
  Saue Madge the Owle, and melancholly Puſſe,
  Light-loathing Creatures, hatefull, ominous.

His mouth, in ſigne of ſilence, vp is bound,
For *Melancholly* loues not many wordes:
One foote on Cube is fixt vpon the ground,
The which him plodding *Conſtancie* affordes:
  A ſealed Purſe he beares, to ſhew no vice,
  So proper is to him, as *Avarice*.

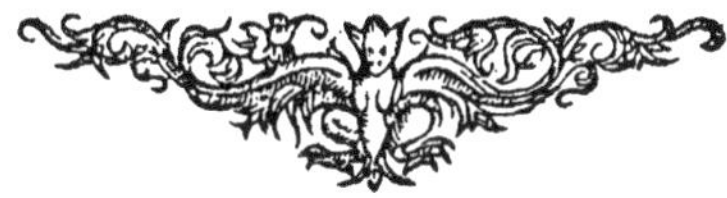

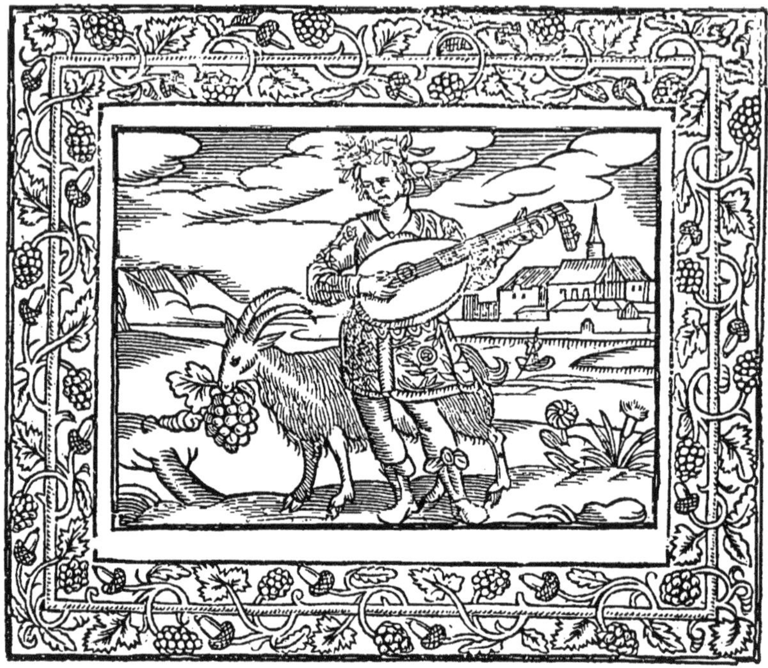

THE Aierie *Sanguine*, in whoſe youthfull cheeke,
The *Peſtane Roſe*, and *Lilly* doe contend:
By nature is benigne, and gentlie meeke,
To Muſick, and all merriment a frend;
As ſeemeth by his flowers, and girlondes gay,
Wherewith he dightes him, all the merry May.

And by him browzing, of the climbing vine,
The luſtfull *Goate* is ſeene, which may import,
His pronenes both to women, and to wine,
Bold, bounteous, frend vnto the learned ſort;
For ſtudies fit, beſt louing, and belou'd,
Faire-ſpoken, baſhfull, ſeld in anger moou'd.

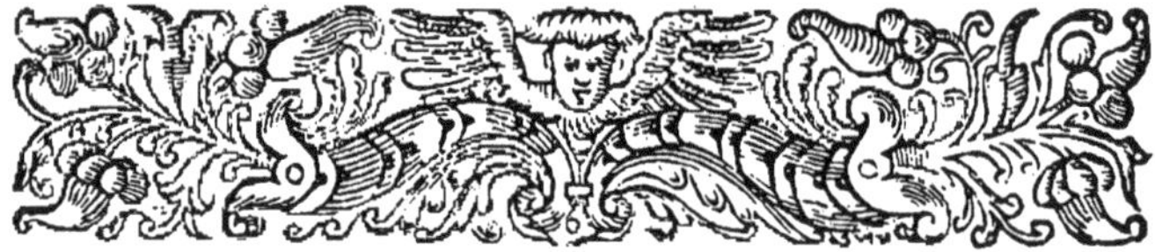

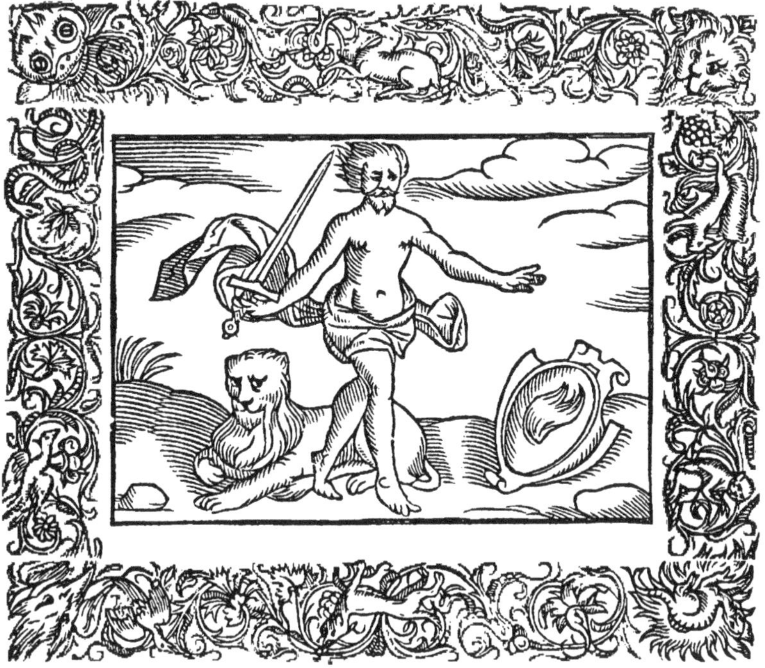

NEXT *Choller* ſtandes, reſembling moſt the fire,
Of ſwarthie yeallow, and a meager face;
With Sword a late, vnſheathed in his Ire:
Neere whome, there lies, within a little ſpace,
A ſterne ei'de Lion, and by him a ſheild,
Charg'd with a flame, vpon a crimſon feild.

We paint him young, to ſhew that paſſions raigne,
The moſt in heedles, and vnſtaied youth:
That Lion ſhowes, he ſeldome can refraine,
From cruell deede, devoide of gentle ruth:
Or hath perhaps, this beaſt to him aſſign'd,
As bearing moſt, the braue and bounteous mind.

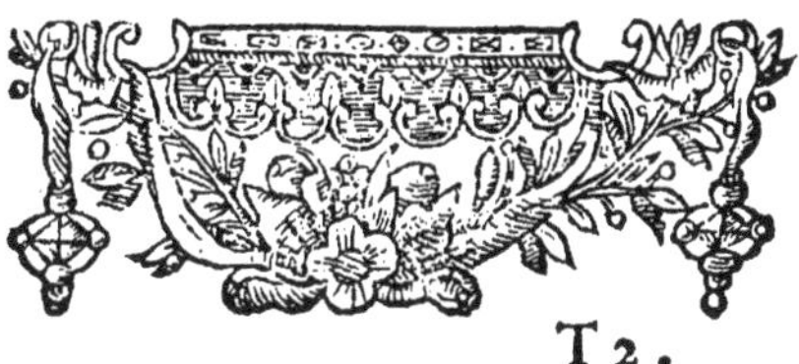

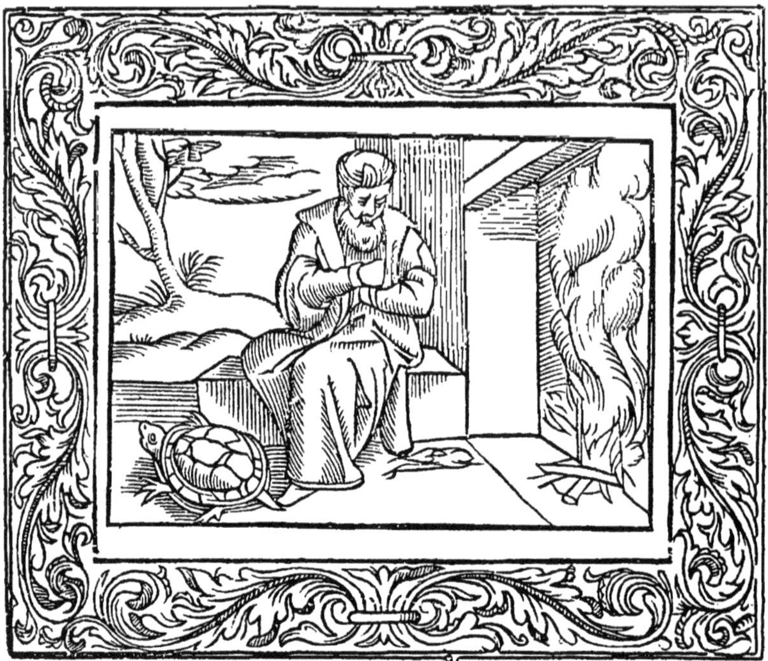

HEERE *Phlegme* ſits coughing on a Marble ſeate,
As Citie-vſurers before their dore:
Of Bodie groſſe, not through exceſſe of meate,
But of a Dropſie, he had got of yore:
His ſlothfull hand, in's boſome ſtill he keepes,
Drinkes, ſpits, or nodding, in the Chimney ſleepes.

Beneath his feete, there doth a *Tortoiſe* crall,
For ſloweſt pace, Sloth's Hieroglyphick here,
For Phlegmatique, hates Labour moſt of all,
As by his courſe araiment, may appeare:
Nor is he better furniſhed I find,
With Science, or the virtues of the mind.

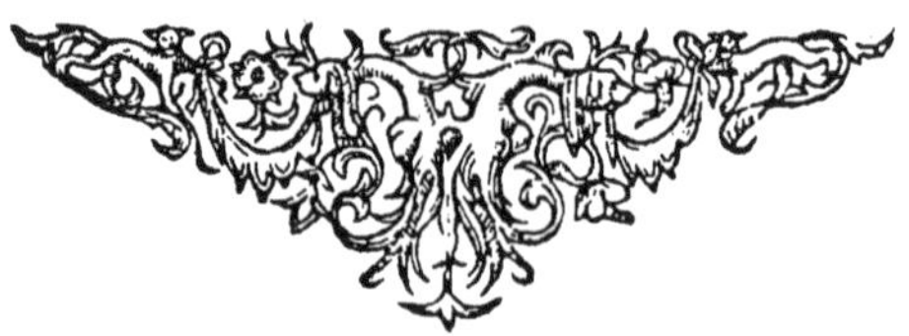

Ad

Ἰησοῦς.

Σὺ ἡ οἶς. Thou art that ſheepe.

Anagramma G: Camdeni. aut incerti cuiuſpiam.

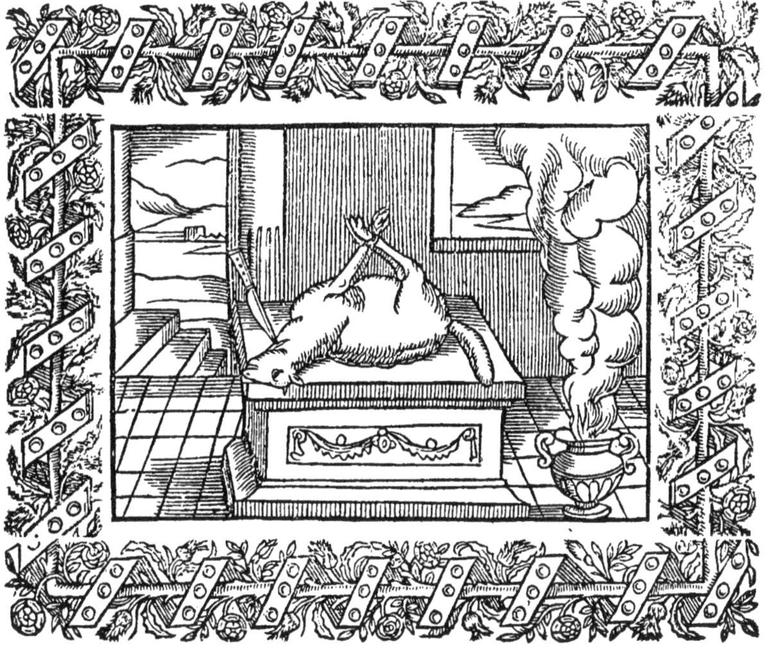

THE ſillie *Lambe*, on Altar lieth bound,
Prepared readie, for the Sacrifice,
Who willingly awaites his mortall wound,
Without reſiſtance, or helpe calling cries,
To mooue the tender hearted to relent,
Or heauens to heare a dieng Innocent.

Thou art (deere Lord) this Lambe, who for our guilt, *Eſai* 53.7.
Forſook'ſt the Throne, of higheſt Maieſtie, *Acts* 8.32.
And gau'ſt thy blood, for ſinners to be ſpilt,
Frend to thy foes, high in humilitie:
And is this creature innocent, and dumbe,
Till Lion-like, thou ſhalt to Iudgment come.

Redemptor noſter homo naſcendo, agnus moriendo, Leo reſurgendo, et ad cœlos aſcendendo, aquila facta eſt.

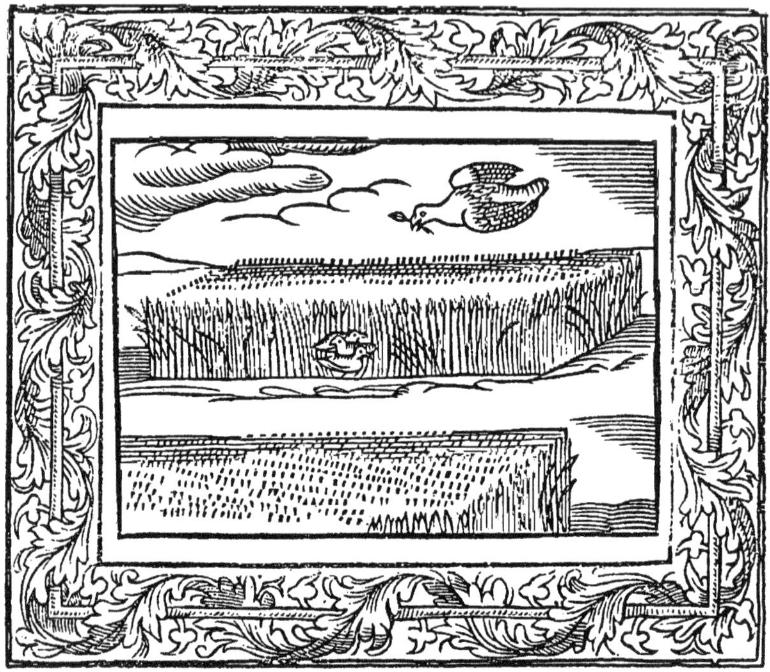

THE *Partrich* building in the ripened wheate,
Did charge her young, (while ſhe abroade did fiie,
With tender care, to ſearch about for meate,)
To marke the talke, of thoſe that paſſed by:
Ere long there came, the owner of the corne,
Who ſaid by frendes, next day it ſhould be ſhorne.

There is no daunger, quoth the old one yet,
Be ſtill a while, I once abroade againe,
Then heard they, he his kinſmen would intreate,
Without delay, to fell that feild of graine:
Some feare there is, quoth Damme, but if he ſaies,
Hee'le come himſelfe, then time to goe our waies.

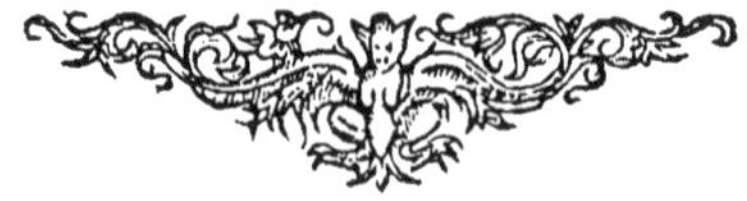

Matrimonium

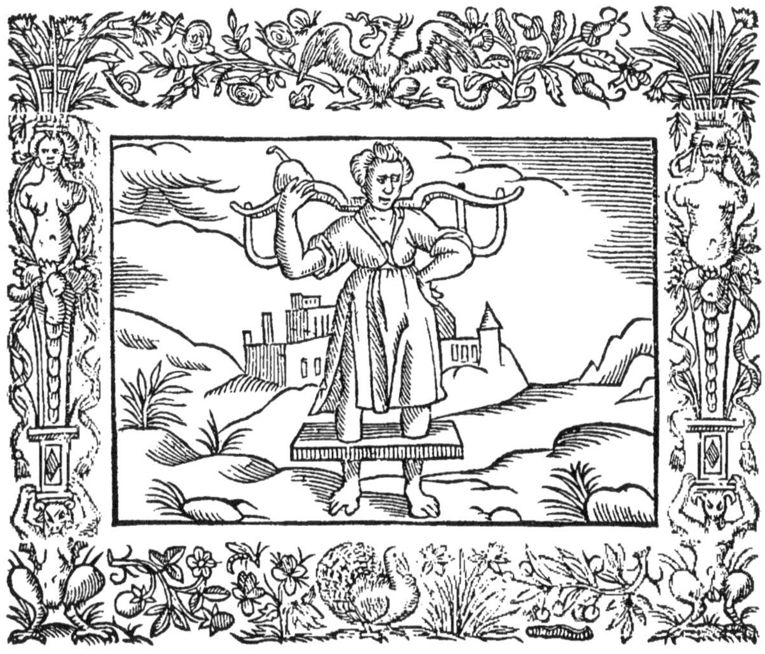

WHO loueth beſt, to liue in *Hymens* bandes,
And better likes, the carefull married ſtate,
May here behold, how *Matrimonie* ſtandes,
In woodden ſtocks, repenting him too late:
The ſervile yoake, his neck, and ſhoulder weares,
And in his hand, the fruitefull *Quince* he beares.

The ſtocks doe ſhew, his want of libertie,
Not as he woont, to wander where he liſt:
The yoke's an enſigne of ſervilitie:
The fruitefullnes, the *Quince* within his fiſt,
Of wedlock tells, which * *SOLON* did preſent, * Plutarch.
T'*Athenian* Brides, the day to Church they went.

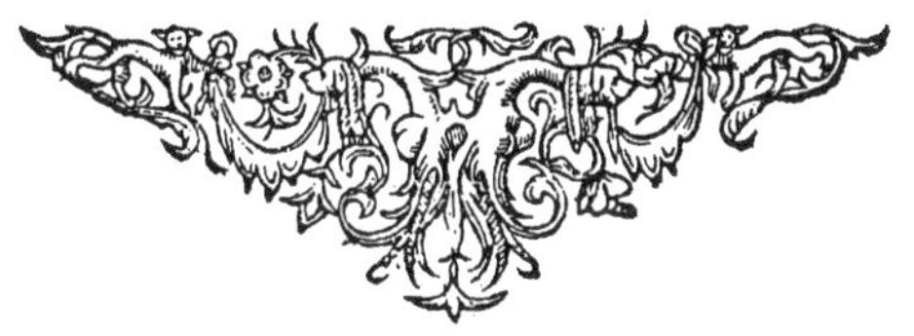

Sed

Ad Lesbiam.

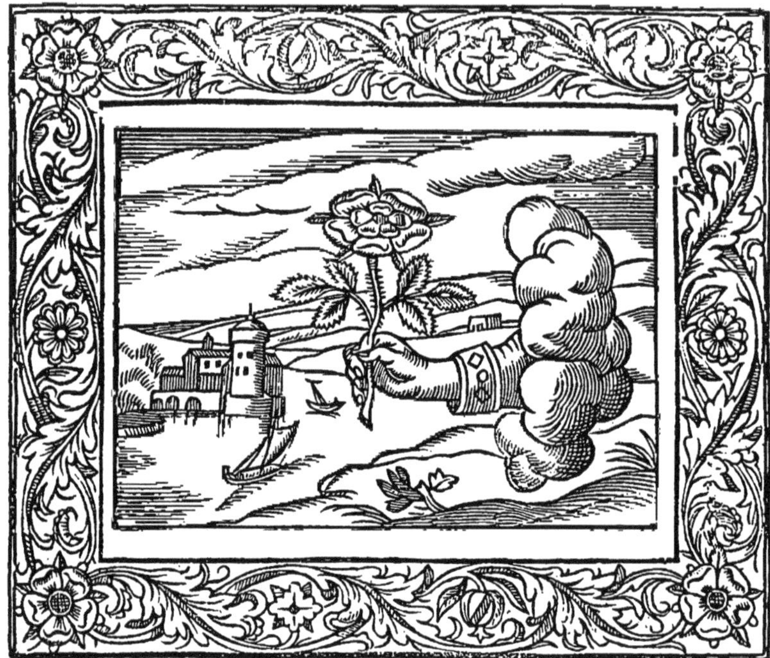

LESBIA, that dost th' *Elysian Rose* excell,
Or *Cyprian Goddesse*, for a beauteous grace;
Forgiue me, here that I so plainlie tell,
Dum licet iniusto subtrahe colla iugo *Propert: 2. 5.* My loues long errors, wandring in thy face:
Thy face that takes, like that *Dædalian* maze,
All eies thereon, that shall with wonder gaze.

Though fairest faire, thou beest yet like the Snow,
Or shamefast Rose, thou inwardly art cold,
Nor can the beames, that gentle Loue doth throw,
Exhale the sweete, thy bosome doth enfold:
As thou art faire, so wert thou *Lesbia* kind,
My wronges had di'de, and none had knowne thy mind.

Ovid: Epist: 13. *Sive latet Phœbus, seu terris altior extet,*
Tu mihi luce dolor, tu mihi nocte venis.

Veritas

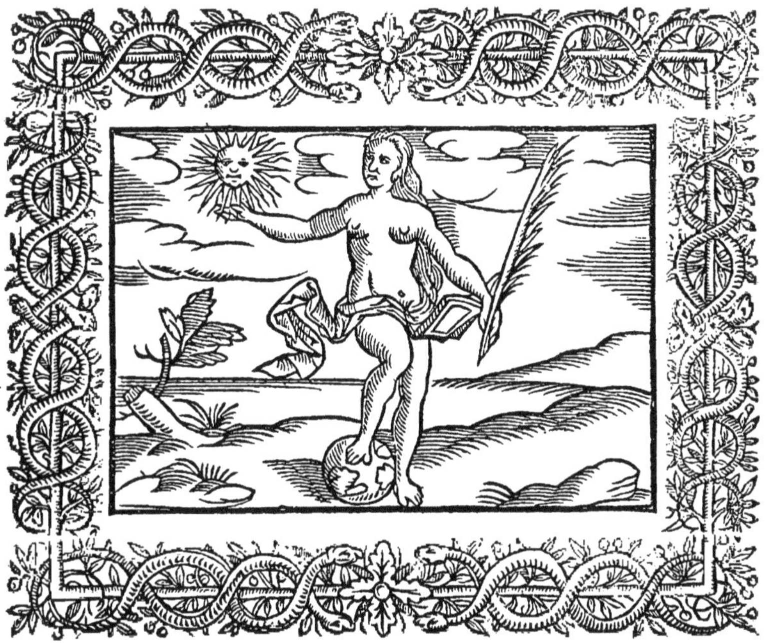

A BEAVTEOVS maide, in comly wiſe doth ſtand:
Who on the Sunnes bright globe, doth caſt her eie:
An opened booke, ſhe holdeth in her hand,
withall the Palme, in ſigne of victorie;
Her right foote treadeth downe the world belowe:
Her name is TRVTH, of old depainted ſo.

Her nakednes beſeemes ſimplicitie:
The Sunne, how ſhe is greateſt frend to light:
Her booke, the ſtrength ſhe holds by * hiſtorie:
The Palme, her triumphes over Tyrants ſpite:
The world ſhe treads on, how in heaven ſhe dwels,
And here beneath all earthly thing excells.

* Hiſtoria cuſtos illuſtrium virorum virtutis, teſtis malorum sceleris, benefica in omne humanum Genus: *Diodorus Siculus. 1. Bibliothec:*

Inter Auguſti Numiſmata.

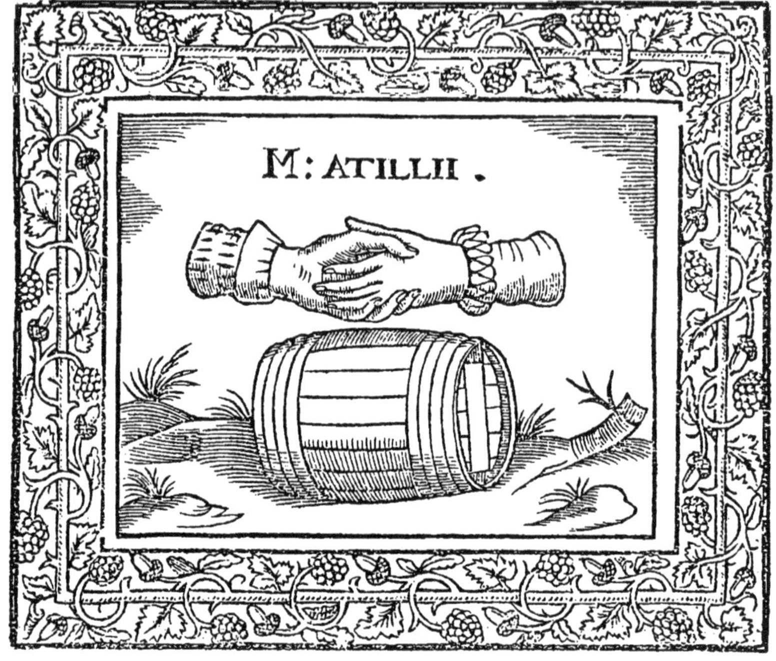

Vide hiſtoriam M: Attilii Reguli in Cic: officiis.

OF CONCORD firme, the *Romans* in their coine,
This ſymbole gaue, their peace about to make,
That as their hands, in one their hearts ſhould ioine,
And ſooner firſt, they would their liues forſake,
Then treachr'ouſly, their vow and promiſe breake,
Though to their foe, if they the word did ſpeake.

Fides etiam perfidis præſtanda, Ambroſ:

Card: Iulianus: vide Bohemorũ Annales. et Foxium in ſuo Martyrolog:

For lo, the Lord who ſecrets all doth knowe,
With vengeance moſt, doth plague the faithles wight:
As that ſame " *Card'nall*, prou'd not long agoe,
Who in the feild againſt his faith would fight:
With God and man, the truth accepted is;
Oh! let not heathen, vs excell in this.

Nec regnis poſt ferre fidem. *Silius*: *lib*: 11: Et optimus ille Militiæ cui poſtremum eſt primumque tueri Inter bella fidem *Idem lib*: 14.

Nàm illis promſſiis ſtandum quis non videt? quæ coactus quis metu, aut deceptus dolo promiſerit. Cicero in offic:

Publica Romulides pacturi fœdera iungunt
Concordes geminas oreque corde manus.
Ingens crede nefas hoſtiles fallere dextras,
Quod pœnas meruit vindice ſæpe Deo.

Ex Baſ: noſtro.

Iuſtitia

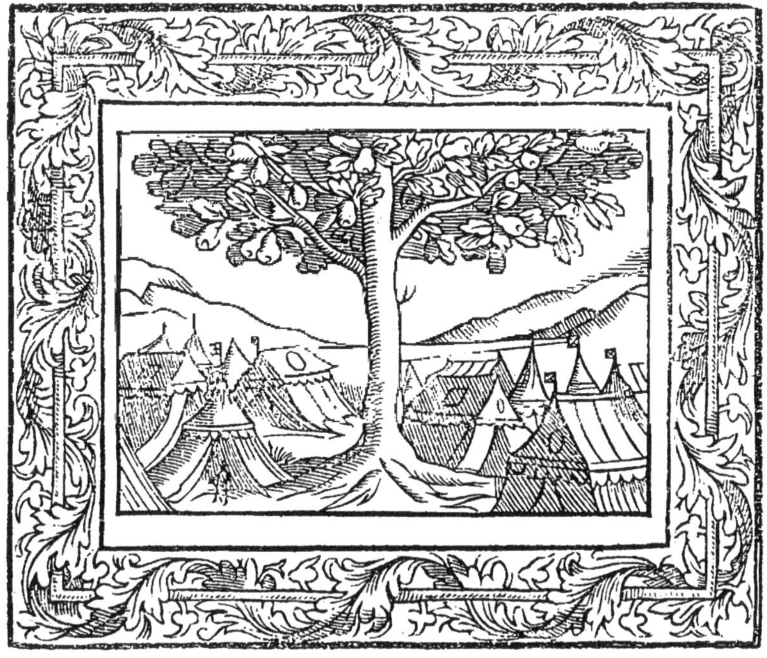

WHEN *SCAVRVS* forth the Roman youth did lead,
    To proue their valour on the common foe:
Within his Campe, in authors as I read,
A pearetree laden with the fruit did grow,
    Which at's departure, kept the wonted ſtore,
    As full remaining as it did before.

A mirror for commaunders in our age,
Who deeme it honour, and a ſouldiers guiſe,
To vſe on foes all * villanous outrage:
Rapes, murders, rapines, burnings robberies:
    And greateſt part of valour to conſiſt,
    Like ſavage bruites, in ſpoyling what they liſt.

Memoriæ tradiderit Scaurus pomiferam arborẽ quam in pede caſtrorum fuerat cõplexa metatio postero die abeũte exercitu intactis fructibus relictam. Front, *Srata gem: cap.* 3.

* In omne ſas nefaſque avidi aut vænales, non ſacro non prophano abſtinentes. *Tacitus. 2. hiſt:*

Nemo pullum rapiat, ovem nemo contingat, ſegetẽ nemo deterat, olenm, ſal, lignum nemo exigat, annona ſua contentus ſit. *Vopiſc. in Aur.*

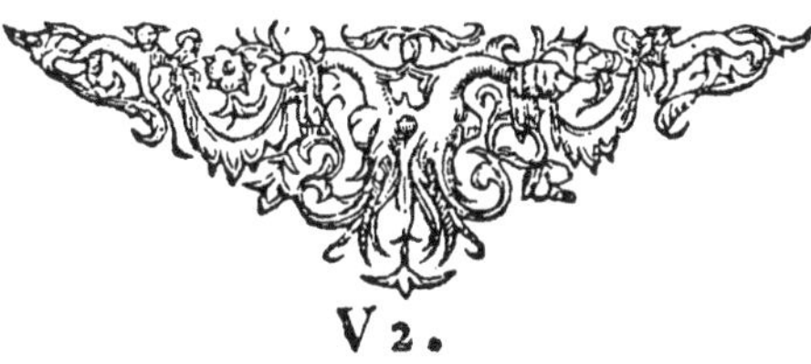

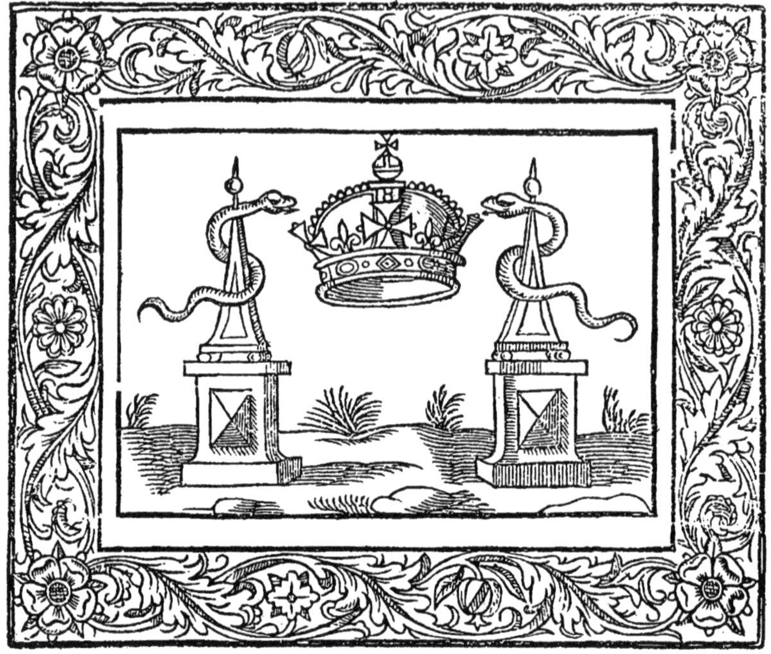

THE auntient Romans by their Temples vſ'd,
To paint a ſerpent, or ſuch hideous thing:
That holy places, might not be abuſ'd
By children, whom they told, that theſe would ſting:
And made beleue they liu'd, to that intent,
To Sacred things they ſhould be reverent.

pingo meos angues: *Perſ;* Vile Traytor, of ſome Hyrcane Tiger bred,
Such Serpents ſtill, thy Soveraignes crowne do guard:
Iovi cura est veneranda principis *Theocritus.* But think not as the other, theſe are dead,
Like child or foole: but that they are prepar'd,
With mortal ſtings, to be reueng'd on them,
That ſhall abuſe, tha'nointed Diadem.

Tacitus. 1. Annal: Proditores etiam iis quos ante ponunt inviſi ſunt.

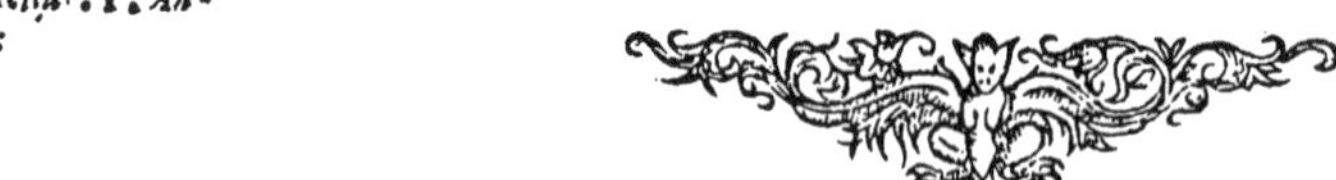

Dolis

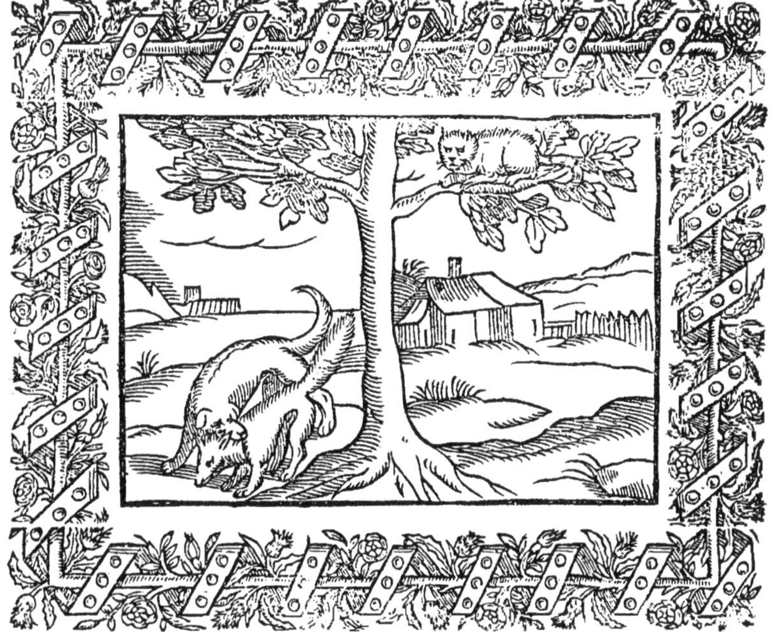

Ex Æsop fab.

THE Cat and Foxe, while that a lone they sate
Consulting, Regnard thus began to boast,
And soberlie to tel vnto the Cat,
His shiftes, when danger did assaile him most:
The Cat said, one is proper vnto me
If worst should come, that is to take a tree.

Meane time of hounds, there came a yolping crew,
Who found the Foxe: Pusse trusting to her clawes,
And seeing him torne in peeces, in her view,
Said to her selfe, after alitle pause;
One honest shift is better now I see,
Then all thy cunning in extremitie.

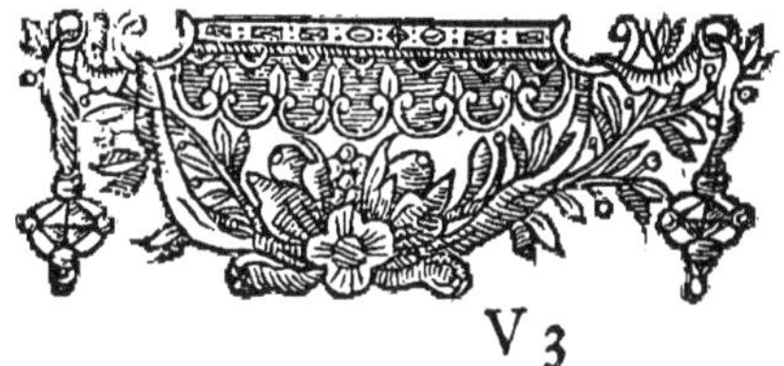

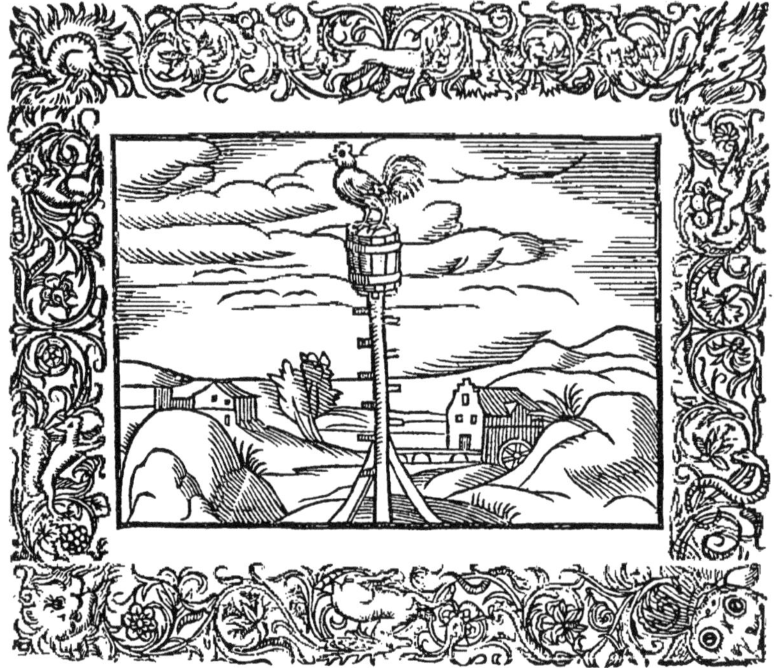

A BEACON ſtanding on the Rocky ſhore,
Vpon whoſe top, a cock to ſit you ſee:
Gods Miniſters doth ſhew, ſhould evermore,
Stand Sentinell; and howerly watchfull be,
Vpon their flock, defending every port,
Whereto the foe, is likelieſt to reſort.

Super ſpeculam Domini ego ſum ſtans iugiter per Diem. Ezech. 3

Speculatoré dedi te. Eſai 21.

For many are the ſtratagems of ſinne,
And Sathan labors ſtill with might and maine,
Within our ſoules, a landing place to win:
It is your partes, with fervent prayer againe;
And faith the ſpirits ſword, and all yee may,
To keepe his malice, from your flocks away.

Ex Baſil: noſtro ad Principem.

Peccatis totos ne vos ſopor opprimat altus,
Excubias perago nocte dieque pias:
Cumque gregi Dæmon Marte inſidietur aperto,
Littore ab æquoreo tæda cavere iubet.

Gregor. Hom. 19. in Ezech:

Quiſquis populi ſpeculator ponitur, in alto debet ſtare per vitam, vt poſſit prodeſſe per providentiam.

Vindicta

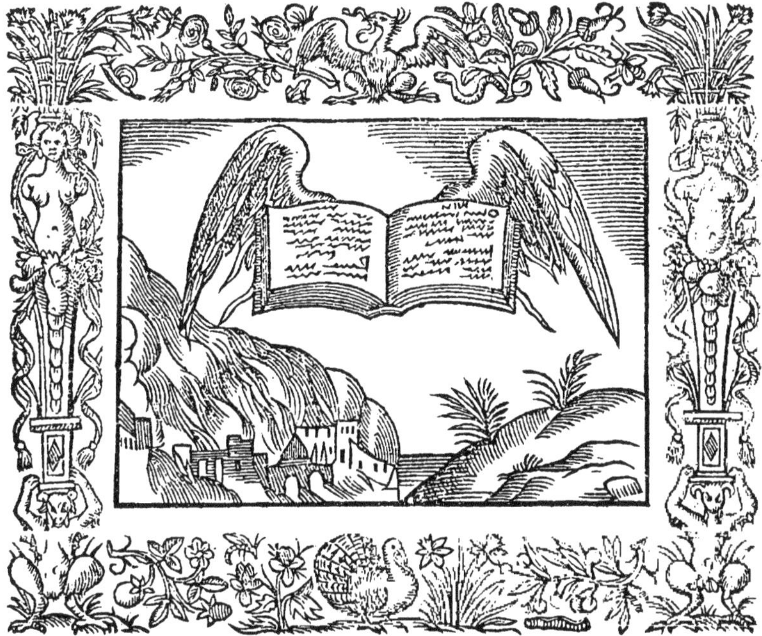

WHILE ſinfull *Sodome* dreades the heavenly fire,
And Nero trembles at his ſhadowes ſight:
This booke, the Herald of * th'Almighties Ire,
Doth on the howſe, of every ſwearer light:
To puniſh iuſtly, ſo prophane a ſinne,
With all the plagues, that are containd therein.

Zachar: 3.

A warning good for ſwearers, and for thoſe,
That think ſuch ſinne, their actions only grace:
And him the man, that can with feareful oathes,
Blaſpheme the Lord of heaven vnto his face:
But know prophane, ere many yeares be paſt,
A plague will come, with winged ſpeede at laſt.

Periurii pœna divina exitium, humana dedecus *Cicero*. 2 *de legibus*.

In prolem dilata ruunt periuria patris.
Et pœnam merito filius ore luit: *Claudian*:

Dum Sodoma immiſſos horret ſibi cœlitus ignes,
Terga ſua et Nemeſi dat paricida Nero:
Advolitans cœlo liber hic requievit in illum,
Numina periuro qui vocat ore Dei.

Ex Baſilico noſtro.

Eternitas

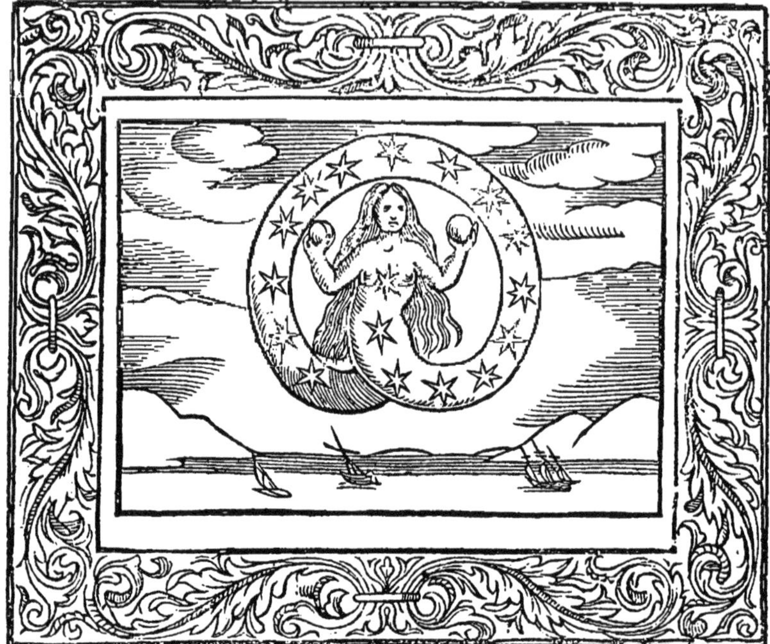

A VIRGIN faire, purtraicted as you ſee,
With haire diſpred, in comelie wiſe behind:
Within whoſe handes, two golden balls there be:
But from the breſt, the nether partes are twin'd
Within a ſtarrie circle, do expreſſe,
Eternitie, or *Everlaſtingnes*.

ETERNITIE is young, and never old:
The circle wantes * beginning and the end:
And vncorrupt for ever lies the gold:
The heaven her lightes for evermore did lend,
The Heathen thought, though heauen & earth muſt paſſe.
And all in time decay that ever was.

In æterno nihil præteritum eſt, neque venturum. *Phil. Iudæus.*

Cic: 1. de Natura Deorum.

Fuit quædam ab infinito tempore æternitas, quam nulla circumſcriptio temporum metiebatur; ſpatio tamen qualis ea fuerit intelligi non poteſt.

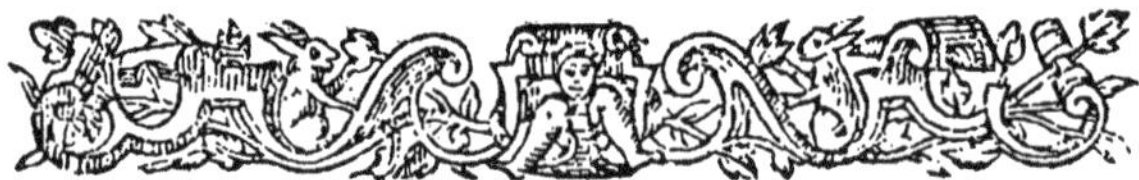

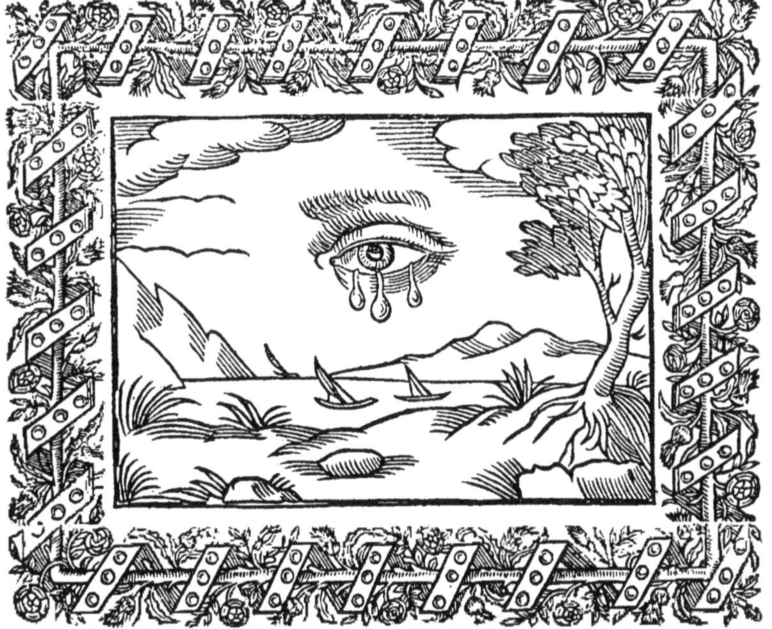

Incerti. Ex pergula Regia.

LOOKE how the *Limbeck* gentlie downe diſtil's,
In pearlie drops, his heartes deare quinteſcence:
So I, poore Eie, while coldeſt ſorrow fills,
My breſt by flames, enforce this moiſture thence
In Chriſtall floods, that thus their limits breake,
Drowning the heart, before the tongue can ſpeake.

Great Ladie, Teares haue moou'd the ſavage feirce,
And wreſted Pittie, from a Tyrants ire:
And drops in time, do hardeſt Marble peirce,
But ah I feare me, I too high aſpire,
Then wiſh thoſe beames, ſo bright had never ſhin'd,
Or that thou hadſt, beene from thy cradle blind.

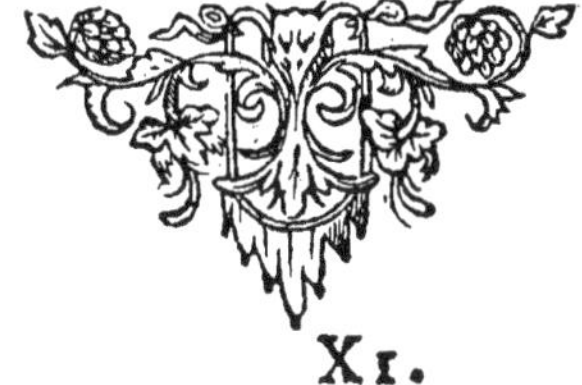

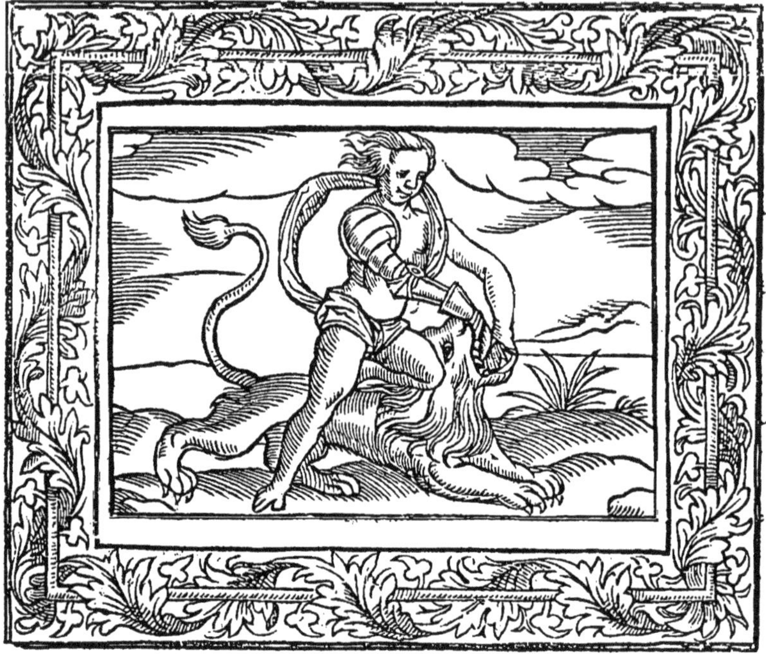

LYSIMACHVS adiudged once to die,
By sentence iust, for that he poisoned,
CALISTHENES his maister privilie,
And lieng long in dungeon fettered
To end his daies, did in the end request,
He might be throwne, vnto a savadge beast.

The which was straight of *ALEXANDER* graunted,
And naked he vnto a Lion cast,
But hauing one arme closely arm'd, vndaunted,
By th'vpper Iaw, he holdes his foe so fast,
That downe his throate, that armed arme he sendes,
And even the heart-stringes, from the bodie rendes.

Which bold attempt, when *ALEXANDER* knew,
Thy life is thine, *LYSIMACHVS* quoth he,
Besides I giue, (as to thy valour due,)
My frendship here, my Scepter after me:
For thus the virtuous, and the valiant spright,
Triumphes o're Fate, and Fortunes deadliest spite.

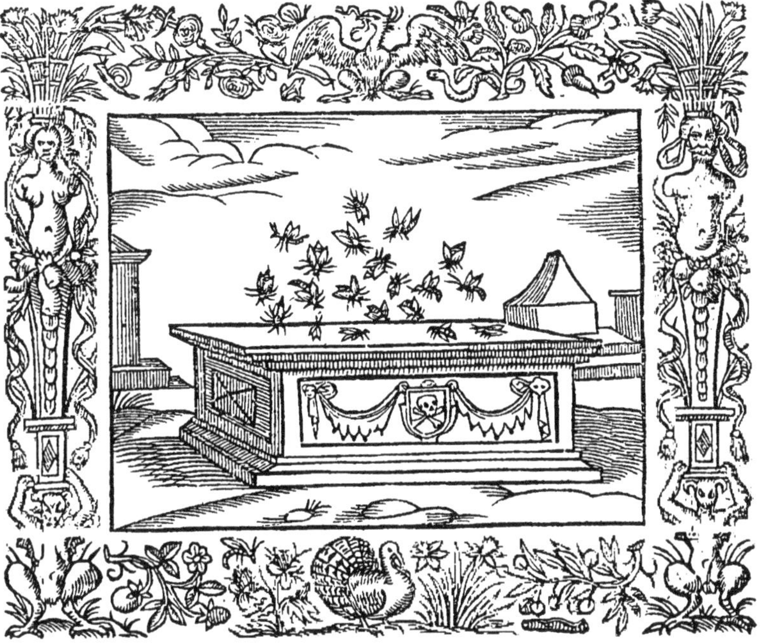

WEE doe adore by nature, Princes good,
And gladly as our Parents, them obey,
But loath the * Monſters, that delight in blood,
And thinke their People ſent them for a prey:
To whome the Lord, doth in his Iudgment ſend,
A loathed life, or elſe a fearefull end.

* Leo rugiens et Vrſus eſuriens, princeps impius ſuper populum pauperem: *Pro*: 25.

Nihil tam firmũ eſt, cui non ſit periculum etiam ab invalido: *Curtius lib.* 7.

Once *NERO'S* name, the world did quake to heare,
And *ROME* did tremble, at *DOMITIAN'S* ſight:
But now the Tyrant, cauſe of all this feare,
Is laid full low, vpon whoſe toombe do light,
To take revenge, the *Bee*, and ſummer * *Flie*,
Who not eſcap't ſometime his crueltie.

* Otioſus enim Muſcas necare ſolet: hinc illud: Ne Muſca quidẽ cum Imperatore.

Sponte pios Reges reveremur, at arte Tyrãnos,
Arte regunt iidem, funere et arte cadunt:

Vellicat extinctum eum turba togata NERONEM,
Muſcula et illudit, DOMITIANE tibi.

Baſilic: Doron.

De Tyranno IOB loquens, ſonitum ait terroris ſemper eſſe in auribus illius. *Iob*. 15.

—ſollicito bibunt
Auro ſuperbi; quam iuvat nuda manu
Captaſſe fontem

Seneca.

Ad generum Cereris ſine cæde et ſanguine pauci
Deſcendunt Reges, et ſicca morte Tyranni.

Iuvena: Satyr: 10

Ad pijssimum Iacobum magnæ Britanniæ Regem.

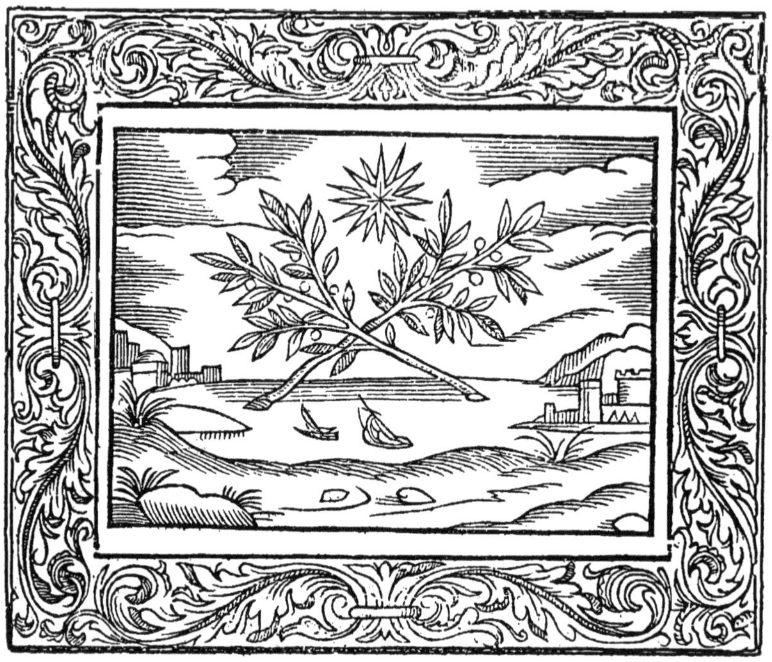

BVT thou whose goodnes, Pietie, and Zeale,
Haue caus'd thee so, to be belou'd of thine,
(When envious Fates, shall robbe the Common weale,
Of such a * Father,) shalt for ever shine:
Not turn'd as * *Cæsar*, to a fained starre,
But plac'd a * Saint, in greater glory farre.

With whome mild *Peace*, the most of all desir'd;
And learned Muse shall end their happie dayes;
While thou to all eternitie admir'd,
Shalt liue a fresh, in after ages praise:
Or be the Loade-starre, of thy glorious North,
Drawing all eies, to wonder at thy worth.

* Bonus Princeps nihilo differt a bono patre.

* Hanc animam interea cæso de corpore raptam Fac iubar vt semper Capitolia nostra forumque Divus ab excelsa prospectet Iulius æde. *Ovid: Metamor: 15*

* Pietate, et Iustitia, Principes Dij fiunt. *Augusti dictum. apud Senecam in Ludo.*

Te tua sed Pietas omni memorabilis ævo,
Sidus ad æterni Cæsaris vsque feret:
Iustitia occumbet tecum, quia Musa, Fidesque
In patriam, raris pax et habenda locis.

Ex Basil: nostro.

Icon

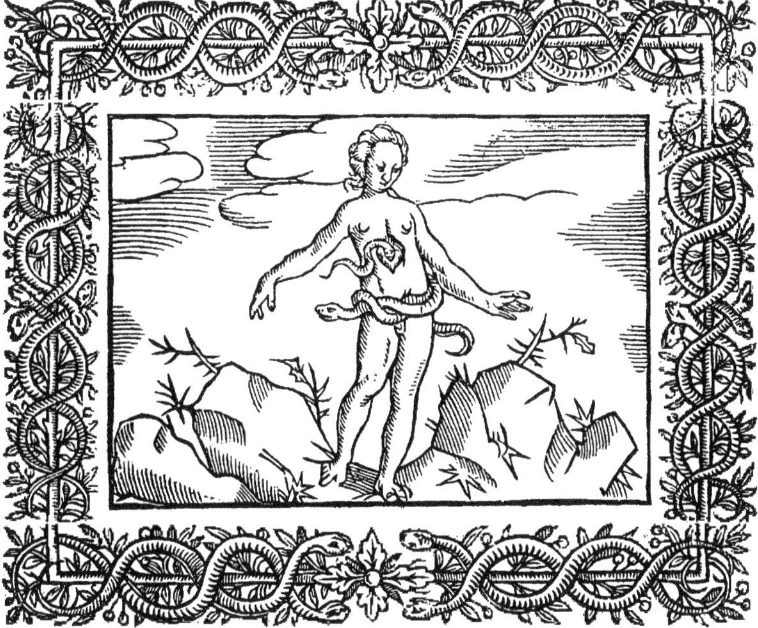

A YOVNG man blind, black, naked here is ſeene,
Ore Mountaine ſteepe, and Thornie Rock to paſſe,
Whoſe heart a Serpent gnawes with furie teene,
Another's wound about his waſt; alas,
Since *ADAM'S* fall, ſuch our eſtate hath bin,
The liuely picture of our guilt and ſinne.

His age denotes youthes follies and a'miſſe,
His blindnes ſhewes, our want of wiſedomes ſight;
Sinnes deadly waies, thoſe dang'rous ſtepps of his,
His nakednes, of grace depriued quite:
Hell's power the Serpent, which his loines doth girt,
A * Conſcience bad, the other eates his heart.

Heu quantũ miſero pœnæ mens conſcia donat *Lucan:*

* Grave pondus Conſcientia. *Cicero lib: 3. de natura Deorum.*

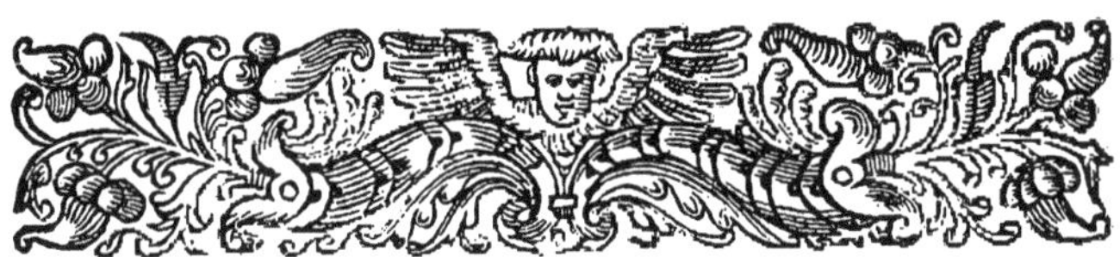

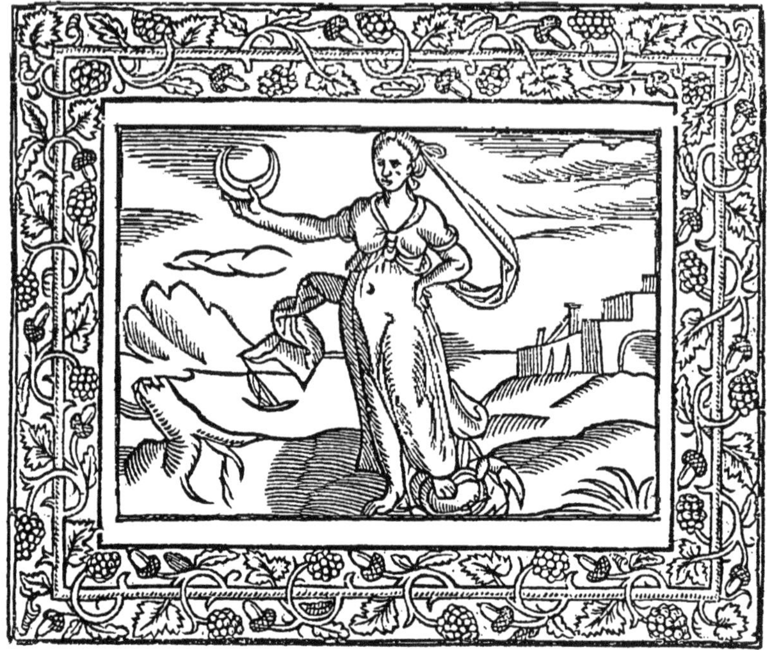

INCONSTANCIE with fickle foote doth stand,
Vpon a *Crab*, in gowne of palie greene,
A shining Cressaunt shewing in her hand,
Which as her selfe, is changing ever seene:
That cullour light, she borrowes from the Sea,
Whose waues continue, never at a stay.

Forward, and backward, *Cancer* keepes his pace,
Th' inconstant man, so doubtfull in his waies,
The private life, one while will most embrace,
In travaile then, he listes to spend his dayes:
Which was the Kitchin, that he makes a Tower,
Then downe goes all togeither in an hower.

In

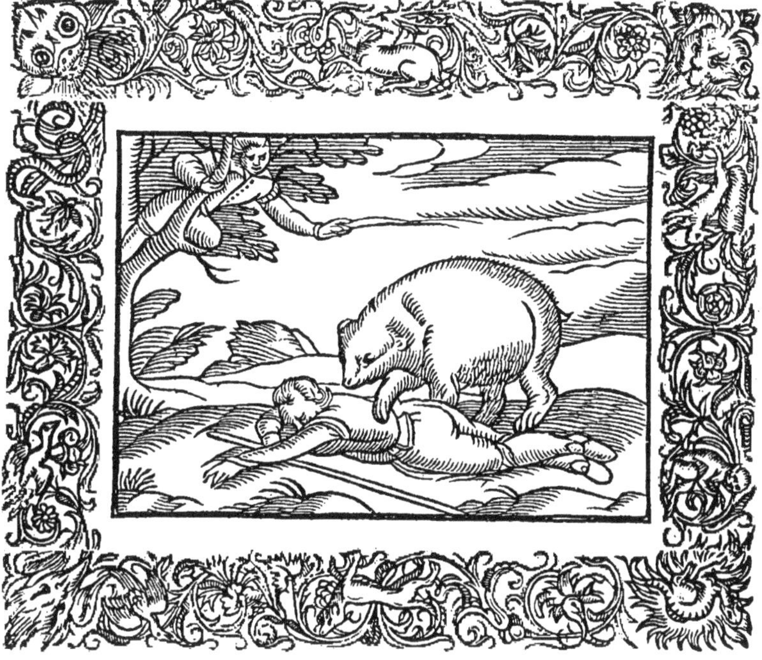

TWO frendes there were that did their Iourney take,
And by the way, they made a vow to either,
What ere befell, they never would forſake,
But as ſworne brethren, liue and die togeither:
Thus wandring thorough deſerts, here and there,
By chance they met, a great and vgly *Beare*.

Ex Æſopi fabu:

At whome, amazed with a deadly feare,
One leaues his frend, and climbeth vp a tree:
The other, falles downe flat before the *Beare*,
And keepes his breath, that ſeeming dead to be,
The *Beare* forſooke him, (for his nature's ſuch,
A breathles bodie never once to touch.)

The beaſt departing, and the daunger paſt,
The dead aroſe, and kept along his waie:
His fellow leaping from the tree at laſt,
Askt what the *Beare*, in's eare did whiſpring ſay,
Quoth he, he bad me, evermore take heede,
Of ſuch as thou, that faillſt in time of neede.

Levitas

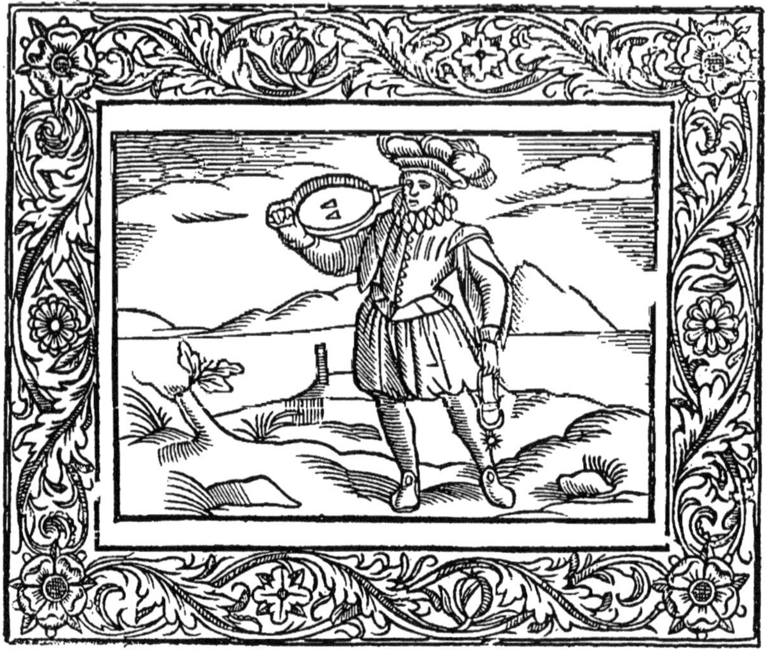

A YOVTH arraid, in ſundry cullors light,
And painted plumes that overſpred his creſt:
Deſcribes the varieng and fantaſtique wight,
(* For like our mindes, we commonly are dreſt:)
Eccleſiaſt: His right hand holdes, the bellowes to his eare,
His left, the quick, and ſpeedie ſpurre doth beare.

Such is Capriccio, or th'vnſtaied mind,
Whome thouſand fancies howerly doe poſſeſſe,
For riding poſt, with every blaſt of wind,
In nought hee's ſteddie, ſaue vnſtablenes:
Muſitians, Painters, and Poetique crew,
Cæſ: Ripa perugino. Accept what *RIPA*, dedicates to you.

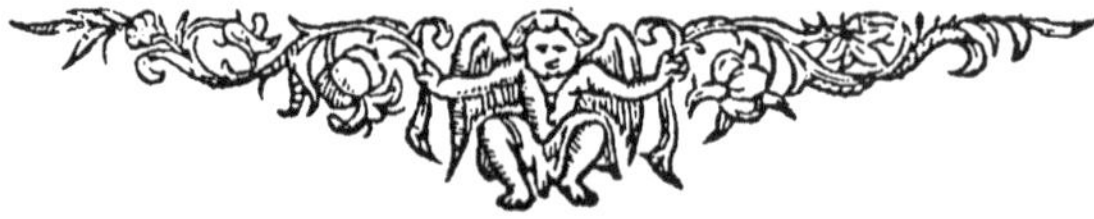

Adhuc

Ad D. M. L. nobilem quandam Italam Mediolanensem quinquagenariam, quæ puero vix 15. annos nato non ita pridem nupsit. Iocosum. Pasquini.

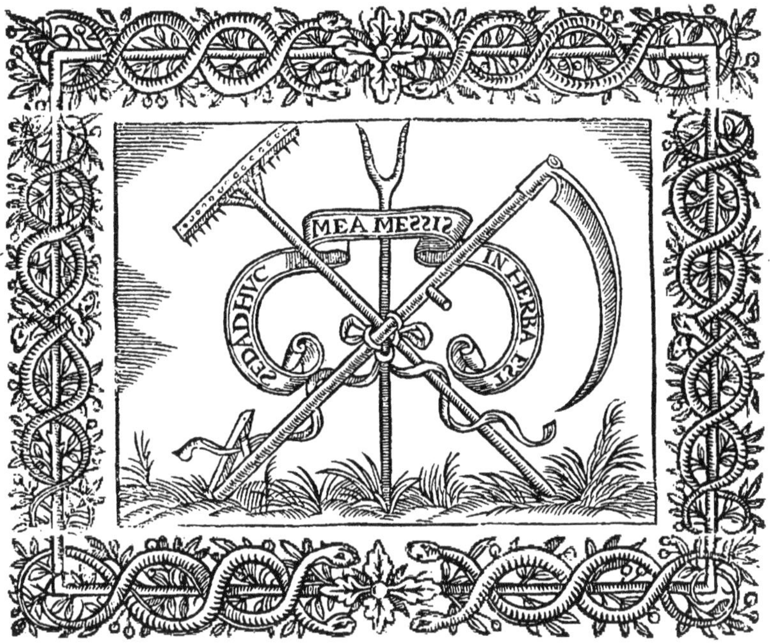

ADMIRED Ladie, I haue mused oft,
In silent night, when you haue beene in bed,
With your young husband, wherevpon you thought,
Or what conceipt possest your carefull head,
Since he we know, as yet had never seene,
His tendrest yeares, amounted to fifteene:

No question but you grieued inward much,
As doth the Miser, in a backward yeare:
When others reape, to see your harvest such,
And all your hopes, but in their blade appeare:
Ladie, let henceforth nought disease your rest,
For after-crop's doe sometime prooue the best.

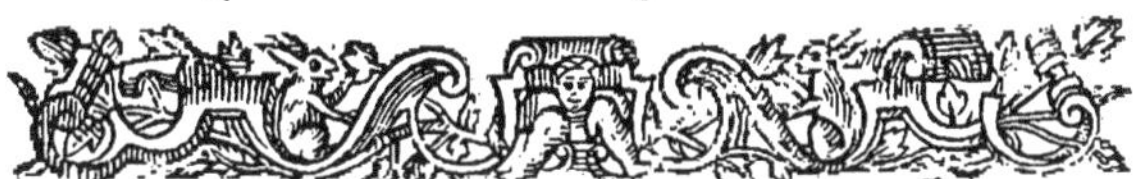

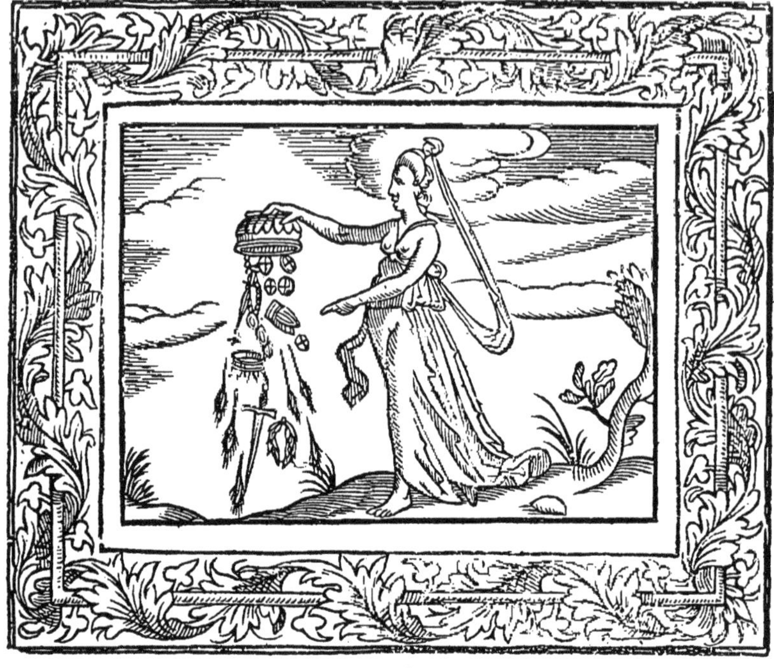

WHAT louely Goddeſſe do mine eies behold?
That powers ſuch plentie with her bounteous hand:
Her name is *BRYSVS*, whome the Greekes of old, *Priſchlinus in Perſium.*
As Queene of dreames ador'd within their land:
Whome if they ſeru'd, devoutly as they ſhould,
They made no doubt, of hauing what they would.

And well may *BRYSVS*, be a Goddeſſe thought,
So many who with fancies vaine deceiues:
Whome when ſhe to fooles Paradice hath brought,
For golden Apples, ſcarce ſhe giues them leaues:
To viſions vaine, and dreames then take no heede, *Non augurabimini, non obſervabitis ſomnia. Levitic: 19.*
Which had in Chriſt, their ending as you reade.

Somnia fallaci ludunt temeraria nocte, *Tibullus 34.*
Et pavidas mentes falſa timere iubet.

Cerno Deæ effigiem, cuius ſed dicito? BRYSVS, *Baſilic. Doron.*
Quam numen credunt ſomnia vana ſuum:
Fundit opes varias: ſtultos ſpe lactat inani,
Quos bullis ditat craſtina luſa dies.

Libidinis

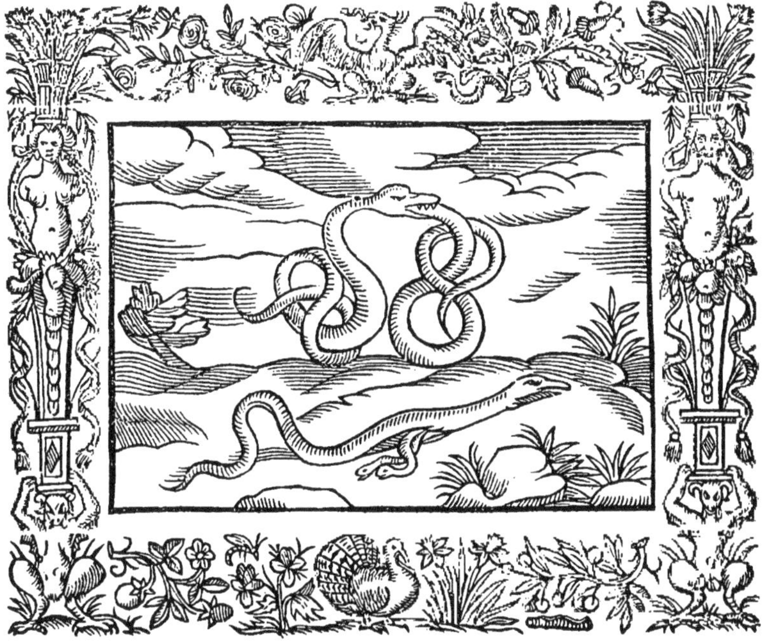

THE *Viper* when he doth engender, loe,
Thus downe the females throate, doth put his head,
Which of ſhe bites, as learned Authours ſhow,
And ne're conceiues, before the male be dead:
Eke when ſhe forth, her poiſonous broode doth ſend,
Her young ones likewiſe, bring her to her end.

Thrivet: in Apotheg:

Of Beaſtly luſt, th' effectes herein perceiue,
How deadly, and how dangerous they be,
Of life and ſoule, that doe at once bereaue,
Turning abundance into beggery:
Daughter of Sloth, vile cancker of the mind,
Leauing repentance, and foule ſhame behind.

Sævus criminum ſtimulus libido eſt, quæ nunquam manere quietum patitur affectum, nocte fervet, die anhelat.

Bernard: de Abel et Cain.

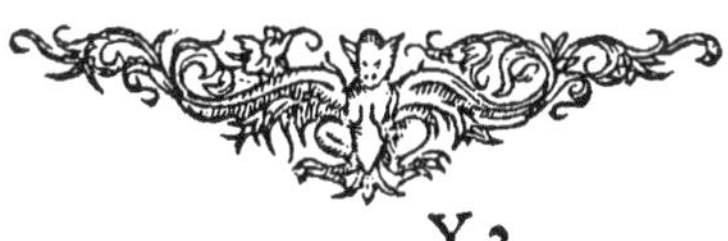

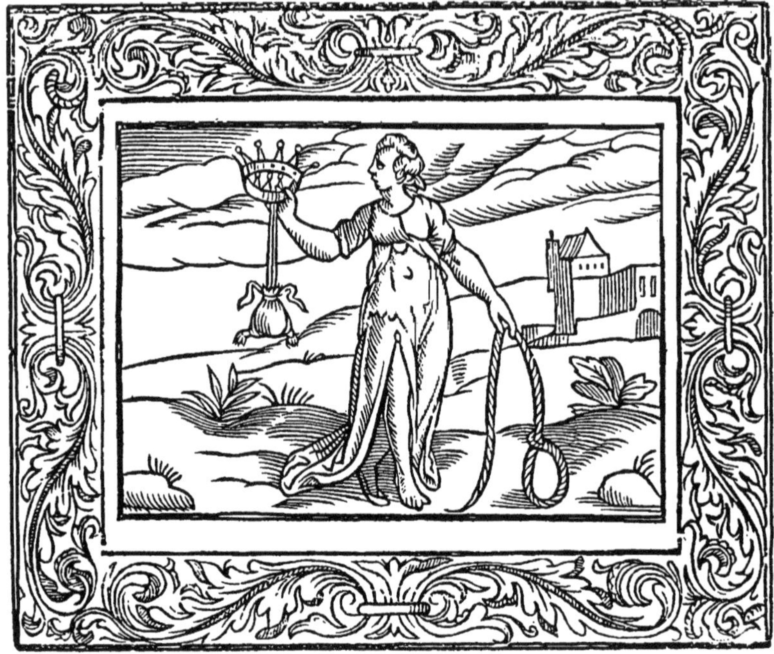

Ex Epigrammate græco vetusto:

A WOFVLL wretch, that languisht in dispaire,
Withouten frendes, and meanes of living here,
A halter tooke, to make an end of care,
The while beneath hid treasure doth appeare:
Which to his lot assign'd, by fortunes doome,
He takes, and leaues his halter in the roome.

The owner after missing of his pelfe,
For deadly greife, his heapes and hopes were gon,
The others halter takes, and hanges himselfe:
Fortune thus dallies ever, and anon
O're-swaieng all, with Scepter in her fist,
And bandieth vs, like balls which way she list.

Fortuna vitrea est, cum splendet frangitur: *Publius*

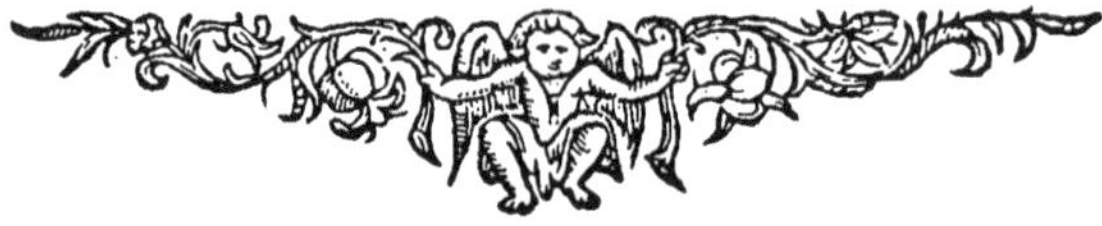

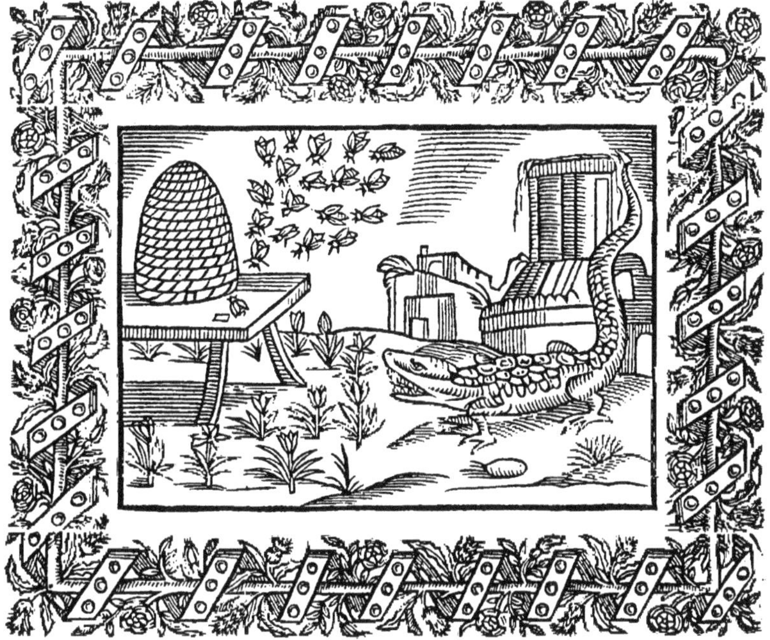

THE *Crocodile* along th' Ægiptian *NILE*,
That lurkes to make the paſſenger his pray,
The moſt of all delightes, to robbe and ſpoile
The Hunny-hiues, were he not kept away
By *Saffron* planted, round on every ſide,
Which this ſlie theife, could never yet abide.

This *Crocodile*, I count the Ghoſtly foe,
Who evermore lies watching, to devoure
Our *Hopes* encreaſe, that in the ſoule doth grow,
Did not the grace divine, this *Saffron* flower
(Moſt wholeſome herbe) prevent his deadly ſpight,
And guard the Garden, ſafely day and night.

Vnde Crocodili nomen habet παρὰ τὸν κρόκον δειλεῖν: i. quod Crocum maxime timeat, Nam Apiarij in Ægypto (teſte Plinio,) circum alvearia Crocum conſerunt ne a prædone iſto decipiantur:

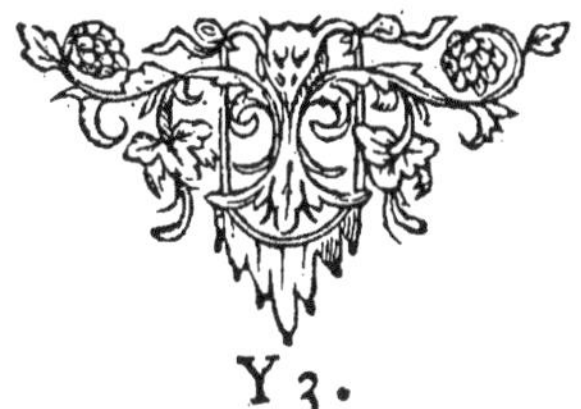

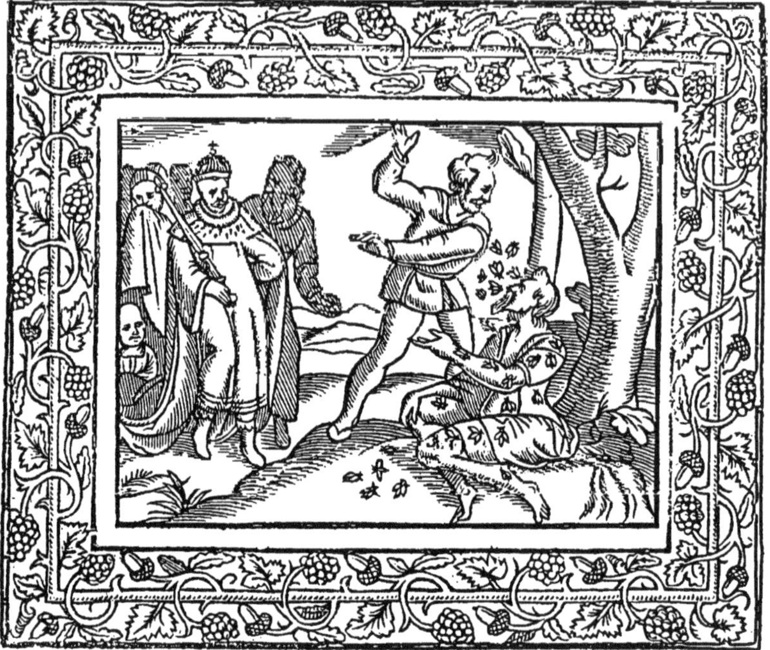

WHEN as *TIBERIVS CÆSAR* past along
The streetes of *Rome*, by chaunce he did espie
A Lazar poore, who there amid the throng,
Did full of sores, and loathsome vlcers lie,
About the which, so busie was the flie:
That moou'd with pittie, *CÆSAR* willed some,
Stand by to kill them, as they saw them come.

Whereat the wretch, did suddainely replie,
These flies are full, pray let them yet alone,
For being kill'd, a fresher companie,
More hunger pincht, would bite me to the bone:
So when the wealthy Iudge, is dead and gone:
Some starued one succeedes, who * biteth more,
A thousand times, then did the full before.

* Caninum legis studium dixit *Columella lib:*

Quemadmodum vis morborum pretia medentibus, sic fori tabes pecuniam advocatis fert. *Tacitus Annal: 11.*

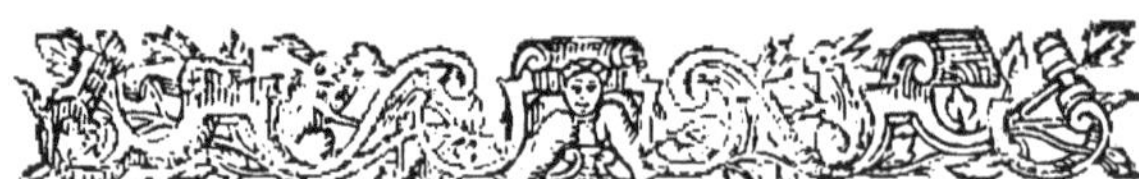

Silentij

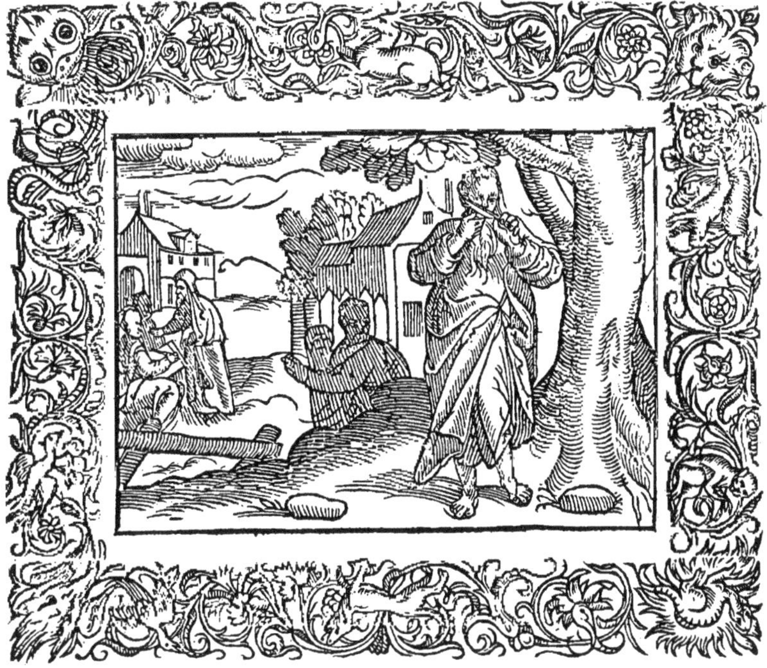

LOE *SOLON* here th' Athenian ſage doth ſtand,
The glorie of all *GRECIA* to this day,
With courage bold who taketh knife in hand,
And with the ſame, doth cut his tongue away:
But being ask'd of ſome, the reaſon why,
By writing thus he anſwer'd by and by.

Oft haue I heard, that many haue ſuſtained,
Much loſſe by talke, and laviſhnes of tongue,
Of ſilence never any yet complained,
Or could ſay iuſtly, it had done him wrong:
Who knowes to ſpeake, and when to hold his peace,
Findes feweſt daungers, and liues beſt at eaſe.

Angerona Dea præſes ſilentij apud Romanos, obſignato ore ãtiquitus effiⅽta eſt

Res omnium difficillima ſilere et audire: *Gellius lib*: 1.

Quingennium ſilentium in Pythagoræ ſchola quã ἐχεμυθίαν vocabant, teſte Laertio indicebatur. *Laertius lib*: 22.

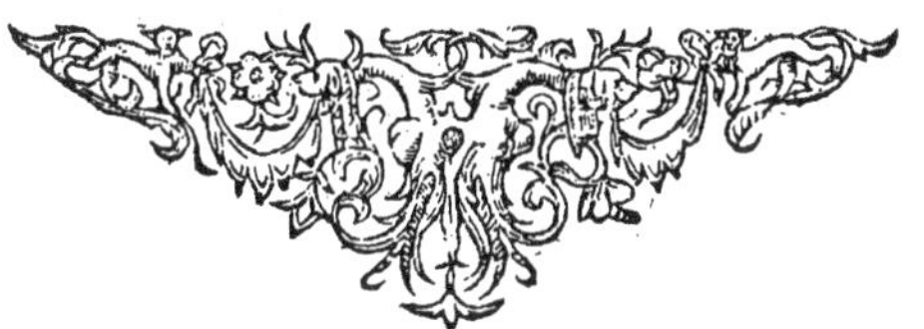

Vini

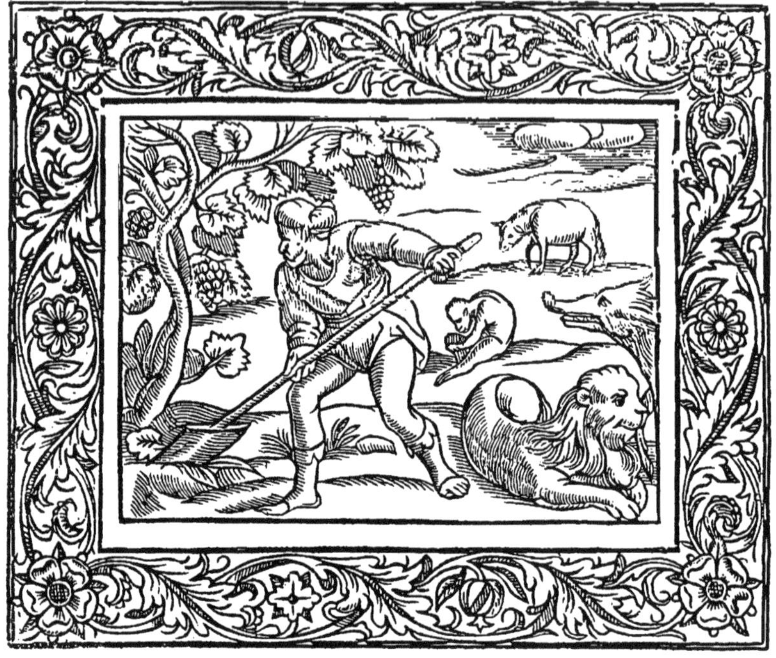

THE husbandman, laid ſometime to his vine,
To make it beare, the donge of ſundry beaſtes,
Whoſe virtue ſince, hath quite poſſeſt the wine,
As may appeare, at many drunken feaſtes:
One * Lion-like, doth quarrell with his hoſt,
Stares, ſweares; breakes windowes, or behacks the poſt.

Ape-like you ſee, the ſecond merry ſtill,
Or whot with luſt, he never thinkes of ſleepe:
Another * ſwiniſh, feeles his ſtomach ill:
The fourth is ſoft, and ſimple as the ſheepe:
A Romane ſage, did ſometime thus expreſſe,
In briefe th' effectes, of loathſome Drunkenes.

* Vina dabant animos — *Ovid: Metam:* 12.

--- geminata libidine ſurgit *ibidem.*

* --- Affigit humo divinæ particulā auræ. *Horat: lib: Serm:* 2. *Satyr:* 2.

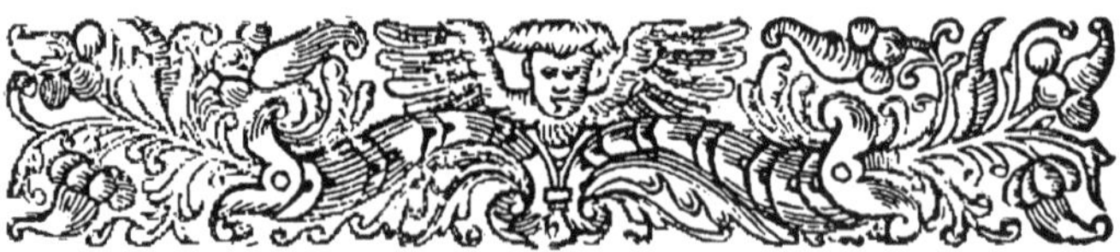

Nec

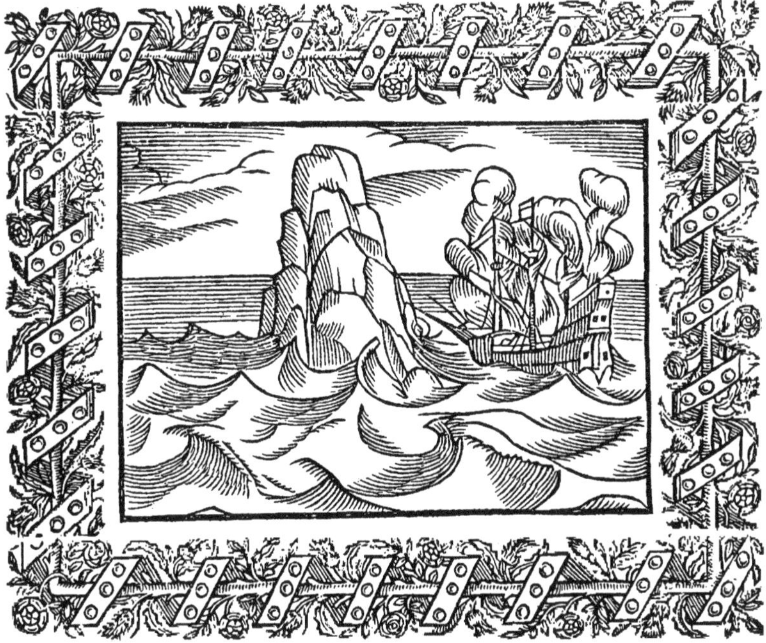

AMID the waues, a mightie Rock doth ſtand,
Whoſe ruggie brow, had bidden many a ſhower,
And bitter ſtorme; which neither ſea, nor land,
Nor *IOVES* ſharpe-lightening ever could devoure:
This ſame is *MANLIE CONSTANCIE* of mind,
Not eaſly moou'd, with every blaſt of wind.

Neere which you ſee, a goodly ſhip to drowne,
Herewith bright flaming in a pitteous fire:
This is *OPINION*, toſſed vp and downe,
Whoſe Pilot's *PRIDE*, & Steereſman *VAINE DESIRE*,
Thoſe flames *HOT PASSIONS*, & the *WORLD* the ſea,
God bleſſe the man, that's carried thus away.

Vide Lipſium de Conſtantia.

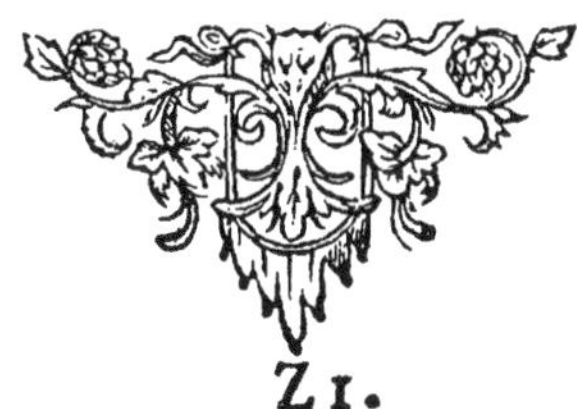

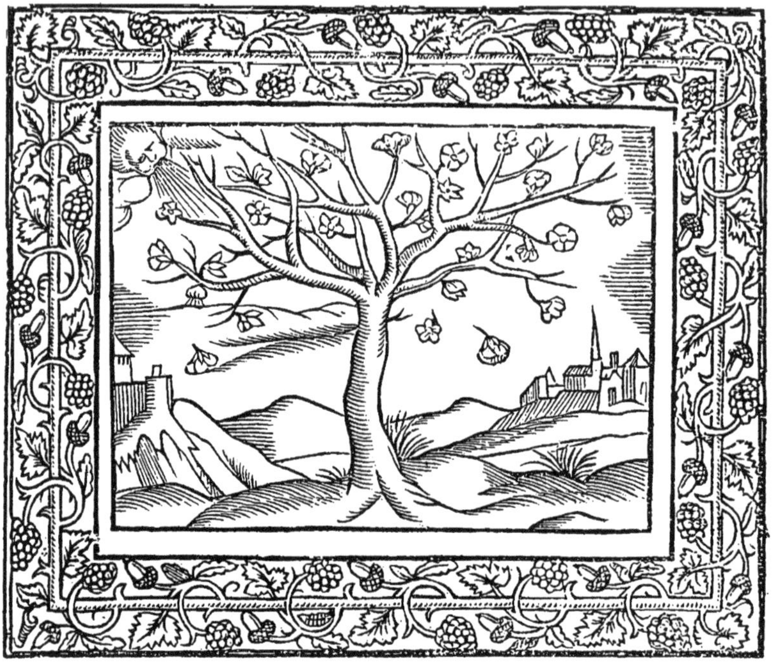

WHILE gentle *Zephire*, warmes the tender ſpring,
And *Flora* glads all creatures at her ſight:
The *Almond-trees*, ere any leaues they bring,
Vnfold their pride, their bloſſomes red and white:
But withered ſoone, vnto the ground they fall,
Or yeild their fruite, the leaſt and laſt of all.

So many children in their tender yeares,
Doe promiſe much by towardlines of wit,
From ſuch, yet ſeldome any fruite appeares:
When as ſome plodder, that below doth ſit,
Of whome both frendes, and maiſter did diſpaire,
As hindmoſt hound doth ſooneſt catch the Hare.

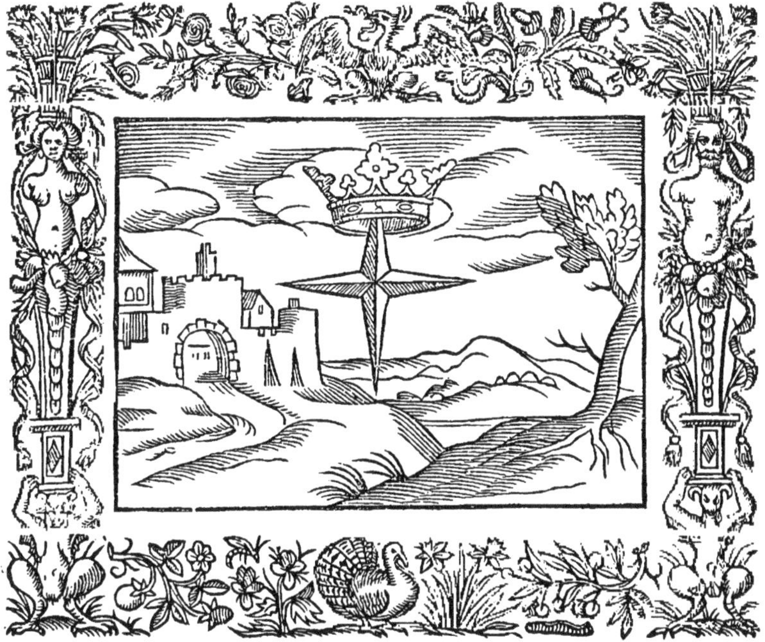

BY raſh attempt, who iniures mightie men,
Or by baſe deede, incurres the Princes Ire,
Doth often wiſh, it were to doe agen,
And that his hand, perhaps were in the fire,
That fought againſt him, or with Libell baſe,
Sedition ſow'd, or ſlaunder in diſgrace.

Principes non irritãdos. *Proverb:* 25.15.

For as this Engine, where the ſame doth light,
Like *IOVE'S* ſwift-thunder, merciles it ſtrikes,
And by the roote, rends vp rebellion quite:
The wiſer man, will then aware the pikes,
And frame himſelfe, to liue without offence,
Firſt * God to ſerue, and afterwardes his Prince.

* Let the firſt care, be of God, & divine thinges. *Ariſt: politic:* 7. *Cap:* 8.

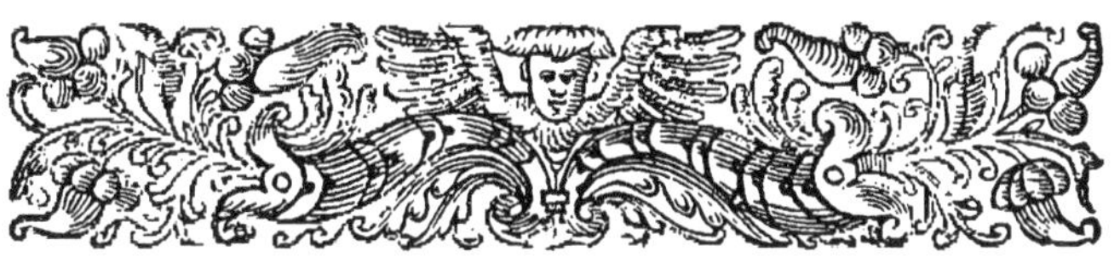

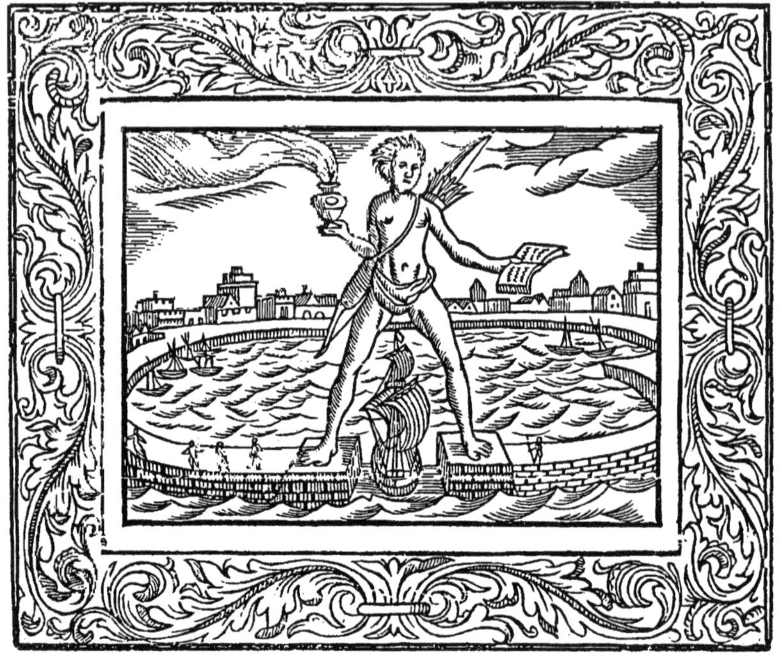

THE Monuments that mightie Monarches reare,
COLOSSO'S ſtatues, and Pyramids high,
In tract of time, doe moulder downe and weare,
Ne leaue they any little memorie,
The Paſſenger may warned be to ſay,
They had their being here, another day.

But wiſe wordes taught, in numbers ſweete to runne,
Preſerued by the liuing Muſe for aie,
Shall ſtill abide, when date of theſe is done,
Nor ever ſhall by Time be worne away:
Time, Tyrants, Envie, World aſſay thy worſt,
Ere *HOMER* die, thou ſhalt be " fired firſt.

Scindétur veſtes, geminæ frangentur et aurum, Carmina quem tribuent fama perennis erit: *Ovid: Amor: Eleg: 10.*

" Exitio terras cum dabit vna dies: *Ovid:*

Ergo cum ſilices, cum dens patiatur aratri
Depereant ævo, carmina morte carent.
Cedant carminibus Reges, Regumque Triumphi,
Cedat et auriferi ripa beata Tagi.

Ovid: Eleg: vltim:

Pro

Henrici 4. Angliæ Regis, Symbolum.

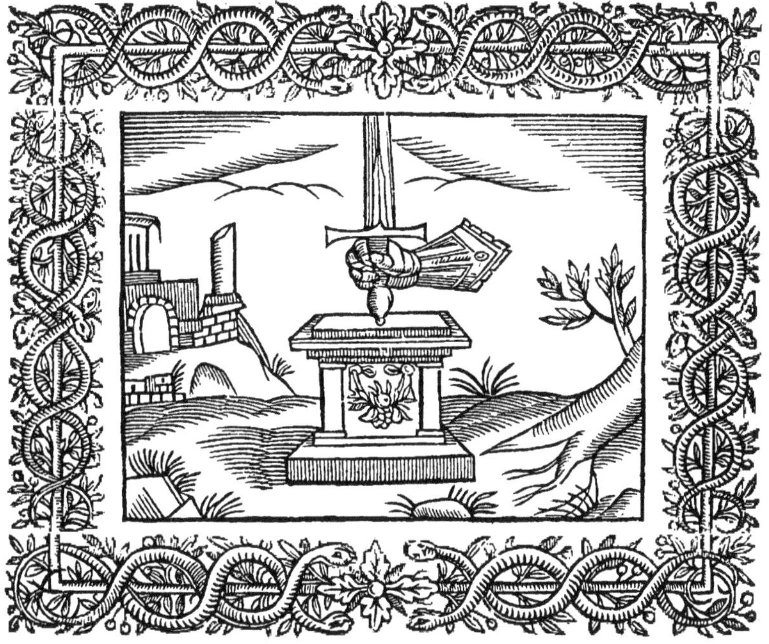

THE Monarches good, that doe deſerue the name
Of " Countrie Parents, by their loue and care
Of common-wealth, and to defend the ſame
From publicque harmes, by wiſe foreſight, prepare:
 * By louing heartes, are guarded ſurer farre,
 Then ſome vnweldie *SWIZZE*, or *IANIZAR*.

HENRY this once, thy Royall Impreſe ſtood,
To ſhew, thy foe ſhould find thee readie preſt,
For Church, and Country, to diſpend thy bloud,
When daunger, or occaſion did requeſt,
 And further, though the Trumpet ſterne did ceaſe,
 Thus evermore, to goe prepar'd in *PEACE*.

" Patres Patriæ

* Non ſic excubiæ, nec circumſtantia tela, quam tutatur amor. *Claudian: ad honor.*

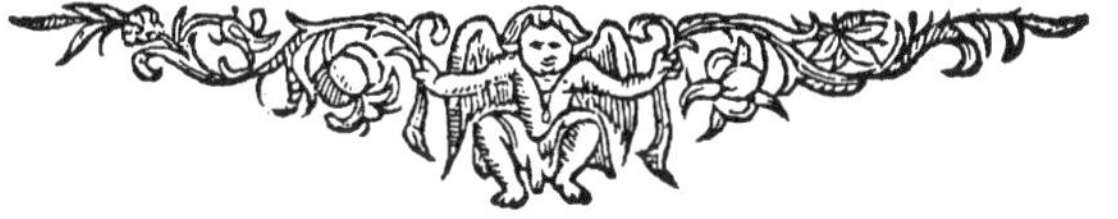

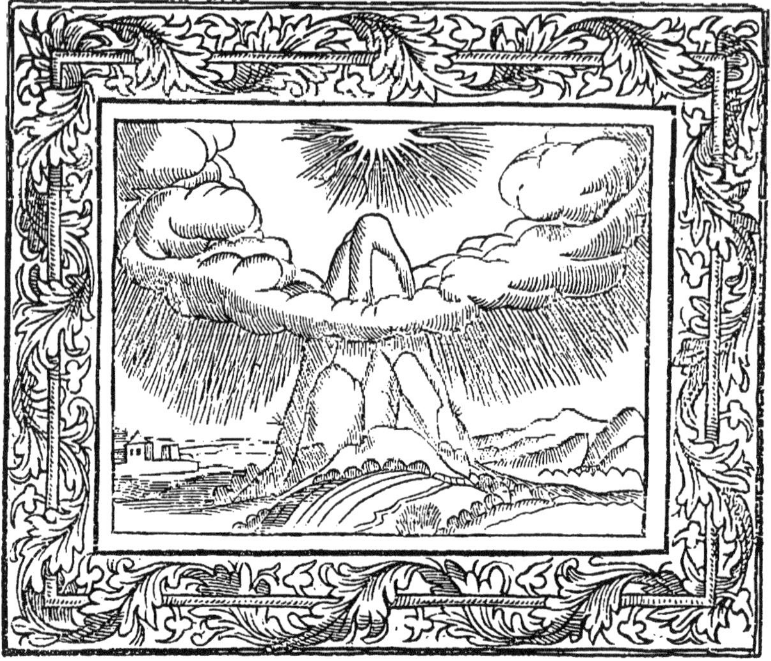

THE godly mind, that hath ſo oft aſſaid,
The perils that our frailtie here amate,
Through heauenly wiſedome, is no more afraid
Of Fortunes frowne, and bitter blaſtes of Fate:
For though in vale of woes, her dwelling be,
Her nobler part's aboue vntouch't and free.

For mortall thinges doe find their change below,
And nought can here defend vs from the ſhower,
Now greateſt windes doe threate our overthrow,
Our golden morne anon begins to lowre:
And while our hopes, are yet but in their ſap,
Their buds are blaſted by the Thunderclap.

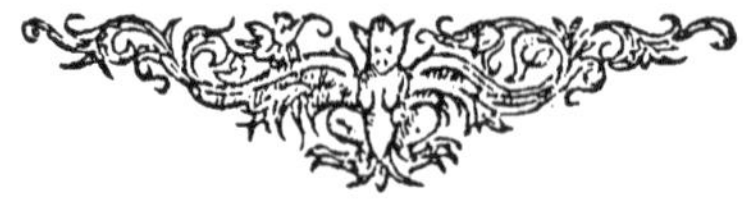

Ordo

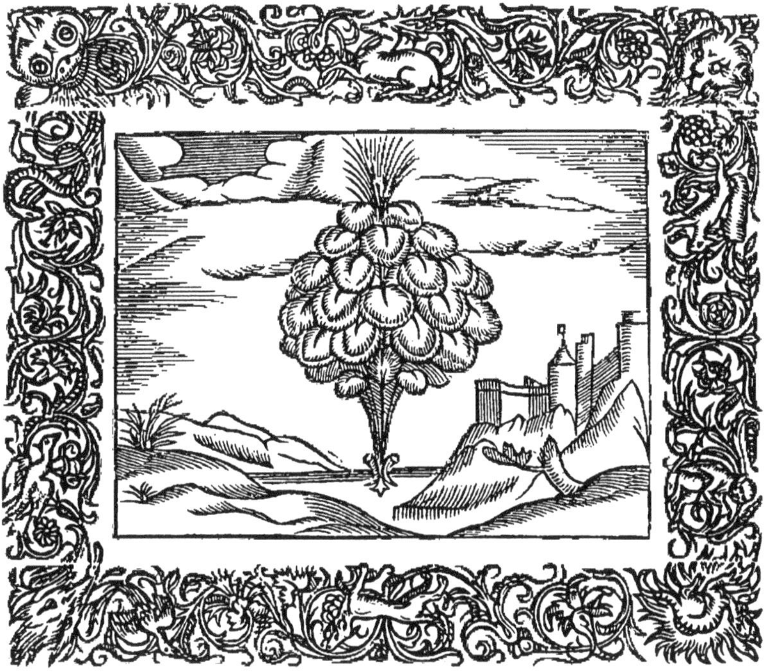

THE Common-wealth, whoſe Baſe is firmely laid
 On eveneſt ground, of Iuſtice and the right,
By time or chaunge, in vaine we ſee aſſaide,
But where affection overſwaies with might:
 Confuſion there, all vnto havock bringes,
 And vndermines, the thrones of mightieſt Kinges.

The Impreſe of King Stephen.

Our Engliſh *STEPHEN*, did take vnto him this
Faire falling Plume, reſembling beſt of all,
The new eſtabliſh't goverment of his,
Whereas each feather keepes his ranck and fall:
 So ſhould that ſtate, (let Fortune doe her worſt,)
 As faire, and firme, as ever at the firſt.

His

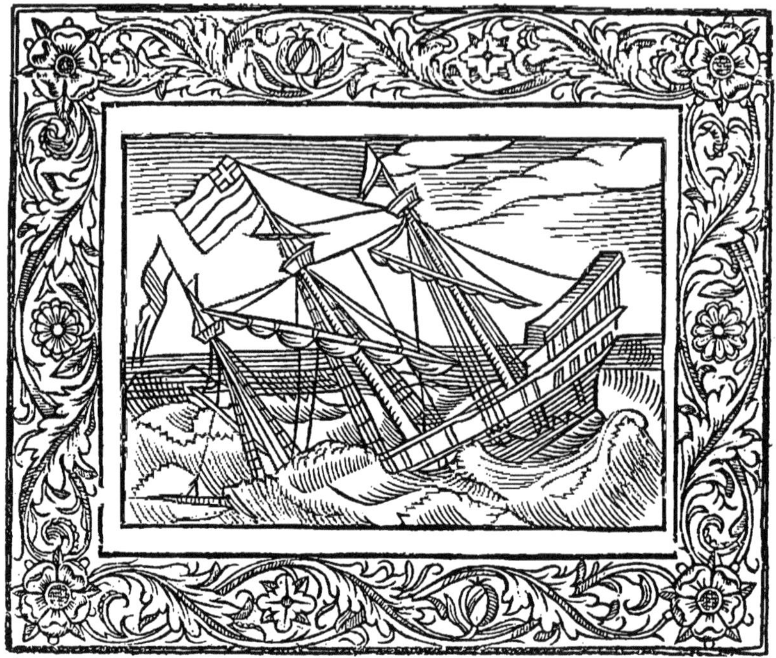

THE valiant mind, whome nothing can diſmay,
The loſſe of frendes, of goods, or long exile
From natiue countrie, perils on the Sea,
Night-watchings, hunger, thirſt, and howerly toile,
Takes courage, and the ſame abideth faſt,
With reſolution, even vnto the laſt.

Such ſhew'd himſelfe, *ÆNEAS* vnto thoſe
Of his poore remnant, on the *Tyrrhene Seas*;
When even diſpaire, their eies began to cloſe,
* We greater bruntes, haue borne (quoth he) then theſe:
And God, (my Mates,) when he ſhall pleaſe will ſend,
Vnto our greateſt miſeries an end.

* O paſſi graviora Deus dabit his quoque finem. *Virgil: Æneid:* 2.

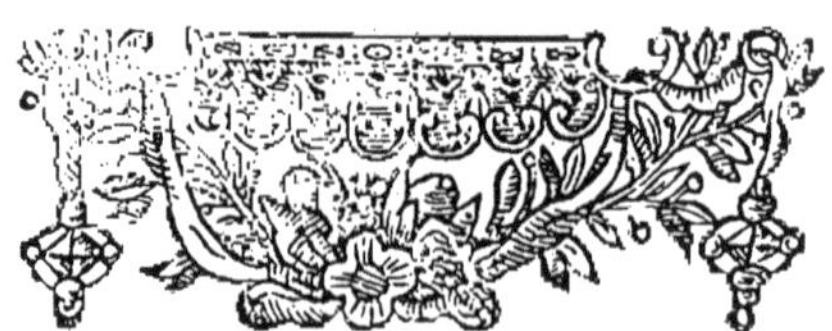

In

In vos hic valet.
Nicolas VVhite.

Anagramma Authoris.

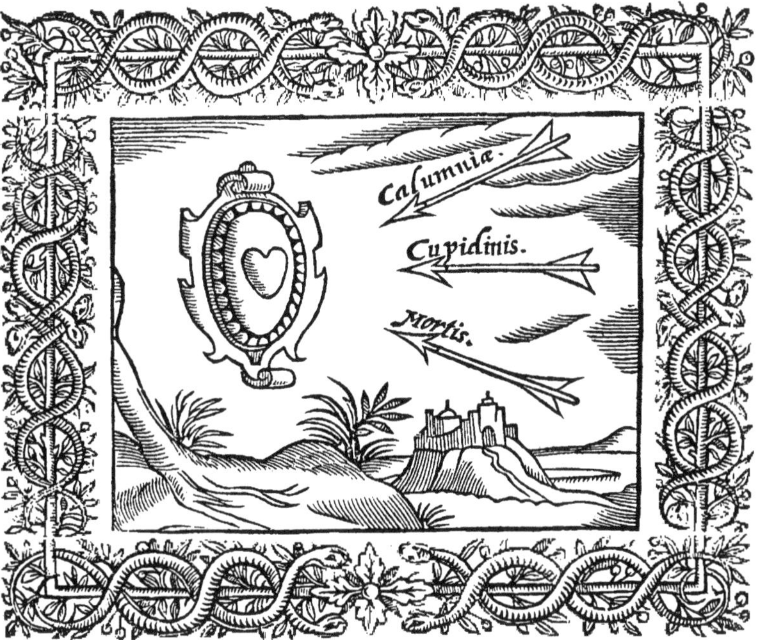

WHO ſtriues to keepe a heart and conſcience pure,
Devoide of vice, and inward guilt of Sinne:
Is guarded by his Innocence more ſure,
And witneſſe of an honeſt mind within,
Then if he were in compleate armour clad,
* Or Bow and quiver of the Moore he had.

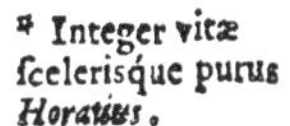
* Integer vitæ ſcelerisque purus *Horatius.*

For Innocence reſembled by the *WHITE*,
And manly courage by the conſtant heart,
Way not a ſtraw the force of *SLAVNDERS* might,
DEATHES Ebone ſhaft, or *CVPIDS* golden dart:
When, whome Affection, or their guilt doe wound,
Even at the firſt, are ſtricken to the ground.

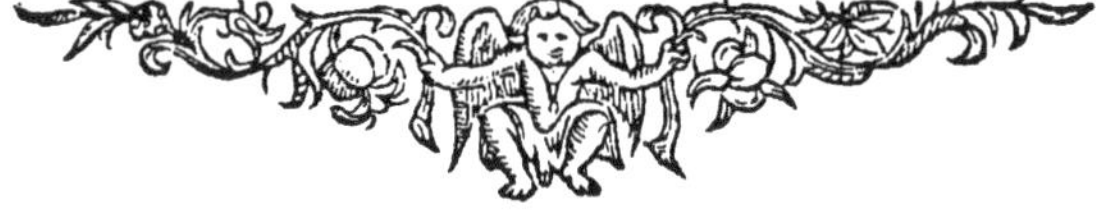

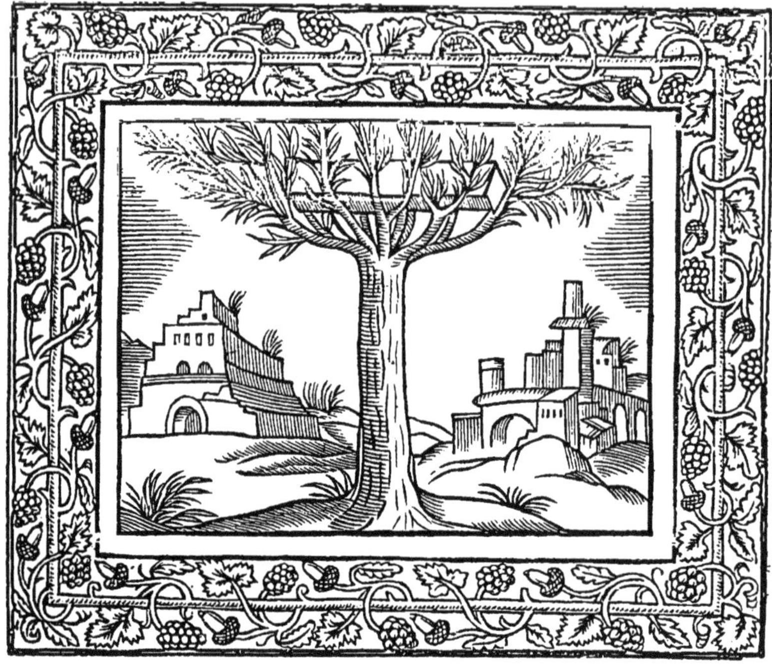

THE *Cipreſſe tree*, the more with weight oppreſt,
The more (they ſay) the braunch will vpward ſhoot,
Plini: in Hiſtor: natural:
And ſince the bodie doth reſemble beſt,
A Columne ſtrong and ſtately from the roote:
The Auntients would, it ſhould the Impreſe be,
Of Reſolution, and true Conſtancie.

Though Fortune frowne, and doe her worſt to bend,
Th' vndaunted ſpirit with her wearie weight,
His vertue yet, doth ever vpward tend,
And he himſelfe, ſtandes irremooued ſtreight,
Laughing to ſcorne, the paper blaſtes of Fate,
That would remooue, or vndermine his ſtate.

Excelſus animus non movetur minis, aut Fortunæ ſævientis procellis. *Seneca.*

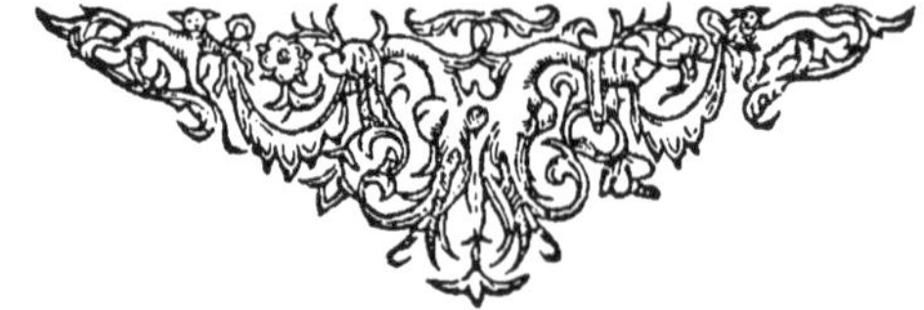

Vane

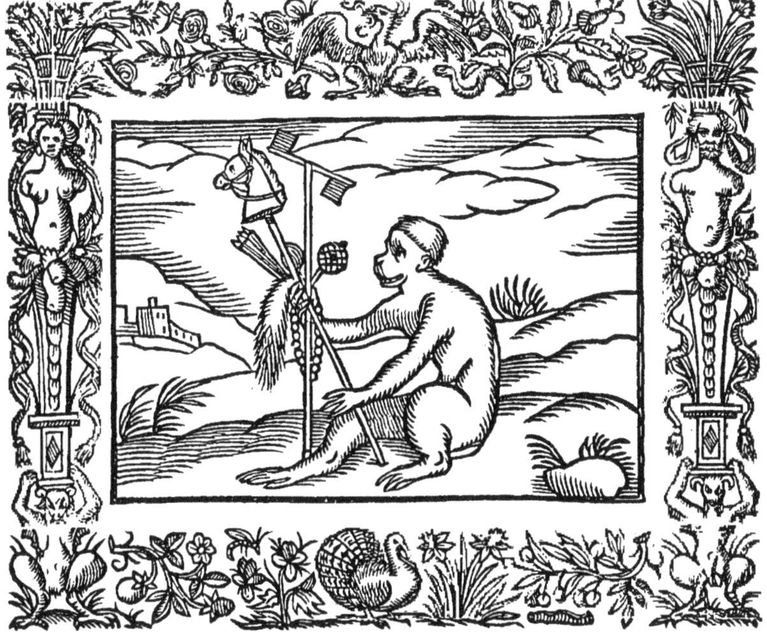

RICH *NAVPALVS*, hath ſecretly convaid,
Our Engliſh fleece ſo long beyond the ſea,
That not for wit, but for his wealth tis ſaid,
Hee's thence return'd a worthy Knight awaie,
And brought vs back, beades, Hobbie-horſes, boxes,
Fannes, Windmills, Ratles, Apes, and tailes of Foxes.

And now like *IASON*, vp and downe he goes,
As if he had th' *Heſperian Dragon* ſlaine,
And equaliz'd in worth, thoſe old Heroe's,
That inthe *ARGO* cut the Grecian maine:
Honour thou didſt, but doe his valour right,
When of the fleece, thou dubbeſt him a Knight.

Vellera divendit Belgis laudata Britannûm,
Sed nugas referens NAVPLVS inde domum: *Baſilic: Doron.*
Vellere factus eques, volitat novus alter IASON
Vileſcit (rides) velleris ordo nimis.

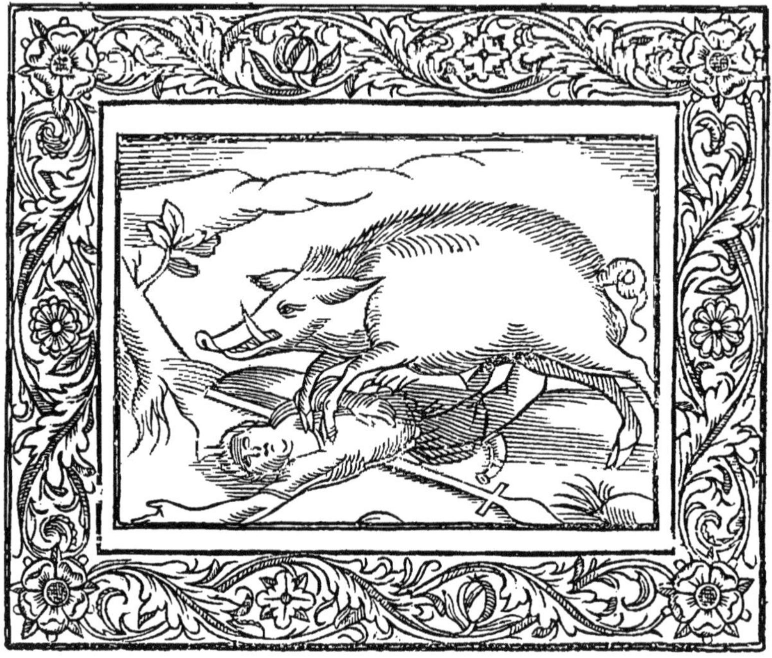

Ovid: Metam 10

I MVCH did muſe, why *Venus* could not brooke,
The ſavadge Boare, and Lion cruell feirce,
Since Kinges and Princes, haue ſuch pleaſure tooke
In hunting: haply cauſe a Boare did peirce
Her *Adon* faire, who better lik't the ſport,
Then ſpend his daies, in wanton pleaſures court.

Which fiction though deviſd by Poets braine,
It ſignifies vnto the Reader this;
Such exerciſe Loue will not entertaine,
Who liketh beſt, to liue in Idlenes:
The foe to vertue, Cancker of the wit,
That bringes a thouſand miſeries with it.

Exoſos Veneri lepores mirâre fugaces,
Silueſtres ceruos, ſetigerumque genus?
Ex animis cecidit vel quod * Cynarëius Heros,
Aut his quod non ſit luſibus aptus amor.

* Adonis.

Zelus

To my Father, Mr. Henry Peacham, of Leverton in Holland, in the Countie of Linc:

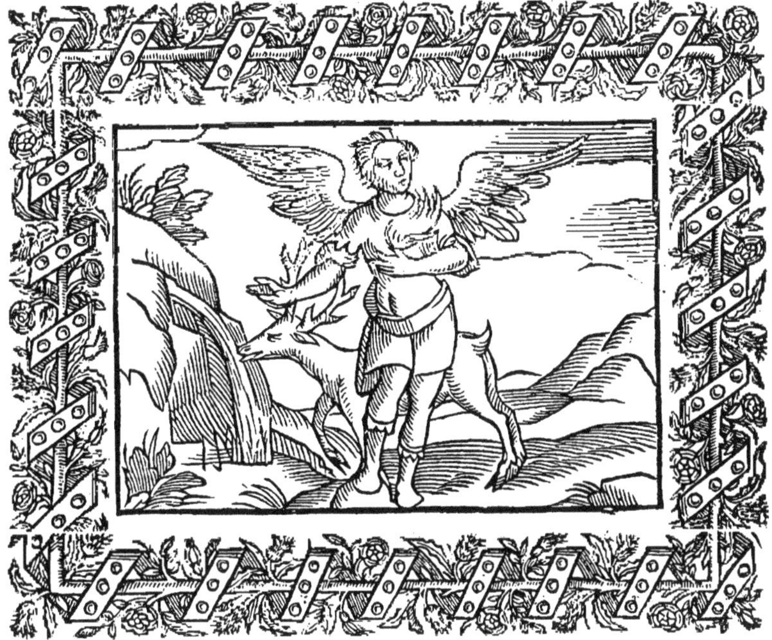

WITH Breaſt enflam'd, and longing heartes deſire,
Thus winged *Zeale*, to heauen-ward caſtes her eie:
And loathing what the world doth moſt admire,
Vpborne by Faith, aſcendes aboue the skie:
Whereby Oh God, thy miſteries we learne,
And all beyond, our reaſons ſight diſcerne.

And as the *Hart* emboſ't, doth long to taſt
The pearly-trickling ſtreame, or Chriſtall fount,
Even ſo the ſoule, by Sinne purſu'de and chaſ'd,
Thee, thee, (oh Lord) deſires, who doſt ſurmount
All treaſures, pleaſures, which we here poſſeſſe,
The ſumme and ſubſtance, of our happines.

Nullum omnipotenti Deo tale eſt ſacrificium, quale eſt zelus animarum. *Gregor: Homil: 12 in Ezechiel:*

Animi acrimonia cum ad Pietatem acceſſerit, zelum parit, zelus autem fidei præſidium eſt. *Nazianzen: orat: 23.*

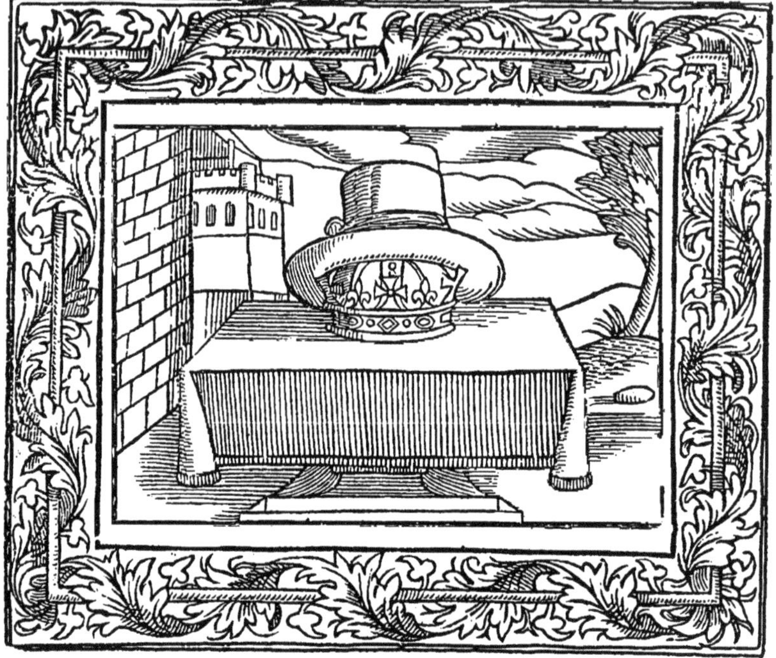

There is more pride, vnder one of their black Bonnets, thé vnder Alexanders Diademe. King Iames in his Basilicon Doron:

Earle Gourie one of the greatest Puritanes of his time in Scotland, in his travailes thorough Fraunce and Italie, vsed with his Diamond, (for the most part) to draw in his Chāber windowe, a man in armour, with a Sword in his right hand, pointing towards a Crowne, adding this or the like word, *Te solum*, which yet rēaines in many places to be seene, what he meant hereby it might easily haue bin ghessed.

VPON a Crowne with pretious Iemmes beset,
Say what's the reason thus a hat we see,
Since Diadem's of Princes ever yet,
From base controule, haue beene exempt and free:
There is a sect, whome *PVRITANS* they call,
Whose pride this Figure fitteth best of all.

Not such I meane, as are of Faith sincere,
And to doe good endevour all they can,
Would all the world of their religion were,
We taxe th'aspiring factious Puritan:
Whose * Paritie, doth worst confusion bring,
And Pride presumes to overlooke his King.

* Paritas confusionis mater. *August:*

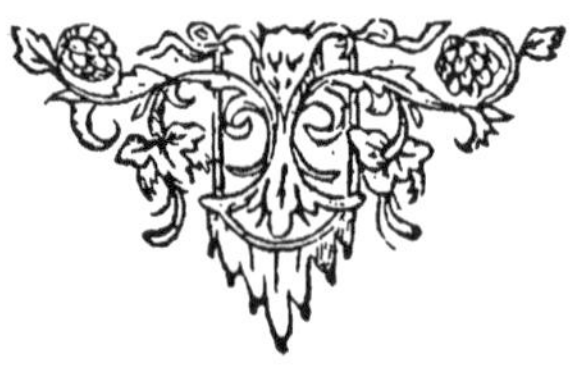

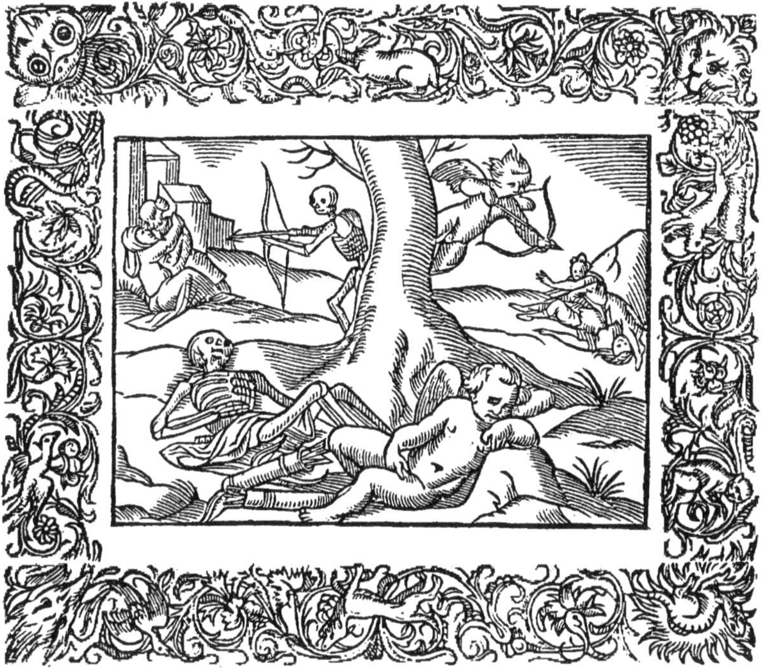

DEATH meeting once, with *CVPID* in an Inne,
Where roome was ſcant, togeither both they lay.
Both wearie, (for they roving both had beene,)
Now on the morrow when they ſhould away,
CVPID Death's quiver at his back had throwne,
And *DEATH* tooke *CVPIDS*, thinking it his owne.

By this o're-ſight, it ſhortly came to paſſe,
That young men died, who readie were to wed:
And age did revell with his bonny-laſſe,
Compoſing girlonds for his hoarie head:
Invert not Nature, oh ye Powers twaine,
Giue *CVPID'S* dartes, and *DEATH* take thine againe.

Hoc idem habet Whitnæus in Embl: quod bona cum illius venia ab Authore etiam mutuatus ſum.

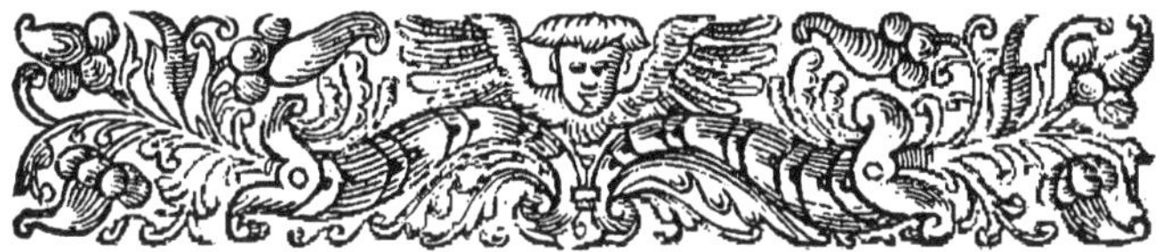

Latet

---VSIANIVS armis Herculis ad postē fixis latet abditus agro. *Horat:*

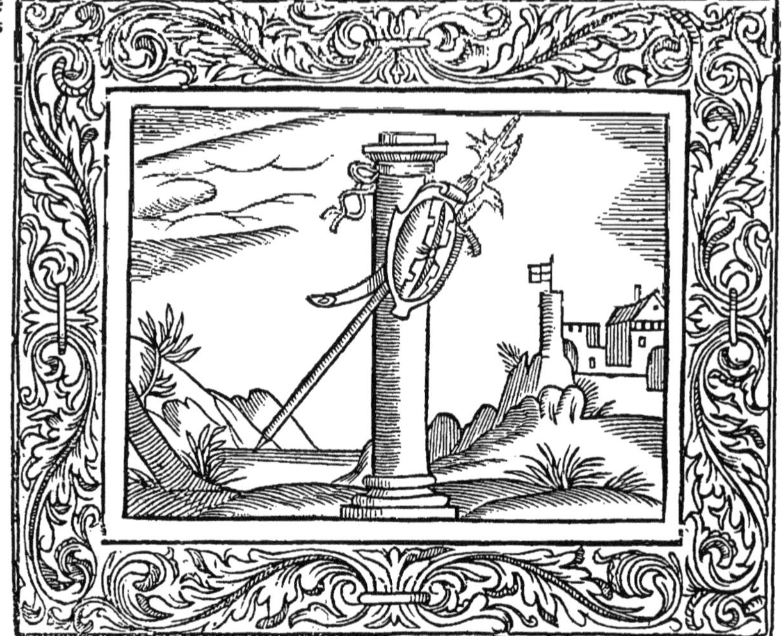

THE valiant mind that once had most delight,
By sea and land to make his prowesse knowne,
And in defence of King, and countries right,
So much his valour, and his vertue showne,
Some wished port, doth at the last desire,
And home whereto in age he may retire.

For infinite's the summe of world affaires,
* Nor new, nor straunge, that doe afflict the mind,
And shew before the day our silver haires,
Yea even before we can experience find:
That frailest man, by course of nature dies,
* Even at his first beginning to be wise.

* Nihil novū sub Sole. *Salomon in Ecclesiaste*.

Γηράσκω δ' αἰεὶ πολλὰ διδασκόμενος. Solon.

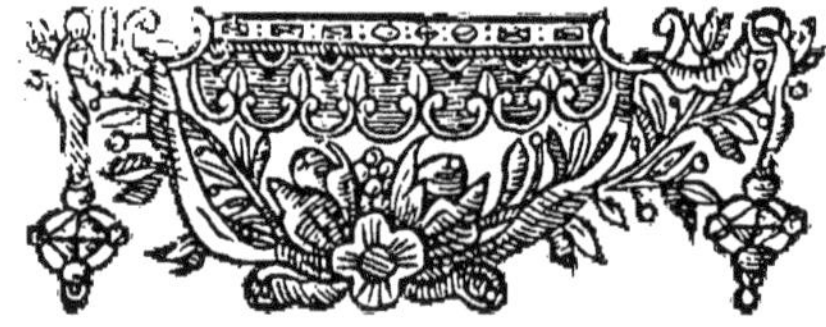

Sine

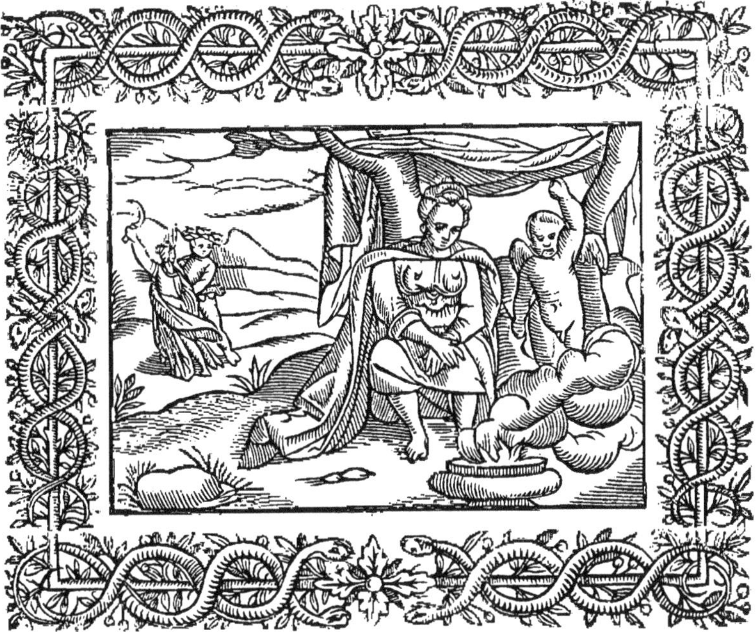

SAY *Cytharæan* maid, why with thy ſonne,
Both handes and feete thou warmeſt at the fire?
Who wont your ſelues, t'enkindle many a one,
With gentle flames, of kindly loues deſire:
I gheſſe cauſe BACCHVS is not preſent heere,
With mirthfull wine, nor CERES. with her cheere.

Where Temp'rance and Sobrietie do raigne,
There luſtfull vice, and pleaſure frozen are:
And vertue beſt, there liketh to remaine;
When often times th' effectes of daintie fare,
And drunken healthes, are quarrelles and debate,
Blaſpheming, whoredome, oathes and deadlie hate.

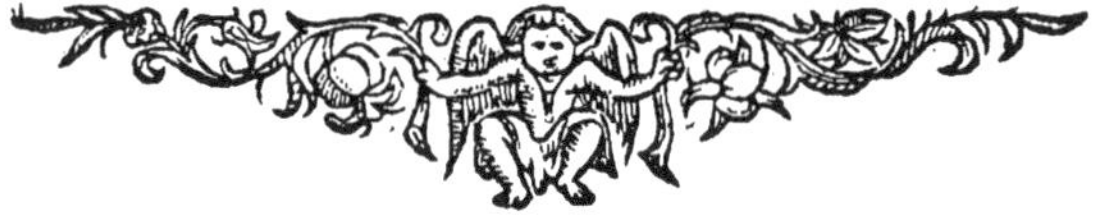

To the no lesse vertuous then faire, Mrs. Anne Dudleie,

è l' nuda DIANA.

Anagramma. Anna Dudleia.

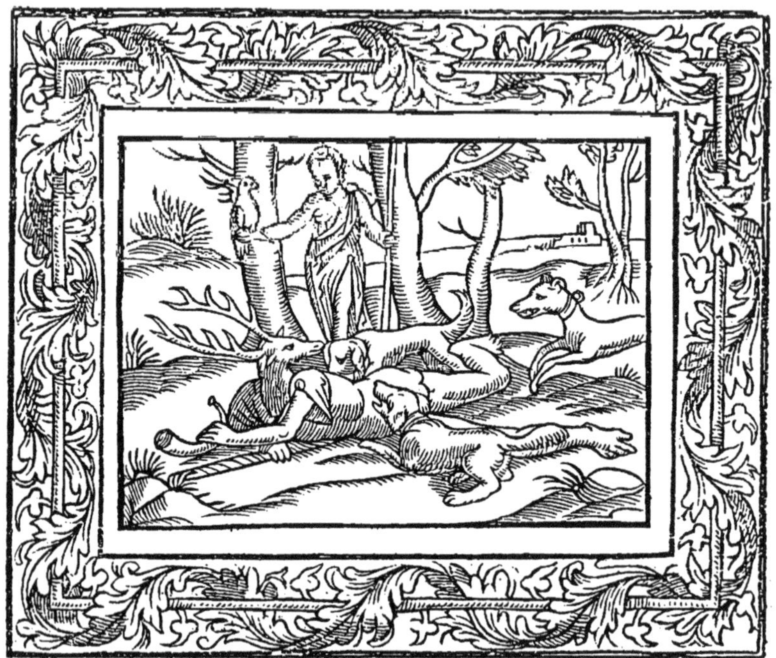

DIANA chast, doth eagerly pursue
With swiftest houndes, the aiery-footed Stagge:
And while they keepe, the merry chase in view,
The woodes with Ecchoʼs thundring, Loue doth lagge
Behind the thickets, and with arrow keene,
Doth lie in waite, to wound this maiden Queene.

But all in vaine he doth his shaftes bestow,
For Labour did this Goddesse faire defend,
And sau'd her harmelesse from his deadly bow,
And poisʼnous dartes: so if thou dost intend,
To overcome the force of *Cupids* might,
Flie Idlenesse, and then he leaues thee streight.

Gratis

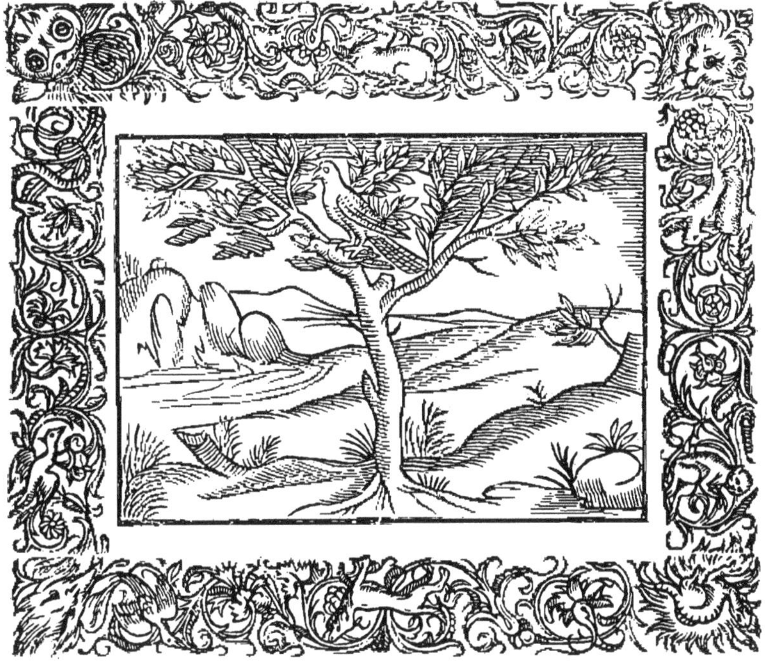

THE gentle Merlion, wearied long with flight,
While on the ſpray in ſhadie groue ſhe ſleepes,
With tender foote, a Larke ſhe holdeth light,
Which till the morning carefully ſhe keepes,
Then lets it goe, and leaſt ſhe ſhould that day
Præie on the ſame, ſhe flies another way.

Such thanckfullnes in bird and beaſt we find,
By Natures firſt inſtinct obſerued ſtill,
When worſer, man in benefits is blind,
Nay oftentimes, for good will render ill:
And rather ſeeke ingratefully his blood,
That ſau'd his life, or daily gaue him foode.

Fallitur egregio quiſquis ſub principe credit
Servitium, nunquam libertas gratior extat, *Claudian 3. Stilic. com.*
Quam ſub Rege pio ----

Anagramma Nominis Authoris.

Hinc ſuper hæc, Muſa.
Henricus Peachamus.

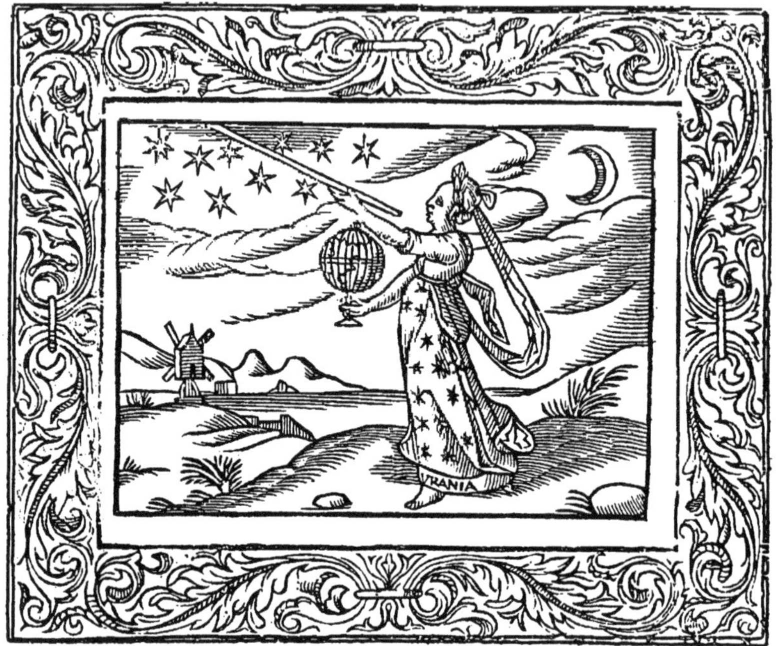

BID now my Muſe, thy lighter taske adieu,
As ſhaken bloſſome of a better fruite,
And with *VRANIA* thy Creator view,
To ſing of him, or evermore be mute:
Let muddy Lake, delight the ſenſuall thought,
Loath thou the earth, and lift thy ſelfe aloft.

Repent not (though) thy time ſo idlely ſpent,
The cunning'ſt Artiſt ere he can, (we ſee)
Some rareſt Modell bring to his Intent,
Much heweth off in Superfluitie:
And many a pretious hower, I know is loſt,
Ere ought is wrought to countervaile the coſt.

Movere

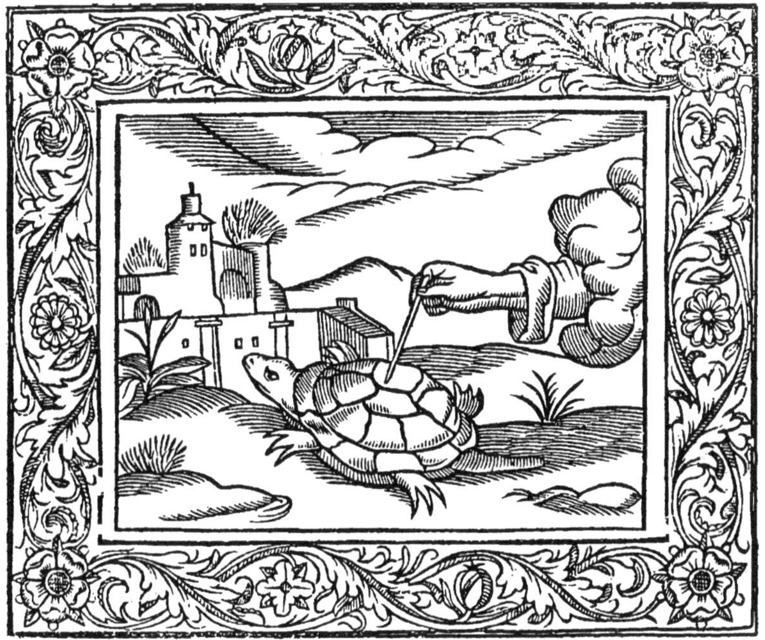

SO quicke of ſenſe as hath experience taught,
The *Tortoiſe* liues within her armed ſhell,
That if wee lay the lighteſt ſtraw aloft,
Or touch that Caſtle wherein ſhe doth dwell,
Shee feeles the ſame and quickly doth retire,
A worke of Nature we do moſt admire,

So many men are in theire Nature prone,
To make the worſt of matters vaine and light,
And for a ſtraw will take occaſion,
In choller mooú'd to quarrell and to fight,
Then meddle thou the leaſt for feare of wrong,
But moſt of all beware a laviſh tongue.

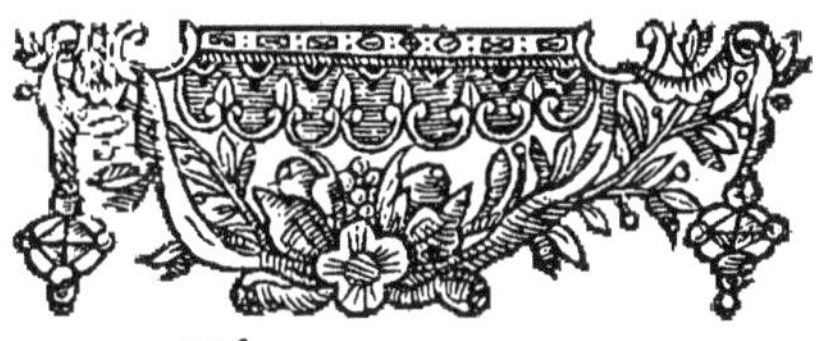

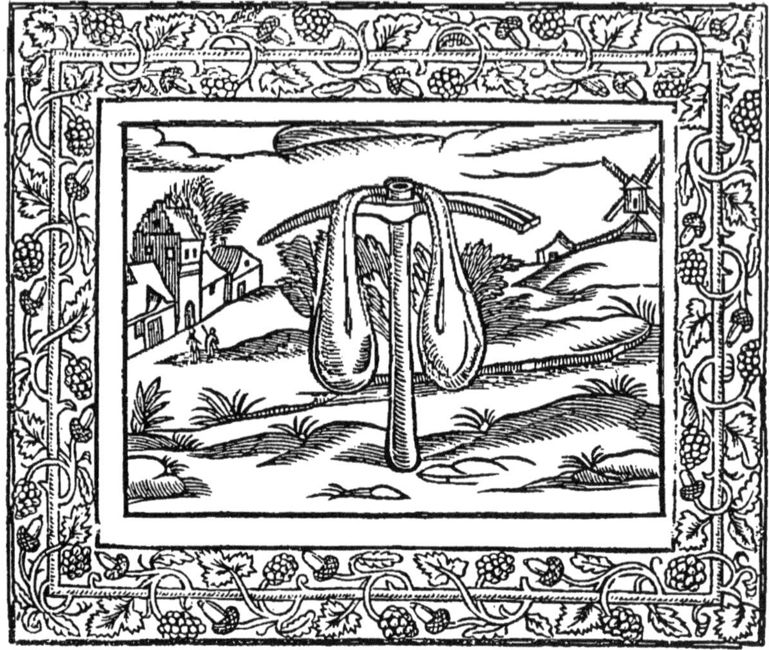

WHAT ſhall we doe? now tell me gentle Muſe,
For we welnigh haue finiſhed our taske,
Thy tender hand could never Mattock vſe,
Full well I wot, nor canſt thou humblie aske
At greatnes gate, or for reverſions ſue,
As beggars, and the baſely minded doe.

Deſire of God but this, when thou art old,
To haue a home, and ſomewhat of thine owne,
To keepe thy ſelfe from hunger and the cold,
And where thou maieſt in quiet ſing alone:
For thinke it hell, * to liue as bird in cage,
At others curt'ſie, in thy latter age.

* Alterius non ſit qui ſuus eſſe poteſt: frequens Paracelſo dictum.

Seneca in octau:

Bene paupertas humili tecto contecta latet,
Quatiunt altæ ſæpe procellæ,
Aut evertit fortuna Domos.

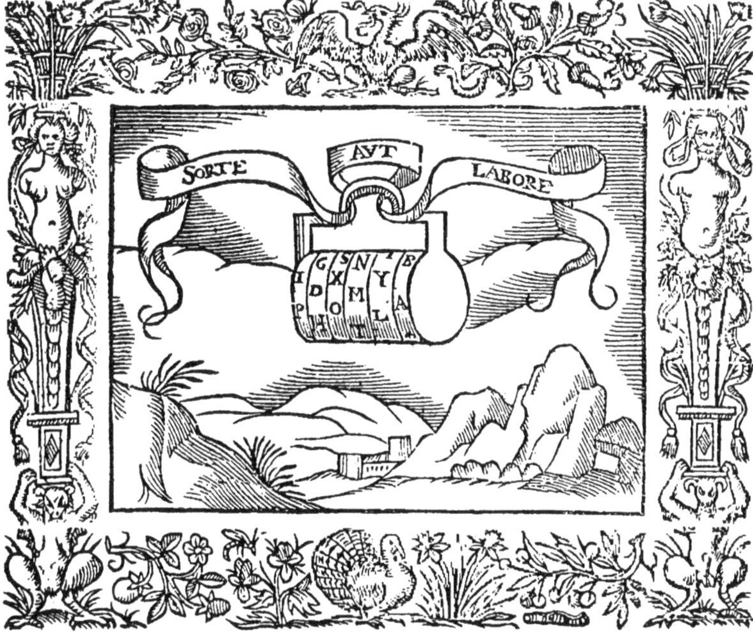

I F neither art, by birth, nor fortune bleſt,
With meanes to liue, or anſwere thy deſire,
With cheerefull heart, on labour ſet thy reſt,
To bring to paſſe the thing thou doſt require,
For lot, or labour, muſt our calling giue,
And find the word, that all doe ſeeke, *TO LIVE*.

Though thouſands haue beene raiſed by their frendes,
By death, by dowries, even when leaſt they thought,
The Lord a bleſſing, ſtill to labour ſendes,
When lightly come, doth lightly goe as oft:
And goodes ill got, by vſe, and wicked gaine,
Doe ſeldome to the ſecond heire remaine.

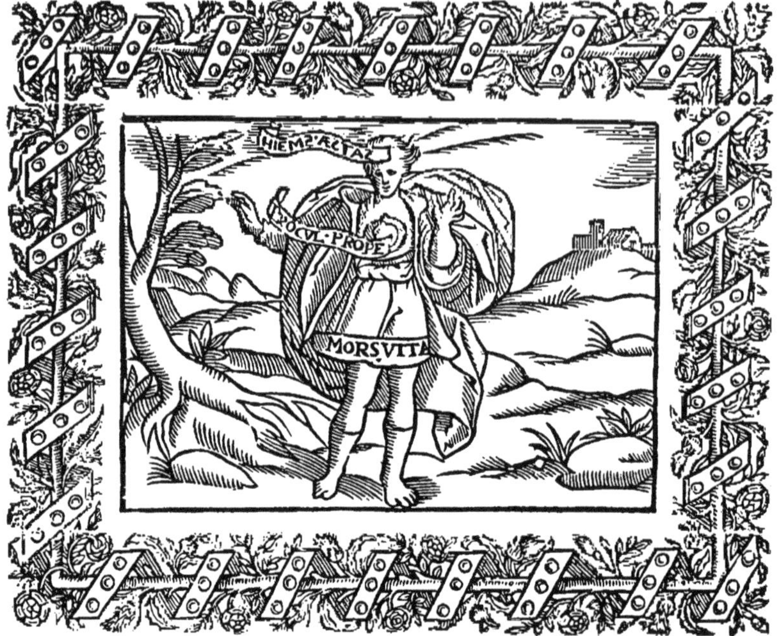

THERE was in Rome a goodlie ſtatue fram'd
Of youthfull hew, attraied all in greene,
Which of the people was *TRVE-FRENDSHIP* nam'd:
Winter and Sommer, on his brow were ſeene:
Within his breaſt, his heart did plaine appeare,
Whereon theſe wordes were written, FARRE, and NEERE.

Vpon his skirt, ſtoode *LIFE* and *DEATH* below,
To teſtifie in life and death his loue,
That farre and neere, with open heart do ſhow,
Nor place, nor ſpace, true frendſhip ſhould remoue:
* Winter and ſommer, whatſoever came,
In faire or foule, we ſhould be ſtill the ſame.

* Delicata eſt Amicitia quæ amicorum fœlicitatẽ ſequitur: *Hieron: ſuper Mich: Prophetam.*

Heſiod: Μηδὲ πολύξεινον μηδ' ἄξεινον καλέεσθαι

Hieron: in Epiſt: ad Ruffinum. *Obſecro te ne amicum qui diu quæritur, vix invenitur, difficile ſervatur, pariter cum oculis, mente amittas.*

Nulli

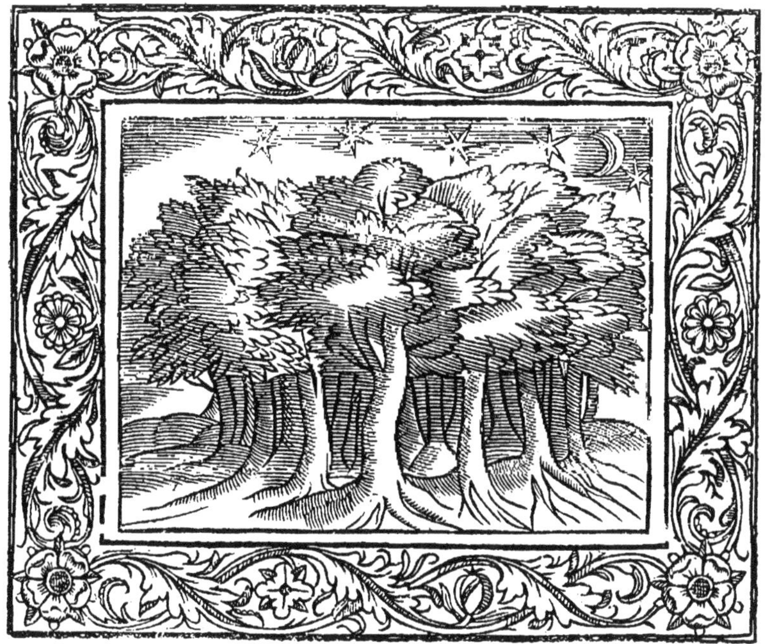

A SHADIE Wood, pourtraicted to the ſight,
With vncouth pathes, and hidden waies vnknowne:
Reſembling *CHAOS*, or the hideous night,
Or thoſe ſad Groues, by banke of *ACHERON*
With banefull *Ewe*, and *Ebon* overgrowne:
Whoſe thickeſt boughes, and inmoſt entries are
Not peirceable, to power of any ſtarre.

Thy Impreſe *SILVIUS*, late I did deviſe,
To warne the what (if not) thou oughtſt to be,
Thus inward cloſe, vnſearch'd with outward eies,
With thouſand angles, light ſhould never ſee:
For fooles that moſt are open-hearted free,
Vnto the world, their weakenes doe bewray,
And to the net, the firſt themſelues betray.

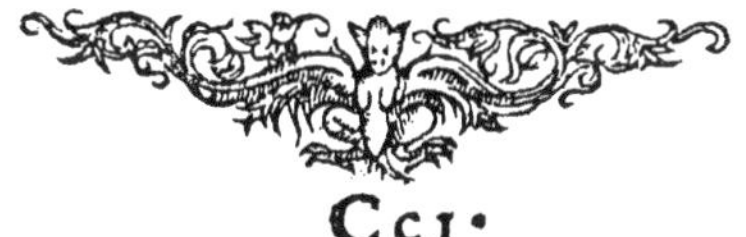

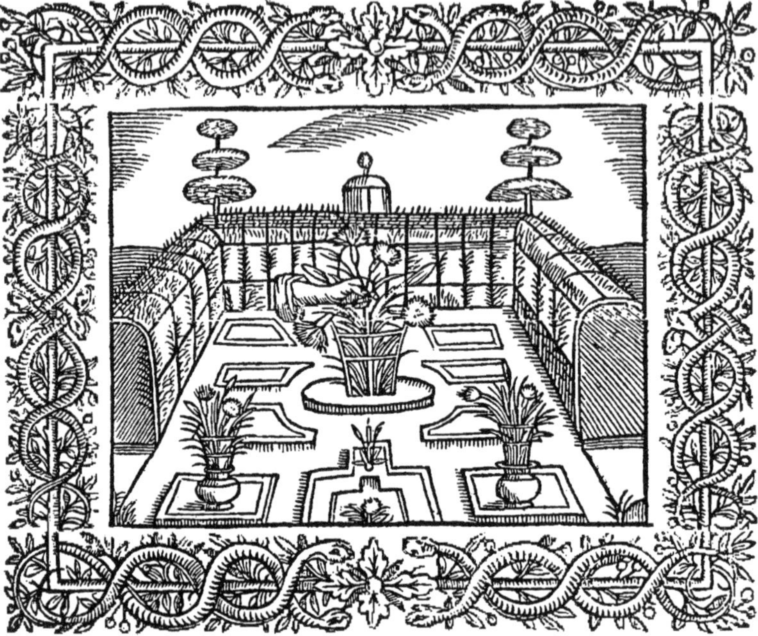

A GARDEN thinke this spatious world to be,
Where thou by God the owners leaue dost walke,
And art allow'd in all varietie,
One only flower to crop from tender stalke,
(As thou thinkst good) for beautie or the smell,
Or some one else, whose beautie doth exell.

This only flower, is some one calling fit,
And honest course wherein to leade thy life,
Thy selfe applieng carefully to it,
Or else the heedie choosing of thy wife:
Wherein thou wisely dost thy selfe preferre,
Or to thy ruine ever after, erre.

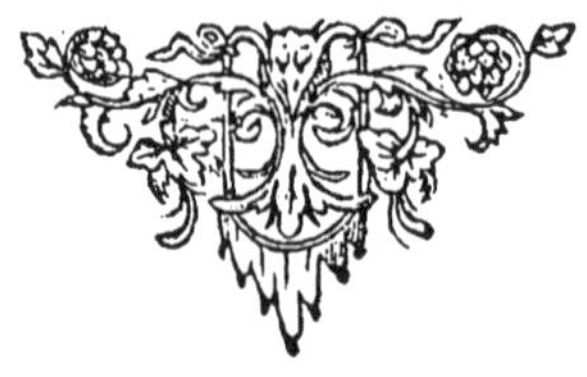

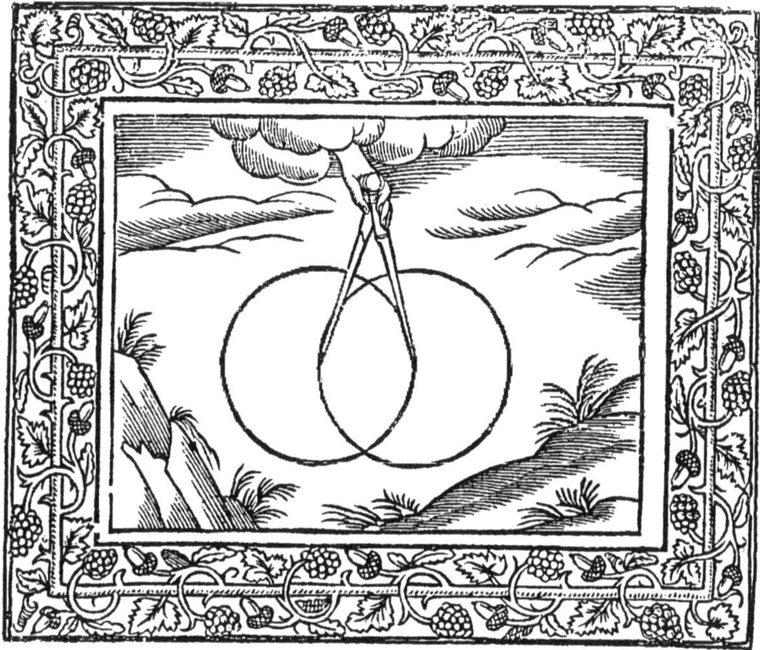

EXESSE we loath, of want we most complaine,
The golden meane we prooue to be the best,
Let idle fits refresh thy daylie paine,
And with some Labour exercise thy rest,
For overmuch of either, duls the spright,
And robs our life, of comfort and delight.

If that thou wouldst acquaint thee with the Muse,
Withdraw thy selfe, and be thou least alone,
Even when alone, as *SOLON* oft did vse,
For no such frend to Contemplation,
And our sweete studies, as the private life,
Remote from Citie, and the vulgar strife.

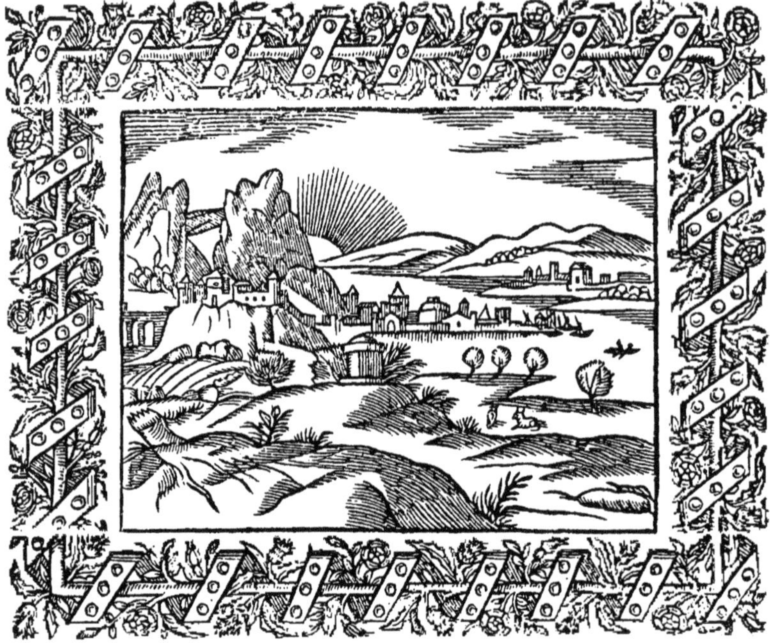

WERT thou thy life at libertie to choose,
And as thy birth, so hadst thy beeing free,
The Citie thou shouldst bid adieu, my Muse,
And from her streetes, as her infection flee:
Where *CHAOS* and *CONFVSION* wee see,
Aswell of language, as of differing heartes,
A bodie severed in a thousand parts.

Thy solitarie * Academe should be
Some shadie groue, vpon the *THAMES* faire side,
Such as we may neere princely *RICHMOND* see,
Or where a long doth siluer *SEVERNE* slide,
Or *AVON* courtes, faire *FLORA* in her pride:
There shouldst thou sit at long desired rest,
And thinke thy selfe, aboue a Monarch blest,

* A wood neere Athens, wherein the Phylosophers vsed to studie.

There

There moughtst thou sing thy sweete Creators praise,
And turne at quiet ore some holy booke;
Or tune the Accent of thy harmelesse laies
Vnto the murmur of the gentle brooke:
Whiles round about thy greedy eie doth looke,
  Obseruing * wonders in some flower by,
  This bent, that leafe, this worme, that butterflie.

* τὸ θαῦμαστον in re minima esse pulchre dixit. *Aristoteles*.

Where mightst thou view at full the Hemisphære
On some faire Mountaine, in a Summers night,
In spangles there embraudered is the * *BEARE*,
And here the *FISH*, there *THESEVS* * louer bright,
The watry *HYADS*, here deceiue our sight,
  ERIDANOS, and there *ORION* bound,
  Another way the silver *SWANNE* is found.

* Vrsa maior and minor.

* Ariadne.

Or wouldst thou Musick to delight thine eare,
Step but aside into the neighbour spring,
Thou shalt a thousand wing'd Musitians heare,
Each praising in his kind the heauenly King:
Here *PHILOMEL*, doth her shrill TREBLE sing,
  The *THRVSH* a TENOR, off a little space,
  Some matelesse *DOVE*, doth murmur out the BASE.

Geometry or wishest thou to learne,
Obserue the Mill, the Crane, or Country Cart,
Wherein with pleasure, soone thou shalt discerne
The groundes, and vse of this admired Art,
The rules of *NVMBRING*, for the greatest part,
  As they were first devis'd by Country Swaines,
  So still the Art with them entire remaines.

If lou'st thy health, preferre the Country Aire,
Thy Garden fore the Pothecaries shoppe,
Where wholesome herbes, shall it at full repaire,
Before a Quint'sence, or an oily droppe:
There groweth the *Balme*, there shooteth *Endiue* vp:
  Here *Pæonie* for th' *Epilepsie* good,
  There *Dill*, and *Hysope*, best to stanch the bloud.

The cooling *Sorrell*, and the *Perslie* whot,
The *Smallage*, for a bruise, or swelling best,
The *Mercurie*, the formost in the Pot,
The *Lavander*, beloued for the Chest,
The *Costmarie*, to entertaine the guest,
The *Rosemarie*, and *Fenel*, seldome set,
The lowlie *Daisie*, and sweete *Violet*.

Nor Princes richest *Arras* may compare
With some small plot, where Natures skill is showen,
Perfuming sweetely all the neighbour aire,
While thousand cullors in a night are blowne:
Here's a light Crimson, there a deeper one,
A Maidens blush, here Purples, there a white,
Then all commingled for our more delight.

Withall (as in some rare limn'd booke) we find,
Here, painted Lectures of Gods sacred will,
The *Daisie*, teacheth lowlines of mind,
The *Camomill*, we should be patient still,
The *Rue*, our hate of vices poison ill,
The *Woodbine*, that we should our frendship hold,
Our Hope, the *Sav'rie*, in the bitterst cold.

Yet loue the Citie, as the kindly Nurse
Of all good Artes, and faire Civillitie:
Where though with good, be intermix't the worse,
That most disturbe our sweete Tranquillitie:
Content thy selfe, till thine Abillitie,
And better hap, shall answere thy desire,
* But Muse beware, least we too high aspire.

* Vive tibi, et longe nomina magna fuge: *Ovid*: 1 *Trist*. 4.

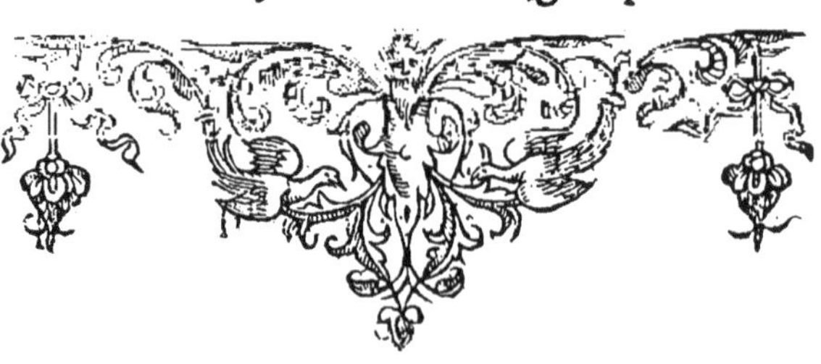

Omnis

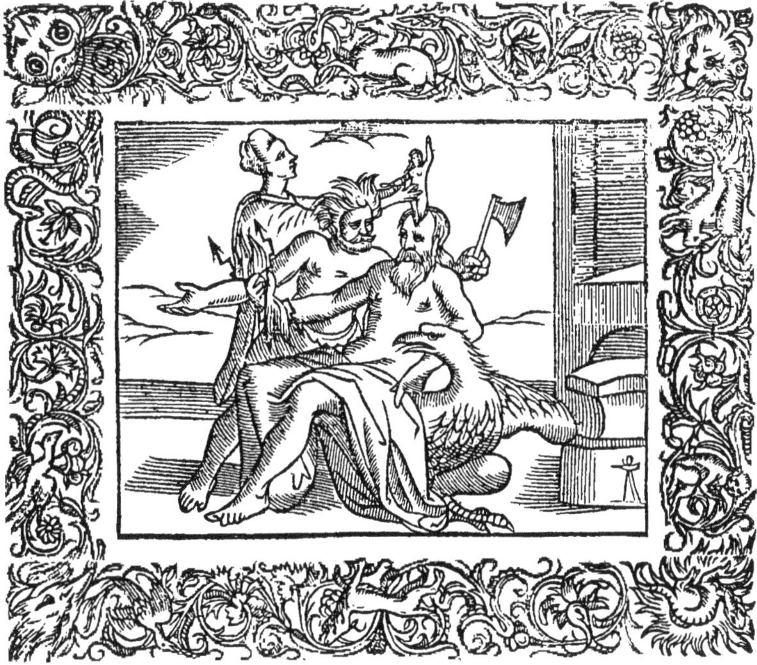

THE Poets faigne, *IOVE* to haue beene with child,
But very ſtraunge, conceiu'd within his head,
And knowing not, his burthen how to yeeld,
Lo! *MVLCIBER* doth bring the God abed,
By cutting with an Axe, his skull in two,
When iſſueth *PALLAS* forth, with much adoe.

By *PALLAS*, is all heavenly wiſdome ment,
Which not from Nature, and our ſelues proceedes,
But is from God, immediately ſent,
(For in our ſelues, how little goodnes breedes)
That threefold power of the Soule againe
Reſembling God, reſideth in our braine.

Some wits of men, ſo dull and barren are,
That without helpe of Art, no fruite they bring,
Whoſe Midwife muſt be toile, and endleſſe care,
And Conſtancie, effecting every thing:
And thoſe who wanting Eloquence, are mute,
Some other way like *IOVE* muſt yeeld their fruite.

Divina

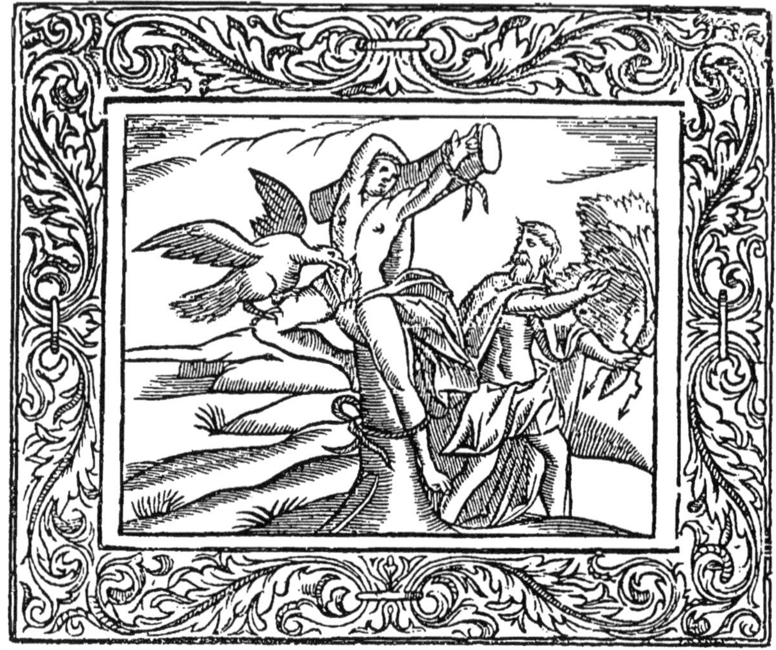

THE greedie Eagle here, vpon the tree,
PROMETHEVS heart with teene doth præy vpon,
But this example doth admonish thee
On wretches poore to haue compassion:
To pitie those, on whome doth fortune frowne,
And Tyrant-like, not more to crush them downe.

when the Oake's downe, every one gathers stickes. *Schol: Theocrit:*

Minimum debet liberé, cui nimium libet. *Seneca in Troad:*

This pleaseth God, this Pietie commaundes,
Nature, and Reason, * bids vs doe the like,
Yea though our foes, doe fall into our handes,
Wee should * haue mercie, not in malice strike:
Who helpes the sick, and pities the oppressed,
He liues to God, and doubtlesse dieth blessed.

* Ignoscendo auxit magnitudinem pop: Romanus. *Salust:*

* Severitas amittit assiduitate authoritatem. *Seneca 1 de Clementia.*

Pulchrum est eminere inter illustres viros,
Consulere patriæ, parcere afflictis,
Fera cæde abstulere, tempus atque iræ dare;
Orbi quietem, Sæculo pacem suo,
Hæc summa virtus, petitur hac Cœlum via.

Seneca in Octavio.

Homo

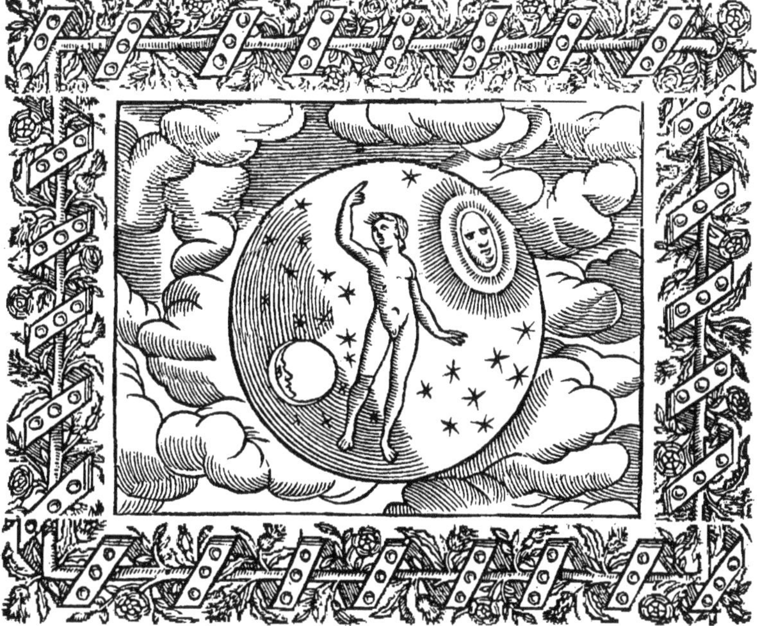

HEARE what's the reaſon why a man we call
A little world? and what the wiſer ment
By this new name? two lights Cœleſtiall
Are in his head, as in the Element:
Eke as the wearied Sunne at night is ſpent,
  So ſeemeth but the life of man a day,
  At morne hee's borne, at night he flits away.

Of heate and cold as is the Aire compoſed,
So likewiſe man we ſee breath's whot and cold,
His bodie's earthy: in his lunges incloſed,
Remaines the Aire: his braine doth moiſture hold,
His heart and liver, doe the heate infold:
  Of Earth, Fire, Water, Man thus framed is,
  Of Elements the threefold Qualities.

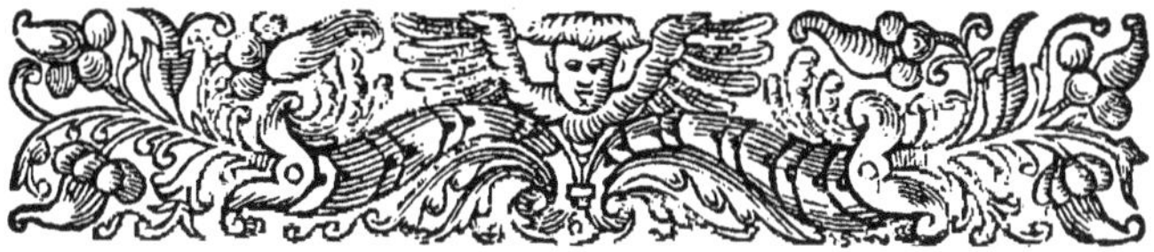

And as we fitly *INFANCIE* compare
Vnto the *SPRING*, so *YOVTH* we liken may
To lazie *SVMMER*, whot devoid of care:
His middle Age to *AVTVMNE*, his decay
To *WINTER*, ſnowie white, and froſtie gray,
For then his vigor failes, his heate is cold,
And like the ſapleſſe Oake he dieth old.

Vini natura.

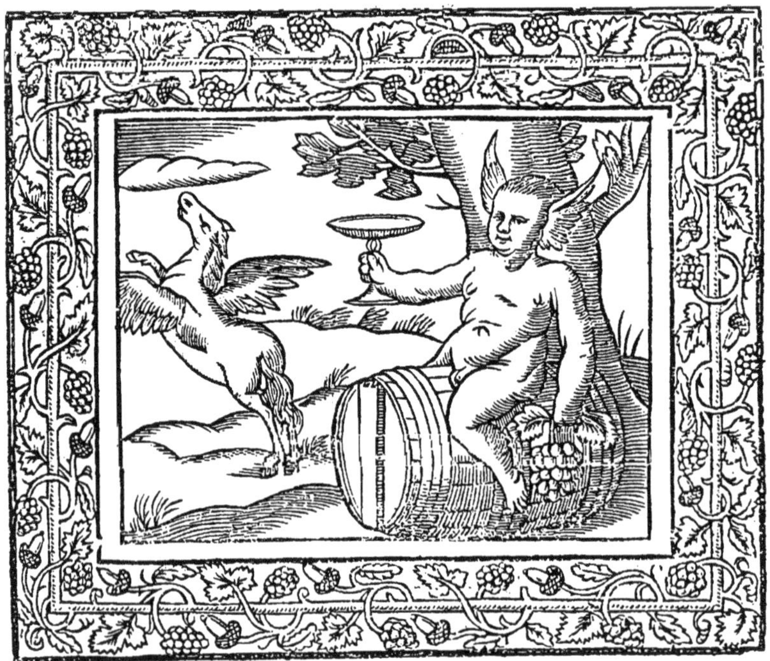

BEST *BACCHVS* Ivie thy faire brow befits,
Thy winges withall, that proud *Gorgonean* horſe:
Becauſe thou addeſt vigor to our wits,
Heate to our blood, vnto our bodie force:
Mirth to our heartes, vnto the dullard ſpright
A quick Invention, to the Sence delight.

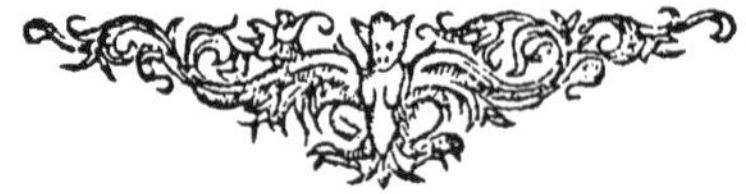

Vnum

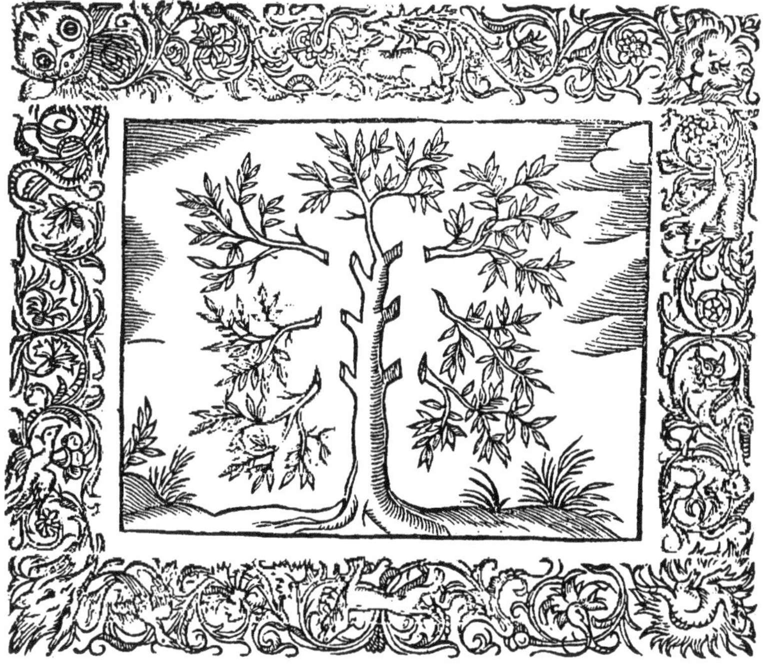

THE Husband good, that by experience knowes,
With cunning skill, to prune, and when to plant,
Muſt lop the Tree where ranck abundance growes,
Aſwell as helpe the barren in her want:
Elſe happilie, when Summer ſeaſon's paſt,
With leaues he may goe ſatisfie his taſt.

Even ſo the wit, that ranckly doth abound,
With many fancies but it ſelfe deceiues:
And while it ſeemes in ſundry Artes profound,
In no one good it's fruitfull, but in leaues:
Then ſome one calling chooſe, whence good may growe,
And let the reſt, as * needeleſſe branches goe.

* Vellem in Adoleſcente quod āputem. *Cicero 1 de Oratore.*

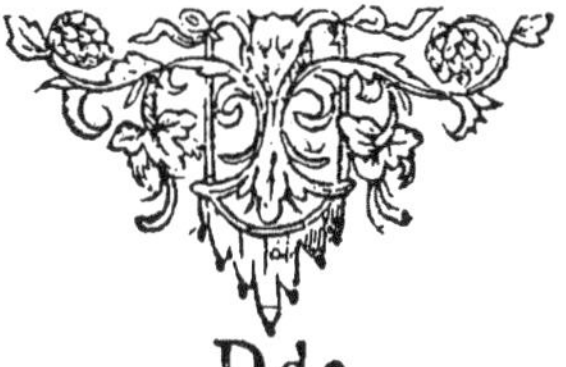

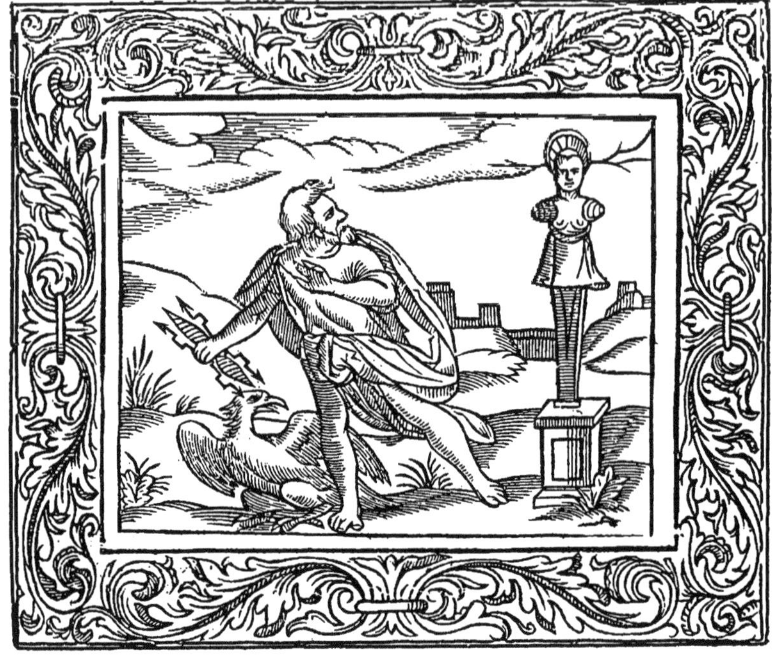

Symbolũ fuit Erasmi Roterodami quod licet Crambe a Poetis nostris toties repetitum, illius postremo memoriæ dedico consecroque.

A PILLAR high, erected was of stone,
In former times, which *TERMINVS* they nam'd:
And was esteem'd, a God of every one:
The vpper part, was like a woman fram'd,
Of comely feature downe vnto the brest,
Of Marble hard a Pillar was the rest.

Which when *IOVE* passed by, with sterne aspect,
He bad this God remooue, and get him gone,
But *TERMINVS* as stoutly did neglect
His heste, and answer'd, I giue place to none:
Varro. I am the bound of thinges, which God aboue
Hath fixt, and none is able to remooue.

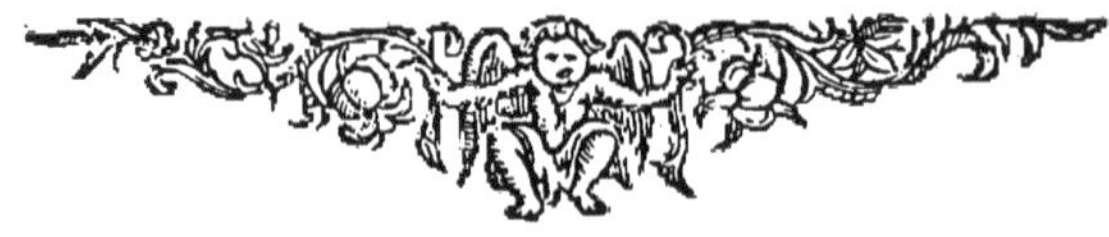

Fortuna

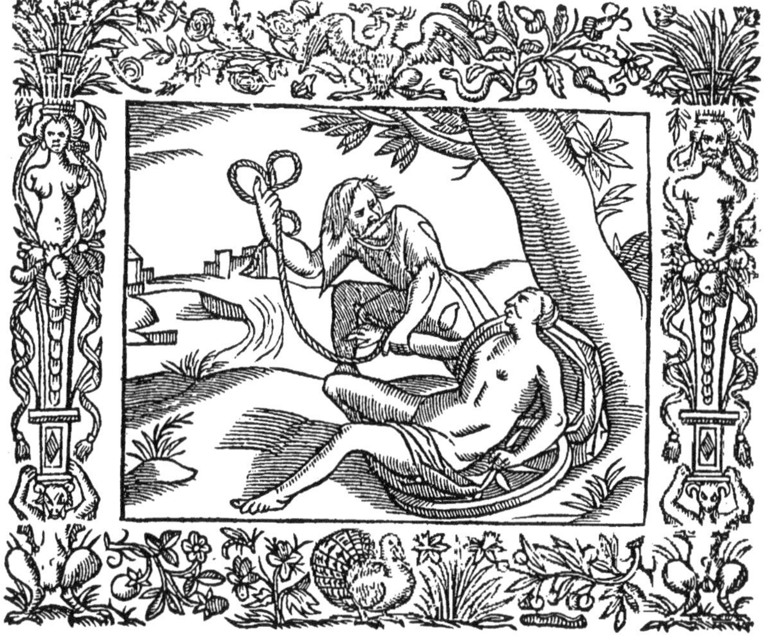

HEERE Povertie, doth conquered Fortune bind,
And vnder keepes, like *HERCVLES* in aw,
The meaning is, the wiſe and valiant mind,
In Povertie eſteemes not Fate a ſtraw:
* And though a while this angry Goddeſſe frowne,
She vtterlie ſhall never caſt him downe.

* Non eſt fortuna ſæpius tentanda. *Iul: Cæſar Comen. lib: 4.*

If Wiſdome haue but what the corpes doth craue,
Convenient foode and raiment for the back:
And libertie to liue, not like a ſlaue
Here in this world, ſhe little elſe doth lack:
But can contented in her cottage ſing,
In greater ſafetie, then the greateſt King.

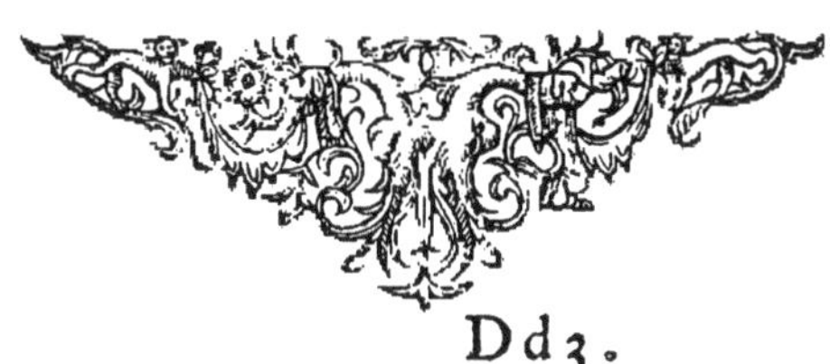

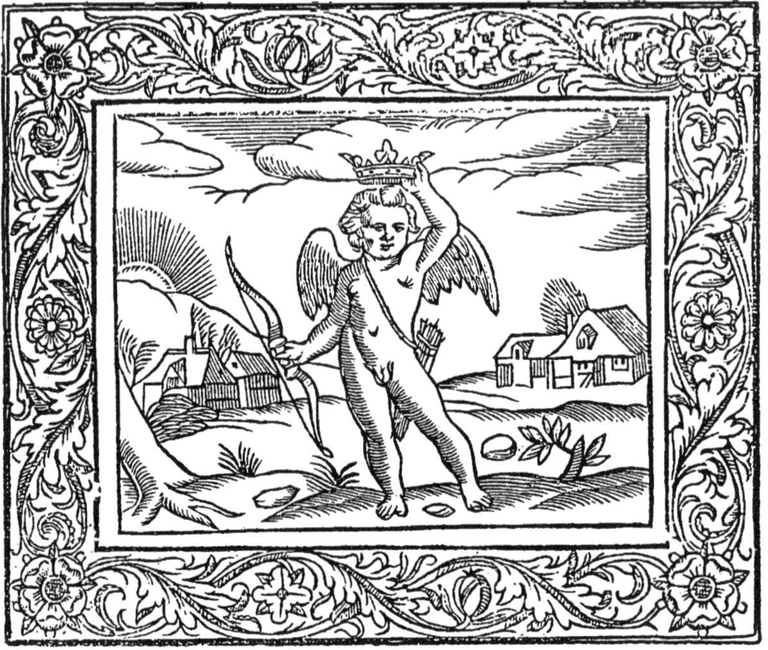

THE awfull Scepter though it can compell
By powerfull might, great'st Monarches to obay:
Loue, where he listeth, liketh best to dwell,
And take abroade his fortune as he may:
Ne might, or gold, can winne him thence away,
Whereto he is through strong affection led,
Be it a Pallace, or the simplest shedde.

But *VENVS* Infant, dred of all beneath,
Imperious feare from my sweete Saint remooue,
And with thy soft Ambrosial kisses, breath
Into her bosome meeke, and mildest Loue
With melting Pitie, from thy Queene aboue:
That she may reade, and oft remember this,
And learne to loue, who most beloued is.

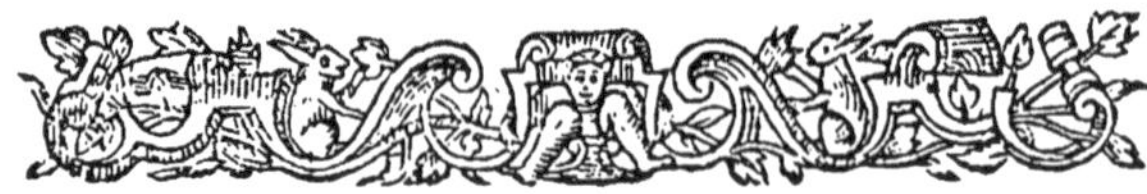

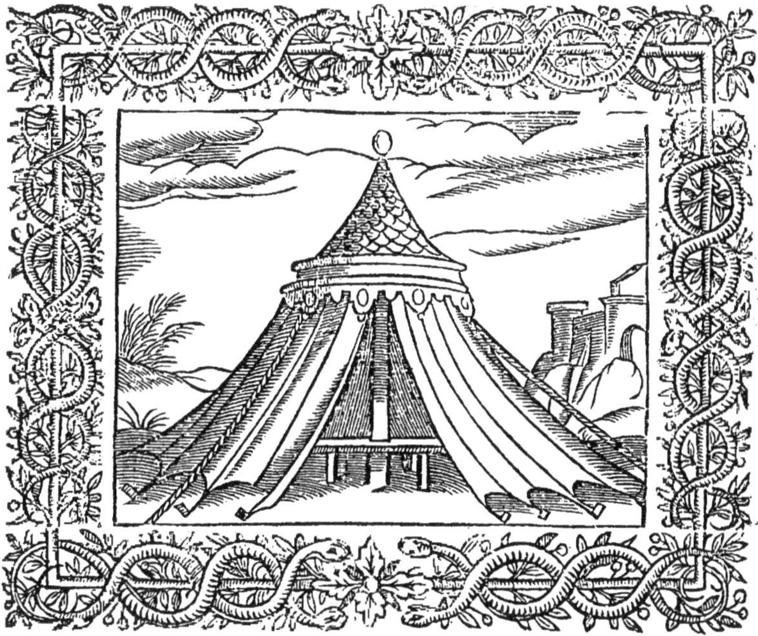

NOR house, nor home, hath wretched man on earth,
Ne ought he claimeth iustly as his owne:
But as a * Pilgrim wandring from his birth
In Countries straunge, and Deserts wild vnknowne,
Like * *RECHABITE*, or those Tartarian * *HORDES*,
Whose vastest Region but a Tent affordes.

Betime hence learne we wisely to supplie
Our inward wantes, ere hence we flit away:
And hide in Heauen, that treasure carefully,
Which neither Moth, nor Canker shall decaie:
In * following state, eke not to spend our stock,
Where oft for merit, we but gaine a mock.

* *1 Pet: Cap: 2 11*

* *Ieremie 35. 7.*

* Companies of Tartars, and subiects of the great CHAM, liuing in Tentes in the wildernes, without Ciuilitie, togeither with their wiues, children, and cattle, neuer abiding in one place, but ranging and robbing vp and downe where they list.

* Sequor nil consequor. dictum Ariosti.

Sapientiam

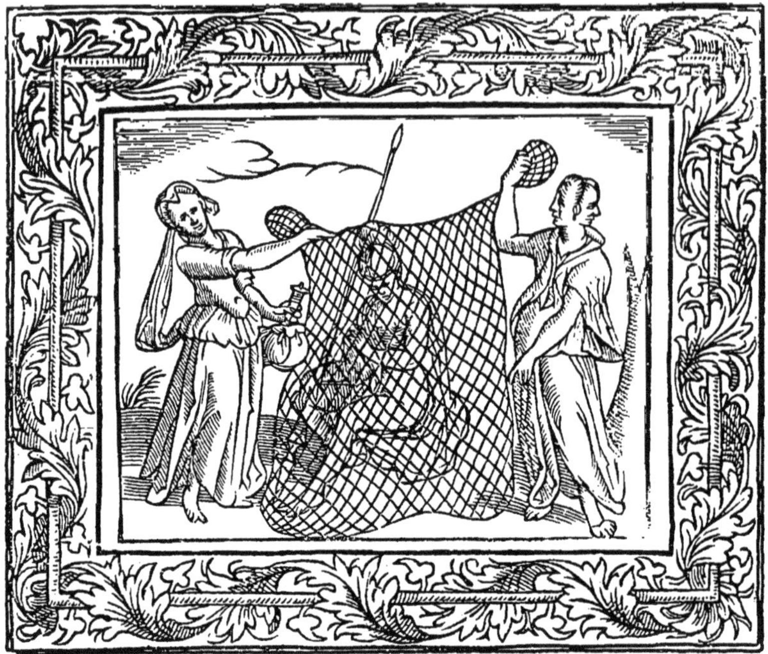

AH pitie *PALLAS*, who hath thee enwrapt?
And in a ſnare, thus brought thee to diſtreſſe:
The wiſeſt now I ſee may be entrapt,
And Vertue ſtoope to Fortunes fickleneſſe:
Nor Scholler-ſhip, or wit, at all times can
From ſad diſaſter, keepe a mortall man.

The loue of Money, and Diſſimulation,
Hold thee *MINERVA* tangled in their ſnare:
For now the world, is growne to ſuch a faſhion,
That thoſe the wiſeſt, that the richeſt are,
And ſuch by whome the ſimpler ſhould be taught,
Are in the net, like *PALLAS* ſooneſt caught.

Perſonam

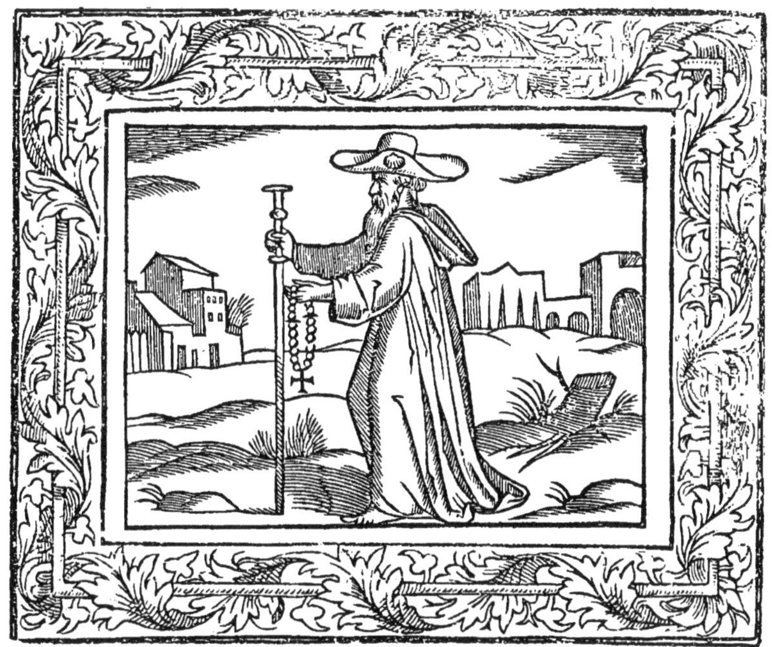

THE Hypocrite, that doth pretend in ſhow,
 A feigned Zeale of Sanctitie within,
Eſchew betime, nor haue with ſuch to doe,
Whoſe hoodes are but the harbour of their Sinne,
 And humbleſt habits, but a falſe diſguiſe,
 To cloke their hate, or hidden villanies.

No *HIRCAN* Tyger, *ERYMANTHIAN* Beare,
So arm'd with malice, thirſtie after blood,
To high eſtate aſpiring, as they are,
The worſt of men, nay man it is too good.
 Where *LVCIFER* did openly rebell
 To God, theſe Traitors even within the Cell.

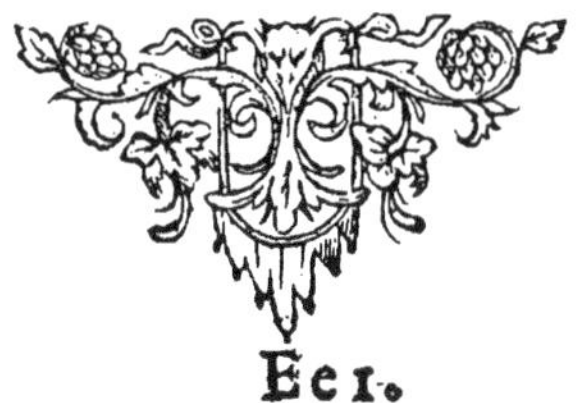

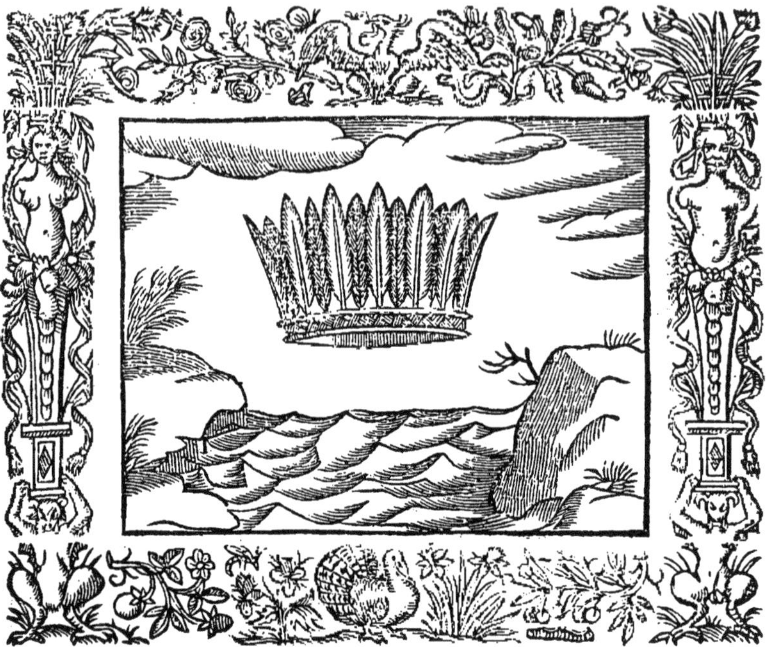

THE cheifest good, (ah would so good it were)
That most imagine Honours bring with them,
We pick from others praises here and there,
So patch herewith an Indian Diadem
Of Parrats feathers, vocall favours light,
And Plumes indeede, whereto we haue no right.

He is not honourd that Discents can show,
Nor he that can commaund a numerous traine,
Nor he to whome the vulgar lout so low,
Nor he that followes Fashion light and vaine,
Saluting windowes, and around doth wheele,
Like *VRSA MAIOR*, starres from head to heele.

We honour him, whose Actions not deface,
The Glories which his Ancestors haue wonne,
By Cowardise, or vicious liuing base,
Ne wrong for Passion, or Affect hath done:
In whome at once, Artes, Bountie, Valour, dwell.
Contending each which other should excell.

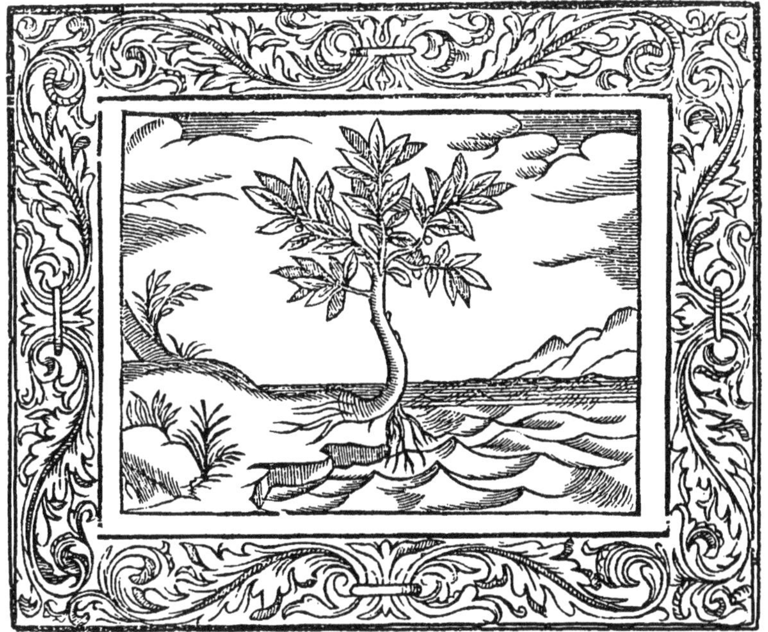

THE *Laurel* greene, that long in ſafetie ſtood
By PENEVS ſtreame, the Muſes chaſt delight,
Oft water'd by the *NAIAD'S* of the flood,
And oft reuiued by her " Louer bright,
The Waue aſſaileth with her ſwelling might,
And overthrowes in time, (but who doth know
Their miſerie, that neere to Greatnes grow.)

" PHOEBVS, whome the Poets feigne to haue loued the Bay, vnder the name of DAPHNE.

This ſacred Bay, is Learning and the Artes,
In former times that flouriſhed at will,
Now waſh'd and worne by ſome, even to the heartes,
Who ſhould haue ſuccour'd and vpheld them ſtill,
Who eate the Corne, but throw the Chaffe to Skill:
And what the Church had once to holy vſes,
Serues them to pride, and all prophane abuſes.

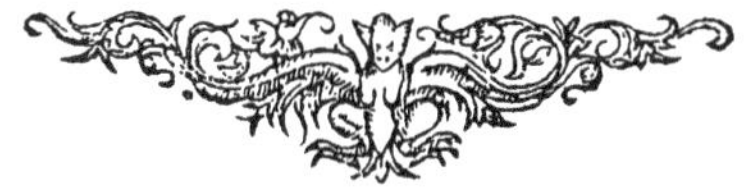

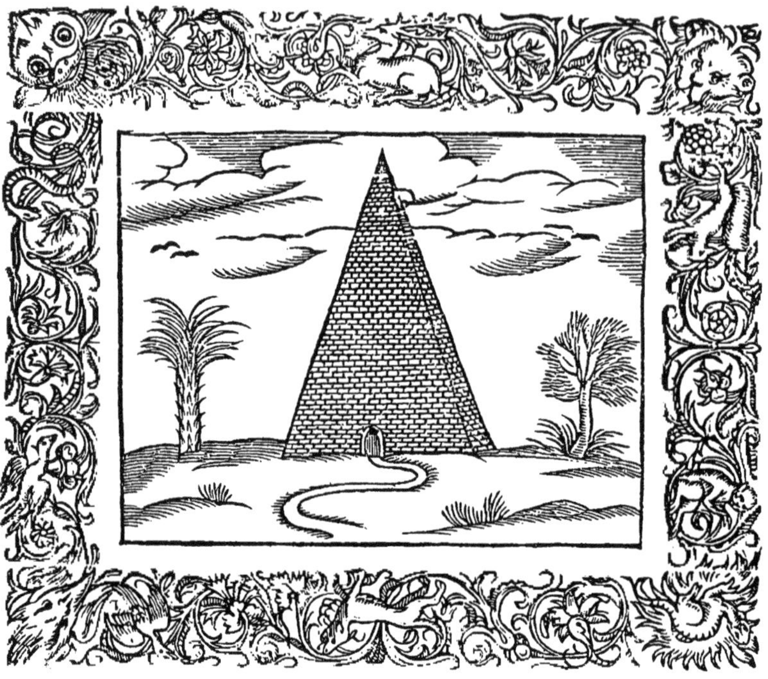

IF that thy Fortunes haue their heigth attain'd,
And bid thee not on greatnes *BASE* to feare,
Let not with that preferment thou hast gain'd,
Vnwonted Pride, or Insolence appeare:
But how much higher thou art plac'd in sight,
So much the lesse affect thy state and might.

For Honors, know, but lend Ambition winge,
And like false mirrours, make vs seeme too greate,
Vpborne by vulgar breath, (the vainest thing,)
Till all be melted by the Soveraigne heate:
That left abandon'd, in a trustlesse aire,
We drowne within an Ocean of dispaire.

Nil

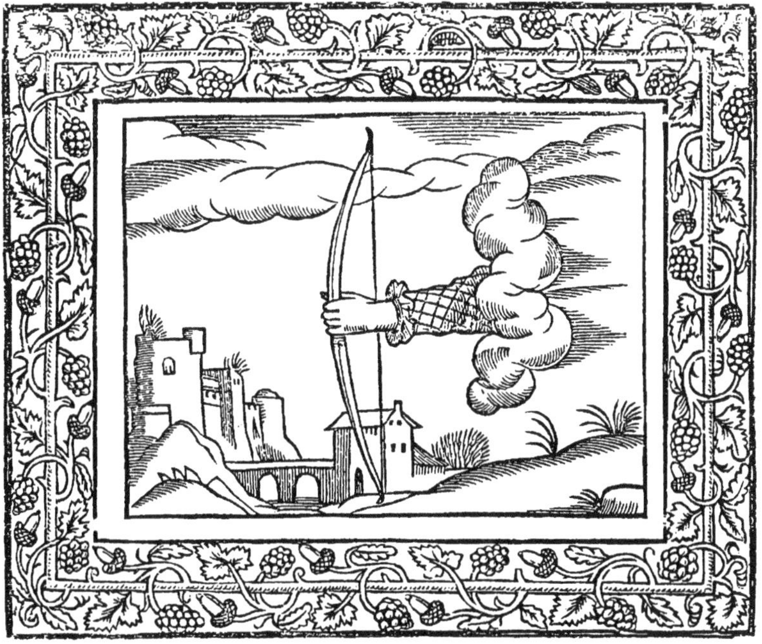

FIRST trie thy ſtrength, and ponder well the end,
Ere thou attempt'ſt a buiſines of weight,
By triall made of wit, thy wealth, or frend,
Who can adviſe, or iudge of thy conceipt:
Thou elſe but haſteſt, to thy loſſe and ſhame,
While abler Iudgments, beare away the game.

Hence nobleſt houſes, their decay haue knowne,
And greateſt Clerkes in vaine opinions err'd,
And wits too heavy-rancke beene overthrowne,
Who elſe in time, mought well haue beene preferr'd:
Withall we taxe, the glorious foole that crakes,
Yet good at nothing, that he vndertakes.

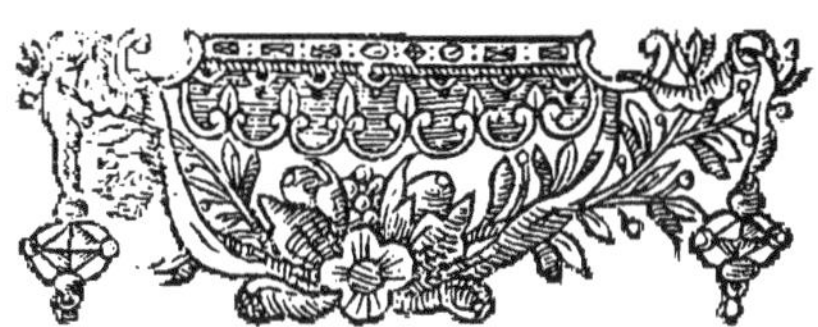

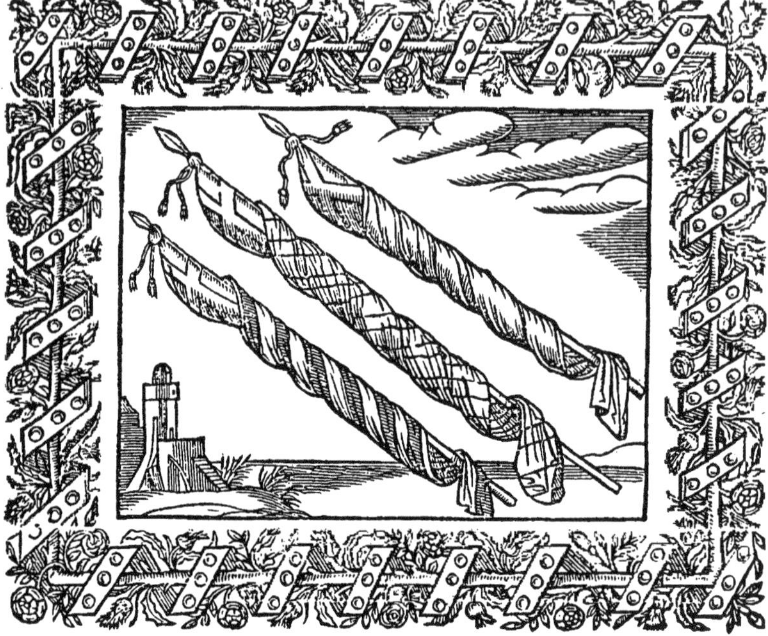

THE valiant mindes, that doe delight a farre,
By vertuous deede to make their prowesse knowne,
Who not of * Fathers Actes ambitious are,
But of the braue Atcheiuements of their owne,
Thus as their Ensignes folded vp vnshowne,
In Peace reiected, or forgotten lie:
Till new Alarmes, advance them out on high.

* Nam genus et proavos &c. *Ovid: Metamorph:* 13.

But Wisedome ever armed with Fore-sight,
Then rateth Valour at her weight in gold,
For though the ease-full world her merit slight,
She seees aloofe the storme. How Malice old
Plaies loose a while to get the better hold,
And bids vs arme, when least we thinke of knocks,
For * Foes asleepe, (they say) the Divell rocks,

* A Proverbe well knowne in the low Coũtries

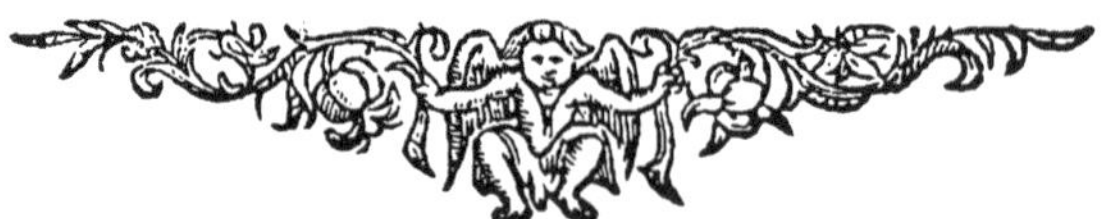

Tantò

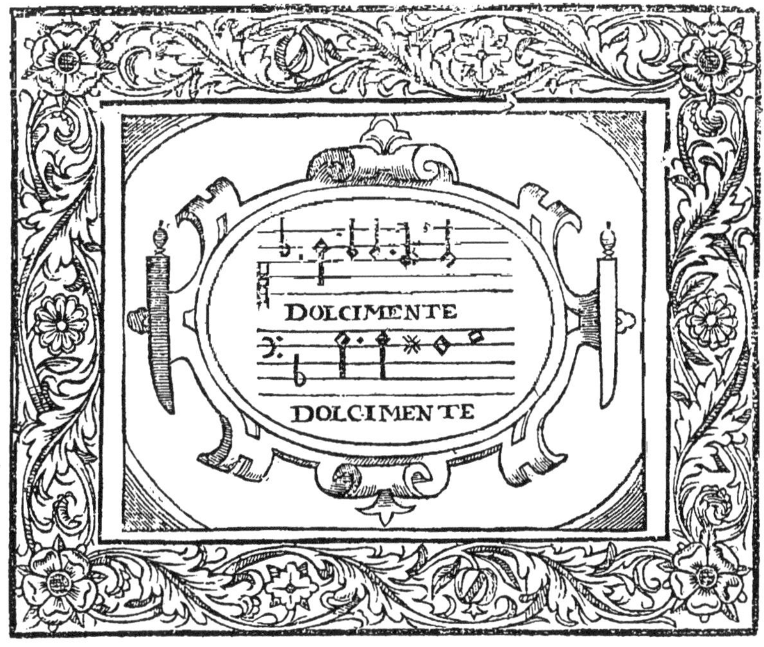

THE mortall strifes that often doe befall,
Twixt louing Bretheren, or the private frend,
Doe proue (we say) the deadliest of all:
Yet if * compos'd by concord, in the end
They relish sweeter, by how much the more,
The Iarres were harsh, and discordant before.

How oft hereof the Image I admire,
In thee sweete *MVSICK*, * Natures chast delight,
The * Banquets frend, and * Ladie of the Quire;
Phisition to the melancholly spright:
Mild Nurse of Pietie, ill vices foe;
Our Passions Queene, and * Soule of ALL below.

* The first Discord here taken is from the eleuēth to the tenth, that is from b fa b mi, vnto alamire, a tenth to f fa vt in the Base, The second from the ninth, or second to the 8. or vnison.

χαῖρε * φυὴν ἐρόεσσα * χοροίτυπε * δαιτὸς ἑταίρη. *Homer: in Hymnis, Musicam aliquens.*

* According to the opinion of Pythagoras.

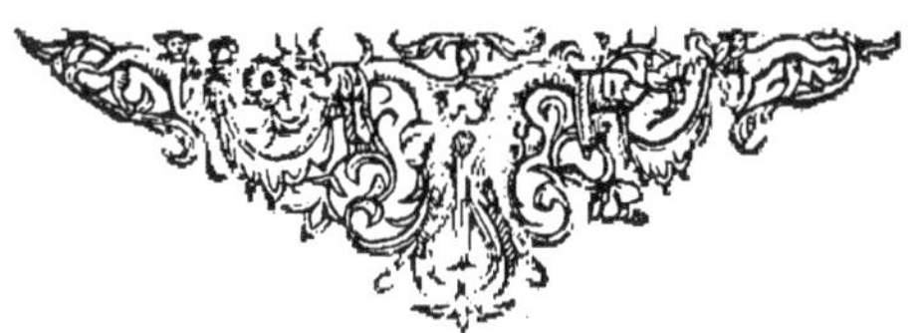

Per

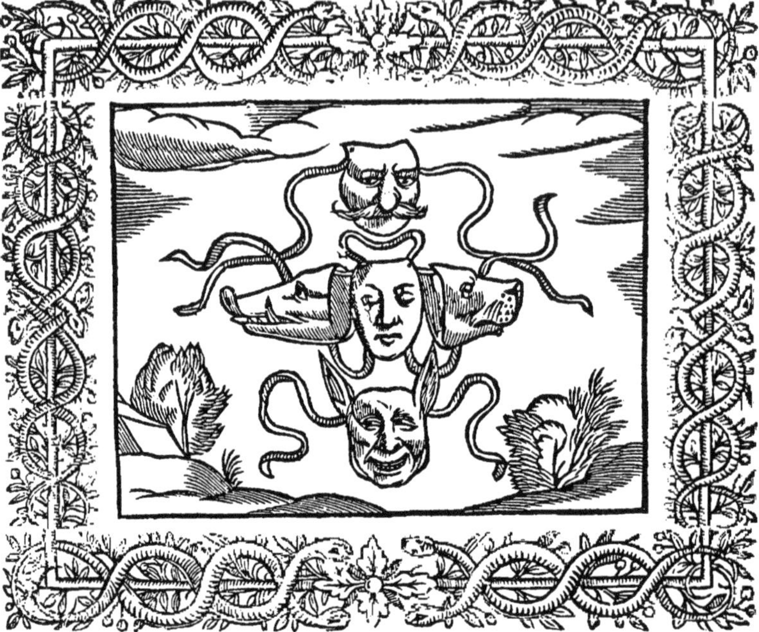

THE worldly wretch, that day and night doth toile,
And tire himſelfe in bodie and in minde,
To gather that by all deviſes vile,
He muſt be faine ere long to leaue behinde:
All ſhapes like *PROTEVS* gladly entertaines,
No matter what, ſo that they bring the gaines.

Abroade Religion, Flatterie at the Court,
Plaine dealing in the Countrie where he dwells,
Then Gravitie among the wiſer ſort,
Where Fooles are rife, his Follie moſt excells:
Thus every way transforme himſelfe he can
Saue one, in time to turne an honeſt man.

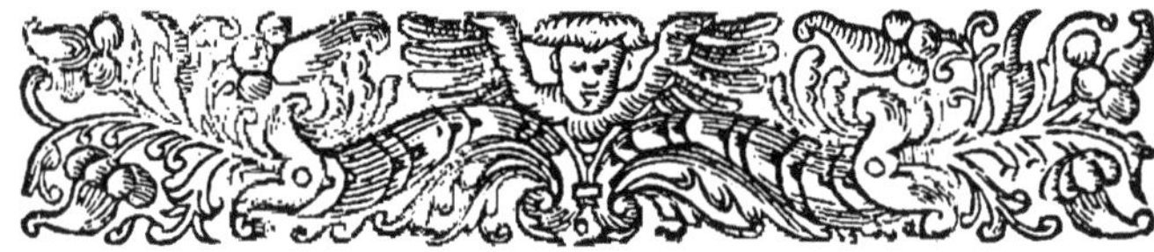

Aula

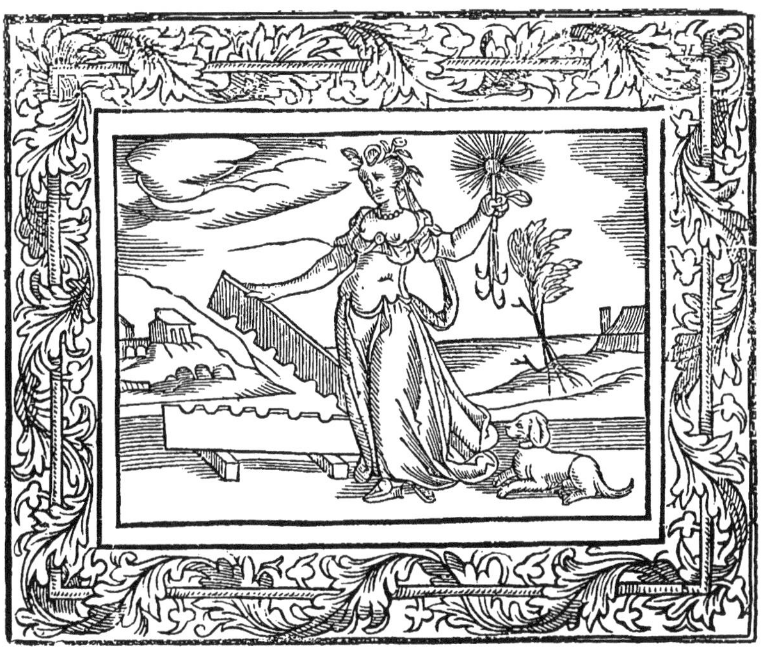

WITH mightie men, who likes to ſpend his prime,
And loues that life, which few account the beſt,
In hope at length vnto his heigth to clime,
By good deſert, or thorough Fortune bleſt,
May here behold the Modell of his bliſſe,
And what his life, in ſumme and ſubſtance is.

A Ladie faire, is FAVOVR feign'd to be,
Whoſe youthfull Cheeke, doth beare a louely bluſh, *Cеſare Ripa in Iconologia.*
And as no niggard of her courteſie,
She beares about a Holy-water bruſh:
Where with her bountie round about ſhe throwes,
Faire promiſes, * good wordes, and gallant ſhowes.

* Byſſina verba. *Plutarch: in Apothegi*

* Aureæ compedes. *Alciatus.*

* Cui omnia principum honesta atque inhonesta laudare mos est. *Tacitus Annal*: 3.

Seneca in Thyeste.

Herewith a knot of guilded hookes ſhe beares,
With th' other hand, a paire of * Stocks ſhe opes,
To ſhew her bondage: on her feete ſhe weares
Lead-ſhoes, as waiting long vpon her Hopes:
 And by her doth the fawning Spaniel lie,
 The Princes bane, the marke of * Flatterie.

Stet quicunq; volet potens
Aulæ culmine lubrico
Me dulcis ſaturet quies;
Obſcurus poſitus loco
Leni perfruar otio

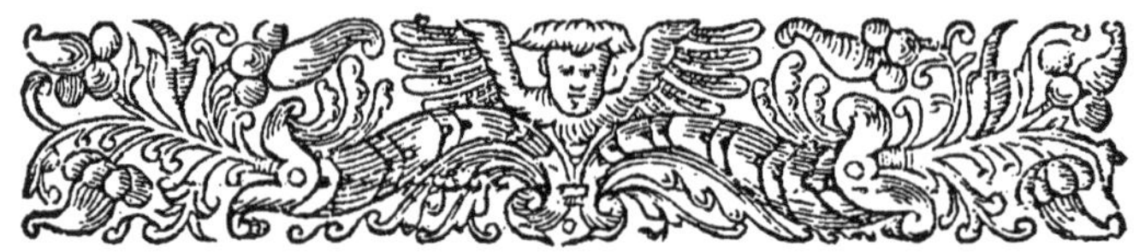

The

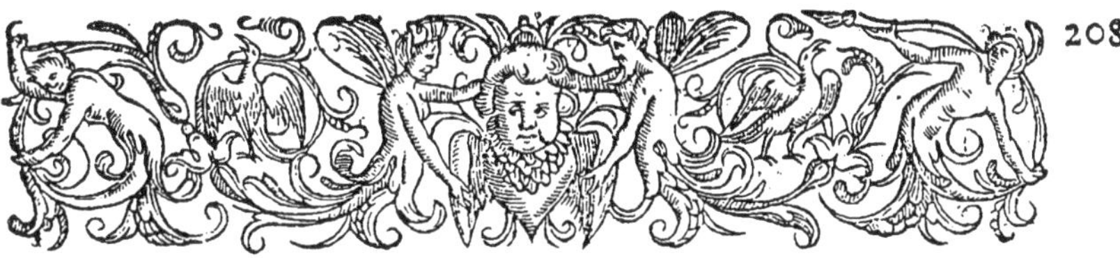

The Authors Conclusion.

AS then the Skie, was calme and faire,
The Windes did ceaſe, and Cloudes were fled,
AVRORA ſcattered *PHOEBVS* haire,
New riſen from her Roſie bed:
At whoſe appoach the * Harlot ſtrew',
Both meade, and mountaine, with her flowers:
While *ZEPHYRE*., ſweeteſt odours threw,
About the feildes, and leavie bowers.

* FLORA ſometimes a famous Harlot in Rome, and after Goddeſſe of flowers, in whoſe honour they kept their feaſtes called FLORALIA.

The Woods and Waters, left their ſound,
No tend'reſt twigge, was ſeene to mooue,
The Beaſt lay couched on the ground,
The winged People perch'd aboue,
Saue *PHILOMEL*, who did renew,
Her wonted plaintes vnto the Morne,
That ſeem'd indeede, her ſtate to rue,
By ſhedding teares vpon the Thorne.

When I as other taking reſt,
Was ſhew'd (me thought) a goodlie plaine,
With all the ſtore of Nature bleſt,
And ſituate within the Maine,
With Rocks about environ'd quite,
But inward round, in rowes there ſtood,
Aſwell for profit, as delight,
The Trees of Orchard, and the Wood.

The builder *Akorne* long agoe,
To *DODONÆAN IOVE* adioin'd,
And there the loftie *Pine* did grow,
That winged flies before the Wind:
LEVCOTHOE that wounded bleedes,
Nor wanting was, nor that ſame Tree,
That beares the ſtaine, in fruite and ſeedes,
Of *THISBES* woefull Tragœdie.

The Mulberie.

The *Elme* embracing *BACCHVS* ſtood,
And there the *Beech* was alſo plac't,
That gaue the golden Age her foode:
Though we eſteeme it, but as maſt;
The *Walnut*, praiſed for her hew,
The *Aſh*, the beſt for helue, and ſtaues,
The *Eugh*, vnto the bender trew,
The *Sallow* ſoft, that water craues.

* Eraſmus in his Commentaries vpon St. Hierom affirmeth Cherries to haue been knowne to theſe partes of Europe little aboue two or three hundred yeares, being firſt brought from CERASVNTIS a Citie of PONTVS, whēce they haue their name.

Th' vnblaſted *Bay*, to conqueſts due,
The *Perſian Peach*, and fruitefull *Quince*:
And there the forward *Almond* grew,
With * *Cherries* knowne no long time ſince:
The *VVinter-Warden*, Orchards pride,
The * *PHILIBERT*, that loues the vale,
And red *Queene-Apple*, ſo envi'de,
Of Schooleboies, paſſing by the pale.

* The Filbert ſo named of PHILIBERT a king of FRANCE, who cauſed by Arte, ſundry kindes to be brought forth, as did a Gardiner of OTRANTO, in Italie by cloue Gilliflowers, and Carnations, of ſuch cullours as we now ſee them

With many moe, of me forgot,
Vpon the which the Aëry crew,
Each in his kind, and order ſat,
And did his wonted note renew;
The long-liu'd *Eagle*, *IOVE* forſooke,
And hither in a moment flew,
Who to the *Oake*, himſelfe betooke,
As King, his multitude to view.

And *IVNOS* Bird, not farre away,
Diſplaid her *ARGVS* hundred eies;
By him ſat perched on a ſpray,
The *Swanne*, that ſweetly ſinging dies:
The *Crane*, who Centinell hath ſtood,
The *Herne*, high'ſt ſoarer in our ſight,
The *Pheaſaunt* fetch'd from *PHASIS* flood,
With *Faulcon* for the Kings delight.

* Thracia pel'ex *Seneca in Herc: fur:*

The *Turtle* here to each did tell,
The loſſe of his beloued mate,
And ſo did * *THRACIAN Philomel*,
In ſweeteſt tunes, her bitter Fate:
Ne wanted there the envious *Stare*,
The theeviſh *Chough*, and prating *Iay*,
The *Raile*, and froſtie *Feldefare*,
And *Larke* abroade by breake of day.

Within there was a Circlet round,
That raiſ'd it ſelfe, of ſofteſt graſſe,
No Velvet ſmoother ſpred on ground,
Or Em'rald greener ever was:
In mid'ſt there ſate a beauteous Dame,
(Not *PAPHOS* Queene, ſo faire a wight)
For Roſes by, did bluſh for ſhame,
To ſee a purer, red and white.

In Robe of woven Silver fine,
And deepeſt Crimſon ſhe was clad:
Then diaper'd with golden twine,
Aloft a Mantle greene ſhe had,
Whereon were wrought, with rareſt skill
Faire Cities, Caſtles, Rivers, Woods;
And here, and there, emboſs'd a hill
With Fountaines, and the Nymphes of Floods.

A maſſie Collar ſet with ſtones,
Did over all, it ſelfe extend,
Whereon in ſparkling Diamonds,
SAINT GEORGE, her Patrone did depend;
A Crowne Imperial on her head,
One hand a bright drawne Sword did hold,
The other (moſt that made her dredd,)
Three Scepters of the fineſt gold.

While proudly vnderfoote ſhe trod,
Rich Trophæies, and victorious ſpoiles,
Atchieued by her might abroad:
Her name is *EMPRESSE OF THE ILES*:
There Charriots were, that once ſhe wanne,
From *CÆSAR*, ere ſhe was betraid,
With ſtandards gat from Pagans, whan
She lent the Holy Land her aide.

Here ſaw I many a ſhiver'd launce,
Swordes, Battle-axes, Cannons Slinges,
With th' Armes of *PORTVGAL*, and *FRAVNCE*,
And Crownets of her pettie Kinges:
High-feathered Helmets for the Tilt,
Bowes, Steelie Targets cleft in twaine:
Coates, Cornets, Armours richly guilt,
With tatterd Enſignes out of *SPAINE*.

About her now on every Tree,
(Whereon full oft she cast her eie,)
Hung silver Sheildes, by three and three,
With Pencill limned curiouslie:
Wherein were drawne with skilfull tusch,
Impresa's, and *Devises* rare,
Of all her gallant Knightes, and such
As Actors in her Conquestes were.

Eke some of Queenes, and Ladies too,
As pleased their Invention best,
(For wit of woman, much can doe,)
Were fastned vp among the rest,
In sundry tongues, whose Motto's old,
And names, though scarcely could be read,
She wishd their Glories mought be told,
To after times, though they were dead.

Great EDVVARD third, you might see there,
With that victorious Prince his sonne:
Next valiant IOHN of LANCASTER,
That SPAINE, with English overran:
And those braue spirits Marshalled,
The first that of the Garter were,
All Souldiers, none to Carpet bred,
Whose names to tell I must forbeare.

Fourth HENRIES Sunbeames on the Cloude,
Fift HENRIES Beacon flaming bright,
YORKES Locke, that did the Falcon shroude,
Was here, so were his Roses white:
The Marshal MOVBRAIE NORFOLKES Duke,
Yet liuing in great HOVVARDS blood,
With valiant BEDFORD, Symboles tooke
As pleas'd them, to adorne the Wood.

By whome the BEAVCHAMPES worne away,
And noblest TALBOT, scourge of FRAVNCE,
With NEVILS whome could nought dismay,
Left Reliques of their Puissance:
The loyal VERE, and CLIFFORD stout,
Greate STRONGBOVVES heire, with BOVRCHIER, GRAY,
Braue FALCONBRIDGE, and MONTACVTE:
Couragious ORMOND, LISLE, and SAY.

With

With other numberlesse beside,
That to haue seene each one's devise,
How liuely limn'd, how well appli'de,
You were the while in Paradise:
Another side she did ordaine,
To some late dead, some liuing yet,
Who seru'd ELIZA in her raigne,
And worthily had honour'd it.

Charles E: of Nottingham L: Admiral. Thomas E: of Suffolke, and L: Chamberlaine. George E: of Cumberland. L: Willowghby. Sir Philip Sydney Sir Ihon Norris. &c.

Where turning, first I spide aboue,
Her owne deare PHOENIX hovering,
Whereat, me thought, in melting Loue,
Apace with teares mine eies did spring;
But Foole, while I aloft did looke,
For her that was to Heauen flowne,
This goodly place, my sight forsooke,
And on the suddaine all was gone.

With griefe awak d, I gaz'd around,
And casting vp to Heauen mine eie,
Oh GOD I said! where may be found,
These Patrones now of Chivalry,
" But Vertue present and secure,
" We hate, when from our knowledge hid,
" By all the meanes we her allure,
" To take her dwelling where she did.

Now what they were, on every Tree,
Devises new, as well as old,
Of those braue worthies, faithfullie,
Shall in another Booke be told.

FINIS.

1612.

www.ingramcontent.com/pod-product-compliance
Ingram Content Group UK Ltd.
Pitfield, Milton Keynes, MK11 3LW, UK
UKHW051127260726
13967UKWH00010B/2899